Animal Thinking

Contemporary Issues in Comparative Cognition

Strüngmann Forum Reports

Julia Lupp, series editor

The Ernst Strüngmann Forum is made possible through the generous support of the Ernst Strüngmann Foundation, inaugurated by Dr. Andreas and Dr. Thomas Strüngmann.

This Forum was supported by funds from the
Deutsche Forschungsgemeinschaft (German Science Foundation)

Animal Thinking

Contemporary Issues in Comparative Cognition

Edited by

Randolf Menzel and Julia Fischer

Program Advisory Committee:
Nicola Clayton, Julia Fischer, Randolf Menzel, and
Sara Shettleworth

The MIT Press

Cambridge, Massachusetts
London, England

Series Editor: J. Lupp
Assistant Editor: M. Turner
Photographs: U. Dettmar
Design and realization: BerlinScienceWorks

MIT Press books may be purchased at special quantity discounts
for business or sales promotional use. For information, please email
special_sales@mitpress.mit.edu or write to Special Sales Department,
The MIT Press, 55 Hayward Street, Cambridge, MA 02142.

The book was set in TimesNewRoman and Arial.
Printed and bound in the United States of America.

Library of Congress Cataloging-in-Publication Data

Ernst Strüngmann Forum (8th : 2010 : Frankfurt am Main, Germany)
Animal thinking : contemporary issues in comparative cognition / edited by
Randolf Menzel and Julia Fischer.
     p.   cm. — (Strüngmann forum reports)
"Eighth Ernst Strüngmann Forum held Sep. 26–Oct. 1, 2010, Frankfurt am
Main."
Includes bibliographical references and index.
ISBN 978-0-262-01663-6 (hardcover : alk. paper)
1. Cognition in animals—Congresses. 2. Animal navigation—
Congresses. 3. Decision making in animals—Congresses. 4. Social
behavior in animals—Congresses. 5. Animal communication—
Congresses. I. Menzel, Randolf, 1940– II. Fischer, Julia, 1966– III. Title.
QL785.E67   2010
591.5'13—dc23
                                                              2011018644

10 9 8 7 6 5 4 3 2 1

Contents

The Ernst Strüngmann Forum

Founded on the tenets of scientific independence and the inquisitive nature of the human mind, the Ernst Strüngmann Forum is dedicated to the continual expansion of knowledge. Through its innovative communication process, the Ernst Strüngmann Forum provides a creative environment within which experts scrutinize high-priority issues from multiple vantage points.

This process begins with the identification of themes. By nature, a theme constitutes a problem area that transcends classic disciplinary boundaries. It is of high-priority interest, requiring concentrated, multidisciplinary input to address the issues involved. Proposals are received from leading scientists active in their field and are selected by an independent Scientific Advisory Board. Once approved, a steering committee is convened to refine the scientific parameters of the proposal and select the participants. Approximately one year later, a central meeting, or Forum, is convened to which circa forty experts are invited.

Preliminary discussion for this theme began in 2009, when the Board expressed interest in topics related to an earlier meeting, "Animal Mind–Human Mind" (Griffin 1982). The Board was keen to learn what progress had been made on the central questions raised at that gathering: What kind of conscious experience do animals have? In which sense do animals plan, expect, decide between options, communicate, and evaluate their own behavior and that of group members?

In response, Randolf Menzel and Julia Fischer proposed this Forum to assess the state of the art in comparative cognition. By focusing on four specific areas (navigation, planning and decision making, communication, and social knowledge), their aim was to clarify points of disagreement and evaluate progress within each area, as well as to compare the structure of the problems and issues across areas. Could common principles across species and areas be found and, by assessing present experimental paradigms, could new avenues for experimental research be proposed? In December 2009, Nicola Clayton and Sara Shettleworth joined them on the steering committee to identify the key issues for debate and select the participants for the Forum, which was held in Frankfurt am Main, Germany, from September 26 to October 1, 2010.

It is important to understand that the activities and discourse surrounding a Forum begin well before participants arrive in Frankfurt and conclude with the publication of this volume. Throughout each stage, focused dialog is the means by which participants examine the issues anew. Often, this requires relinquishing long-established ideas and overcoming disciplinary idiosyncrasies that might otherwise inhibit joint examination. However, when this is accomplished, new insights can emerge.

This volume conveys the synergy that arose from a group of diverse experts, each of whom assumed an active role, and is comprised of two types of contributions. The first provides background information on key aspects of the overall theme. These chapters have been extensively reviewed and revised to provide current understanding of the topics. The second (Chapters 5, 9, 13, and 18) summarizes the extensive group discussions that transpired. These chapters should not be viewed as consensus documents nor are they proceedings; they are intended to transfer the essence of the discussions, to expose the open questions that still remain, and to highlight areas in need of future enquiry.

An endeavor of this kind creates its own unique group dynamics and puts demands on everyone who participates. Each invitee contributed not only their time and congenial personality, but a willingness to probe beyond that which is evident, and I wish to extend my gratitude to all. A special word of thanks goes to the steering committee, the authors of the background papers, the reviewers of the papers, as well as the moderators of the individual working groups: Sara Shettleworth, Nicky Clayton, Bill Searcy, and Joan Silk. To draft a report during the Forum and bring it to its final form in the months thereafter is no simple matter, and for their efforts, I am especially grateful to the rapporteurs: Jan Wiener, Amanda Seed, Brandon Wheeler, and Keith Jensen. Most importantly, I wish to extend my sincere appreciation to Randolf Menzel and Julia Fischer. Their guidance throughout this project was invaluable.

A communication process of this nature relies on institutional stability and an environment that encourages free thought. The generous support of the Ernst Strüngmann Foundation, established by Dr. Andreas and Dr. Thomas Strüngmann in honor of their father, enables the Ernst Strüngmann Forum to conduct its work in the service of science. In addition, the following valuable partnerships are gratefully acknowledged: the Scientific Advisory Board, which ensures the scientific independence of the Forum; the German Science Foundation, which provided financial support for this theme; and the Frankfurt Institute for Advanced Studies, which shares its vibrant intellectual setting with the Forum.

Long-held views are never easy to put aside. Yet, when this is achieved, when the edges of the unknown begin to appear and gaps in knowledge are able to be defined, the act of formulating strategies to fill these becomes a most invigorating exercise. It is our hope that this volume will convey a sense of this lively exercise and play its part in furthering research on comparative cognition.

Julia Lupp, Program Director
Ernst Strüngmann Forum
http://www.esforum.de

List of Contributors

Kristin Andrews   Department of Philosophy, York University, Toronto, ON M3J 1P3, Canada

Verner P. Bingman   Department of Psychology, Bowling Green State University, Bowling Green, OH 43403, U.S.A.

Redouan Bshary   Institute of Biology, University of Neuchâtel, 2009 Neuchâtel, Switzerland

Peter Carruthers   Department of Philosophy, University of Maryland, College Park, MD 20742, U.S.A.

Dorothy L. Cheney   Department of Biology, University of Pennsylvania, Philadelphia, PA 19104, U.S.A.

Ken Cheng   Department of Biological Sciences, Macquarie University, Sydney NSW 2109, Australia

Morten H. Christiansen   Department of Psychology, Cornell University, Ithaca, NY 14853, U.S.A.

Nicola Clayton   Department of Experimental Psychology, University of Cambridge, Cambridge, CB2 3EB, U.K.

Michael C. Corballis   Department of Psychology, University of Auckland, Auckland 1142, New Zealand

Anthony Dickinson   Department of Experimental Psychology, University of Cambridge, Cambridge, CB2 3EB, U.K.

Nathan Emery   School of Biological and Chemical Sciences, Queen Mary, University of London, London E1 4NS, U.K.

Julia Fischer   Cognitive Ethology Laboratory, German Primate Center, 37077 Göttingen, Germany

Paul W. Glimcher   Center for Neuroeconomics, New York University, New York, NY 10013, U.S.A.

Christoph Grüter   Laboratory of Apiculture and Social Insects, Department of Biological and Environmental Science, University of Sussex, Falmer BN1 9QG, U.K.

Onur Güntürkün   Institute of Cognitive Neuroscience, Biopsychology, Ruhr-University Bochum, 44801 Bochum, Germany

Robert R. Hampton   Department of Psychology and Yerkes National Primate Research Center, Emory University, Atlanta, GA 30322, U.S.A.

Susan Healy   Schools of Psychology and Biology, University of St. Andrews, St. Andrews KYI6 9JP, U.K.

Charlotte K. Hemelrijk   Biological Centre, University of Groningen, 9751 NN Haren, The Netherlands

Kay Holekamp   Department of Zoology, Michigan State University, East Lansing, MI 48824, U.S.A.

Lucia F. Jacobs   Department of Psychology, University of California, Berkeley, CA 94720–1650, U.S.A.

Kathryn J. Jeffery   Institute of Behavioral Neuroscience, Department of Cognitive, Perceptual and Brain Sciences, University College London, London WC1H 0AP, U.K.

Keith Jensen   Biological and Experimental Psychology, Queen Mary, University of London, London E1 4NS, U.K.

Alex Kacelnik   Department of Zoology, Oxford University, Oxford OX1 3PS, U.K.

Felice Di Lascio   Institute of Biology, University of Neuchâtel, 2009 Neuchâtel, Switzerland

Hanspeter A. Mallot   Institute for Neurobiology, University of Tübingen, 72076 Tübingen, Germany

Daniel Margoliash   Department of Organismal Biology and Anatomy, University of Chicago, Chicago, IL 60637, U.S.A.

Randolf Menzel   Institut für Biologie, Freie Universität Berlin, 14195 Berlin, Germany

Nora S. Newcombe   Department of Psychology, Temple University, Philadelphia, PA 19122, U.S.A.

Michael J. Owren   Department of Psychology, Georgia State University, Atlanta, GA 30302, U.S.A.

Derek C. Penn   Department of Psychology, University of California, Santa Monica, CA 90403, U.S.A.

Josef Perner   Department of Psychology, University of Salzburg, 5020 Salzburg, Austria

Ana Pinto   Institute of Biology, University of Neuchâtel, 2009 Neuchâtel, Switzerland

Tabitha Price   Cognitive Ethology Research Group, German Primate Center, 37077 Göttingen, Germany

William A. Searcy   Department of Biology, University of Miami, Coral Gables, FL 33124, U.S.A.

Amanda Seed   School of Psychology, University of St. Andrews, St. Andrews, K416 9JP, U.K.

Robert Seyfarth   Department of Psychology, University of Pennsylvania, Philadelphia, PA 19104, U.S.A.

Murray Shanahan   Department of Computing, Imperial College London, London SW7 2AZ, U.K.

Sara Shettleworth   Department of Psychology, University of Toronto, Toronto, ON M5S 3G3, Canada

Joan B. Silk   Department of Anthropology, University of California, Los Angeles, CA 90095, U.S.A.

Jeffrey R. Stevens   Center for Adaptive Behavior and Cognition, Max Planck Institute for Human Development, 14195 Berlin, Germany

Sabine Tebbich Department of Cognitive Biology, University of Vienna, 1090 Vienna, Austria

Christoph Teufel Brain Mapping Unit, Department of Psychiatry, University of Cambridge, Cambridge CB2 3EB, U.K.

Erica van de Waal Institute of Biology, University of Neuchâtel, 2009 Neuchâtel, Switzerland

Brandon C. Wheeler Cognitive Ethology Laboratory, German Primate Center, 37077 Göttingen, Germany

Jan Wiener Department of Psychology, Bournemouth University, Poole, Dorset BH12 5BB, U.K.

Markus Wild Insitut für Philosophie, Humboldt-Universität zu Berlin, 10099 Berlin, Germany

1

Animal Thinking

An Introduction

Randolf Menzel and Julia Fischer

The topic of this Strüngmann Forum—animal thinking—was not formulated as a question—"Do animals think?—but rather as a statement. One might question whether we have already gone too far by making such a statement, but this obviously depends on what we mean by "thinking." If one believes that thinking refers only to mental processes accessible through human conscious recollection, then thinking must be strictly reserved for our species alone. The issue of whether animals experience conscious recollections in some similar way dominated the debate at an earlier meeting of the Dahlem Konferenzen, the forerunner to the Ernst Strüngmann Forum. At that meeting, Donald Griffin, who edited the resulting volume, "Animal Mind – Human Mind" (Griffin 1982), was concerned that ignoring or eliminating the possibility of animals experiencing some sort of consciousness might be perceived as being narrow-minded and unscientific. In his words (Griffin 1982:3):

> In areas where data are few and of limited relevance, dogmatic negativity can easily limit what scientists even try to investigate, and thus perhaps delay or prevent important insight and discoveries.

This kind of argument was, and still is, suspected of being anthropocentric, and perhaps even guided by simple-minded "folk psychology." Indeed, comparing animal thinking with the form of thinking that humans consciously experience is, in an epistemological sense, fraught with risk and unfair to any animal species, including humans. Aware of such potential shortcomings, Griffin tried to avoid these pitfalls by motivating participants to focus on experimental paradigms and their conceptual background.

Thirty years later, we continue to struggle with the question of how to judge the mental life of other species. Do we grant animals too much intelligence, or too little? Should we distance ourselves from the idea that animals possess intelligence? Can we reasonably tackle the inner workings of other species' minds, and how can we best conceive an animal mind?

Since the advent of the cognitive revolution in the 1960s, animals have been viewed as goal-seeking agents that acquire, store, retrieve, and internally process information at many levels of cognitive complexity. This cognitive turn paved the way for an immensely productive research program. While this field benefited from insights into the proximate causes of animal behavior, awareness grew of the importance of taking a species' evolutionary history and ecological adaptation into account, an insight which led to a multitude of field studies with a large range of animal species. Studies in the field and in the lab are now performed in concert to compensate for their respective limitations. It is this combined approach which makes current cognitive behavioral studies so rich. This volume provides multiple and paradigmatic examples for such combined studies.

The conceptual frame of current cognitive behavioral studies acknowledges the multiple levels of neural processing and mental operations but struggles with the borderlines between more behaviorist and more cognitive accounts. Two principles became apparent in the discussions across the four groups:

First, problem-solving strategies that appear similar across animal species do not allow us to conclude that similar neural and/or mental operations are at work, particularly when the comparison crosses the line between animals and humans. However, such comparisons can be highly inspiring and may lead us to working hypotheses that need to be scrutinized, not only with respect to animal but also human cognition. After all, an important aspect of the cognitive turn was the demystification of human cognition, which led to the rejection of an immaterial homunculus inside our heads.

Second, modern science is guided by the parsimony argument. In biology, the doctrine of the simplest and intellectually most economic explanation is complicated by the fact that we do not know what is more or less simple or economical for a particular brain. Elemental forms of cognition, such as stimulus-response connections and a large range of memory items stored in isolation, are interpreted as being more likely to be implemented than composed representations that are handled together in working memory. Sometimes this argument is combined with the notion that small brains or small volumes of parts of the brain favor "simpler" solutions. The scale applied here follows formal principles; for instance, how many parameters or processes might be involved. However, in most cases we do not know whether it involves more or fewer neural processes to encode (e.g., space as a cognitive map or as a combination of seemingly simple rules and picture memories). The same argument can be made for many cognitive faculties; for instance, for decision making, planning, tool manufacturing, intentionality. As the theoretical physicist Jean-Claude Pecker (2004:185) stated:

> The principle [of parsimony or Occam's razor] can both be used to eliminate unnecessary irrelevancies, but also to constrain the development of imaginative theories.

The issue of where to set the criterion to distinguish imagination from scientific evidence continues to be a matter of debate; some argue that the field of animal cognition suffers from mushrooming "just so" stories and armchair speculation, even in the scientific literature (see Penn, this volume). Anecdotes are powerful because they provide motivation for enquiry. Ideally, they lead to carefully designed experiments that test the conjectures encapsulated in anecdotal observations of animal behavior, but they certainly cannot substitute for rigorous and skeptical enquiry. The reports and discussions presented in this volume provide multiple examples of the ongoing struggle to avoid unfounded complex interpretations as well as to not get stuck in the simplistic assumption that animal minds are just information storage devices bound to external stimuli and sensorimotor associations.

This Strüngmann Forum brought together experts from the fields of animal behavior, neuroscience, computational cognition, cognitive science, and philosophy to discuss the state of the art in animal cognition research. Our goal was to identify key questions at the frontier of present research, and to push the boundaries of knowledge by discussing how these questions could be translated into experiments and observations. Together with the members of the program advisory committee, Sara Shettleworth and Nicky Clayton, we identified four highly active areas of research: navigation, decision making and planning, communication, and social knowledge. These fields differ strikingly in terms of their maturity and integration with other disciplines, as both the sections' chapters and respective group reports document. The former two fields are characterized by emerging integration of behavioral analysis with neuroscience, whereas the latter two are more strongly embedded in the discourse of "what makes us human." Possibly because of this difference, there was great variance in the types of controversies and debates.

In the navigation group (Wiener et al., this volume), discussion focused on how specific sensorimotor connections and cognitive processes are integrated to guide animals to the intended goals, to allow them to localize themselves, and to perform shortcutting travels between locations. Debate centered on the structure and use of a cognitive map. Paradigms were identified in a "navigation toolbox" to allow low- and high-level cognition to be separated in the navigation of different animal species: in walking and flying animals, in middle-range and far-ranging navigation, as well as in laboratory or field studies. The comparison between walking and flying insects (ants and bees) turned out to be particularly informative. An additional component of navigation is pursued in the first chapter by Randolf Menzel, who addresses the question of how navigation and communication about locations is combined in honeybees. Kathryn Jeffery contributes an overview of the neural mechanisms that support navigation in the three-dimensional world of a rat. This chapter is a testimony to the fact that neuroscience is one of the closest partners in addressing questions at the mechanistic level. Verner Bingman makes the case for viewing animal navigation as intelligent behavior. At the meta-level, he raises the interesting question: Would animal navigation be less interesting if it were "less intelligent"? The group report on animal navigation (Wiener et al., this volume) delivers the "navigation toolbox"—an analysis of the components important in animal navigation—as well as suggests how and in which way these components are integrated to produce navigational behavior, meaning more controlled by global matching procedures (e.g., of worldwide gradients) rather than a representation of spatial relations.

The second group focused on how we may conceptualize decision making, planning, and knowledge of one's own epistemic states in animals. Tony Dickinson addresses goal-directed behavior, which refers to the fulfillment of an animal's current motivational states, and contrasts it with "future planning," which refers to behaviors that serve the fulfillment of possible future needs. One key issue concerns how experiments need to be designed to uncover planning for the future in animals, and whether such experiments can uncover episodic-like memory indicative of mental time travel. Two theories are presented (the mnemonic-associative theory and the mental time travel theory) to guide future studies. Jeffrey Stevens makes the case for an integration of evolutionary and psychological approaches in animal cognition. Specifically, he argues that the "bounded rationality approach" (i.e., the acknowledgment that simple mechanisms typically suffice to produce adaptive behavior) is also of great relevance for the present field of research. Robert Hampton discusses whether animals know what they know, and how we know whether they know what they know. The key issue here is whether any of the experiments in this field require a meta-representation of an animal's knowledge states, or whether the observed differences in behavior are due to the fact that the animal does one thing when it knows the solution and another when it does not. The group report (Seed et al., this volume) summarizes this controversy as well as other key issues, such as the fundamental question of "what is a decision" to more difficult issues of declarative and implicit knowledge and the repercussion for animal consciousness.

The section on animal communication begins with a foray into the murky waters of "information" by Julia Fischer, who comes to the conclusion that the concept of information is indispensible to understand the receiver's part in the communicative dyad. In addition, she argues that pitting motivational against referential communication effectively sets up a false dichotomy. Christoph Grüter discusses the emerging properties of the collective action of social insects and the importance of communication to achieve such collective action. He attempts to relate collective decision making in insect societies to unsupervised phenomena in other species, including humans, technical communication networks, and neural nets. Michael Corballis straddles boundaries between groups, as he links language to episodic memory. Obviously, information is the key concept in animal cognition research and, indeed, this group spent a great deal of time discussing the value of information for animal communication studies (Wheeler et al., this volume). Perhaps, however, a somewhat fuzzy and commonplace understanding of information is more productive than trying to resolve the issue of what constitutes information, as it frees up capacities for more interesting issues, such as the insight that a great deal of signaling behavior can be understood without the need of invoking elaborate cognition. In contrast, cognition is important when it comes to the processing of and response to signals, as well as when animals need to integrate information from different sources.

The fourth section is devoted to social cognition. Redouan Bshary begins with a plea for a broader quantitative research program to gain further insights into the socio-cognitive abilities of a greater range of taxa. Through computational modeling, Charlotte Hemelrijk challenges the notion that complex social behavior requires complex cognition. Her models suggest that relatively simple sets of rules can generate a number of behavioral patterns observed in nonhuman primates. Dorothy Cheney discusses the mechanisms and adaptive value of having long-term bonds, and presents field research that addresses the emergence of contingent cooperation in wild primates. The group report (Jensen et al., this volume) discusses recent advances and problems in the field of theory of mind research.

It is important to understand that controversies about concepts, design of experiments, or interpretations of collected data were not avoided during our discussions, and they often found their way into the reports. In our view, such controversies are of particular value since they reveal the filters in our mind; that is, the often unspoken bias toward a favored idea or concept. Equally, it is important to note that everyone shared a strong desire to understand the species-specific ecological conditions and selective pressures behind the cognitive processes. Our goal was to avoid generalization across species based on superficial similarities, to gain from the insights collected by well-controlled experiments with different animal species, and to be skeptical about single case observations that appeal to a general public audience. This general attitude of the participants reflected the understanding that animals possess a range of representations of the world, and that the ability to make inferences is a key component of animal thinking. Having said that, it is also important to note that the group reports are not consensus documents; presented views are not necessarily shared by all members of the groups. Likewise, the individual chapters may sometimes reveal a somewhat provocative tone, which we have purposely retained to foster further discussion and debate.

The best part about writing this editorial introduction is that it gives us the opportunity to acknowledge the invaluable contributions of several people. First, we would like to thank the moderators of the discussion groups—Sara Shettleworth, Nicky Clayton, Bill Searcy, and Joan Silk—for ensuring that each group worked their way through the sets of questions which they had identified for themselves at the onset. The rapporteurs—Jan Wiener, Amanda Seed, Brandon Wheeler, and Keith Jensen—did a fabulous job in bringing into shape the "train wrecks" of sketches and notes that resulted from the long and sometimes quite controversial discussions. The staff of the Ernst Strüngmann Forum performed at their usual level of perfection, and we note this because we did not have to worry about anything related to organization; everything was perfectly managed. In addition to the many other things she did, Marina Turner compiled the reference list—no mean feat. Julia Lupp steered us expertly through the process of planning and conducting this meeting. She is the heart and soul of the Forum, and we deeply appreciate her contribution to the success of this meeting. In closing, we wish to thank the Ernst Strüngmann Foundation for their steadfast support of these very special meetings.

Navigation

2

Navigation and Communication in Honeybees

Randolf Menzel

Abstract

Honeybees navigate and communicate in the context of foraging and nest selection. A novel technique (harmonic radar tracking) has been applied to foraging behavior. On the basis of the data collected, a concept that assumes an integrated map-like structure of spatial memory was developed. Characteristic features (long-ranging landmarks) and local characteristics are learned during exploratory flights. Route flights and information about target destinations transferred during the waggle dance are integrated into the map-like memory, enabling bees to make novel short-cutting flights between learned and communicated locations and to perform decisions about their flight routes. Cognitive terminology is applied to describe these implicit knowledge properties in bee navigation.

Introduction

Animals know where they are and where they want to go next. The question, however, is: What do "know," "want," "where," and "what next" mean in this context?

Ants following an outbound pheromone track are motivated to collect food at the terminal of the track. A male moth flying upwind within the female pheromone plume is seeking to find the female of the same species to copulate. The food-searching fiddler crab *Uca* rushes back to its hole on the sandy beach when it is disturbed. If the ant crosses a pheromone trail of a different species, the moth detects the female plume of another moth species, or *Uca* sees another nearby hole, none of these species will be distracted from their specific goal-seeking behavior. In all of these cases, the animals are in a defined motivational state (outbound foraging run, seeking to copulate, searching in the vicinity of the shelter): they seek a goal, they "know" where they are (at a particular location relative to the goal), and they perform a behavior that brings them to it. The neural instructions applied under these conditions are dominated by external stimuli and innate information. These stimuli and instructions define the current state, the goal, and the next performances. Thus the knowledge base guiding such elementary forms of navigation can be conceptualized as sensorimotor links that are activated and inactivated by motivational states— neural states which represent the goal are guided rather stereotypically by external stimuli, and involve a minimal set of memories. Navigation, in even these elementary forms, involves the integration of multiple sensory inputs and memories of different time spans. The current state of sensory input needs to be compared with the past, so that advances or deviations from the direction toward the intended goal will be recorded. This goal-seeking behavior is continuously updated according to motivational states, external stimuli, and the animal's own motor performance. Decisions are being made between options (continue, terminate, reverse, alter behavior), and it is quite obvious that no single external stimulus alone defines which decision will be made. Drawing on multiple sensory inputs, neural operations are performed that lead to the appropriate selection of adaptive behavior. However, the neural operations underlying these elementary forms of navigation can be thought of as isolated functions which independently control decision making and behavior selection. In most cases of navigation, guidance by external stimuli will be much more complex, motivational states are less strictly defined, multiple goals may be available, individual learning leading to large ranges of memories will be more important, and selection procedures between possible behaviors will be richer. How do we conceptualize the neural processes underlying these more complex forms of navigation? As extensions of the elementary operations with just a few more components, like richer memory, added? The alternative would be to allow conceptually for novel operations on the level of representations that are thought to combine multiple forms of instructions (innate and learned) and provide neural substrates for planning, decision making, and behavior selection.

Integration across sensory input can be rather simple or extremely complex in navigating animals. Likewise, memory structure can be quite simple (e.g., in the egocentric form of path integration) and complex, as in serial picture memories and cognitive maps. At which level do we need to assume processing on representations, and which terms are adequate in capturing such processes? These questions will be addressed in experiments with the honeybee.

The Bee Case

The social life of these animals and their unique way of communicating locations in the environment (waggle dance communication; von Frisch 1965) allows access to the structure of their navigational memory. Honeybees are central place foragers, as are many Hymenopteran insects, which need to learn the location of their nest. They navigate over a range of several kilometers and allocate their foraging activity according to changing environmental conditions, optimizing the energy and time budget invested in collecting food (Seeley 1995). In theory, the central place foraging strategy allows them to cope with the necessary adaptations through egocentric path integration mechanisms. An animal leaving the hive on an exploration flight or in response to dance communication needs only to register the rotatory components of its flight relative to celestial cues and/or far distant visual cues (e.g., the profile of the horizon), weigh it against the distances flown in the respective sectors, continuously integrate these parameters, and return safely to the hive by subtracting 180°. It was indeed believed in the past that this is the only strategy applied (Wehner and Menzel 1990). In that case, an animal transported to an unexpected site and released there should be lost. However, this is not so. We do not yet fully understand what the structure of navigational memory in honeybees is; however, it is clear that egocentric path integration cannot be the only mechanism and may not even solely exist in its egocentric form. I shall argue in favor of a memory structure that integrates multiple levels of representations, provides the information for novel short-cutting flights, and allows the bee to make decisions between potential goals.

Tracking the Flight Paths of Navigating Bees

Sydney Brenner once said that "progress in science depends on new techniques, new discoveries, and new ideas, probably in that order." Thus, let us first consider the methods applied in honeybee navigation studies, then new discoveries, and finally new ideas. The most commonly applied paradigm used in honeybee navigation experiments, besides the study of dance communication, is based on the conflict that arises in foraging bees when they are transported to an unexpected site and then released (catch-and-release procedure combined with observing vanishing bearings). In such a situation, bees are removed from ongoing behavior. Observation of their initial flight path at the release site (vanishing bearings) show that they fly as if they had not been displaced: hive-departing bees fly in the direction they would have taken from the hive to the feeder, feeder-departing bees 180° to this direction, hive-arriving bees as if they need to repeat the flight toward the hive, and feeder-arriving bees in a similar way as if they need to continue flying toward the feeder.

The distribution of vanishing bearings taken at the release site has been interpreted as reflecting an egocentric vector memory established by the bee during training along a route to the feeder (Wehner and Menzel 1990). The distance component of that vector could not be determined with this method, but it was reasonable to assume that bees fly according to their vector memory, including the distance measure. It was also assumed that the bees are lost after applying the egocentric vector information. When the full flight path of capture-and-release bees was monitored using the harmonic radar technique, it was found that bees are not lost (Figure 2.1; Menzel et al. 2005). They first apply the vector information, then go through a phase of searching, and then return home to the hive over distances that do not allow them to use any beacon at the hive. Since the study area did not provide any far distant cues for orientation (e.g., a characteristic profile of the horizon), local cues must have provided the necessary information for successful homing. Such information could be associated home-directed vectors with particular local cues and/or learned spatial relations between local cues and those characterizing the home location.

Four additional observations are important:

1. Bees returned from all directions around the hive.
2. Some bees flew first to the feeding site and then, without landing, along the learned route back to the hive.
3. Bees not trained to a far distant feeder performed equally well and returned from all directions to the hive.
4. Bees recruited by a dancing bee returned home equally well after applying the vector information they received from the dancer (as shown in Figure 2.1).

These observations support the conclusion that bees locate the hive and the feeder from any location within the range of the release site (several hundred meters), they decide between two destinations, and they have established their spatial knowledge not during trained route flights but rather during their exploratory behavior early in the life of a foraging bee.

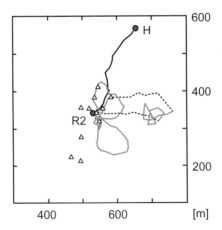

Figure 2.1 Radar track of a bee that was recruited by a dancer, indicating a feeding place 200 m to the east. The recruited bee was caught when leaving the hive (H), transported to a release site (R2) 300 m south of the hive, equipped with a transponder for harmonic radar tracking and released. It flew first 200 m to the east (dashed line), searched there briefly (gray line), returned to the release site (upper dashed line), and after some systematic searching (gray line) returned home along a straight flight (black line) (after Menzel et al. 2005).

Bees Learn Allocentric Features during Exploration Flights

Before initiating foraging flights and attending dances, bees learn a range of environmental properties during exploratory orientation flights. These properties relate to the sun compass (time of day and the local ephemeris function), the calibration of their visual odometer, the immediate surroundings of the hive (picture memory as established from specified view points), and the further distant layout of the landscape. The first excursions from the hive bring the bee in narrow loops into the surrounding environment (Capaldi et al. 2000). One component of these flights is certainly path integration—making sure that they are able to return to the starting point, the hive. In its minimal form, path integration may rely on an egocentric reference system, but the fact that path integration is a component of the first exploratory flights does not mean that these flights can be adequately explained by egocentric reference. Through recent experiments (Fuchs et al., pers. comm.), we found that bees return home faster after their first exploratory flight when released in the explored sector, as compared to releases in the unexplored sector. We also observed that successive exploratory flights of the same bee are directed into different sectors around the hive, which suggests that bees apply a strategy of sequentially exploring the whole area around the hive in a systematic manner. The information gathered during these systematic exploratory flights allows them to return safely from any release site within the range of the explored area, because trained route flights are not necessary for the fast and directed homing flights from all directions around the hive (see above).

Additional information about the memory established during exploratory flights comes from experiments in which bees from colonies located in different environments were tested for their search behavior in the same environment, and were found to perform significantly different patterns of search behavior (Greggers and Lehman, pers. comm.). As in the exploratory flights, it turns out that long-stretching landmarks (boundaries between extended areas, landmark arrays, distributed cues, and other cue gradients) embedded in the sun compass guide the search behavior most reliably. An analysis of the search flight patterns of animals from different environments indicates two strategies: generalization and transfer. In generalization, bees that were exposed to partially matching landscape structures between the home area and test area searched at these matching structures more strongly than bees which had not experienced such structures. In transfer, the search patterns in the test area resembled extended landmark features of the home area relative to the sun compass. Bees performed search patterns that replayed the geometric structure of their home area, although the test area did not contain any of these structures. Thus the search behavior was not guided by the structures they were exposed to in the test area, but rather by the memory of extended landmark features of their home area.

From these observations, we conclude that exploratory flights of young bees are indeed learning flights during which allocentric landmark features are stored in memory. Such a memory would provide the information an animal needs to return from any location within the explored area after it has spotted itself relative to the stored features. Again, one might interpret these findings as indicating the recognition and application of home-directed vectors associated to particular landmarks during exploratory flights. In such a case, bees should only be able to apply home-directed flights. However, bees that had learned a feeding site may fly from the release site first to the feeding place and then back home to the hive (see above). Are bees able to perform novel short-cutting flights to several locations?

Novel Flight Vectors Are Derived from Two and Three Experienced Locations

Consider the following experiment (Menzel et al. 1996): We trained the same group of bees to two different locations in the morning and in the afternoon. Then we collected bees at the moment when they departed from the hive and transported them to the incorrect feeding site (in the morning they were released at the afternoon site and vice versa). Here they vanished toward the hive indicating that they used the local landmarks to identify the location, switched motivation (they were collected when motivated to fly out to the feeder), and retrieved the correct vector memory for return flights to the hive. Obviously the vector memory from route flights is rather flexible and can be switched by context stimuli. We next asked which direction hive-departing bees take when released halfway between the morning and afternoon feeding sites, a site they had not been trained to before, one which they may have explored only during orientation flights, but not during training. Half of these bees behaved according to their working memory: they flew into the direction they would have taken from the hive, if they had not been displaced. The other half flew toward the hive. In my view, these results indicate a geocentric map-like memory structure, but the evidence was weak since we determined only vanishing bearings.

In a recent experiment using radar tracking, we trained bees to two feeders at the same time (Figure 2.2). When released at an unexpected site (R), they are confronted with several options for their decisions. They may apply the content of their working memory (outbound or inbound vectors to the feeder, vector from Fa to Fb) or they may refer to a geometric, relational memory and fly directly to one of the three locations: Fa, Fb, or the hive (H). We found that animals caught on arrival at a feeder (e.g., feeder Fa) initially performed either a flight along a vector that would have brought them from the other feeder to the capture feeder Fa (flight path 1, an appropriate behavior if they mistook the release site for the other feeder Fb), or a vector flight that would have brought them back from the capture feeder Fa to the hive (flight path 2). After some searching, which brought them into areas other than the release site (schematically depicted in Figure 2.2 as location S), the bees selected one of three possible flights to one of the two feeders (flight path 3 or 4) or directly back to the hive (flight path 5). After arriving at the other feeder (Fb), they flew either to the capture feeder or back to the hive. During the tests, no other animals were present flying around either of the feeders; only local cues were available. Two strategies appear to be applied: vector flights as if the animal had not been transported to an unexpected release site (flights 1 and 2), and novel flights to one of three locations, the feeders, and the hive.

The simple rule, which assumes the recognition and application of an associated home-directed vector, cannot explain these findings. One may argue against a geocentric structure of the navigational memory by proposing that vector integration is performed over long distances. If this were the case, however, only vectors anchored at the hive would have been learned during route flights; all other vector flights would have to be derived from vector integration. Displaced bees would then recognize a landmark previously associated with a particular homing vector. This vector would provide the basis for adding vector memories from the hive to each of the two feeders. The other flight

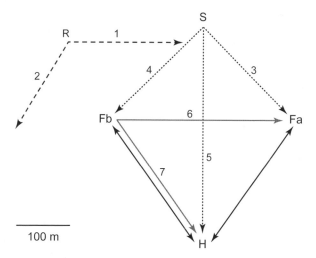

Figure 2.2   Bees trained simultaneously to two feeders (Fa, Fb, black lines) over distances of 300 m were individually released at several unexpected release sites immediately upon arrival at the respective feeder. One test situation is schematically shown in which bees were released at R after they had just arrived at Fa. Before their release at R, a radar transponder was attached. Initially, two vector flights appeared (dashed lines 1, 2). After some searching, which brought the bee to a different location (schematically depicted as location S), the bee chose between three novel flights, which brought it first to either feeding site (dotted lines 3, 4) or directly back to the hive (H, dotted line 5). If they arrived at one of the feeders, they continued by either flying to the other feeder (gray line 6) or directly back to the hive (gray line 7). During the experiment both feeders were closed, no landmarks were available at either of the two feeder locations, and all other bees were caged.

vectors (to each of the feeders and the hive, as well as between the two feeders) may also result from vector integration. If the bee performs this kind of vector integration, it would in fact relate its flights to a network of vectors, a spatial representation that differs from a geocentric map only in the assumption that the space between the endpoints of the vector operations is, in a sense, empty. Are memories of locations empty of meaning to bees?

Communicated and Learned Vectors Are Integrated into a Common Frame of Reference

In the waggle dance, a bee executes fast and short forward movements straight ahead on the vertical comb surface, returns in a semicircle in the opposite direction, and starts the cycle again in regular alternation. Each waggle dance involves several of these cycles (von Frisch 1965). The length of the single waggle runs and the number of sound pulses correlate with the distance flown to reach the source, and the angle of the waggle phase relative to gravity correlates with the direction of the foraging flights relative to the sun's azimuth in the field and sun-linked patterns of polarized skylight. Thus, by encoding the visually measured distance and the direction toward the goal, the waggle dance allows colony members to share information about the distance and direction toward a desirable goal. Are just instructions about flight vectors communicated?

Above it was argued that the navigational strategies applied by foraging bees cannot be fully appreciated if one assumes a hive-centered egocentric form of spatial memory. Instead, however, it seems that the exploratory orientation flights of young bees lead to a map-like spatial memory that appears to be derived from repetitive exposure to the same landmarks from different viewpoints. Given this capacity and the fact that bees are recruited by a dancing bee only after they have performed their exploration flights, it is tempting to assume that bees attending a dance might recall from their memory of landmarks and homing vectors a corresponding outbound vector that is related to expected landmarks. Under these conditions, neither the dance behavior nor the flight path of a recruited bee would be guided solely by two independent measures (direction and distance) but rather by an "expectation" of arriving at a particular location. A component of this "expectation" would be the route to be followed, as embedded in the map-like memory.

We performed an experiment in which a few bees danced for a feeding place at 650 m distance from the hive and two groups of potential recruits had visited two different (and currently exhausted) unscented feeding places, also at 650 m distance but at an angle of either 30° or 60° to the dance-indicated site (Figure 2.3). The communication process was video recorded and the flight paths of the recruits were radar tracked. Irrespective of the angular difference between the feeding place of the dancing bees (FD) and the feeding place of the trained bees which were recruited (FT), recruits flew either to FD or FT heading off

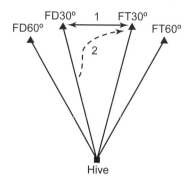

Figure 2.3 Experimental design and schematic representation of the main findings of an experiment in which recruits chose between a dance-indicated place and a place previously learned. FD: feeding place of the dancing bees. FT: feeding place of the trained bees that were recruited. Two groups of bees were trained over distances of 650 m from the hive: one group to FD (2 bees, the dance-performing bees), the other to FT (about 20 bees, the recruits in the test situation). Between the hive and FD and the hive and FT, there was either a 60° or 30° angular difference. After training the large group of bees to FT for a few days, FT was closed for a day and the bees experienced an empty feeder. On the test day, the two FD bees danced for FD, no food was provided at FT, and the FT place was devoid of any visual cues. FT bees were recruited by the dances and flew either to FD or FT (see text). In the 30° test situation, some recruits performed cross flights (1) after arriving at either FD or FT. Recruits on the way to FD may also deviate from their flights about half way and fly over to FT (Menzel et al. 2011).

in the respective directions immediately after leaving the hive, indicating that they had already made a decision to follow the dance information or their own route memory while still inside the hive. The direction toward FD and FT was chosen at equal frequency in the 60° group; bees of the 30° group flew to FT four times more frequently than to FD. Recruit flights toward FD require more dance-following than flights toward FT in both groups (on average 25 vs. 14 dance rounds for FD and FT flights, respectively). Recruits of the 30° group on average followed fewer dance rounds, possibly because the small difference in angular information reminded them of their learned route and they left the dance ground earlier. In the 30° group, some of the recruits deviated from the course toward FD during their outbound flights and crossed over to FT. Most importantly, after arriving at either FD or FT, they frequently performed cross flights to the respective other location. Notice that bees arriving at FT (a location that was not marked by any local cues during the experiment) performed novel short-cutting flights to FD, the location indicated by the dance, although these animals on average followed fewer dance rounds than those which headed out directly to FD. This finding indicates that the observation of fewer dance rounds provides enough information about the location of FD but probably less stimulation to motivate the recruit to apply this information first.

From these observations we conclude that recruits (a) already relate the location of FD to that of FT during the communication process inside the hive and (b) apply a memory of the locations FD and FT which allows them to fly from one location to the other, following a direct novel shortcut if the flight trajectories do not differ too much. It thus appears that recruits compare the information received during dance communication with their own spatial memory, either on the level of potential flight vectors or locations.

Obviously, dance communication involves a motivational and an instructive component; the former requires less information from the dancer, the latter more. The motivational component appears to remind a recruit about its own foraging experience. The signals included in this form of communication are certainly manifold (olfactory, gustatory, acoustic, vibratory). It is well documented that floral odors carried by the dancer stimulate recruits to leave the hive, and if the odor reminds them about their own foraging goals, they return to these feeding sites (von Frisch 1965; Grüter and Farina 2009, Grüter this volume). Thus floral odors may have a particularly high potential to motivate recruits to take up their own foraging again, but this does not diminish the importance of the spatial communication process. Following multiple waggle runs allows for the possibility of averaging across the rather large scatter of the directional and distance measures of the dance. Indeed we found that the directional scatter in the flights of recruits is smaller than expected from the scatter of the directional measure in the dance (Riley et al. 2005).

Is the Bee Dance a Form of "Language"?

Karl von Frisch used the term "dance language" and may have understood this in an allegorical or metaphorical sense. Premack and Premack (1983) stated that the honeybee dances should not be called a language, based on the argument that there is no evidence that the bees can judge whether their dances conform to anything in their surroundings. They also stated that there is no evidence yet for chain communication whereby an animal picks up on the received information without itself experiencing the primary signals inducing the dance. In his studies of dance communication within a swarm, Lindauer (1955) did not observe a bee changing its dance pattern until it had actually visited the second cavity, and these observations were verified more recently by Visscher and Camazine (1999), who observed no higher attraction of bees to dances that indicated the same location as the one for which they had previously been dancing. However, they also found that it takes a swarm longer to get started with the flight to a new nest site if a decision must be made between alternative nest sites and present arguments for some form of collective "quorum sensing" (Seeley and Visscher 2004), indicating that some form of "evaluation" of the incoming information is performed by those individuals in the swarm that guide the whole swarm.

Communication codes can be of three kinds: indexical, iconic, or symbolic (Peirce 1931; Bierwisch 2008). The bee dance certainly contains indexical components, a property particularly strongly expressed by the odor and taste of the nectar fed to recruits. Iconic codes refer to the relation between the code and the object to be communicated, and is strongest for rather similar characters of code and object. Without a doubt, the bee dance is iconical in structure and evolution. Symbolic codes emerge from the relation between the conventions to read the code and do not require any similarity or causal relation between the object (content of information) and its code. The convention can be explicitly defined (e g , as in traffic signals) or developed implicitly, as is the case in human language (Manfred Bierwisch, pers. comm.).

The bee dance combines the first two codes for different messages. The vector components may be based on an iconic code, whereas the quality of the food source or potential nest site may be communicated by indexical codes. Both of these components are determined predominantly by innate mechanisms. Is there a symbolic component in the bee dance?

To address this question, we would need to know what kind of neural or mental states dancing and recruited bees refer to when they transmit and receive the communication signals characterizing the location with particular properties. Do they communicate only the motor performances to be applied for reaching the goal, or do they consult their memory about the location of the site in the same geometric reference frame? Do dancers read out their memory of the experience of the site or do they just convert a stereotypical measure of quality (of the food source, of the potential nest site) into dance parameters?

A first step toward answering these questions has been made by the experiments reported above. We tentatively conclude that dance communication includes a symbolic component because recruits relate their own spatial experience to the information received from the dancing bee.

Discussion

Animals rely on multiple sensory inputs, multiple forms of memory, and different behavioral strategies to travel from one location to the other. It has been a rewarding enterprise to explore the multiple domains of sensorimotor connections separately, but does such a research strategy capture the neural and mental processes adequately? By following such an approach, I believe that we may miss the major functions of navigation altogether. Locations are more than just the endpoint of travel: they are qualified to the animal (e.g., nest, feeding place with particular properties, potential new nest site) and are selected as places to stay or to travel to, depending on the animal's motivational states. In addition, they are related to each other in space. Bees report about such locations and evaluate the reports according to their own knowledge and motivation. They decide whether to apply the information received or ignore it. Thus far we can only speculate about additional processes, such as comparison of received information from multiple reports. Just addressing the question of how navigational memory is organized with respect to spatial relations certainly does not do justice to the problem.

In the spatial domain, honeybee navigation cannot be adequately conceptualized by assuming isolated functions (e.g., egocentric path integration, route learning, instruction, and application) about the vector components in dance communication. Instead, our data clearly document that multiple navigational experiences are integrated in a spatial memory that allows the relating of the characteristics of the locations and their spatial relations. The concept developed on the basis of these data was inspired by the model developed by Jacobs and Schenk (2003) (see Figure 2.4), in which a coarse map (bearing map) is established by relating far-ranging landscape features (gradients) to the sun compass. In our experiments, gradients are irrigation channels, boundaries between agricultural fields, tree lines, and roads. Bees learn these gradients and generalize them when translocated to a different landscape. Isolated islands of sketch maps are thought to be placed into the bearing map and provide snapshot memories of topographic arrangements of landmarks, possibly from one or many vantage points. Such snapshot memories have been studied in great detail at the nest site and the feeding place (e.g., Collett and Graham 2004), but it is still not known whether the idea of a retinal-fixed memory and the assumed routines of reducing mismatch captures the properties of these memories. Since bees travel along routes multiple times when foraging, we added route memory to the Jacobs–Schenk model. Route memories combine both gradient and sketch properties. They are embedded in the sun compass and gradients, replacing one or the other feature if one is missing (e.g., when the sky is fully overcast); they contain an uninterrupted sequence of snapshot memories (Menzel et al. 2010); and the vector components are both tightly stored in working memory and communicated in the waggle dance. This

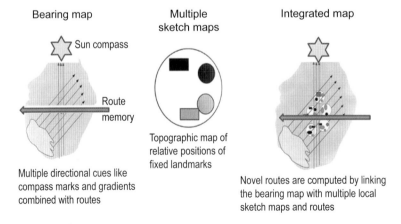

Figure 2.4 Concept of spatial memory structure in the honeybee adopted from Jacobs and Schenk (2003) (see text).

concept assumes that the integrated map does not provide the same information at different locations. In fact, it can be full of "white regions" that lack sketch map memories and are characterized only by the coarse gradient map. Thus far, evidence for this property is lacking, although it has been proposed that the spatial memory of a lake is characterized as a "white region" (Gould and Gould 1982; but see Wray et al. 2008).

I do not hesitate to use the terms "knowledge," "compare," "expect," and "decide" when describing the assumed processes in the bee mind. These terms do not refer to any higher-order mental processes but rather capture the neural operations in working memory that underlie decision-making processes at the level of implicit forms of knowledge. An essential component of such neural processes will be a common representation of experienced and communicated spatial relations, specific characteristics of these locations, and the motivational state of the individual. We interpret our data as documenting a rich form of a common geocentric memory as the structure of navigational working memory and conclude that vector information from the waggle dance is incorporated into such a common memory.

In human language, symbolic codes can be used in different contexts giving rise to semantic and syntactic properties. Applying a loose terminology, one may understand the context dependence of the bee dance (dances for food, for water, for resin, for a new nest site) as an expression of semantic and syntactic components, and describe it in grammatical terms. Would that have any relevance for the communication process between bees? Given our ignorance of the "mental" state of the dancing bee, we should avoid using the term "language" because the metaphorical connotations of this term are too easily overlooked. I suggest that "indexical" or "iconic" communication with symbolic components is a more appropriate descriptive term to characterize the informational status of the dance.

3

Navigating in a Three-Dimensional World

Kathryn J. Jeffery

Abstract

A central theme in the study of animal navigation has been the extent to which such navigation requires the formation of an internal representation of space, the so-called "cognitive map." Although its properties remain disputed, it is now generally accepted that a map-like representation exists in the brain, and neurobiological studies, conducted in tandem with behavioral investigations, have done much to elucidate the neural substrate of the map as it operates in two dimensions. However, to date little is known about how the map encodes real-world, three-dimensional space. Using recent neurobiological and behavioral findings, this issue is explored here. It is argued that the navigational problems in three dimensions are qualitatively as well as quantitatively different from those in two dimensions, and evidence suggests that, perhaps for this reason, horizontal and vertical space are processed separately in the vertebrate brain. The possible adaptive consequences of such an anisotropic encoding scheme are outlined.

Introduction

Navigation has been one of the most intensively studied aspects of animal cognition in the past century because it is a fundamental competence, and because it requires engagement of a number of processes that are also relevant to cognition more generally, such as memory and planning. A central theme in spatial cognition research has been whether there exists an internal representation of allocentric (world-centered) space, the so-called "cognitive map" (Tolman 1948). With the advent of single neuron studies in freely behaving animals, evidence has steadily accrued that this is undoubtedly the case: there is an internal representation of space in the mammalian brain, located in the hippocampal formation and surrounding regions. This representation has many of the properties to be expected of a map, and thus the hippocampal spatial representation is often referred to as the "cognitive map."

Although self-localization, navigation, and the cognitive map have been well studied in two dimensions (2D), the world actually exists in three dimensions (3D). Even animals that are constrained to move over a surface, because they cannot swim or fly, frequently travel over undulating terrain, which complicates distance-measuring (odometry). In addition, many animals, including our evolutionarily distant ancestors (fish) and our close relatives (monkeys and apes), travel freely through volumetric space, as when swimming, gliding or flying, climbing through burrow systems, or swinging through trees. While we humans lost this capacity temporarily, we have recently regained it with the development of undersea, air, and space exploration and, most recently, virtual reality worlds in which we, or our avatars, can "move" freely in all dimensions. Given that so many of our evolutionary ancestors moved through volumetric space, the brain is likely to have evolved a mechanism long ago for representing space in all three dimensions, and not just two of them. However, the question of how this might be achieved has remained unexplored. In this chapter, I address the question of whether the cognitive map is three dimensional, like the world is, or whether it is two dimensional and encodes only horizontal space.

Surprisingly, the question of the 3D structure of the cognitive map has received relatively little attention to date, partly because of the technical difficulties of collecting behavioral and neural data in three dimensions, and partly because it has been assumed that encoding of the vertical dimension is probably just like encoding of the other two. However, encoding three dimensions is fundamentally different from encoding two, qualitatively as well as quantitatively. Recent evidence suggests that the vertical and horizontal components of space may be represented differently, and perhaps separately, in the vertebrate brain; that is, the cognitive map is *anisotropic*. This chapter reviews the neural basis of the cognitive map and examines the question of whether it encodes 3D space, and if so, whether this encoding is indeed anisotropic, and why this might be.

The Cognitive Map in Two Dimensions

The core neural substrate of the mammalian cognitive map is the place cell system, discovered by O'Keefe and colleagues in the hippocampus of freely moving rats in the early 1970s (O'Keefe and Dostrovsky 1971). In this experimental paradigm, recordings are made of the activity of single neurons detected by chronically implanted, in-dwelling electrodes, while animals explore an environment (Figure 3.1a). Place cells are hippocampal neurons that become active in spatially localized regions of the environment, known as place fields, and are thought to encode collectively a representation of the environment and the animal's location within it. Following the discovery of place cells, neurons in surrounding brain regions were discovered that respond to head direction

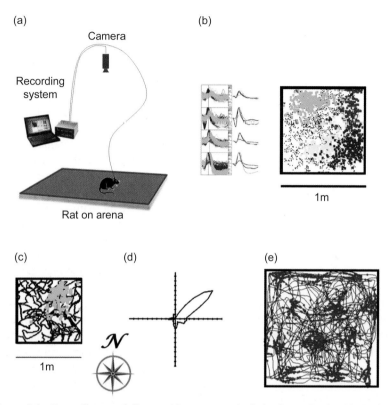

Figure 3.1 Recording spatially sensitive neurons in behaving animals. (a) Typical experimental setup. A rat explores an arena, foraging for food, while recordings of single neurons are made. The signals (action potentials emitted by single neurons) from chronically implanted electrodes are conveyed via a thin recording cable to the recording system. Meanwhile, an overhead camera tracks the position of the animal. (b) An example of a set of single neuron data. The waveforms on the left are action potentials, whose signals were collected simultaneously on four electrodes. Because the potentials from different neurons have slightly different shapes, it is possible to determine which signals came from which cell (color-coded on the figure). The pictures on the right show the action potentials represented as dots, with each dot color coded as for the waveforms and each placed on the location of the rat at the moment the cell fired. These neurons, which were hippocampal place cells, concentrated their action potentials ("spikes") in a spatially localized region of the environment. Note that different neurons concentrated their spikes in different places, so the environment as a whole is represented by the neuronal population. (c–e) Comparison of data from (c) a place cell, (d) a head direction cell, and (e) a grid cell. An arbitrary north is depicted by the compass rose. (c) The place cell has a single firing location ("place field") as shown by the concentration of spikes (green spots) in one part of the arena. (d) The head direction cell's activity is shown as a polar plot of firing rate against head direction. Note that firing rate increases markedly when the rat's head is facing north–east. (e) The grid cell, like the place cell, also lays its action potentials (red dots) down in focal parts of the environment, but unlike the place cell it has multiple place fields and these are arranged in a regular array, suggesting they may function like hexagonal "graph paper."

(for a review, see Taube 2007), hence their name "head direction cells." These cells are thought to function in, among other things, the orientation of the place cell map. Most recently, neurons called "grid cells" have been identified in the entorhinal cortex, upstream of the hippocampus (Hafting et al. 2005), whose function seems to be to encode directionally tagged distances.

The findings of place cells, head direction (HD) cells, and grid cells suggest that the brain is equipped with the essential tools with which to construct and use a map: a compass (HD cells), an odometer (grid cells), and the map itself (place cells). Anatomically speaking, the main direction of information flow is HD cells → entorhinal grid cells → hippocampal place cells, with return connections from hippocampus to the deep layers of entorhinal cortex. Study of these cells, and how they interact, can reveal important clues as to how animals encode space. What follows is a brief discussion of their properties as documented in 2D space, followed by a look at how these neurons may help us understand the encoding of 3D space.

The Place Cell Map in Two Dimensions

We begin with the place cells and the question of how the place cell "map" appears to be constructed from incoming sensory inputs. An example of the remarkable, spatially localized activity—the place field—of a place cell is shown in Figure 3.1b. Early studies of place cells rapidly determined that they are anchored to physical—often visual—features of the environment, because translation or rotation of such features caused place fields to move accordingly (O'Keefe and Dostrovsky 1971; Muller and Kubie 1987). It seems that for place cells, the boundaries of an environment are especially important for anchoring. This was confirmed by a study of O'Keefe and Burgess (1996), in which an environment was transformed by squashing or stretching it; the place cell map also squashed or stretched, although by a lesser amount, suggesting that the place cell map may be attached to the environment by its "edges."

What about place fields that are not *at* the boundaries of the environment, and thus lack its direct sensory (e.g., tactile) inputs? How do they manage to localize their activity so precisely? How does a given cell determine when the rat is at the correct distance from the walls and that it should start firing? A priori two broad possibilities arise, which can be classed as nonmetric versus metric. According to the nonmetric view, place cells are driven by inputs that may correlate with distances and directions but do not directly encode them. For example, if a cell responds to a set of stimuli, such as a visual snapshot (i.e., the exact view from a particular vantage point in the box), and cannot fire in the absence of these specific stimuli, this would constitute nonmetric spatial encoding: although the firing is spatially localized, no distances or directions are explicitly represented. One could not do trigonometry, for example, with such an encoding scheme. On the other hand, if the cell also fires in that same location in the dark when the animal can be shown (by interventional manipulations) to be using only self-motion cues (also known as *path integration* cues), then the cell must be using metric encoding. This is because the only way that visual and self-motion cues resemble each other is that they convey the same information about position; that is, they are *isomorphic*, or informationally equivalent (Gallistel 1990) in the metric domain. Both kinds of sensory information, visual and path integration, are thus converted to a signal that "means" distance (or direction).

The metric view, by contrast, supposes that the cells receive information that explicitly encodes metric information (i.e., distances and directions with respect to fixed features of the environment). Thus, a place cell whose field is destined to be somewhere near the center of the environment receives explicit information about distance and direction from the anchoring boundaries. Initial evidence suggested that place cell encoding in the horizontal plane is probably metric, because the cells indeed show the same patterns of activity both when visual cues are available, in which case they control the activity of the cells (Muller and Kubie 1987), or unavailable, in which case the cells use path integration (Jeffery 2007). Furthermore, place fields are often positioned at a fixed distance from a barrier that is located *behind* the animal (Gothard et al. 1996), again suggesting a distance calculation based on self-motion. The source of direction information is thought to be from a system known as the HD system, while the distance information may come from odometric processes that are combined with the directional signal in a set of neurons known as the grid cells. Head direction and grid cell systems are discussed further below. A more comprehensive description of how place, head direction, and grid cells cooperate to form the place cell map has been given by Jeffery (2007) and Moser, Kropff, and Moser (2008).

The Head Direction Cell Compass in Two Dimensions

Head direction cells typically show remarkably precise responsiveness to the orientation of the animal's head (not body), as shown in Figure 3.1d. They are found in a network of peri-hippocampal structures including lateral mammillary nuclei, anterior thalamus, dorsal pre-subiculum (also called post-subiculum), and retrosplenial cortex. Damage to any of these structures impairs navigation and also, for reasons that are not yet understood, impairs memory for life events in humans. Different cells prefer different head directions, and thus the cells can be thought of as a collection of tiny compasses, each one indicating a different direction. However, the population as a whole always acts coherently, which may allow a unique "sense of direction" to be possessed by the animal at any given moment.

A similar question arises with HD cells as for place cells: How does a HD cell manage to orient its firing so accurately? To compute one's orientation, it is necessary to have some kind of anchor that provides a reference direction, together with some means of updating computed heading following movement.

Visual landmarks seem to provide anchors for HD cells, because rotation of these reliably rotates the preferred firing directions (Taube et al. 1990b). These cues need to be located at some distance from the animal so that their angular location remains relatively stable as the animal moves around. Indeed, evidence shows that HD cells prefer distal landmarks (Zugaro et al. 2001) and that they perhaps do not use proximal ones at all, since place fields (an indirect measure of HD activity) do not rotate with rotation of intra-maze landmarks (Cressant et al. 1997). When an animal enters a novel environment, the newly encountered landmarks are, if possible, linked to the animal's internal sense of direction, which is maintained as it locomotes from familiar environment to new so that consistent orientations can be maintained across connected environments (Dudchenko and Zinyuk 2005). This linkage may not always occur; sometimes, the HD system as a whole may orient differently in different local environments (Taube and Burton 1995). It is possible that animals with magnetoreception or with a celestial compass might use this as a global signal to orient their HD system, but this has not yet been demonstrated.

To update their heading representation, evidence suggests that HD cells use multiple sources of angular self-motion information, both sensory and motor. On the sensory side, the vestibular apparatus detects angular movement with the semicircular canals, in the inner ear, which work by sensing the inertial flow of fluid induced when the head undergoes angular acceleration in any direction. The resulting signal is integrated to provide velocity and position information. In the horizontal plane, the HD cell signal breaks down following vestibular lesions (Stackman and Taube 1997), and thus this signal is clearly useful in updating the heading calculation of these cells. Other sensory sources of angular self-motion include optic and tactile flow, as well as proprioception. On the motor side, it is thought that a copy of motor commands is routed to the HD system to provide advance warning of an impending movement, enabling the system to respond almost immediately to the change in orientation. Evidence for this advance warning comes from the intriguing observation that the firing directions of HD cells in areas closer to the motor system, such as anterior thalamus, more accurately correspond to the animal's future head position than its current one; that is, they are slightly predictive, on the order of about 40 ms (Blair and Sharp 1995).

The Grid Cell Odometer in Two Dimensions

HD cells were discovered about twenty years after place cells, and it was another fifteen before the likely source of distance information to place cells was determined. Recording one synapse upstream of place cells, in entorhinal cortex, revealed spatially sensitive neurons whose firing is not singular, as with place cells, but occurs as repeating, evenly spaced circular regions spread in a hexagonal grid-like array across the surface of the environment (Hafting et al.

2005) (Figure 3.1e). These astonishing firing patterns strongly resemble graph paper (albeit hexagonal rather than square), and may indeed serve a similar function in the spatial system. Recently, evidence has emerged from an fMRI study for a grid cell network in humans as well (Doeller et al. 2010), suggesting generality of the processing mechanism across mammals.

Different grid cells lay down their fields at different positions, even if they are located adjacently in the brain; however, grids in a given animal in a given environment seem to have the same orientation, suggesting a coherent directional input, almost certainly arising from the HD system. The size of the spacing between the fields is characteristic of cells within a particular dorso-ventral level and is the same for all environments, implying the operation of an intrinsic distance-calculating process. Moving down the entorhinal cortex from dorsal to ventral, the scale of the grids becomes ever larger (Brun et al. 2008). Thus, the grid cell system has the capacity to represent environments of different scales. The stable orientation and distance properties make grid cells a likely candidate for the source of metric information to place cells. Consistent with this idea, place cells also increase their scale progressively from dorsal to ventral regions (Kjelstrup et al. 2008).

The question of exactly what kind of information the grid cells convey to place cells, and how, is as yet unresolved. Like place cells, grid cells also stretch and compress their fields as the environment is deformed (Barry et al. 2007). Therefore, they also appear to be anchored to the environment, perhaps by means of the more recently discovered "border cells" in entorhinal cortex (Solstad et al. 2008) and subiculum (Lever et al. 2009), whose firing lies along the boundaries of the environments. They also "remap" (change their firing patterns) when the contextual environment is changed (Fyhn et al. 2007; Alenda et al. 2010), again suggesting some consonance with the place field map. Thus, it seems likely that the activity of grid cells combines to form local, discrete firing fields in the place neurons. However, inactivation of the hippocampus (where the place cells are) causes the grid pattern to break down (Bonnevie et al. 2006), which makes a bidirectional effect seem likely. One possibility, proposed by O'Keefe and Burgess (2005), is that place cells feed their information back to the entorhinal cortex to anchor grid cells, and that grid cells in turn provide (by virtue of their evenly spaced fields) odometric information to place fields.

Place cells, HD cells, and grid cells have been well studied in flat environments, but the world, of course, is not actually flat. As noted earlier, all species have at least some vertical component to their travel, and those that can swim, climb, glide, or fly often spend much of their time traversing all three dimensions. An important issue, therefore, is how these cells operate when the animal moves into the third, vertical dimension. Based on findings from these neurons, the next section explores this question.

The Cognitive Map in Three Dimensions

Why should spatial representation in three dimensions be any different from navigation in two? There are several reasons. First, it is far more complex. In two dimensions, both heading (direction subject is facing) and bearing (direction subject is traveling) can be described with relatively few numbers, let's say, 360 at a resolution of one degree. In a volumetric space, this value, at the same resolution, increases to 130,000 (i.e., 360^2). A similar explosion in descriptive load occurs with the position parameter. Second, gravity means that navigation in the vertical dimension requires more energy; thus the vertical component of a journey makes a much bigger contribution to the cost of that journey. Third, to aid locomotion, the body plan of most animals is asymmetric in the vertical dimension (i.e., there is a "right way up" for the vast majority of living organisms), and this constrains how animals move and may therefore constrain how they map space. Finally, and perhaps most importantly, rotations in three dimensions have different properties from rotations in two in that they interact, which makes them order-dependent ("noncommutative"). This has implications for how a compass system could remain stable in three dimensions. As we will see, the brain may have solved this problem by keeping the vertical dimension separate and processing it differently.

Place Cells in Three Dimensions

Relatively few data exist concerning how place-coding neurons respond to excursions made into the vertical dimension. An early study of rat place cells, made on a surface that could be tilted (Knierim and McNaughton 2001), explored whether the fields would slowly shrink and disappear as the tilting surface moved through their (putatively) globular firing fields. This did not happen: although there was some slight responsiveness to slope, inasmuch as cells altered their firing patterns ("remapped") when the floor was tilted, there was no evidence of true 3D tuning.

Place fields, however, appear to show *some* sensitivity to height above ground, though less so than sensitivity to horizontal position. We made place cell recordings on both a helical track (akin to a spiral staircase) and a pegboard (like a climbing wall) (Figure 3.2; Haymann et al. 2011); in both kinds of apparatus, firing was modulated by how high the (horizontally oriented) animal was above the ground. Firing, however, extended over much greater vertical than horizontal distances, suggesting that the scale of the spatial map is greater in vertical space than horizontal space. Alternatively, it may be that place cells use nonmetric (and less-sensitive) encoding in the vertical dimension. It should be noted that in both kinds of apparatus, the animal's body maintained a horizontal posture while it was climbing. This may be important, as we will see below in the discussion on rotation.

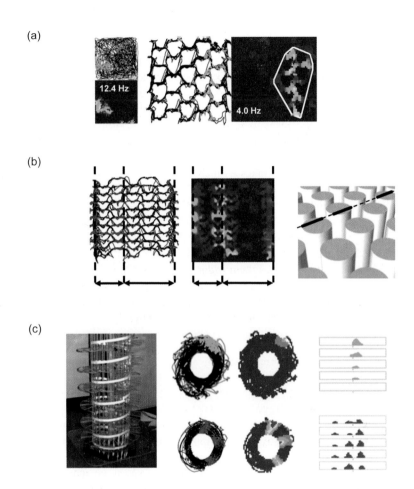

Figure 3.2 Responses of place and grid cells to travel in the vertical dimension, adapted from Hayman et al. (2011). (a) Place cell on the pegboard. Photo (left) shows a rat climbing on the pegs. Middle panel shows the raw data: the path of the rat is shown in gray and the cell spikes as small green spots. Right panel shows the same data as a contour plot (peak in red) with a white line to reveal the extent of the field. Note that the field shows vertical as well as horizontal delimitation. (b) A grid cell on the pegboard. Note that on the pegboard, the firing is aligned vertically as stripes. The middle panel shows the contour plot of the stripes, revealing more clearly the variable inter-stripe distance. The right panel shows a hypothesis about the origin of the stripes: namely, that they represent transections through an intrinsically columnar array of firing fields. (c) A place and a grid cell on a helical track (apparatus as shown in photo). The middle, circular plots show the track as seen from an overhead camera, showing the singular firing field of the place cell (top) and the multiple fields of the grid cell (bottom). When firing is decomposed into individual coils (right plots) and linearized to produce a firing rate histogram, it can be seen that the place cell's firing is vertically delimited whereas the grid cell seems to fire on all coils.

It remains to be seen whether place fields will turn out to be truly 3D (i.e., globular) in a volumetric environment where animals can move freely. There may also be ecological differences, in that animals that use surface locomotion (e.g., rats) may encode volumetric space differently than animals that can move freely in all dimensions (e.g., bats). Since ambulating bats evidently have both place cells (Ulanovsky and Moss 2007) and grid cells (Yartsev et al. 2010), telemetric recordings made as they fly will be particularly illuminating.

Head Direction Cells in Three Dimensions

Two issues must be addressed concerning directional orientation in 3D: How is heading initially computed by HD cells, and how is it updated following rotations? In 2D, heading can initially be established by carry-over of the internal direction sense (maintained by path integration) from the last known heading, or by static landmarks, or both. The same is probably true for 3D, though this has yet to be established. There is, however, an additional cue available in 3D, in the form of terrain slope, which can orient the place cell map (Jeffery et al. 2006) and therefore almost certainly the HD cells. The mechanism by which this acts is unclear. It could be a static cue, acting via gravity detectors, such as the otolith system in the vestibular inner ear together with visual and proprioceptive cues to surface inclination, or it could be a dynamic cue acting via proprioception and kinesthesis as the animal moves around. Experiments with moving versus stationary animals in light and in darkness are needed to address this question.

What about updating? The problem of updating heading following rotations in 3D is complicated. Rotations take place about an axis or, equally, within a plane, where the axis is orthogonal to the plane. This makes rotation a 2D process, unlike translation, with the consequence that rotation in a given plane has a component in each of the other two orthogonal planes. This is shown in Figure 3.3, where it can be seen that the translation of each point in the rotated object has a component in all three planes (X–Y, Y–Z, and X–Z).

Rotations in the three orthogonal planes are described in egocentric terms as "yaw," "pitch," and "roll." For an upright subject, as shown in Figure 3.4, yaw refers to rotations in the horizontal plane about a vertical axis, pitch to rotations in the sagittal plane about the transverse axis, and roll to rotations in the coronal plane about the antero-posterior axis. As there is no complete, convenient set of equivalent terms for rotations in an earth-centered frame of reference, the discussion below will use the egocentric terms together with additional information to orient the planes with respect to the environment.

Updating 3D heading signals has an added complexity because of these interactions between rotational planes; this means that a sequence of rotations in two orthogonal planes produces the same outcome as a single rotation in the remaining orthogonal plane. For example, the rat in Figure 3.5a began a sequence of turns by facing north and finished it by facing west, which amounts

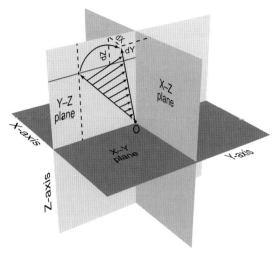

Figure 3.3 Rotations in 3D space. Each of the three spatial dimensions is referenced to one of three orthogonal planes, with each plane being defined by the two axes that bound it: X–Y, Y–Z and X–Z. The large arrow starts in the Y–Z plane and rotates (curved arrow) to its final position. The location of the arrow tip has thus moved in the X-axis (δX), Y-axis (δY) and Z-axis (δZ). If rotation is thought of as translation of a set of points (small arrows), where the translation distance for each point is proportional to its distance from the center of rotation (O), then it can be seen that the set of translations that comprise this rotation has a component in all three planes.

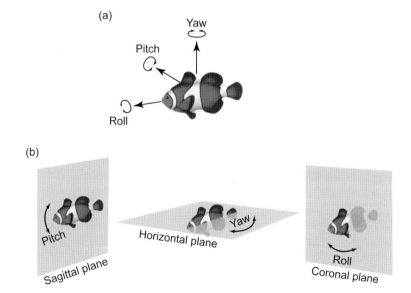

Figure 3.4 Rotational reference terms: (a) the three axes of rotation; (b) the three equivalent planes of rotation.

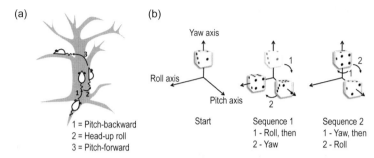

(a)

(b)

Yaw axis

Roll axis

Pitch axis

1 = Pitch-backward
2 = Head-up roll
3 = Pitch-forward

Start

Sequence 1
1 - Roll, then
2 - Yaw

Sequence 2
1 - Yaw, then
2 - Roll

Figure 3.5   Interactions among 3D rotations. (a) Interaction of rotations in three dimensions as a rat climbs a tree, sidling around the trunk in the process. Although the animal has ended up on the branch with an orientation that represents a 90° counterclockwise yaw with respect to the starting heading, it never actually executed a yaw rotation. Thus, for HD cells to maintain a veridical representation of heading they need to adjust themselves during the vertical roll in step 2. This would not be the case, however, if the animal executed a horizontal roll (e.g., about the branch of a tree). Thus, the HD responses to roll need to be modulated by how the roll is oriented relative to vertical. (b) The noncommutativity of rotations in three dimensions. From a starting position (left), the die can undergo a roll followed by a yaw (middle), or a yaw followed by a roll (right). The different ordering of the two rotations results in a different final position and a different final orientation of the die.

to a counterclockwise yaw rotation, even though it did not execute a yaw at any stage of the process. Thus, the order of rotations matters: the end result is not the same for rotation *A* followed by *B* as it is for *B* followed by *A* (technically, it is said that rotations do not commute). This can be seen by rotating a polarized object, such as the die in Figure 3.5b, in 90° increments: first in the roll axis, then in the yaw axis, versus yaw followed by roll. Note that although the rotations in that example are described using allocentrically anchored axes, the same happens if the rotations are described in egocentric terms.

What does this mean for HD cells? It appears that HD cells do not provide a true 3D heading signal. Although, as we have seen, HD cells indicate heading in the horizontal plane and are sensitive to yaw rotations in this plane, they are not sensitive to pitch and roll rotations (Taube et al. 1990a). An experiment with rats climbing up a mesh wall on the inside of a cylinder found that HD cells maintained their firing as a rat moved from the horizontal to the vertical plane and thenceforth reacted on that plane as though the rotations were taking place on the horizontal plane (Stackman et al. 2000). This suggests that HD cells refer their firing to the animal's plane of locomotion and treat this as if it were horizontal. Firing on opposite sides of the cylinder was reversed: a cell that fired, for example, when the animal was facing directly up on one of the panels would fire when the animal was facing down on a panel on the opposite side of the apparatus, and both of these directions were also consistent with the firing on the arena floor. The cells thus did not treat the plane of locomotion in isolation; they also took into account the relationship of that plane to the arena floor. The same geometric transformation that would map the arena floor onto each wall of the apparatus also described the transformation of the HD signal. Interestingly, the signal seemed to disappear completely when the animal was inverted (Calton and Taube 2005), and a behavioral experiment showed that animals also lost the ability to undertake map-based navigation while inverted (Valerio et al. 2010).

What does this mean for the animal's ability to orient in 3D? Clearly, HD cells do not suffice to allow this. There are cells elsewhere in the brain that are sensitive to pitch (Stackman and Taube 1998), but there is as yet no evidence that the signals from these are integrated with the HD signal to provide a true 3D compass heading. In any case, because the HD signal is not referenced to earth-horizontal, a complicated transformation would be needed to extract 3D heading from the mix of planar heading signals coming from the "horizontal" and vertical heading systems. Furthermore, the silencing of the HD signal in inverted locomotion suggests that the system is perhaps trying to avoid certain kinds of unstable state. In the next section, it is suggested that vertical and horizontal heading signals are kept separate to avoid the problem of noncommutativity.

Grid Cells in Three Dimensions

What about grid cells in 3D? The metric properties of grid cells offer a way to determine whether distance measurements in vertical space are encoded differently from horizontal space in the mammalian cognitive map. It might have been predicted a priori that grid cells would form grids in the vertical dimension as well as the horizontal, resulting in a lattice-like array of firing fields. In fact, recordings made on the helical track and the pegboard, described above for place cells, found that the cells showed their usual periodicity in the horizontal plane but, amazingly, did not seem to be modulated at all by height (or at least, very little). This produced a remarkable striped firing pattern when the animals were on the pegboard (Figure 3.6). Thus, it seems that grid cell odometry did not operate in the vertical dimension on these structures.

Two possible explanations may account for the failure of grid cells to account for vertical travel in this experiment. The first is that there is a distinction to be made between vertical odometry while an animal remains horizontal (as on the pegboard and the helix) and odometry when the animal's plane of locomotion (i.e., the plane of its feet) is also vertical (e.g., when climbing a mesh), and it may be that the limitation to vertical odometry applies to the former but not to the latter. In other words, perhaps the odometer cannot determine distances in the direction orthogonal to the plane of the animal's body. Second, it may be that the odometer does not measure distances in the direction of gravity, but only distances orthogonal to gravity (i.e., in the earth-horizontal plane).

If grid cells are not measuring vertical distances traversed, what *are* they measuring? Do they measure distance traveled in the earth-horizontal plane

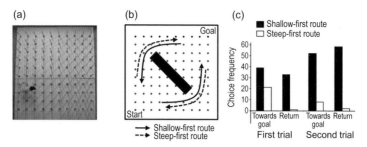

Figure 3.6 Anisotropic route choice in rats, from an experiment reported in Jovale-kic et al. (2011). Rats were trained on the pegboard (a) to shuttle between a start and goal corner. When a barrier was introduced, rats had the choice of taking either a route with a steep segment first followed by a shallow segment, or a shallow segment first followed by a steep segment (b). Rats strongly preferred the shallow-first route (c) on both test trials.

alone, or do they measure surface distance traversed, which would be longer on, say, hilly terrain? The limited available experimental data on 3D path integration predict both possibilities; optic flow and locomotor cues (e.g., footstep counting) convey information about surface travel, whereas data from HD cells suggest that the frame of reference, as discussed above, may be the plane of locomotion rather than earth-horizontal (Stackman et al. 2000). On the other hand, the vestibular apparatus encodes movements relative to the inertial frame of reference of the earth's gravitational field, and data from insects suggests extraction of the earth-horizontal component of travel (Wohlgemuth et al. 2001). Thus, the question has not yet been resolved.

Is the Cognitive Map Anisotropic?

Based on the evidence from place-coding neurons reviewed above, it is hypothesized here that the brain's representation of allocentric space—the cognitive map—is anisotropic, encoding vertical space differently from horizontal space. Specifically, it is proposed that horizontal space is encoded metrically and vertical space nonmetrically. This hypothesis derives from observations that (a) HD cells do not show sensitivity to pitch rotations, and (b) place and grid cells appear to encode vertical space differently, inasmuch as both cell types show elongated firing fields and grid cells do not show periodicity in the vertical dimension in the same way that they do in the horizontal. Since grid cell periodicity is thought to be the means by which place cells receive distance and direction information, the absence of vertical periodicity in grid cells suggests that the place cell map may not itself be metric in the vertical dimension. Thus, the tentative conclusion is that the cognitive map measures distances horizontally but not vertically. Note that "horizontal" here assumes that the animal is oriented normally (i.e., horizontally), moving around with its feet on a plane parallel to the earth's surface. The situation for climbing a vertical wall may, as discussed above, be different, and this issue needs further investigation.

The anisotropy hypothesis is only tentative at present, because place cells may receive metric inputs other than grid cells, which have not been discovered yet. However, map anisotropy is supported by behavioral studies in both animals and humans. Studies of rats in a 3D lattice maze found that they tended to solve the vertical and horizontal components of the task independently (Grobéty and Schenk 1992), and we have obtained similar findings both in a lattice maze and on the pegboard (Jovalekic et al. 2011). Interestingly, in our study we found that the horizontal components of the tasks tended to be solved first: when offered a choice of flat-steep versus steep-flat routes to the same place, rats invariably chose the flat-steep option, irrespective of whether they were going upward or downward (Figure 3.6), suggesting a preference for executing the less costly part of the journey first. A conceptually similar study in humans found that subjects solved the horizontal part of a journey first in a multilevel building (Hölscher et al. 2006). These effects might not be confined to surface-dwelling animals or to mammals. Holbrook and Burt de Perera (2009) found that fish would separate the vertical from horizontal components of a spatial choice. In their experiment, fish were trained on a Y-maze to choose between a left up-slanted tube or a right down-slanted one, and then tested with the conditions reversed (left-down and right-up). The fish tended, surprisingly, to choose the tube that matched the training condition in its slope characteristics regardless of whether it lay to the left or the right. This suggests not only an ability to separate the vertical from horizontal dimensions, but also a preference for vertical information as being perhaps more salient.

Studies of humans orienting in 3D space find that subjects tend to prefer to reduce the degrees of freedom in their representation. For example, Vidal et al. (2004) found that subjects in a virtual 3D maze performed better if they remained upright and had therefore aligned their egocentric and allocentric frames of reference in one of the dimensions. Similarly, astronauts in a weightless environment tend to construct a vertical reference using visual rather than vestibular (i.e., gravitational) cues and remain oriented relative to this (Tafforin and Campin 1994).

What could be the advantages and disadvantages of an anisotropic map in which horizontal and vertical components are separated? At first glance, this seems like a maladaptive strategy. Although a 2D orientation system is commutative in its operation, by ignoring the third dimension the system is vulnerable to mistakes, in situations like the one shown in Figure 3.5a. Another disadvantage is that 3D vectors cannot be computed with a map that is only metric in the horizontal plane. This can be seen by considering a contour map, in which horizontal information is represented in Cartesian (X–Y) coordinates while vertical information is represented by numbered lines. Although it is possible to locate one's position in 3D on such a map, it is not easy to perform navigational computations such as vector addition, needed for homing, or detour planning.

On the other hand, there are several advantages to allocation of horizontal and vertical components of the map to separate processors. To begin, a planar rather than volumetric map imposes a much smaller representational load (e.g., 360 vs. 130,000 "bins" in the directional example given earlier). Second, the separation of horizontal from vertical means that each component of the map only has, at most, a 2D problem to solve. The horizontal, metric component can compute rotations using a commutative process (e.g., simple integration of successive angular displacements) without needing to process the order in which these occur. The vertical processor only needs some kind of information about height: a one-dimensional property. Unless this needs to be integrated with the horizontal processor for 3D vector calculation, a fairly coarse, non-metric representation of height would suffice for most purposes, at least for surface-traveling animals such as rats and mice (and humans). This is because on a surface, the vertical dimension is yoked to the horizontal: for any given X–Y position, there is only one Z position. Therfore, it may be only necessary to have a coarse representation of height to allow heuristic route calculations to occur (e.g., if route A has more hills than route B for the same horizontal distance, then select route A). Whether or not surface-traveling animals perform precise computations of height traveled, or only use heuristic approximations, is a matter for future research.

Conclusions

This chapter hypothesizes that the cognitive map is anisotropic; that is, the brain has evolved to process horizontal and vertical dimensions separately to reduce representational and computational load. Testing this hypothesis will require studies in both behavioral and neural domains. If confirmed, it will have implications not only for the academic study of cognitive mapping, memory, and executive functions, but also technological design in three dimensions, including architecture, spacecraft design, and virtual reality.

Acknowledgments

This work was supported by grants from the Wellcome Trust (GR083540AIA) and the European Commission Framework 7 ("Spacebrain"). The author would like to thank Theresa Burt de Perera and Eleonore Haussner for helpful comments on a draft of the manuscript.

4

Making the Case for the Intelligence of Avian Navigation

Verner P. Bingman

Abstract

When demonstrated, communication, social cognition, and the ability to solve problems are generally considered hallmarks of animal intelligence. The seemingly routine navigational behavior of birds, reflected in their ability to return to remote goal locations even when displaced to distant, unfamiliar places, would seem to suggest a similarly remarkable ability, which combines learning, memory, and representational manipulation. Why, then, is navigation only rarely discussed together with more traditional examples of intelligence? Two factors have nurtured this neglect: navigation can be understood as a purely computational process through which a simple algorithm can lead to goal-directed behavior, and there is uncertainty about whether the underlying neural organization of navigation has the same quality of a freely associating, distributed network, which would characterize mammalian prefrontal cortex and possibly the avian nidopallium. Indeed, the avian nidopallium and hippocampus seem to be part of dissociable neural systems insofar as they can apparently evolve independently of each other. However, the experimental demonstration that the hippocampus is central for homing pigeons to carry out memory-based, corrective reorientation following a navigational error, and the occurrence of so-called hippocampal path cells, which display prospective-like response properties suggesting their participation in representing future navigational outcomes, combine to show that at least hippocampal-dependent aspects of navigation rise to the level of traditional examples of animal intelligence.

Introduction

With some notable exceptions (e.g., Köhler 1925; Tolman 1948), animal behavior research for most of the twentieth century viewed the behavior of animals as being channeled by genetically determined, innate predispositions (classical ethology) or controlled by the regimented rules of associative learning theory. There was little room to even indulge the possibility of intelligence (I choose not to define intelligence formally, preferring our intuitive understanding of what it means) that would enable, for example, insight learning as applied to problem solving, let alone a consideration that animals may have mental experiences. However, the watershed publications of Griffin's, "The Question of Animal Awareness" (1981) and "Animal Thinking" (1984), legitimized in many ways at least a tolerant discussion of intelligent behavior by animals and even a public declaration by some respected researchers that animals may have mental experiences that resemble thought. Considering what has happened over the last thirty years, Griffin's views can only be considered visionary.

Given that Griffin invested a large part of his research career examining the navigational mechanisms of birds, it is bewildering that in his discussions of intelligence he seems to deny implicitly bird navigation as an indication of intelligence. In "The Question of Animal Awareness," Griffin cites numerous examples of the surprising sensory-behavioral abilities of birds and how they may be applied to navigation. However, he does so only to point out that many of those sensory abilities were skeptically considered by earlier scientists, and therefore, behavioral science is full of surprises and we should not off-hand discount animal intelligence or animal mental experiences. Even today, as researchers consider animal intelligence, the emphasis is on things like problem-solving ability, communication, and social cognition. Rarely is navigational ability brought into the discussion. Why?

The Navigational Map of Homing Pigeons and Migratory Birds: Computability of a Gradient Map

An experienced homing pigeon, taken to a location tens of kilometers away from where it has never been before (Wallraff 2005; Wiltschko and Wiltschko 2003), or an experienced migratory bird, displaced by winds or experimentally transported (Perdeck 1958; Thorup et al. 2007) to a location perhaps thousands of kilometers from the familiarity of a previous migratory journey, displays the remarkable ability to reorient in a goal-directed fashion (Bingman and Cheng 2005). The capacity to determine a goal-directed flight path, even after displacement to distant, unfamiliar locations, is supported by what researchers in the field refer to as the *navigational map*. Much of the discussion on the (not to imply there is only one) avian navigational map has focused on its sensory basis, with atmospheric odors being essential for pigeon homing (Gagliardo et al. 2006) and perhaps geomagnetic cues important for the longer distance navigation of migratory birds (see Bingman and Cheng 2005). However, from the perspective of animal intelligence, of more interest are the properties of the spatial representation that capture the sensory information in the form of a metaphorical map (Bingman 1998). Often overlooked is that a navigational map requires birds to (a) learn and remember some sensory quality(ies) that uniquely defines the spatial location of a goal (e.g., the home loft in pigeons or nesting site in migratory birds), (b) learn and remember how the same sensory quality(ies) predictably varies in space and represent that variation in a map-like fashion, and (c) from a "start" location (e.g., release site in homing pigeons or point of displacement in migratory birds) compare the current sensory inputs with the stored sensory quality of the goal location and then compute a goal-directed trajectory based on that comparison. This navigational ability has all the elements of true problem solving:

- by exploring their environments, animals learn how some physical/chemical stimulus(i) uniquely characterizes a goal location(s) and predictably changes in space,
- the information is then durably stored in memory, and
- the same information is then later applied in a spontaneous (nontrial and error) fashion to solve the problem of computing a goal-oriented response when confronted with the novel sensory inputs (challenge) of a displacement site.

Why is this type of navigation behavior rarely brought into discussions of animal intelligence?

Although the properties of a map can be difficult to define, the essential, adaptive feature of any map is that it enables corrective reorientation and the computation of novel routes to goal locations (O'Keefe and Nadel 1978). In free-flying birds, the conventional assumption is that, from locations distant and unfamiliar relative to the goal location, the navigational map is characterized by at least two intersecting sensory gradients (Wallraff 1974). Using homing pigeons as an example, passing through the home loft would be at least two environmental gradients with differing directional axes. For explanatory purposes, it is easiest to assume that the gradient axes are perpendicular to each other, although in reality this need not be the case (Benhamou 2003). For example, a gradient in the intensity of stimulus X would increase to the north and decrease to the south of the loft; a gradient in the intensity of stimulus Y would increase to the east and decrease to the west. After displacement to some unfamiliar location, a pigeon could compare the local values of gradients X and Y with the values at the home loft. Knowing how the intensity of X and Y change in space, the pigeon could then determine its displacement relative to the home loft in the X and Y plane and compute a homeward vector or at least direction (for a fuller explanation, see Wallraff 2005). Adopting this gradient model, it should be clear that bird navigation, at least from distant, unfamiliar sites, can be reduced to a simple algorithm by which comparing current inputs with stored data of the goal location is used to compute a direction and perhaps distance toward home. In my view, the almost Turing machine-like quality of the computations that can support navigation renders it less recognizable as what researchers would generally consider intelligent; after all, a machine can do it as can a neural network model (Jones and Bingman 1996). By contrast, a New Caledonian crow spontaneously fashioning a rod as a hook to access a goal object defies any kind of simple computational modeling and is immediately recognized as a prototypical example of intelligent behavior (Weir et al. 2002), supported perhaps by some kind of mental experience. Does the computational accessibility of a gradient map render it less intelligent?

Gradient Map and Compass Model: How Universal?

In the context of intelligent behavior, a possible source of misunderstanding is the assumption of a *gradient* navigational map. As a gradient, it logically follows that a bird could simply follow the gradient to its goal location, reducing the cognitive demands to simply discriminating locally in what direction stimulus quality changes and then moving in a direction that reduces the difference in local stimulus quality with the memorized stimulus quality at the goal along the lines of a servo-mechanism. However, in birds it is well demonstrated that the map provides only relative positional information; once a bird determines its location relative to home, it engages compass mechanisms, using the sun or earth's magnetic field, to then orient in the goal direction (Wallraff 2005; Wiltschko and Wiltschko 2003). The dissociation between map and compass is easily demonstrated using phase-shift experiments, altering a bird's internal sense of time leading it to misinterpret the position of the sun. When phase-shifted (most studies have been carried out in homing pigeons), birds will orient in the wrong direction relative to the goal indicating that they do not follow a gradient but simply use the gradient data to determine relative position and then a dissociable compass to goal orient. The presumptive gradient map of birds has the properties of a modern GPS system.

Birds are certainly not the only global navigators; sea turtles are similarly successful at navigating with remarkable precision over considerable distances. However, a perhaps naïve assumption is that birds, with their substantially larger forebrains, are likely to possess computational abilities that differ from sea turtles, and this difference could manifest itself as differences in the representational strategies used to guide navigation (Bingman and Cheng 2005). There is accumulating evidence that the navigational ability of sea turtles relies, in part, on the detection and interpretation of variation in the earth's magnetic field (e.g., Lohmann et al. 2004). However, there is no evidence that sea turtles adopt the same kind of map and compass *representational* strategy as birds. To the best of my knowledge, a phase-shift or any manipulation designed to uncouple a map-like positional sense from a compass-like directional sense has never been carried out in sea turtles, leaving open at least the possibility that sea turtles may behave more like gradient-followers than true navigators. Lohmann (2007) has also proposed that geomagnetic-based navigation in sea turtles could function well without assuming anything like a bi-coordinate map assumed to be used by birds. The point is that successful global navigation from point A to point B can be potentially supported by different spatial representational strategies, which may vary in their flexibility and complexity. Based on field observations and experimental studies in experienced homing pigeons and migratory birds, avian long-distance navigation appears to be characterized by a level of map-like flexibility not demonstrated at the same scale in other animal groups; a capacity seemingly equal to tool manufacturing in its spontaneity and complexity.

Considering Brain Organization and the Centrality of the Hippocampus

Leaving aside navigation for the moment, it is worth noting that although one can comfortably approach the question of animal intelligence from a purely behavioral perspective (see above), the properties of any animal intelligence can only be fully understood if examined as well from a neural/mechanistic perspective. As such, if we assume that the strongest case for animal intelligence can be found in nonhuman primates (my apologies for the moment to members of the Corvidae), then it is inevitable that the prefrontal cortex, together with its connections to body-centric regions of the parietal cortex and emotion-regulating areas of the limbic system, is taken as the essential brain system that supports intelligent behavior and, if they exist, conscious mental states. Given that only mammals possess a prefrontal and parietal cortex, does that mean that animal intelligence can only be found in mammals? The absence of a neo(iso) cortex in birds could then lead one to reject carelessly the notion of intelligent avian behavior, including their navigational behavior. However, research in a variety of corvid species over the last ten years or so belie the notion that a prefrontal cortex is necessary for intelligent behavior (e.g., Weir et al. 2002; Dally et al. 2006). In fact, the functional properties of the nidopallium (Rose and Colombo 2005; Güntürkün 2005) of the avian forebrain are remarkably similar to mammalian prefrontal cortex, suggesting convergent evolution in designing, but not necessarily the design, of a neural architecture that can support intelligence. However, what is interesting about the prefrontal cortex and perhaps nidopallium (not enough is known about how nidopallial neuronal populations are coupled to each other) is that they are both extensively connected to other forebrain regions and composed of neuronal populations, at least in prefrontal cortex, generally characterized as operating as a freely associating, distributed network shaped by learning experiences. These brain areas, which are thought to support problem-solving ability and eventual mental states, are notable for their lack of specificity (modularity in a generic sense might be a better word); that is, they are not part of a well-defined, linearly organized neural circuit that is partially dissociable from other portions of the forebrain. As such, the freely associating, distributed quality of prefrontal and possibly nidopallial organization could be viewed as a necessary property of a neural system that supports intelligence.

By contrast, an example of a truly modular-like neural system is the song acquisition and production regions of the songbird brain (Zeigler and Marler

2008). Here, a series of well-defined and semi-isolated brain regions are dedicated to the acquisition of a discrete behavioral output in closed-ended learners (species of songbird that can acquire songs throughout their life spans, including mimics, are certainly more "creative," but they still rely on the same dissociable neural circuit). Although impressive from a number of perspectives, bird song and its dependence on experience and memory rarely qualifies it as a major player in discussions of animal intelligence. Could the modularity of its underlying neural circuitry contribute to its non-inclusion? Returning to navigation and spatial cognition in general, the vertebrate hippocampus is almost an iconic brain structure that would necessarily be central to any discussion of navigation as intelligent. Do the properties of the hippocampus and connected structures reflect the kind of free-associating, diffuse neural network of a prefrontal cortex or the modularity of the avian song system, and should it matter?

How does the hippocampus contribute to the navigational behavior of birds? Most of the work examining the relationship between the hippocampus and long-distance spatial navigation has been carried out in homing pigeons (Bingman et al. 2005). Perhaps surprisingly, the learning and operation of the homing pigeon navigational map, under conditions where it is known to be dependent on variation in the distribution of atmospheric odors, is not dependent on the hippocampus. Where the hippocampus is crucial is when homing pigeons navigate with the use of familiar landmarks or landscape features, typically when they are closer to the loft. A simplified summary then indicates that the homing pigeon navigational map, presumably represented as two intersecting stimulus gradients, is hippocampal independent. Insofar as we wish to equate the hippocampus with intelligent spatial behavior (see below), the intuitive sentiment that any kind of *computable* behavioral flexibility does not satisfy an essential criterion of intelligence (see above) would be supported and lead one to exclude the navigational map from a discussion of intelligence. By contrast, although not nearly as spectacular, landmark- or landscape-based local navigation of distances perhaps extending to 25 kilometers—navigation whose conceptually geometric (but still computational?) rather than gradient properties resemble those of the cognitive map of O'Keefe and Nadel (1978)—is hippocampal dependent. As such, should this latter form of navigation, which would also likely be applied when navigating to local goal locations such as memorized cache sites in food-storing birds, be more suitable for inclusion in discussions of example intelligent behavior?

What about long-distance migration? I have been treating the idea of a navigational map as if there is only one kind, an assumption that is almost certainly an oversimplification. Although I am comfortable assuming that any navigational map would be represented as a bi-coordinate grid, the nature of the sensory information that fills the grid may vary (Bingman and Cheng 2005). For example, how might a navigational map based on atmospheric odors in homing pigeons differ from a navigational map hypothetically based on the earth's magnetic field in long-distance migrants, and could that be of any relevance for hippocampal involvement and notions of intelligence? Here the data are scant with respect to the hippocampus. However, Healy et al. (1996) first document-ed an experience-influenced, relatively larger hippocampus in one migratory species of European warbler compared to a nonmigrant species. In line with the observations of Healy et al. (1996), in some species, migratory populations tend to display superior spatial memory ability compared to nonmigrant popu-lations of the same species (Cristol et al. 2003; Pravosudov et al. 2006), and those differences can correlate with variation in hippocampal anatomical fea-tures (Cristol et al. 2003). These findings suggest that the hippocampus might be more involved in aspects of long-distance navigation which characterize migrants compared to the more modest distances of pigeon homing, although the hippocampus of homing pigeons is also larger than in nonhoming strains of domesticated pigeons. Alternatively, because migrants have at least two famil-iar territories (breeding and over-wintering sites) within which they will need to navigate locally, the hint of a broader role of the hippocampus in migrants may be explained by a greater demand for local, landscape-based navigation (see, however, Healy and Krebs 1991).

The hippocampus can be viewed as a nodal structure for a kind of flex-ible, map-like navigation whereas the nidopallium can be viewed as a structure likely important for behavior more recognizable as "intelligent." Can the spa-tial hippocampus and intelligent nidopallium be truly functionally dissociated? First, it must be noted that although not directly connected, there are several brain regions that share anatomical connections with both the hippocampus and nidopallium (cf. Casini et al. 1986 and Leutgeb et al. 1996). In addition, it is noteworthy that food-storing bird species have been reported to outperform non- or lesser-storing species on spatial tasks (e.g., Kamil et al. 1994), an abil-ity associated with larger hippocampal volumes (Krebs et al. 1989; Sherry et al. 1989). This observation has nurtured the idea that hippocampal-dependent spatial memory, at least with respect to cache memory, is dissociable from other types of memory and, now taking that a step further, perhaps other types of intelligence.

Migrant birds potentially offer some important insight into this issue. Migrant songbirds appear to have generally smaller forebrains than nonmi-grants (Sol et al. 2010; Winkler et al. 2004), although there are potentially confounding variables that make the connection between forebrain volume and migration less than certain. The laboratory of Gustav Bernroider has now taken this observation to a higher resolution by demonstrating that, at least in one sample of North American and Eurasian species, nidopallium volume is considerably larger in non- and short-distance migrants while the hippocam-pus tends to be larger in long-distance migrant species (Figure 4.1) (Fuchs et al. 2010). These findings support other behavioral work (see above) offering evidence that a hippocampal spatial system and a nonspecified, intelligent ni-dopallial system can evolve independently and are functionally dissociable; this speaks directly to the idea of discrete cognitive systems in the spirit of

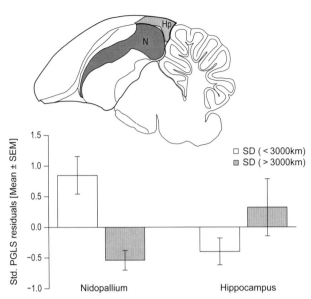

Figure 4.1   Dissociation of hippocampal and nidopallial cognitive systems. Top: Schematic of a sagittal section through the avian brain highlighting the location of the nidopallium (N) and hippocampus (Hp). Bottom: Residuals (deviation from expected means) from phylogenetically corrected, generalized least square regressions (PGLS) using telencephalon volume as a predictor of nidopallium and hippocampus volume in a group of sampled songbird species. Note that the nidopallium is significantly larger than the hippocampus in non- and short-distance migrants (SD, < 3000 km migratory distance) whereas the hippocampus tends to be larger in long-distance migrants (LD, > 3000 km migratory distance). Standard error bars shown. See Fuchs et al. (2010).

Sherry and Schacter's (1987) dissociable memory systems. Although perhaps overly speculative, the same data support the idea that evolution can address the challenges of seasonality either by promoting hippocampal-dependent spatial abilities in support of navigation, which enables migration and escape from seasonally harsh environments, or by promoting nidopallial intelligence to enable birds to problem-solve their way through, for example, a harsh winter. (I am not sure where food-caching fits into this, but it may represent a situation where strong selection has led to both enhanced hippocampal-spatial memory and presumptive nidopallial planning/social cognition.)

Corrective Reorientation, "Path Cells," and an "Intelligent" Hippocampus

Having indulged in some perhaps undisciplined speculation on the nature of avian hippocampal and nidopallial cognitive systems, I would like to combine the findings from two experiments to make the case that at least some aspects of the avian hippocampal spatial system has the properties of intelligence.

Gagliardo et al. (2009) trained control and hippocampal-lesioned homing pigeons to home from two locations. Initially, homing from those locations would engage the pigeons' hippocampal-independent navigational map and compass mechanisms, and no detectable difference was found in their homing ability. The point of the training, however, was to enable the pigeons to learn the landmark and landscape features associated with the path home. By doing so, the pigeons were trained to learn a landmark-based map of the local environment, a map known to be hippocampal dependent. On the critical test releases, pigeons were subjected to a phase-shift manipulation. Because pigeons will initially rely on their navigational map and compass to determine a homeward bearing even from a familiar training site, the effect of the phase shift would initially lead the birds in a direction away from the homeward direction. The question was whether the pigeons learned a hippocampal-dependent landmark or landscape map, which would enable them to recognize the experimentally induced navigational error quickly and allow them to reorient in a homeward direction. Using GPS-data loggers attached to the backs of the pigeons, the recorded flight tracks (see Figure 4.2 for examples) showed that while both groups generally flew in a direction away from home upon release, the control pigeons more quickly executed a corrective reorientation and took a more direct path home. One of the more striking observations was that the hippocampal-lesioned birds routinely crossed the boundary between land and sea (the experiments took place near Pisa, Italy) suggesting that this spatially salient landscape boundary meant little to pigeons that lacked a hippocampus. This finding alone may not suggest that the hippocampus is part of an "intelligent system" as popularly understood, but it certainly suggests in an intuitive way that a pigeon without a hippocampus is less flexible and more likely to perseverate using a spatial mechanism, in this case the sun compass, to guide its navigational behavior when other inputs (e.g., landscape information) clearly indicate that the flight trajectory is wrong. As pointed out to me by Ken Cheng, the poor ability of the hippocampal-lesioned pigeons to abandon a failing navigational subroutine (sun compass orientation) for a potentially more successful one (landmark navigation) would indicate an impaired capacity to solve a problem in an unusual circumstance; an ability often considered a hallmark of intelligence.

Under a very different experimental setting, my lab has studied the spatial response properties of hippocampal neurons as homing pigeons move (navigate) through a maze environment to arrive at locations that reliably offer food (Hough and Bingman 2004; Siegel et al. 2006). What I wish to highlight here is the occurrence of a type of neuron that preferentially responds either in a restricted location along a path that leads to a goal location (local path cell) or along an entire corridor that leads from one goal location to another (integrated path cell; see Figure 4.2). (As an aside, this type of neuron is overwhelmingly found in the left but not right hippocampus and is thus relevant to discussion of the relationship between brain lateralization and intelligence.) The response

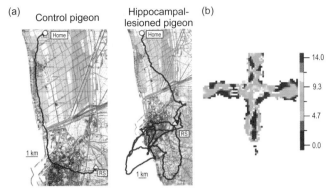

Figure 4.2 Homing pigeon corrective reorientation and hippocampal-integrated path cells supporting the proposal of navigation as intelligent. (a) Flight path reconstructions (red lines) of a control (left) and hippocampal-lesioned (right) pigeon when released from a familiar training site following the purposeful imposition of a navigational error by subjecting the pigeons to a phase shift of the light dark cycle. Note the relatively rapid reorientation of the control bird and the seemingly aimless wandering of the hippocampal-lesioned bird, including flight over the sea, before reorienting homeward. RS (triangle) identifies the release site; HOME (circle) identifies the location of the home loft; the scale bar is located at bottom left of each track (see Gagliardo et al. 2009). (b) Rate map of a hippocampal, "integrated path cell" showing the heightened (red, firing rate scale, spikes/sec, on right) firing rate of a single neuron as the pigeon moved (navigated?) through two of the corridors connecting goal (food) locations at the end of each maze arm. What is not shown is that the increased firing along the north–south corridors primarily occurred *only* when the pigeon was moving out of a maze arm toward the next feeding site; thus the seemingly prospective quality of this kind of neuron. See Siegel et al. (2006).

properties of path cells suggest that they are crucial in representing goal-directed navigational routes. More compelling in the context of intelligence, the neurons do not respond simply to where the pigeon is (a characteristic of the hippocampal place cell of rats) nor the direction the pigeon is moving. Rather, the best descriptor for at least some path cells is that they code for the interaction of where a pigeon is *as well as where it is going* (Siegel et al. 2006). The prospective quality of these neurons seductively suggests that *if* pigeons experience mental states about their spatial future, then the hippocampus with its path cells would be a necessary part of the supporting neural architecture.

Homing pigeons, when purposely manipulated to fly in a wrong direction, can rely on a learned, memory-based representation of local landmarks or landscape features to reorient in a goal-directed fashion; a memory representation that has all the properties of a cognitive map as described more than thirty years ago by O'Keefe and Nadel (1978). (As another side note, but related to an earlier point, an interesting, open question is whether corrective reorientation in migratory birds (Thorup et al. 2007) would be similarly dependent on the hippocampus, or if the kind of gradient map presumably used by long-distance migrants could support reorientation independent of the hippocampus.) The capacity for corrective reorientation can be explained in part by the presence of path cells, which have a notable prospective quality. I leave it to the reader to decide if this combination of behavior and neural representational power rises to the level of tool construction in New Caledonian crows as a demonstration of intelligence and perhaps even a candidate for conscious awareness.

Conclusion

One of nature's greatest spectacles is the seemingly routine but nonetheless alluring migration of birds. Carrying out a goal-directed flight of potentially thousands of kilometers and challenged by winds that can blow them hundreds of kilometers off course, experienced migrants engage a navigational system that enables them to return year after year to within a few meters of the previous year's nesting site. Less spectacular but better understood is the range of map-like and compass abilities of homing pigeons. But why is navigational behavior neglected in discussions of animal intelligence?

I have avoided any attempt to define intelligence, preferring to rely on our intuitive understanding of what it means. This can be viewed as a weakness, but using that intuitive understanding I have tried to make the case that at least aspects of hippocampal-dependent navigation rise to the standard of intelligent behavior, leaving open to discussion how a computational gradient map should be viewed. Many of the ideas presented are highly speculative and may not withstand closer scrutiny or future experimental findings. However, one consequence of recognizing hippocampal-dependent spatial behavior as intelligent would be to de-emphasize the importance of any particular kind of neural organization (i.e., neocortical or nidopallial) as necessary for flexible, nontrial and error problem-solving ability. By doing so, this would allow us to consider intelligence more thoughtfully in perhaps unlikely places such as navigational behavior in sea turtles and bees (e.g., Menzel et al. 2005).

Acknowledgments

My sincere thanks go to Gustav Bernroider and Anna Gagliardo for the many engaging conversations regarding avian navigation and the nature of animal intelligence. Special thanks to Ken Cheng and Sue Healy for their very helpful comments on an earlier draft of the manuscript. Roman Fuchs, Anna Gagliardo, and Ryan Peterson prepared the figures; Diana Klimas helped with editing. Portions of this work were funded by NSF grant IOS-0922508, and the support of NSF is gratefully acknowledged.

First column (top to bottom): Sara Shettleworth, Jan Wiener, Kate Jeffery, Hanspeter Mallot, Vern Bingman, Sue Healy, Jan Wiener
Second column: Vern Bingman, Nora Newcombe, Randolf Menzel, Nora Newcombe, Ken Cheng
Third column: Randolf Menzel, Sue Healy, Lucy Jacobs, Sue Healy, Sara Shettleworth, Kate Jeffery

5

Animal Navigation

A Synthesis

Jan Wiener, Sara Shettleworth, Verner P. Bingman, Ken Cheng,
Susan Healy, Lucia F. Jacobs, Kathryn J. Jeffery,
Hanspeter A. Mallot, Randolf Menzel, and Nora S. Newcombe

Abstract

Navigation, the ability to organize behavior adaptively to move from one place to another, appeared early in the evolution of animals and occurs in all mobile species. At the
simplest level, navigation may require only movement toward or away from a stimulus,
but at a more sophisticated level, it involves the formation of complex internal representations of the environment, the subject's position within it, the location of goals, the
various routes from current position to goal and possible obstacles along the way. The
vast array of navigational capabilities in various species has made it challenging for
students of comparative cognition to formulate unifying frameworks to describe and
understand these capabilities, although the variety also confers an exciting opportunity
for asking comparative questions that are hypothesis driven.

A unifying framework, the *navigation toolbox*, is proposed to provide a way of
formulating common underlying principles that operate across many different taxa. The
toolbox contains a hierarchy of representations and processes, ranging in complexity
from simple and phylogenetically old sensorimotor processes, through the formation
of navigational "primitives" such as orientation or landmark recognition, up to complex cognitive constructs such as cognitive maps, and finally culminating in the human
capacity for symbolic representation and language. Each element in the hierarchy is
positioned at a given level by virtue of being constructed from elements in the lower
levels and having newly synthesized spatial semantic contents in the representations
that were not present in the lower levels. In studying individual species, the challenge is
to determine how given elements are implemented in that species, in view of its particular behavioral and anatomical constraints. The challenge for the field as a whole is to
understand the semantic structure of spatial representations in general, which ultimately
entails understanding the behavioral and neural mechanisms by which semantic content
is synthesized from sensory inputs, stored, and used to generate behavior.

Introduction

Navigation is one of the most fundamental problems that animals and humans confront. It is based on a complex interplay of a large number of different processes and components, and requires the integration of spatially relevant information across sensory modalities, the formation and retrieval of memories, and the selective activation of task-specific representations. Thus, navigation comprises a paradigmatic case of cognitive functions operating across several levels of complexity ranging from sensorimotor loops to higher forms of cognitive processing.

Because navigational tasks are performed by most animal species, in a wide variety of environmental conditions, over very different spatial scales, and using a variety of sensorimotor systems, the analysis of navigation poses an exciting but difficult challenge for comparative cognition. That such a variety of sensory inputs and motor outputs could all be subserved by the same general mechanisms seems a priori unlikely. Nevertheless, some fundamental processes may have been conserved by evolution, whereas others may have evolved convergently in different taxa. Comparison of animal species and their associated environmental adaptations provides us with vital information about the potential representations and processes that are involved in navigation and is a key strategy in identifying both the general as well as task- and species-specific components.

Comparative studies of navigation in a wide range of species have revealed certain processes which appear to be fundamental, inasmuch as they appeared early in evolution and have persisted, and other processes that seem to be more recent and more complex. Furthermore, evidence, some of it reviewed in this chapter, suggests that the more complex and recent processes are, in many (if not all) cases, synthesized from the older and simpler processes. This can be concluded not only from behavioral studies which look at the different abilities displayed by different animals, but also by studies of the underlying neurobiology and of how these processes are organized in the brain. These considerations have led us to propose a taxonomy of navigational processes, organized hierarchically, to try and capture the elements of this synthetic process. This taxonomy, which we call the "navigation toolbox," forms the basis for organizing the subsequent discussion of what we know, and what we have yet to discover, about how animals and humans navigate. Having outlined the processes in the toolbox, we then use it as the basis to explore the synthetic processes that gave rise to the higher-level elements before concluding with an examination of how these tools may be used in decision making and planning.

The Navigation Toolbox

The toolbox that we propose (Figure 5.1) was compiled by considering findings in the literature on animal behavior and neuroscience concerning navigation and its building blocks. It comprises a collection of processes and representations ("tools") that have been identified by various research enterprises as contributing to navigation in species of different kinds. Each species has access to a subset of the tools in the toolbox, and it uses these tools to construct navigational behaviors. We acknowledge that alternative typologies and vocabularies exist in other disciplines, such as the spatial ontologies proposed by computer scientists (e.g., Kuipers 1978, 2000), the space syntax developed by architects (Hillier and Hanson 1984), the concepts employed by geographers and used in applied sciences that rely critically on the analysis of spatial relationships such as geographic information system (GIS) and cartography, the formulations of mathematicians working in metric geometry or topology, and even the long-standing philosophical debate about absolute and relative space. Ultimately, intensive cross-disciplinary discussion is needed to delineate the points of correspondence and difference among these approaches. Many of the differences may derive from the different data types considered, as well as differing assumptions and goals in the various fields.

The toolbox is organized hierarchically, distinguishing between lower-level sensory processes and higher-level processes thought to operate on the lower-level components. This is, inevitably, an artificial and hence imperfect hierarchy; for convenience we have made it discrete, whereas in reality there is no clear dividing line between simpler and more complex processing capabilities. However, we hope the organization of the toolbox may be useful for students of navigation in thinking about how complex behaviors are synthesized from more elemental processes in the nervous system.

Level	Level 1 Sensorimotor toolbox	Level 2 Spatial primitives	Level 3 Spatial constructs	Level 4 Spatial symbols (uniquely human)
Elements	Vision Audition Olfaction Touch Kinaesthetic Proprioception Magnetic cues Thermoreception ...	Landmarks Terrain slope Compass heading Local heading Panorama Boundaries Posture Speed Acceleration ...	Cognitive map Self-localization Goal-localization Frames of reference	External maps Wayfinding signage Human language
		Contextual information (e.g., motivation, odor)		
	▼	▼	▼	▼
Behavior supported	e.g., Taxes, kineses	e.g., View matching, beacon navigation	e.g., Cogn. mapping, path planning	Communicating spatial information

Figure 5.1   The navigation toolbox.

Navigational elements (representation or processes) are assigned to different levels of the hierarchy according to two principles:

1. Elements at a given level are synthesized by integration of elements at lower levels.
2. Elements at a given level possess new spatial semantic content not present in the lower levels.

Although the first principle is intuitively obvious, the second requires some explanation. By "spatial semantic content" is meant the "meaning," in spatial terms, of the given element; in other words, how the content of that element relates to some real-world parameter. Examples could be heading, distance, or "place." An example of "new spatial semantic content" might be construction of a position vector by integrating information about distance with information about direction. Not only is the new representation synthesized by integration of elements at lower levels, it also contains additional spatial information. With this new, semantically richer representation, it is possible to perform more sophisticated navigational feats, such as homing or shortcutting. Thus, the hallmark of navigational complexity is the synthesis of internal representations. We will return to this point in the discussion of cognitive mapping.

The navigation toolbox has four levels:

1. *The sensorimotor toolbox* comprises different sensory modalities (e.g., vision, olfaction) and simple motor processes (e.g., approach and avoidance), and provides information relevant for locomotion and navigation. In mammals, these processes take place in, or near, primary sensory or motor cortices. The elements of the sensorimotor toolbox are also involved in other, nonspatial behaviors (e.g., mating, predator avoidance, tool use, or social interaction).
2. *Spatial primitives* are a set of representations that animals build, using the sensorimotor tools in Level 1. For example, an animal may combine the pattern of optic flow, computed in the visual system, together with linear acceleration signals extracted from the otolith organs in the inner ear, to help construct a representation of velocity. Velocity is a spatial primitive in the sense that while it is metric, being a measure of distance traveled per unit time, it does not in itself contain positional information. It can, however, be used to *compute* position, a Level 3 representation. Another example is landmark identification, another higher-order process that may make use of several sensory modalities. Again, landmarks in themselves do not contain positional information, but can be used to compute position if the animal can determine their relative distances and directions with respect to itself. These navigational building blocks are formed using integrative processes (discussed in detail later in the chapter).

3. *Spatial constructs* are even higher-level, more complex, spatial representations constructed from the spatial primitives (Level 2). An example could be position, calculated by identifying landmarks and determining their distances and directions—all Level 2 processes in our hierarchy—and using these to create a representation of current location by a process known as piloting. In a complementary manner, velocity signals computed using Level 2 processes can be used to update a positional calculation, by interaction with the piloting process. Moreover, by relating such positional calculations with landmarks, an integrated representation of space can be formed at Level 3. As with Level 2, the underlying integrative processes in Level 3 are explored later.

4. *Spatial symbols*, including human language and graphic representations, allow for external storage and interindividual communication of Level 3 spatial constructs.

Generating Behavior with Navigational Tools

A given organism does not need all of the tools, or even all of the levels in the toolbox, to generate navigational behavior. Spatial behavior can be supported by any or all four levels of the navigation toolbox, as follows:

- The sensorimotor toolbox can support spatial behavior that is based purely on sensory processes, or sensorimotor loops. Examples of such behavior are taxes and kineses (e.g., positive phototaxis in flies), which do not require forming representations of space or spatial concepts, as may occur in the higher levels of the navigation toolbox. All that is required is simple detection of a stimulus, such as light or odor, and then organization of movement either proportional in its intensity (kinesis) or toward or away from that stimulus (taxis).

- At the level of spatial primitives, information from the sensory toolbox has been integrated to form simple representations that may lack positional information, but which are useful in some kinds of navigation, and are used to build complex spatial representations. At this level, simple locomotion and navigational behavior (such as centering by keeping optic flow equal on the two visual hemispheres, beacon navigation, or view matching) is supported (see Shettleworth 2010b, Chapter 8), but the assembly of more spatially complex internal representations is not yet implied.

- The third level of the navigation toolbox, spatial constructs, consists of representations that are built from the spatial primitives. At its more sophisticated level, integration of primitive nonspatial processes, such as landmark identification, together with primitive relational information, such as the relative distances and directions of landmarks, can result in a spatial memory structure (an internal representation of space) that is in many ways map-like, and is often referred to as a "cognitive map." The extent to which animals of various kinds do or do not possess a memory organized like a cognitive map has been the source of lively debate over many years (see below).

- The fourth level of the toolbox, the spatial symbols, allows for unique behavioral feats in humans, such as navigating to an arbitrary place given a street address anywhere around the world. However, more importantly, humans exhibit the ability to communicate their navigational computations, to a high level of sophistication, to other humans, via maps, language, and mathematics. Map drawing exists, to a very restricted degree, in other species (e.g., bees) as does vocal communication, but the level attained by humans far surpasses anything seen in the rest of the animal kingdom in its flexibility and productive power.

Spatial behavior supported by Level 2 (spatial primitives) and Level 3 (spatial constructs) of the navigation toolbox is of particular interest for comparative cognition: at these levels, we are able to move away from species-specific mechanisms toward general principles of navigation. For example, migrating birds may have access to magnetoreception whereas insects are capable of perceiving polarization patterns in the sky. Despite these differences on the sensory level (Level 1), both sources of information are utilized or integrated to derive semantically equivalent information about space—a compass heading (Level 2). Similarly, honeybees and desert ants rely primarily on different sensory cues (optic flow and proprioception) to estimate the distance that the animal has traveled (odometry). Bees flying over a large range of local cues and following long-ranging landmarks, however, are equipped with the capacity to integrate these spatial structures in such a way that they localize themselves and navigate to the intended goal by novel shortcuts (see Menzel, this volume). Differences occur not just on the sensory but also the motor side. An example is the navigation behavior of the desert ant *Cataglyphis* which, when running over a featureless landscape, seems to primarily rely on an elementary form of path integration, whereas ants navigating in a landscape rich in local cues, such as *Melophorus bagoti*, appear to learn sequences of turns in relating measures of path integration with these cues in their rather stereotypical foraging routes. These examples illustrate that the processes operating during navigation are heavily constrained by the animal's action space.

One might think of these higher-level representations (compass heading or distance) as being *supramodal* (i.e., independent of or "lying above" specific sensory modality) and of having meaning (semantic content) independent of the neural implementation. Such abstractions allow not only comparison across species, but also for interactions between students of natural and artificial navigational agents.

The navigation toolbox thus provides an organizational framework that allows for more systematic cross-species comparisons of higher-level principles supporting spatial navigation, independent of species-specific implementations. We suggest that by attempting to fit the diversity of navigational inputs and outputs seen among species into this proposed framework, we will make significant progress in understanding the similarities and differences in their navigational (and cognitive) abilities. However, having extracted general principles, it is then important to consider whether and how species-specific constraints influence information processing. For example, does an animal's action space and complexity of neural integration determine the set of spatial primitives that are used by the animal? In addition, what is the influence of the animal's navigation range, and how do the properties of its habitat influence how it uses the spatial primitives and spatial constructs available (Figure 5.1, Levels 2 and 3)?

Before examining the integrative processes that lie behind the construction of these navigational elements, let us consider the four levels in the toolbox in more detail.

Level 1: Sensorimotor Processes

The simplest level of the navigation toolbox contains a set of sensory and motor processes that can support simple navigational processes, such as taxes. These sensory processes are used to build higher-order tools in the toolbox and will not be considered further here. Increasing evidence supports the notion of top-down modulation of sensory processing, and it may be that some kinds of simple navigational process, such as template matching for view-based navigation, might occur at very early stages of neural processing, such as primary sensory cortical areas.

Level 2: Spatial Primitives

Many navigational phenomena, particularly those seen in laboratory settings using small-scale environments, can be explained by one or more mechanisms which are more sophisticated than simple sensory-driven Level 1 processes such as taxes, but are nevertheless spatially still relatively unsophisticated (i.e., belonging to Level 2 of the navigation toolbox). Spatial primitives are considered to exist at a level of complexity above sensorimotor elements for two reasons: (a) they are synthesized *from* Level 1 elements, and (b) they have spatial (or proto-spatial) semantic content not present in those elements.

An example of a spatial primitive is landmark recognition. The majority of species that have been studied to date rely on landmarks, at least some of the time, to help organize their spatial behavior; thus this competence seems to be phylogenetically old, although landmark recognition may require different levels of processing sophistication: an ant may simply recognize a landmark as being a particular retinal pattern as part of a panorama (Collet and Collet 2002). In this case, the "snapshot" is a code of the place or viewpoint from which it has been taken. In addition to this snapshot memory, primates might have a multimodal, viewpoint-independent representation built using object-processing capabilities in the perirhinal cortex. Here, one landmark memory may be used in the recognition of more than one place, and the places recognized may be remote from the actual landmark position. Landmark identity, being (usually) multimodal, is a semantically different category from a simple stimulus pattern impinging on a sense organ. Note, however, that the simplest forms of recognition (e.g., odor detection or the ant landmark recognition example above) could be considered as bordering on Level 1 processes, reinforcing the notion that this is not a hierarchy to be taken too rigidly. However, while a landmark may be necessary for spatial navigation, it is not sufficient inasmuch as it contains no spatial information; unless the goal is *at* the landmark, the animal needs other information in order to navigate. In this sense, the landmark, being space-free, is a spatial primitive. If the goal is at the landmark, then a simple kind of navigation (e.g., beacon homing) is supported, and evidence suggests that many species can do this.

Spatial primitives can support behavior that looks remarkably complex to an observer. Navigation by view matching provides an example: it requires a representation of the goal (a standard, e.g., a snapshot or a panorama recorded at the home location) and a record of the current location. According to the snapshot model (Cartwright and Collet 1982) the difference between the standard and the current record is computed by a comparator, resulting in an error. This error is thought to drive the movement of the navigator and in this way the error is reduced. View matching can thus be conceptualized as a servomechanism (Cheng 2006). Beacon navigation requires landmark identification, which may be a higher-order object recognition process, but the behavior that follows is simple approach or avoidance. At a more sophisticated level, a turning movement could be organized to the left or right on the basis of a perceived stimulus; this introduces the beginnings of true spatial (i.e., relational) processing and such behavior lies on the boundary between Levels 2 and 3.

Navigating along a well-known route is another example of behavior supported at Level 2, allowing animals to reach distant destinations even if these are beyond the current sensory horizon. It can be explained assuming spatial primitives, such as a string of beacons or landmarks, to identify the place at which a particular turn has to be conducted. These turns can be informed by motor responses associated to the place. A series of such recognition-triggered responses, therefore, is sufficient for explaining route navigation. Importantly, such processes do not require the operation of a cognitive map, although this does not in itself rule out that some animal species use a map, even in route following, if one is available.

Heading calculation is another well-known example of what we call here a spatial primitive. Many species are able to extract earth-relative directional information from either magnetic or celestial compass cues. Behavioral and neurobiological studies in the laboratory have additionally revealed the existence of local orientational reference frames which are conferred by local cues such as distal landmarks. Heading calculation is an interesting process from a theoretical point of view because it may require the bringing together of very different sensory information streams (directional cues, e.g., with respect to a compass, landmarks and multimodal self-motion cues) to synthesize a semantically new, supramodal representation (such integration processes are discussed in more detail below). As with landmarks, heading alone is of limited use in navigation but is of very great use when combined with other spatial primitives, such as distance leading to an integration of traversed path (i.e., path integration), for example, in the formation of goal or homing vectors. In its basic form, path integration integrates rotational and distance information (both spatial primitives), resulting in a home vector (i.e., a working memory representation of the distance and direction to the home or to other places encountered during travel). When heading home, the animal moves so as to reduce this home vector to zero. It may be debated whether such a home vector represents a spatial primitive or a spatial construct (see next section). If, however, the status of the path integration measure is associated with other spatial primitives, such as landmarks, this would allow the formation of long-term representations of metric relationships between different places in the environment. In this case, path integration undoubtedly becomes part of a spatial construct.

Level 3: Spatial Constructs

Having established a collection of relatively primitive tools which animals may have access to for navigational purposes, we focus now on Level 3: the spatial constructs. As with the previous levels, the elements in this level are characterized by having been synthesized from lower-level elements and by having new semantic content. An important new semantic category is that of *position*, a relational term that implies specification of a subject or an object by means of adjacencies or neighborhoods, distances, or bearings to other memory items. We will call such relations a frame of reference without implying that it has to take the form of a metrical coordinate system. As such, one of the most interesting and contentious issues has been the extent to which it is appropriate to place, in this level, a representation that could be considered map-like.

A good example of a spatial construct is the local vector (Collet and Collet 2002). In executing a local vector operation, contextual cues, such as a view, are associated with path integration to enable travel in a particular compass direction. A view of the surrounding scene, one spatial primitive, serves as the trigger to execute a behavior that relies on another spatial primitive, a compass upon which a direction of travel is derived. Local vectors based on the current state of path integration have been well demonstrated in desert ants (*Cataglyphis*: Collet et al. 1998; *Melophorus*: Legge et al. 2010). It is possible that route-following behavior consists of a string of such local vectors, with the end of one local vector providing the initial conditions (e.g., the appropriate view) to trigger the next (Trullier et al. 1997; Cheng 2006). If such associations between places and local vectors are spread in the vicinity of a goal, they can support homing from an area exceeding the sensory horizon, or catchment area, of a single snapshot marking the home (Cartwright and Collet 1987).

A closely related example is that of path integration. As discussed in the last section, path integration can be viewed as a spatial primitive combining velocity and heading over the course of a journey so as to maintain a constant, ongoing representation. Alternatively, when combined with landmark information, it can be seen as an example of a spatial construct including relational information of landmarks. The exact nature of this representation has not been fully elucidated and may vary according to species or settings: it could be a vector (e.g., the distance and direction back to a home base at a particular location or to another known position) or it could be a location in a cognitive map (see below). If the path integrator transiently fails, or if the animal has just arrived in the environment, it can undertake a position fix using a different set of spatial primitives: namely, available landmarks together with their computed distances and directions. The process of taking a position fix from familiar landmarks is, as mentioned earlier, known as piloting.

The sophistication of Level 3 constructs also allows for navigation toward unseen goals. Insofar as a given species uses such relational spatial constructs, goals can be defined as attractive locations in the spatial reference system, and the task for the animal is to reach the goal from its current location. For spatial behavior at Level 3, it is assumed that the goal cannot be approached simply by steering toward a beacon at the goal or executing a set of landmark-stimulated responses or a learned sequence of body turns. Instead, Level 3 constructs are relational, whereby more than one spatial primitive is required to be integrated to solve the spatial problem.

The Cognitive Map

In the section on spatial primitives, we explored navigational behaviors that can be achieved with relatively simple processes, such as view matching and beacon homing. Other navigation behaviors, in contrast, cannot be explained without reference to a spatial memory in which places are related to one another in a common reference frame. Such a reference frame-based spatial memory system is usually called a *cognitive map*. This is an interesting class of spatial semantic information that is likely possessed by humans (Gillner and Mallot 1998; Hartley et al. 2003), and for which the existence in other animals has been disputed (Bennett 1996; Shettleworth 2010b).

The strongest evidence for the operation of a cognitive map, in the sense of a connected allocentric representation of familiar space, has been seen as the ability to take a shortcut or a novel route under conditions in which path integration, view matching, and beacon orientation can be excluded. While the exclusion of these processes is difficult to achieve experimentally, this can be demonstrated, for example, when an animal is displaced from a goal-oriented route and needs first to self-localize, on the basis of local cues, and then to correct for its displacement in order to reorient toward a goal. What kind of memory structure would allow an animal to relocate its position relative to the goal and subsequently compute a corrective direction to the goal? It can be argued that only a spatial representation with features that resemble a map could enable such corrective reorientations. The critical feature of this representation which makes it map-like is its ability to support spatially relational processes: self-localization and vector calculation.

Thus, the term "cognitive map" has frequently been used to refer to internal spatial representations that organize spatial knowledge about different locations in the world by relating them to one another either by adjacencies or in a common reference frame. The term originated in experimental psychology with Tolman (1948) and was memorably utilized in a widely cited book by O'Keefe and Nadel (1978). While the concept of cognitive maps has been criticized for being used too often as a metaphor without reference to mechanisms, researchers working on navigation in the field where the animal is allowed to navigate in an open space find *map* a useful concept and see evidence for *cognitive maps* in several species and settings (see Menzel and Bingman, both this volume).

The organization of spatial information in the mammalian (rat) brain can also be seen in terms of mapping. In fact, the place and grid cell systems in rats constitute a neural substrate of metric information/coordinate system (see Jeffery this volume; Hafting et al. 2005). Similarly, functional brain imaging studies in humans navigating large-scale virtual environments demonstrate that novel shortcutting or route-planning behavior recruits a different cortical network than route-following behavior (e.g., Hartley et al. 2003); the "map task" used in this and similar studies can be solved with a memory based on place adjacencies, leaving the possibility that the underlying "map" is not using metric coordinates but only a simpler graph structure (Gillner and Mallot 1998).

As discussed above, cognitive maps need to encode spatial relations between locations in the environment, either as a graph of adjacent places or via an allocentric reference frame. Spatial behavior specified in Level 3 of the navigation toolbox—such as self-localization, goal-localization, and the formation of a plan designed to get to the goal (cf. definition of spatial planning below)— require such relational knowledge. Although spatial relations between places can be encoded in a topological (i.e., nonmetric) graph-like format, in which places are represented as nodes and transitions between places are represented as edges (graph-theoretic representation), the inclusion of metric information appears to be crucial to explain a number of behavioral findings (Menzel, this volume).

In humans, evidence of metric information in spatial long-term memory is debatable (see, however, Schinazi et al. 2009). For example, Foo et al. (2005) trained subjects to walk along two straight paths from a starting point, thereby acquiring clear knowledge of distances and directions of each path. When re-leased at the end of one path, shortcutting to the end of the other path was poor (for an analogous study in dogs, see Chapuis and Varlet 1987). Note that this shortcutting is not a type of path integration but requires metric recombination of local distance and angle information from long-term memory. The question about the amount of metric information encoded in the cognitive map remains controversial. A challenge for the future will be to answer a number of ques-tions that are related to this point:

1. Is metric knowledge a prerequisite for cognitive maps?
2. Is metric knowledge equivalent to cognitive maps?
3. How does local and global metric information relate to the concept of the cognitive map?

A different notion of the map has been suggested for birds. Often discussed in the context of bird navigation is a map, referred to as the "navigational map," formed by intersecting stimulus gradients that form a bi-coordinate sys-tem by which any point in space is characterized by a unique combination of coordinates (Wallraff 2005). These coordinate values could provide a global allocentric reference frame with respect to which items of spatial long-term memory (places, landmarks, "home") could be represented (for further details, see Bingman, this volume).

Some of the controversy on the nature of the cognitive map may arise from a confounding of separable functions which must be integrated for novel short-cutting but which may be used independently. For example, it may be neces-sary to analyze separately the cognitive map component derived from distrib-uted cues, such as compass bearings and gradients, from those derived from discrete cues, as done by the parallel map model for the integration of such cues (Jacobs and Schenk 2003; reviewed in Menzel, this volume). Because of the necessity of an underlying distributed cue representation (i.e., a bear-ing map) for shortcutting, it may be difficult to demonstrate true cognitive map shortcutting in small laboratory settings. In the notable exceptions (e.g., Roberts et al. 2007), the experimental space is characterized by an extreme paucity of discrete cues, which may force the animal to rely on bearing-map function, even in the relatively small space of a laboratory maze. In contrast, free-flying birds and insects may naturally recruit a strategy based on such distributed cues, which would enable them to shortcut flexibly. Therefore, one of the challenges for future navigation research is to develop well-controlled laboratory experimental paradigms that will allow us to distinguish spatial be-haviors supported by Level 2 processes and Level 3 processes.

Level 4: Spatial Symbols

The final class of navigational elements in our hypothetical navigation toolbox is an almost uniquely human capacity: the ability to use external symbols to represent space. This ability allows semantic information to be developed beyond that which can be achieved by the neural navigation systems embedded in the brain. Two classes of symbolic manipulation are particularly important in this regard: language and mathematics. Here we concentrate primarily on language, because its role in ordinary day-to-day spatial navigation processes has been the focus of intensive recent study.

Are There Uniquely Human Navigational Strategies? Is There a Role for Language?

Humans have a distinctive, and arguably unique, capacity for symbolic representation and communication (see Figure 5.1, Level 4). Symbolic systems include language, of course, but also encompass more spatial systems such as gesture, sketching, drawing, and external maps. In the context of comparative cognition, two questions need to be considered. First, to what extent does the availability of Level 4 have a top-down influence on the prior levels? This classic issue concerns the extent to which language (as well as other symbolic systems) influences thought. Second, to what extent does the availability of Level 4 extend or augment the capabilities available in species that only have access to the first three levels? That is, are symbolic systems powerful tools for augmenting spatial functioning?

To What Extent Does the Availability of Level 4 Have a Top-Down Influence on Prior Levels?

Thinking about this question has concentrated almost exclusively on spatial language. It is interesting that there are some notable design mismatches between space and language: space is continuous whereas language is categorical; multiple spatial relations are available simultaneously in the world, but must be discussed sequentially in language. Given these considerations, one might suspect that spatial language can be helpful in spatial functioning, but perhaps to a limited extent.

Strong claims have been made that spatial language *shapes* spatial thought (e.g., Levinson 2003). A prominent and often-cited example of such shaping concerns languages that require the use of compass-referenced coordinates to describe spatial relations (e.g., the cup is to the *north* of the plate). By contrast, many other languages describe this spatial relation in a relative fashion (e.g., the cup is to the *right* of the plate). Experiments have been done in which speakers of these contrasting types of languages have been asked to view objects arranged in a line on one table, and then to place them in the same way on a second table after rotating the objects 180 degrees. In many studies, as reviewed in Levinson (2003), speakers of absolute languages maintain the correct compass directions in their reproductions on the second table, while speakers of relative languages use a relative coding internal to the array. However, Li and Gleitman (2002) have shown that these results can be altered through small environmental manipulations so that, for example, speakers of relative languages will produce absolute reproductions when a landmark is available (e.g., a pond at one end of the table). They suggest that there is a great deal of flexibility in spatial representations and thought, so that language picks out certain systems of spatial coding but does not preclude the existence of others (see also Gallistel 2002; Newcombe 2005).

The issue of the uses of spatial language has special resonance in terms of thinking about human development, since, of course, children begin life without having a language and acquire language(s) over the first few years of life. Two lines of research have been important in recent thinking about how spatial language affects spatial development. First, it has been argued that the spatial language which infants hear structures their acquisition of spatial concepts (e.g., Bowerman 1996). For example, Korean children, who hear a language in which the distinction between "tight fit" and "loose fit" is an important semantic contrast, acquire the perceptual and conceptual basis for the distinction, whereas English children do not. A contrasting position is that infants begin with an array of spatial concepts (either innately specified or acquired in the first year) and subsequently map certain of those concepts to the language they hear around them (e.g., Mandler 1996). Data gathered on this issue seem to favor the position that spatial concepts exist before spatial language, but that spatial language draws attention to some of these concepts and dampens others, making the concepts used frequently more available and the ones not used more difficult to activate (see review by Göksun et al. 2010).

Second, Spelke and her coworkers claim (Hermer and Spelke 1996) that language (specifically, productive control of the terms "left" and "right") is essential to being able to use features for reorientation in the geometric module paradigm introduced by Cheng (1986; reviewed by Cheng and Newcombe 2005). Others claim that children younger than 6 years behave like nonlinguistic, nonhuman animals by using geometric information alone to reorient, ignoring useful featural information. They also report a transition to a uniquely human use of features as well as geometry at the age of 6 years (with the advent of the productive use of the words "left" and "right"). However, the failure of toddlers to use features turns out to be specific to the use of extremely small spaces of limited ecological validity (Learmonth et al. 2002). Recently, Twyman and Newcombe (2010) reviewed the extensive literature that has accumulated on this issue, arguing that a variety of evidence indicates that feature use is far more flexible than has been argued by the Spelke group, and that language is not necessary to the development that does occur (although it could be helpful, as could other kinds of experience).

What about symbolic systems other than language? Few, if any, strong Whorfian positions have been taken on the topic of how maps (or other visuo-spatial systems) might mold spatial thinking. Uttal (2000) reviewed how maps affect spatial development, arguing that they are helpful in acquiring abstract spatial concepts and in systematizing spatial thinking. This view, however, merely augments the position related to our second question; it does not take a deterministic stance. Dehaene, Izard, Pica, and Spelke (2006b) claim that the basic geometry of maps is innately available without experience and suggest that maps merely capture knowledge rather than mold it. However, their data from Western cultures show development in the use of some map-relevant concepts that does not occur in their Amazonian population, suggesting a role of cultural input (see Newcombe and Uttal 2006).

Does the Availability of Level 4 Extend or Augment the Capabilities Available in Species that Only Have Access to the First Three Levels?

Spatial language and other spatial symbolic systems seem to aid spatial thought in a powerful way, even if they do not have a strictly determinative effect. For example, babies learn spatial concepts better when the concepts are labeled (Casasola et al. 2009), and, similarly, teaching children a particular spatial word (such as "middle") seems to support their learning of the corresponding spatial concept (Simms and Gentner 2007). Preschool children whose parents use more spatial words (such as "outside" or "corner") show stronger spatial growth than children who do not hear as much language of this kind (Pruden et al. 2010). Spatial thinking in adults is also clearly affected by spatial language (Boroditsky 2001; Casasanto 2008), although some studies of this kind take a turn back in the Whorfian direction.

Maps may be as important as or more important than language in giving human navigation a distinctive quality (Uttal 2000). Maps have been used by humans for millennia (possibly up to 8,000 years), though there have been notable technical advances over the past centuries (e.g., the discovery of a means of measuring longitude and navigation assistant systems that guide navigators to the destination). External maps offload memory and cognitive processing demands, allow for communication and social interaction toward a spatial goal, and highlight areas of ignorance (i.e., territories not explored or separate territories that are known internally but whose relation needs to be determined).

While maps are very elaborate external navigation aids, humans also design and utilize less complex tools to communicate spatial information (e.g., signposts). Such simpler means of communicating spatial information are not unique to humans but are also found in animals. Many animal species, for example, mark their territories with "scent posts" which could be seen as aids to conspecifics in detecting territory boundaries. The most famous example of spatial communication in animals is the waggle dance of honeybees (von

Frisch 1965). In fact, bees use symbolic communication to convey distance and direction information to food locations. However, this is a closed system which lacks the productivity and flexibility found in a true language.

Synthesis and the Navigation Toolbox

The navigation toolbox identifies several sets of processes and representational structures, some taxon-specific and some more general, that can be integrated in the service of navigation. This integration is useful for two reasons. First, for a given type of information, two sensors carrying information of the same semantic content are better than one: the accuracy of detection can always be improved by increasing the number of detectors. Second, as discussed earlier in this chapter, integration of information streams having different semantic content allows for the formation of higher-order representations that allow computations not possible at the lower levels. These two types of integration are discussed in turn.

Integration of Information Streams that Have Similar Semantic Content

In many cases it is advantageous to combine semantically equivalent information sources to derive maximum advantage from all the information available. Homing pigeons, for example, may use both sun compass information and magnetic compass information (both Level 2 primitives, and both belonging to the semantic category of "heading") to compute the direction toward the home. The information sources may even come from the *same* sensory modality (e.g., from two visual landmarks both intermittently visible in foggy conditions). Cue integration presents an interesting problem, however. What should the brain do with these two sources of information? Should it average them, or choose one or the other? If the former, should all sources be given equal weight or should some count more toward the average than others? If the latter, how is the decision made to prefer one over the other?

Bayesian approaches provide a normative framework for modeling how and whether animals should combine versus select information from multiple cues to make inferences or judgments. The importance of the Bayesian approach is its reliance on the existence of "priors," which comprise preconfigured knowledge about the nature of the incoming information. An example of a Bayesian prior would be past experience that a landmark is positionally unstable. Prior knowledge allows a decision maker to discount information known to be unreliable, or at least to rely more heavily on sources known to be trustworthy. Specifically, the Bayesian framework suggests that the available sources of information should be weighted in inverse proportion to their reliability, as measured in terms of variance in the estimate. The principle applies when the animal has multiple sources of information (such as Level 2 primitives) which may be combined and the animal has a past history of relevant experiences (the Bayesian prior) which may be used to weight the current information sources. While Bayesian probability theory has been extensively used in human spatial perception, it has also been proposed for the integration of spatial information in other species (Cheng et al. 2007). It is important to note that controversy remains concerning the value of the Bayesian approach for the explanation of animal navigation behavior. This is because (a) at present there is little evidence for Bayesian integration outside of humans and (b) the Bayesian approach provides a formalism that addresses the statistics of information sources rather than the animals' responses to these sources. While Bayesian approaches are often accepted as useful for hypothesis generation, the direct relation between the formalism and actual behavior is arguable (Jones and Love 2011).

While it is advantageous to combine semantically equivalent information sources in many cases, it sometimes makes more sense to choose one or the other in a winner-take-all (or "first past the post") manner. The question then arises as to how to determine which approach to take. Cheng and colleagues (2007) and Körding (2007) argue that the Bayesian framework predicts the integration of different sources of spatial information only if these sources indicate directions near to each other. If, however, the two sources indicate directions very different from each other, integrating and thus averaging will result in a direction that is indicated by neither of the two sources, which makes integration unreasonable. In cue-conflict experiments, this lack of integration is often exploited to compare the behavioral relevance of different information sources, such as different Level 2 primitives. For example, phase- or clock-shift experiments in homing pigeons result in a large difference (conflict) in the indicated compass direction to the home between the sun compass and magnetic compass—a situation where integration, in the Bayesian view described above, should be unlikely. Indeed, under phase-shift conditions, homing pigeons rely almost exclusively on the sun compass with very little integration of magnetic information in the final behavioral output (Wallraff 2005).

Similarly, studies of place neurons in the rat hippocampus have found that the ensemble location-specific activity will rotate to follow small shifts (10–20°) of a landmark, but will fail to follow large shifts (180°) which introduce a large discrepancy between the landmark and the animal's internal sense of direction (Rotenberg and Muller 1997). Prior history of the landmark also influences how the neurons respond: they will tolerate reasonably large angular rotations of the landmark if the animal did not see these occur, but will not follow the landmark if the animal saw it moved (Jeffery and O'Keefe 1999). An interesting and unresolved question concerns whether the place system is able to reweight the reliability of various cues based on the animal's own internal state. For example, if an animal has been deprived of vision for some time, allowing time for its path integrator to drift, it may be more inclined to tolerate large discrepancies between external and internal cues than if its path integrator was recently reset and hence more reliable.

**Integration of Information Streams that
Have Different Semantic Content**

As well as simply improving detection accuracy for information of a single semantic category, integration can occur when streams of semantically different information converge to form semantically new kinds of information. A prototypical example of integration to form a semantically new representation is the head direction system in rats: vestibular, proprioceptive, motor efferent, and visual signals are combined to form a representation of the orientation of the animal's head. The incoming sensory information is semantically different in nature. Vestibular signals, for example, code for accelerations of the animal's head, whereas visual information conveys the presence and/or location of static landmarks. The Level 2 primitive that results from integrating these Level 1 sensory inputs, the head direction signal, is a supramodal representation because it is not anchored to a particular sensory modality and is not a particular information type; instead, it arises through the convergence of several different kinds. Supramodal representations allow an organism to make use of different kinds of information having different properties. In the case of the head direction signal, the self-motion cues are imprecise but always present, whereas landmarks are very precise but only available sporadically (e.g., when the animal is looking in their direction). By using both, the organism derives an adaptive advantage. Indeed, it can be speculated that the great enlargement of the cerebral cortex during vertebrate evolution derives from the development of multiple supramodal representations in many different domains.

Even more importantly than simply exploiting the advantages of different cue types, the resulting representation is of a semantically different class: "heading," which was not present in the original inputs. This allows the brain to construct signals with new properties and enables an organism greater flexibility in its behavior. In the head direction cell example, the construction of a heading signal permits an animal to navigate even in directions in which there is no specific cue present. Furthermore, it is one of the building blocks to formation of yet another semantically new class of information, the cognitive map, which in turn allows an animal to perform such feats as navigational planning.

Bayesian rules can be used to model integration of semantically different information, just as they can be used to integrate cues of the same "sort." For example, in using head-mounted virtual displays, Warren et al. (2001), found that humans integrated two kinds of information, both providing a heading direction toward an object (beacon). Subjects used both the focus of expansion in optic flow, in which the optic flow pattern expands from the point toward which we face and the identified beacon object. This was shown by dissociating the two cues in virtual reality. In human path integration, both visual cues (optic flow) and cues from the body senses (kinaesthetic and proprioceptive senses) are used (Kearns et al. 2002; Nico et al. 2002).

Bayesian priors might not just affect whether cue combination or choice occurs, but also the hierarchy of cue preference in cases when choice is necessary. Cue-conflict experiments have been a classic method for examining the hierarchy of cue use in spatial problems (e.g., Brodbeck 1994). The hierarchy appears to be dependent on the species, their ontogenetic experience, and on reliability of the cues. For example, when solving spatial problems in the field, free-living hummingbirds use information in a context-dependent manner: They will use the color of a flower, but only if spatial information is not relevant (Hurly and Healy 2002). They will learn the location of a flower relative to other flowers if the other flowers are relatively close (up to 40 cm) but will ignore the information once they are further away (> 40cm; Healy and Hurly 1998). In squirrels, the use of a hierarchy or a majority strategy appears to change by season under natural conditions, suggesting that physiological changes induced by photoperiod and/or experience may constrain or mold the attentional resources available for spatial mapping and hence the final strategy used for orientation (Waisman and Jacobs 2008). In adult humans, the choice of a geometric or featural cue depends on the size of the enclosure (Ratliff and Newcombe 2008). Geometric cues seem to be preferred in smaller spaces, whereas featural cues are followed in larger ones.

In summary, cue integration has the advantage of allowing an animal to maximize its use of information: it can choose the most reliable cues and discount the less reliable; it can use different cues in different ways, depending on their characteristics; and it can combine cues to form supramodal, semantically new representations that allow more sophisticated calculations. For some navigation behavior, Bayesian approaches appear to describe how information can be combined. Determining how general Bayes's rule is in navigation, and how it is implemented at the neural level, remains a challenge for the future.

Cue Integration and Cognitive Mapping

Integrating spatial primitives (Level 2) into spatial constructs (Level 3) is a crucial feature of cognitive mapping. Essentially, different Level 2 primitives, such as landmarks that may define particular locations in space, are related to one another either by adjacency or in a global reference frame (see above section on "The Cognitive Map"). One proposal is a common coding system that integrates location on a coordinate map constructed from distributed cues (the bearing map) with the topological relations of discrete objects (the sketch map) encoded in relation to their location on the coordinate map (the integrated, i.e., cognitive map; Jacobs and Schenk 2003).

Localization of self, other, goal, etc. is a central process of Level 3 and requires either a place representation, which may be recognized from landmarks or some other context in the neighborhood, or a specification of the locality (i.e., frame of reference). It is usual in the field of spatial cognition to distinguish between egocentric and allocentric frames of reference (both Level 3 constructs), where egocentric is self-referred and allocentric (literally: "other-centered") is referenced to the external world. Egocentric frames of reference follow the animal around, as it were, and neurobiological studies in mammals indicate that there are many such reference frames, at least in this taxon, encoded in parietal cortex. The mammalian frames are anchored variously to the eye, head, arm, etc., and need to be integrated for actions to be coordinated. Likewise, there are probably many different allocentric reference frames. Three have thus far been identified: (a) object-centered, in which encoding is specified relative to an object; (b) earth-centered, in which encoding is specified with respect to global latitude/longitude and north/south; and (c) encoding referenced to the local environment (as delineated by boundaries, landmark arrays, etc.). These allocentric frames have been identified in a variety of taxa, including insects, birds, and mammals (Burgess 2006; Lohmann et al. 2008; Nitz 2009).

An open question in navigation concerns whether and/or how integration might take place across allocentric reference frames. This can be examined at the level of the neural substrate and/or at the behavioral level. In the literature on egocentric integration, Anderson et al. (1985) have proposed that interactions between reference frames occur whereby neurons encoding one frame modulate the activity of those in another through a process known as gain field modulation. For example, in monkeys, neurons in parietal cortex that respond to the position of a visual stimulus on the retina are modulated by how the head is oriented with respect to the torso, and their activity thus reflects both parameters. An analogy in the allocentric domain might be found in rodent hippocampal place cells whose response to a boundary is modulated by how that boundary is oriented with respect to direction (Jeffery, this volume).

At the behavioral level, we often see examples of choice rather than integration. Cue dissociation experiments suggest that animals can plan navigational trajectories in more than one reference frame. There are several strategies to utilize the memory of a location encoded by multiple reference frames. An animal could simply pick one frame from the list of remembered frames, or it could orient to frames in a fixed hierarchy of preferences, as seen in juncos and black-capped chickadees, respectively (Brodbeck 1994). An animal could also construct a majority strategy, where the animal chooses the location indicated by the majority (2 of 3) of the remembered frames of reference, with no preference for one frame over another, as has been shown in squirrels (Gibbs et al. 2007; Waisman and Jacobs 2008).

Animals that undertake long-range migration often use an earth-centered allocentric reference frame, but animals with local ranges may have reference frames that are defined by local environmental features. In rodents, data from single neuron recordings suggest that encoding of local environments is metric; that is, it contains information about distances and directions (Jeffery, this volume). An unknown question concerns how independent local reference frames (e.g., patches in a heterogeneous foraging environment or, as in humans, different rooms in an office block) can be related to each other, and whether these between-room relationships are metric or whether they are simply topological (reflecting adjacency relations only). Furthermore, we do not know whether animals are able to represent environments in which they are not currently placed and whether (if so) they do this in a strictly metric way. Recently, research has begun on how spatial maps at local levels can be interconnected and coordinated to allow for navigation in large and complex (and changing) natural environments (Derdikman and Moser 2010), and pursuing this issue is a clear challenge for the future.

Efficient navigation in three-dimensional space requires computing and integrating both horizontal and vertical position. The computation of position in two dimensions requires integration of distance and direction, or (equivalently) distance in two orthogonal directions, in a trigonometric-like fashion. How this is done remained mysterious until recently, when studies of the neural representation of space in mammals revealed the existence of grid cells and so-called conjunctive cells, whose activity seems to combine distance and direction in the horizontal plane (Fyhn et al. 2004; Sargolini et al. 2006). The next question concerns whether the third dimension (i.e., the vertical dimension) is integrated in a similar fashion, using neurons sensitive to distances in all three dimensions. Until now, there are very few experimental data on this. Ecological considerations suggest that many species—those that swim, glide, fly, or climb—would benefit from an integrated three-dimensional representation, because they move freely in volumetric space. On the other hand, the theoretical considerations outlined by Jeffery (this volume) suggest that this would be computationally expensive, so that a modified two-dimensional representation might have to suffice. Resolution of this remains a matter for future research, and comparative studies will be particularly important here.

Using the Navigation Toolbox: Decision, Planning, and Memory Processes in Navigation

As well as self-localization (a sensory process) and orchestration of movement (a motor process), navigation requires decision making, planning, and memory, because there may be more than one way to navigate to a goal, or more than one goal, or the usual route to a goal may be blocked. In cognitive science, planning is usually conceptualized as searching for a path (i.e., a solution) in a problem space. A problem space is a mental representation of the problem containing knowledge of the initial state and goal state as well as possible intermediate states. Our discussion below centers on the questions of how to define decision making and planning in the context of animal navigation. We consider these processes in light of the contributions made by elements in the navigation toolbox.

Decision Making versus Planning

It is useful to distinguish between decision making and planning, although these are often conflated in discussion. Decision making can be defined as choosing between alternative options and, depending on the exact definition, may not require any form of internal representation at its simplest level (for more detailed discussions on definitions of decision making, see Seed et al., this volume). Decision making could thus, in principle, be supported by simple processes in Levels 1 and 2 of the navigation toolbox. By contrast, planning occurs if this choice is informed by simulated future states of the system. In the context of navigation, this means that an animal has to form expectations about future payoff if it makes a particular spatial choice. At its most sophisticated level, navigational planning could potentially involve expectation or simulation of future *location*. The operation of such simulations could be said to involve recruitment of spatial constructs (Level 3) of a map-like representation (the cognitive map), and the question of whether nonhuman animals can do this is so far unresolved (see, however, Menzel, this volume). Next, we discuss what kinds of navigational decision making could take place without the need for a map, and what kinds would need true map-dependent planning.

Mapless Navigational Choices

Many quite sophisticated navigational behaviors can be orchestrated without the need for activation of a cognitive map. Navigating along a well-known route, for example, requires choosing between different options at intersection or choice points. These choices, however, can be informed solely by recognition-triggered responses or servomechanisms (i.e., mechanisms that do not require reference to a planning process as discussed here) nor to any kind of map-based representation. Navigation along a route can therefore be explained by only assuming spatial primitives (i.e., Level 2 of the navigation toolbox) such as landmarks or panoramas to identify a specific choice point, together with an associated local heading to inform about the required movement direction. In the context of this discussion it is important to stress that such choices can therefore be explained without internal simulations of future states and as such, they constitute decision making but not necessarily planning. When these decisions are automatic and not influenced by any representation of a goal, they are said to be *habits*.

Planning, in contrast, requires goal-directed actions. Much of the traditional support for the distinction between habits and goal-directed actions discussed by Dickinson (this volume) comes from studies of rats in mazes and runways. Habits continue automatically even when their outcome is devalued, whereas goal-directed behavior is sensitive to the value of its outcome. For example, if the animal is satiated on the food that it will find at the end of its trip, goal-directedness would mean not setting out, or setting out in search of a different goal. Good evidence that some small-scale spatial behavior has this property has been obtained in laboratory studies with a few species (Dickinson, this volume). To what extent does behavior of other species in more naturalistic spatial tasks provide evidence that it is goal directed in the same sense? The behavior of honeybees, which routinely travel among multiple goals in a flexible way, indicates that bees choose to fly either along novel shortcuts to one of the goals or to apply the memory for a flight direction that would have taken them to the intended goal if they had not been transported to an unexpected location. Honeybees also choose between the information they receive from dance communication and their own experience from former foraging flights. After they have made such a decision they can correct themselves if the outcome did not meet the expectations, and fly along a novel shortcut to the other location, a behavior that meets our definition of planning (see also Menzel, this volume, who interprets these findings as support for planning in relation to a cognitive map).

Navigational Planning Requiring a Cognitive Map

Which experimental paradigms in animal navigation research address planning processes that require a cognitive map? It is generally agreed that to confirm the operation of a cognitive map, it is necessary to demonstrate behavioral planning that has a spatial component (e.g., showing that an animal can compute a novel shortest-path route to a goal).

An example of the minimal test of map-based planning is a route-planning experiment in vervet monkeys (Gallistel and Cramer 1996), in which baited locations are arranged in a diamond shape. When starting from the lower corner, the shortest possible path depends on whether the animals are required to return to the start location. The most efficient path to the upper corner is a zigzag route. If, however, a monkey intends to return to the starting position, because it was baited after the monkey left it, a different route is optimal, resembling a diamond in this traveling salesman task. Choice at one of the baited locations is reportedly influenced in a flexible way by options that are present only later in the navigation task (i.e., the absence or presence of a food reward at the start location). In other words, animals use memory of the options and information about their current state to take different paths according to the circumstances (for a related paradigm in humans, see Wiener et al. 2008).

Experiments like these certainly seem suggestive of the operation of maplike planning processes. However, in situations that require training about each possible path, as in many experiments on small spatial scales (such as in the experiments described above), it seems difficult to provide cognitive map-like knowledge without conditional discrimination training that, for example, in the presence of cue A, path A is the most profitable, in the presence of cue B, path B is, and so on. If the animal then chooses appropriately, depending on whether A or B is present at the start, planning cannot automatically be assumed. Because

Gallistel and Cramer did not describe how their monkeys were trained, their experiment is potentially subject to this objection.

Experiments like these, in which animals can be shown to make decisions informed by the activation of internal spatial representations, are needed to demonstrate the operation of cognitive maps convincingly. The difficulty is that such demonstrations must take place in a single probe trial, because from the second trial onward, rapidly acquired associative reinforcement processes could, in principle, explain successful navigation. However, one-trial processing is difficult to show in animals, because novelty responses often override their goal-directed inclinations on the first probe trial. Thus the question of whether nonhuman animals use map-based planning in navigation is still not fully resolved.

An alternative approach would be to observe internal cognitive representations directly and, indeed, some neurobiological studies are beginning to provide evidence suggestive of spatial simulation processes. Recently, van der Meer and Redish (2009, 2010) provided evidence of this from electrophysiological experiments investigating decision making and planning in navigating rats. The animals were trained to run loops on an elevated track to receive food reward. Between sessions, the rewarded side is varied such that at the beginning of each session, rats were uncertain about the correct choice. During this period of relative uncertainty, rats paused longer at the critical choice points than at other choice points. Moreover, while pausing at the choice points, sequential activation of place cells with place fields around the choice point may be observed (Johnson and Redish 2007). Van der Meer and Redish interpret these findings as rats representing future locations (i.e., simulating the outcome of a spatial decision), which is a crucial aspect of spatial planning. The rats' behavior here seems to be an example of the classic phenomenon of "vicarious trial and error" (VTE), in which animals spend time sampling the cues associated with the options in a difficult discrimination. As discussed by Seed et al. (this volume), one criterion for true decision making is that the latency to choose between options is greater than to accept either one alone. Evidence for behavioral and/or neurological VTE suggests that observations of spatial behavior may provide evidence for decision making according to this criterion.

Because of the difficulties in demonstrating convincingly cognitive mapping in small-scale laboratory settings, it has been suggested that navigation experiments in large-scale spaces, such as the animal's natural habitat (or a city-like environment in the human case), may be a more promising arena for collecting planning relevant data. For example, Wiener and colleagues used large-scale virtual environments to investigate route-planning behavior in humans (Wiener and Mallot 2003; Wiener et al. 2004). They demonstrated that the hierarchical organization of spatial memory influenced participants' route choice behavior and proposed a planning mechanism that uses spatial information at different levels of detail simultaneously. Analogous data might, in principle, be obtained by observing how the paths animals take through their familiar home ranges vary across days and seasons. Short-term changes in routes may appear to reflect planning, for instance, to visit certain kinds of trees when their fruits are available. However, it may be difficult to infer anything about spatial knowledge and plans from such data, which are typically gathered without experimentally manipulating the animals' knowledge or goals (see Janson and Byrne 2007).

In summary, one of the challenges for future navigation research is to develop controlled experiments to investigate spatial planning. According to the definition introduced above, planning requires the animal to form internal representations of simulated future states, given a particular movement decision scenario. Furthermore, spatial (i.e., map-based) planning requires these simulated states to incorporate spatial information, as shown, for example, in the ability to calculate shortest or least-effort paths, or to find novel detours that reveal a knowledge about the spatial relations of connected spaces. One possible way to demonstrate that animals/humans do, in fact, form such representations might be to demonstrate behavioral or physiological responses to the violation of their expectations (which may be conceptualized as "surprise"). An alternative approach, which is just beginning, is to observe the underlying neural processes directly. It may be easier to see future simulations (sometimes called "preplay") in neural activity, although interventional studies would be needed to show that these processes are causally related to navigational behavior. Emerging technologies, such as optogenetic manipulation of neural circuits, will be very exciting in this regard.

Concluding Remarks and Future Directions

Our review of the current status of animal navigation research has focused on overarching principles that arise independently of a given animal substrate. Comparing across a range of species whose navigational competence varies from simple to sophisticated, we note that complex and more phylogenetically recent abilities appear to be synthesized from simple, phylogenetically older ones. Using this observation as a starting point, we organized the panoply of navigational behaviors loosely into a hierarchical framework—the navigation toolbox—which is a collection of processes that can support, either alone or collectively, navigational behaviors of varying complexity. This collection is organized such that elements in higher levels are synthesized from elements in lower levels, acquiring new semantic content in the process.

We argue that the ability to integrate across sensory modalities and semantic classes, so as to generate semantically new information (such as "position"), expanded during brain evolution. It reaches a peak in the human ability to represent spatial information symbolically, using language and mathematics, deriving entirely new semantic content in the process (e.g., multidimensional space, non-Euclidean space, complex space).

The task now, in comparative cognition, is twofold. First, at the level of individual taxa, we need to know how a given element in the navigation toolbox is implemented: in route following or beacon homing, for example, which sensory modalities, and spatial primitives, are recruited to enable decision making? Second, more broadly, we need to understand the underlying neural principles behind certain types of spatial computation. For example, how does the brain do "trigonometry," and is this process the same across all taxa or have multiple solutions evolved independently?

Finally, there remains the open question of whether any animal other than humans make use of the complex internal representation of spatial relations, which is sometimes called a "cognitive map," and even to what extent humans do so. To address this question requires a combination of more sophisticated behavioral experiments, controlling for the possibly occult operation of more primitive processes, and neurobiological studies capable of probing the existence of putative simulation phenomena, such as neural sequence "preplay." Unequivocally, we must be able to undertake sophisticated interventional experiments to disable the processes in question and test hypotheses about spatial representation.

Decision Making and Planning

6

Goal-Directed Behavior and Future Planning in Animals

Anthony Dickinson

Abstract

A distinction is drawn between two forms of prospective behavior, goal-directed behavior and future planning, in terms of the motivational relevance of the goal or outcome of the behavior. Goal-directed behavior is relevant to the animal's current motivational state, whereas future planning refers to action taken in the service of future needs. Two criteria are employed to distinguish goal-directed actions from habitual behavior. Performance must be sensitive, first, to the current incentive value of the goal as assessed by the outcome revaluation procedure (goal criterion) and, second, to the instrumental contingency between the action and the outcome (instrumental criterion). Both associative and cognitive accounts of goal-directed behavior are considered. Discussion of future planning focuses primarily two accounts of the sensitivity of behavior to future consequences: the mnemonic-associative theory and the mental time travel account. Although the avian food-caching paradigm has yielded evidence for mnemonic-associative theory, support for mental time travel in animals comes largely by default. The empirical evaluation of mental time travel awaits a more detailed and articulated specification of the underlying cognitive processes.

Introduction

The problem of intentionality has haunted biology and psychology for centuries. The exquisite adaptation of both animal morphology and behavior appeared to demand the hand of an intentional agent, which in pre-Darwinian times took the form of a divine creator. Thus in his 1691 volume, "The Wisdom of God Manifest in the Works of Creation," John Ray claimed that animals are "acted and driven to bring about Ends which [they] themselves aim not at (so far as we can discern) but are directed to." Of course, two centuries later Darwin vitiated a role for a creator of phylogenetic adaptations by demonstrating how manifest "design" could be brought through a process of selection by consequences, which in case of natural selection were those for reproductive fitness. The challenge to any form of natural intentionality was then fully realized fifty years later when E. L. Thorndike (1911) argued that adaptation through behavioral learning also operated through a process of selection by consequences in the form of his "Law of Effect." According to the Law of Effect, an animal does not perform a behavior that yields a goal with the intent of gaining access to the goal, but rather because past experience with the behavior-goal contingency has simply selected that behavior through a stimulus-response/reinforcement mechanism.

Although readily embracing the elegance of natural selection, both psychologists and biologists have been reluctant to endorse the demystification of intentionality offered by the Law of Effect. Consider one recent example—a fascinating study of foraging by wild baboons (Noser and Byrne 2007). On the basis of observing that the baboons take efficient routes to valuable out-of-sight food resources while ignoring less valuable ones, Noser and Byrne concluded that "our data provide evidence of goal-directed travel and advanced planning during foraging by chacma baboons." However, they cannot fully escape the shadow of the Law of Effect and later acknowledged that "it is possible that the behavior of our baboons was shaped by the repeated experience that rewards from fig trees are larger in the early morning and smaller in the course of the day" (Noser and Byrne 2007:265) The moral of this example is that the intentional status of behavior can rarely, if ever, be determined by the observation in the natural environment. Natural behaviors always appear purposive and goal directed even if the underlying mechanism is selection by fitness or by reinforcement.

Goal-Directed Behavior

Faced with the ambiguous intentional status of natural behavior, my colleagues and I have argued for two criteria in determining whether or not a particular response is goal directed (e.g., de Wit and Dickinson 2009): the *goal criterion* and the *instrumental criterion*.

The Goal Criterion

If a response is to be goal directed, it must not only be "directed" at the goal, it must also be sensitive to whether or not this outcome is currently a goal for the animal or, in the psychological jargon, to the current incentive value of the outcome. If the response were performed irrespective of whether or not its outcome currently has value, it would be a misnomer to characterize it as goal directed. The status of a response with respect to this goal criterion is assessed by the outcome revaluation procedure.

Application of this procedure can be illustrated by the first study to demonstrate the goal-directed status of an instrumental response by the outcome revaluation procedure. Adams and Dickinson (1981) trained hungry rats to press a lever to receive one of two types of food pellet, either a sugar pellet or a grain pellet, while the other type was delivered independently of responding. Having established lever pressing, we then devalued either the pellet that was contingent on the response or the noncontingent pellet by conditioning a food aversion to it. It is important to note that this aversion conditioning was conducted in the absence of the lever so that it could not have a direct impact on lever pressing.

If the lever pressing was truly goal directed, then the rats should have been less inclined to press the lever, when once again given the opportunity to do so, if the contingent, rather than the noncontingent, pellet had been devalued. Only the contingent pellet could have acted as a goal for lever pressing (see discussion of the instrumental criterion below) and, therefore, if this response is goal directed, devaluation of the contingent outcome should have reduced the propensity to perform the response as this type of food pellet would no longer have had the status of a goal. When subsequently given access to the lever again, the rats pressed less if the contingent rather than the noncontingent pellet was devalued, thereby establishing this response as goal directed by the goal criterion. It is important to note that this devaluation test has to be conducted in absence of the outcome so that we can be sure that performance during the test is not subject to the direct selection by its consequences in the manner envisaged by the Law of Effect. If the devalued pellet was presented contingent lever pressing during the test, the reduced performance could be due to the fact that the pellet is no longer capable of directly selecting the response.

Behavioral Autonomy

The importance of the goal criterion is evident from the fact that one and the same response can be both sensitive and insensitive to outcome devaluation depending upon a number of factors. When performance of the response is independent or autonomous of the current value of the outcome in the revaluation test, the response is characterized as a *habit* and, following Thorndike, it is generally assumed that the habit learning involves the acquisition of stimulus-response associations, such as between the sight of the lever and pressing it, through a process of reinforcement by the outcome. Because the animal does not encode or learn about the identity of the outcome in the stimulus-response/reinforcement mechanism, habitual behavior cannot be directly sensitive to a change in value of the outcome. The reality of the distinction between goal-directed and habitual behavior has been firmly established by neurobiological dissociations (Balleine and O'Doherty 2009), which are too numerous to document here in detail. For example, behavior remains goal directed under conditions that normally establish it as habitual (insensitive to outcome revaluation) following lesions of certain prefrontal and striatal structures of the rat.

By contrast, prefrontal and striatal dysfunction in other areas appears to abolish sensitivity to outcome revaluation.

Whether or not goal-directed or habitual control predominates depends upon the training regime (Dickinson 1985). Over-training of a single response often produces behavioral autonomy and habitual control, as does training under a low contingency between response and outcome rates. By contrast, responding remains goal directed in spite of extended training when the animal has a choice between two different responses that yield different outcomes. There is also a marked developmental trajectory for goal-directed behavior in children with instrumental responding by those younger than two years being predominantly habitual (Klossek et al. 2008). Finally, stress promotes the expression of habits over goal-directed action (Schwabe and Wolf 2009).

Although it is generally assumed that goal-directed and habitual learning occur concurrently, we are still uncertain about how these two forms of control interact in determining performance. My colleagues and I have argued that both learning systems contribute to performance so that the overall rate responding is a sum of the goal-directed and habitual components (Dickinson et al. 1995). By contrast, Daw and colleagues (2005) have proposed that behavior is selectively controlled by one processer at a time. The arbitration between the two systems reflects the uncertainty about the value of a response produced by each system with the selected controller being the one that yields the most certain prediction.

Finally, it should be noted that, as yet, no one has distinguished goal-directed from habitual behavior in terms of its overt properties: a goal-directed lever press looks much the same as a habitual one. It is the absence of any overt signature of the intentional status of behavior that requires the deployment of the goal criteria through the outcome revaluation paradigm. Moreover, the concept of the stimulus-response/reinforcement process mediating habitual behavior has supported the development of reinforcement learning algorithms that endow synthetic agents and robots with illusionary intentionality (Sutton and Barto 1998).

The Instrumental Criterion

The second, instrumental criterion is more contentious and is intended to capture the claim that, to be goal directed, the behavior must be "directed" to the goal at a psychological level rather than just at a functional level. This claim is cashed out in terms of sensitivity to the instrumental contingency or, in other words, to the causal relationship between the response and the goal. I argue that, unless the response is sensitive to this relationship, there is little justification characterizing it as "directed" at a goal, at least in terms of the nature of the processes mediating the behavior.

The manifest intentionality of behavior does not necessarily indicate whether it is goal directed by the instrumental criterion. Consider the case of simple approach to a goal, which in terms of its manifest properties, appears to be prototypically goal directed. There is, however, good evidence that in many cases goal approach is not sensitive to the causal relationship between the behavior and access to the goal. In his classic "looking-glass" experiment, Hershberger (1986) fed chicks at a distinctive food bowl to establish it as a goal before placing them in one of two environments that arranged different relationships between the behavior of the chick and the bowl. In the normal environment, the food bowl retreated from the chick at half the rate at which the chicks approached it so that the birds had no problem in catching up to the bowl as they approached it. By contrast, in the "looking-glass" environment the bowl retreated from the chicks at twice the rate at which they approached it so that, to get the food, the birds had to learn to run away from it. When they did so, the bowl caught up to them at twice the rate they retreated from it. This, the birds never learned to do, suggesting that the approach behavior was not under the control of the causal or instrumental relationship with the goal, but rather was a response simply elicited by the sight of a distal stimulus, in this case the food bowl, through its association with food.

The "looking-glass" environment implements what is called the *bidirectional control* for the instrumental status of a response. For a response to be instrumental, an animal must be capable of learning not only the target response (e.g., approach) but also its opposite (e.g., retreat) depending upon which response is required for access to the goal. By this criterion, the instrumental status of the manipulation of levers and similar objects by rats has been established (Dickinson et al. 1996). However, the bidirectional control procedure is not the only way of addressing the instrumental criterion. In fact, any demonstration that the form of the response is controlled by its causal relationship with the goal fulfills this criterion, such as appropriate tool selection or manufacture. For example, Manrique and colleagues (2010) have recently reported that great apes will select between flexible and rigid tools based on which type of tool is required to gain the goal. Similarly, demonstrations that corvids will both select and manufacture the appropriate tools for a task provide evidence in favor of their instrumental status (Bird and Emery 2009; Weir et al. 2002).

The instrumental criterion may be thought to be too stringent because it excludes much behavior that we might wish to characterize as goal directed in terms of its manifest and functional properties, such as approach to a distal stimulus signaling the location of food. For example, Carruthers (2004; see also Allen and Bekoff 1995; Heyes and Dickinson 1995) has challenged the claim that sensitivity to the instrumental contingency is necessary for the attribution of means/ends reasoning and a belief-desire psychology to an animal. As he notes, "why should we not say that the animal behaves as it does because it *wants* something and *believes* that the desired thing can be found at a certain represented location on the (mental) map" (Carruthers 2004:211) and leave the causation implicit, for example, in "flying-in-that-direction action schemata" of a bird. There is, however, little point in arguing about the definition of goal directed in this respect, other than to note that certain behaviors do vary in their sensitivity to the causal relationship with a goal and that such sensitivity adds an important degree of flexibility to the concept of *directedness*, which is the focus of the theoretical discussion of goal-directed behavior in the next section.

Theories of Goal-Directed Behavior

To meet the goal and instrumental criteria, an animal has to learn about and encode the relationship between the response (R) and outcome (O), because in the absence of such knowledge it is impossible for the animal to respond immediately to a change in the incentive value of the outcome. There are three theories of goal-directed behavior, two associative and one cognitive.

Ideomotor Theory

This theory derives from William James' classic account of volition (James 1890) and was developed by Pavlov and his students (Asratyan 1974). The central claim is that the idea or thought of a goal automatically activates the response that caused this outcome in the past. Moreover, it is usually assumed that this activation is mediated by an O-R association. According to this theory, the sight of a particular fruit tree brings to mind the thought of its fruit which then elicits the foraging behavior that enabled the animal in the past to gather this fruit.

The most compelling evidence for the operation of this ideomotor process comes from studies of so-called outcome-specific Pavlovian-instrumental transfer. This transfer reflects the fact that a stimulus which has been associated with a particular outcome is capable of selectively activating a response that has been independently trained with the same outcome. As a result of this training, the stimulus activates a representation of the outcome, which then activates the response through the instrumental O-R association. Although this transfer establishes the role of the O-R association in the control of behavior, it is clear that this process does not mediate the role of the incentive value of the goal in that, surprisingly, the magnitude of the transfer is unaffected by devaluation of the outcome (Rescorla 1994). Rather the O-R association seems to mediate priming of the response rather than its selection for execution.

Associative-Cybernetic Theory

The alternative theory simply reverses the role of the response and outcome. Accordingly, the sight of the fruit tree elicits the thought of foraging in it, which in turn retrieves a representation of its fruit. It is this retrieval process through an R-O association that gives the process its associative character.

Having retrieved the thought of the fruit, its current incentive value is determined, which, if positive, feeds back to activate the response representation, thereby causing its execution. It is this feedback that renders the process of response selection cybernetic, and for this reason, my colleagues and I have characterized this account as an associative-cybernetic model (e.g., Dickinson 1994; de Wit and Dickinson 2009). To the best of my knowledge, this account was first advanced by E. L. Thorndike (1931) and has been developed as a "simulation" model in the field of cognitive science (Sutton and Barto 1981; Hesslow 2002). The feedback process envisaged by the model bears some similarity to Damasio's (1996) "somatic marker" account of decision making. As yet, there is no direct empirical evidence for the contribution of this process to the goal-directed behavior of animals.

Cognitive Theory

The cognitive account has been motivated by the apparent rationality of goal-directed action (Heyes and Dickinson 1990). Although these accounts differ in their detail, in one way or another most assume that goal-directed behavior is mediated by a belief that the response causes the outcome and a desire for the outcome. These two representations are then assumed to interact through a process of practical inference to generate an intention to perform the response. Again, there is little direct evidence in favor of such accounts, although there are empirical claims that rats are capable of causal inferences involving instrumental actions. Without going into details, Blaisdell and colleagues claimed that rats show differential responses to a stimulus depending on whether or not their own behavior had produced it in a way that reflects a causal inference (Blaisdell et al. 2006; Leising et al. 2008; but see Dwyer et al. 2009). Moreover, examples of tool selection or manufacture would require a cognitive account if a role for causal understanding can be convincingly demonstrated.

Future Planning

Over a decade ago, Suddendorf and Corballis (1997) drew the attention of comparative psychology and cognition to an important distinction between different forms of future-directed behavior. The examples of goal-directed behavior that I have so far discussed are limited in two respects. First, the causal relationship between action and outcome operates across a limited temporal interval. Delaying a food reward by more than a minute or so prevents the acquisition of lever pressing by rats (in the absence of "bridging" stimuli) (Dickinson et al. 1992). Second, goal-directed responses gain access to resources that are relevant to the animal's current motivational state: hungry or thirsty rats pressing levers to get access to food or fluids. However, there are numerous examples of animal behavior that, at least at a functional level, appear to transcend both these constraints by taking actions now to yield outcomes that serve future needs states. For example, a variety of birds cache surplus food to recover it hours, days, or even weeks later when hungry. To the extent that such behavior depends upon cognitive processes, it clearly transcends the type of associative goal-directed theoretical machinery outlined above and can be viewed as an example of future planning.

Suddendorf and Corballis made two important claims about future planning that transcend the motivational and temporal constraints on goal-directed action. First, following Bischof-Köhler, they argued that "only humans can flexibly anticipate their own future mental states of need and act now to secure them" (Suddendorf and Corballis 2008). Set within a motivational context, the claim is that the capacity to act in the service of future rather than current needs through future planning is unique to humans. Second, they argued that future planning involves a set of cognitive processes that support *mental time travel.*

Bischof-Köhler Hypothesis

Since Suddendorf and Corballis drew attention to the Bischof-Köhler hypothesis, a number of experimentalists have challenged its claim. The first was reported by Naqshbandi and Roberts (2006), who manipulated the present and future motivational states by giving monkeys a choice between small and large food quantities followed by a period in which water was not available. The rationale assumed that the choice of the large quantity would have induced a state of thirst that could not be immediately satisfied, and thus if monkeys can anticipate a future motivational state of thirst, they should have shown a paradoxical preference for the small food. In accord with this prediction, the monkeys learned to switch their preference away from the large to the small food.

Correia et al. (2007) examined the Bischof-Köhler hypothesis using a food-caching paradigm with scrub jays by explicitly varying relative incentives values of two types of food at caching in the morning and at recovery in the afternoon. The incentive values were manipulated by prefeeding one of the foods to reduce its value through specific satiety. The procedure contrasted the control of caching by the incentive value of a food at the time of caching with that at the time of recovery. On the first day, the birds cached more of the non-prefed, and therefore more valuable food, a choice that reflected the relative incentive values at the time of caching. However, the birds were then prefed the other food just prior to recovery in the afternoon, thereby dissociating the relative values of the two foods at caching and recovery. One food was valuable at the time of caching and the other at the time of recovery. At issue, then, was which food would the jays choose to cache on the second day? The fact that they switched their preference to caching the food that had been valuable at recovery on the previous day rather than the one that was valuable at the time of caching demonstrates that they are capable of acting in the service of a future need state. Therefore, caching was predominantly controlled by the incentive value at the time of recovery rather than the value at the time of caching.

These are just two of a number of studies that have challenged the comparative claims of the Bischof-Köhler hypothesis. However, although this aspect of the hypothesis has not withstood empirical examination, what it has done is to highlight a form of prospective behavior that lies outside the scope of the theories of goal-directed behavior outlined above, which all seek to explain the sensitivity of behavior to the current motivational state. The question then becomes whether or not such future planning requires radically different processes from those mediating goal-directed behavior. The mental time travel theory claims that it does.

Mental Time Travel

The three theories of goal-directed behavior assume that such actions are mediated by some form of generic representation of the relationship between the response and the outcome, be it an O-R or R-O association or a causal belief. Within the taxonomy of human memory, such representations are most akin to what is called semantic knowledge, general factual knowledge about the world, which stands in contrast to another form of human memory, episodic memory (Tulving 1972). Episodic memory supports the recollection of specific past life events. The central claim of the mental time travel hypothesis is that episodic memory and future planning call on a common cognitive resource and that it is this resource that is uniquely human. Indeed, more recently, in their *constructive episodic simulation hypothesis*, Schacter et al. (2008a) have explicitly argued that a function of episodic memory is to allow the simulation of future events through the construction of representations of possible future episodes on the basis of the memories of past ones.

From this theoretical perspective, the issue of whether animals are capable of true future planning comes down to the question of whether the nature of the specific cognitive processes mediates their future-directed behavior. The account offered by the mental time travel theory can be illustrated by reconsidering the processes that enabled the conditions at recovery to control caching by Corriea et al.'s scrub jays. To recap, their jays cached two different types of food in the morning before being given the opportunity to recover them in the afternoon. Importantly, the relative incentive values of the two foods were manipulated at recovery by pre-feeding one of the foods to satiety just before the birds were given access to the caches sites. The critical finding was that on the next caching episode, the birds cached more of the food that had been most valuable at recovery on the preceding afternoon in spite of the fact that the current value of this food had been reduced by pre-feeding just before caching.

Mental time travel theory would explain this sensitivity to the conditions at recovery by arguing that on the second caching episode the birds remembered the recovery events on the previous day, thereby recalling that one type of food had a higher value at recovery. This episodic-like memory of the previous recovery then informed the birds' caching decisions. Although specific processes by which the memory of recovery controls the caching decisions remains unspecified, it is reasonable that the bird should cache more of the food type that it remembers was valuable at recovery.

Although relatively little work has been done to determine the contributions of mental time travel to the control of behavior that has long-term consequences, de Kort et al. (2007) attempted an analysis in the case of food caching. Initially they allowed their jays to cache in one of two cache sites, *A*, while access to the other site, *B*, was blocked. At recovery next day, the bird had access to both sites but found that its caches in *A* had been transferred to *B*. After one more caching and recovery cycle, the birds were given a third opportunity to cache but now both sites were available. At issue was: which site, *A* or *B*, would the bird choose for its caches? According to the mental time travel account, the birds should have shown a preference for caching in *B*. When faced with the opportunity to cache in *A* and *B*, they should have remembered the recovery from *B* on the previous day, a memory that should have biased them to caching in *B*.

The initial results favored the mental time travel account in that the birds did in fact cache more in *B* than *A*. However, this conclusion is based on the assumption that the birds' choice reflected a preference for caching in *B* rather than an avoidance of *A*, but this turned out not to be the case. When a third novel site, *C*, was available during the caching test, the birds cached just as much in *C* as in *B*, although they could not have any memory of recovering from *C*. What they appeared to be doing, therefore, was simply avoiding caching in *A*.

Mnemonic-Associative Theory

How then are we to explain the apparent future planning exhibited by Corriea et al.'s birds? One possibility would be to shift the locus of the episodic-like retrieval. The mental time travel account, at least as I have articulated it, assumes that the animal retrieves a memory of the past outcome of an action at the time when it is deciding whether to perform that action again. An alternative is the theory of long-delay learning developed by Lett (1975), which assumes that the action is recalled at the time of the outcome. The operation of this mnemonic-associative theory can be illustrated again by reference to the Corriea et al. study. Mnemonic-associative theory would assume that at the time of recovery on the first day, the jays recalled caching the two foods in the morning. Because the prefeeding ensured that one of the foods had higher relative value than the other at the time of recovery, the memory of caching this food was associated with a high incentive value, which in turn enhanced the propensity to perform this behavior again through the associative goal-directed mechanisms that I have already discussed. Similarly, the avoidance of the pilfered cache site observed by the de Kort et al. (2007) study is explained by assuming that the memory of caching in the pilfered site at retrieval was associated with the absence of expected caches, a frustrative experience, which would have subsequently punished the propensity to cache in this site again. Indeed, van der Vaart and colleagues (2011) have recently presented a formal model that simulates the results of de Kort et al. using memory-based reward and punishment processes. Furthermore, their simulations demonstrate that the punishment process may not be required as long as the birds have a propensity to avoid returning to recently visited cache sites.

Both mental time travel theory and mnemonic-associative theory assume that episodic-like memory plays a central role in future planning but the mnemonic locus differs in the two theories. According to mental time travel theory, the animal recalls the last experience of the anticipated future outcome at the time when it is planning its actions, whereas mnemonic-associative theory assumes that it is the recall of the actions at the time of a previous outcome that is crucial. The studies of caching that I have discussed so far appear to favor mnemonic-associative theory over mental time travel. Indeed, it is well established that scrub jays retrieve a detailed episodic-like memory of caching particular foods in specific locations at the time of recovery (de Kort et al. 2005). However, there are at least two cases of apparent future planning by animals that are problematic for mnemonic-associative theory in that there is no memory of the action to be recalled.

Following Mulcahy and Call (2006), Osvath and Osvath (2008) demonstrated that great apes, when given an opportunity to gain food from an apparatus that required a tool to operate it, would select an appropriate tool in one context and then transport it to another context containing the feeding apparatus even though an hour or so intervened between the time of selection and the opportunity to deploy the tool. Crucially, Osvath and Osvath also demonstrated that the apes would select an appropriate novel tool for which they could have no prior memory.

The second example again comes from the food-caching paradigm. In a study by Raby et al. (2007), jays learned across a series of days that they received either no food or a particular type of food in one place for breakfast, while receiving a different type of breakfast food in another place on other days. Then, for the first time they were given an opportunity to cache food in the two locations in the evening. Given that the birds could not anticipate where they would be at breakfast time on the next morning, the optimum future planning strategy would be to cache a particular food in the place where it had not been previously available, thereby ensuring that they had at least some food for breakfast the next morning. This future planning is again beyond the explanatory scope of the mnemonic-associative theory because during training the birds could not have any memories of caching in the two locations, and therefore could not have associated memories of these actions with their consequences. However, the birds did in fact show a pattern of caching that matched the optimal future planning.

I have not described these two experiments because they provide unequivocal evidence for mental time travel—clearly they do not. Shettleworth (pers. comm.) has suggested that, rather planning for breakfast, scrub jays may simply have a propensity to cache a particular food type in a given location that differs from the foods that have been previously associated with that location, a strategy that would provide more uniform distribution of resources. Similarly, the apes must have selected the novel tools on the basis of their functionality, which may provide basis for generalization between the training and test tools. Whatever the status of these results is with respect to mental time travel, they share a common strategy of attempting to provide evidence for mental time travel by ruling out the processes of the mnemonic-associative theory. To go beyond this limited strategy, however, we need a more detailed and specific account of how the cognitive and inferential processes of mental time travel enable a recollection of a goal event to select the action that should bring about that event in the future.

Summary

Although there is no doubt that we and other animals have a Cartesian stimulus-response beast machine buried within our psychology, it is also clear that for many animals this machine cohabits with an intentional agent capable of purposive action. Some of the best evidence for this dual psychology comes from advances in our understanding of animal instrumental action. Under certain conditions, instrumental behavior is purely habitual and autonomous of the current value of the goal that established it in the first place. Under others, however, animal action is truly goal directed in that it meets both the goal and instrumental criteria. In such cases, the behavior must be mediated by conjoint representations of the relationship between the action and the goal, whether this be associative or cognitive, and of the current incentive value of the goal.

Goal-directed action can be distinguished from another form of prospective behavior, future planning, in terms of the motivational relevance of the goal. Goal-directed behavior is relevant to the animal's current motivational state, whereas future planning refers to action taken in the service of future needs. The discussion of future planning focused two accounts of the sensitivity behavior to future consequences: the mnemonic-associative theory and the mental time travel account. I belabored the distinction between mental time travel and mnemonic-associative theory because it is clear that an understanding of future planning depends upon a detailed analysis of the psychological processes that enable animals to act for future needs. At present, there is empirical evidence in favor of both theories. However, a theoretical lacuna remains at the heart of mental time travel theory. Whereas the mnemonic-associative theory provides an associative theory to integrate episodic-like recall with action selection, there is no psychological machinery within mental time travel to specify how the appropriate action is selected given the recall of a previous goal episode. Further empirical investigation awaits a plausible account of action selection within mental time travel.

Acknowledgments

I should like to thank the participants of this Ernst Strüngmann Forum for their valuable comments on an earlier draft of this paper. Preparation of the paper was supported by a grant (No. BB/G001057/1) from the U.K. Biotechnology and Biological Sciences Research Council.

7

Mechanisms for Decisions about the Future

Jeffrey R. Stevens

Abstract

Evolutionary and psychological perspectives on decision making remain largely separate endeavors. The bounded rationality approach integrates these two perspectives by focusing on simple, plausible mechanisms of decision making and the cognitive capacities needed to implement these mechanisms. Decisions about the future provide a class of decisions that lend themselves to a bounded rationality approach. Though many different mechanisms may exist for making decisions about the future, only a subset of these mechanisms actually require a representation of the future. The bounded rationality approach helps focus on the cognitive capacities and decision mechanisms that are necessary for a full understanding of decision making about the future.

Introduction

A hungry female chimpanzee spies a termite mound and quickly fashions a branch into a long, thin twig. She then digs to uncover a tunnel in the mound and inserts her twig. Soon, she extracts the twig, revealing a dozen wriggling termites clinging on tightly. The expert angler carefully plucks off and consumes each insect. As she repeats the process, she depletes the soldier termites arriving to defend their nest. When should she leave this hole to either excavate another tunnel or seek a new mound altogether? What decision mechanism does she use to make this choice? What cognitive capacities does she need to implement this mechanism? This foraging situation raises numerous other questions to biologists and psychologists interested in decision making in both humans and nonhuman animals.

Tinbergen (1963) posited four levels of analysis for why a behavior exists: the phylogenetic, functional, developmental, and mechanistic levels. Evolutionary biologists largely focus on why behavioral decisions exist from a functional perspective. For example, what benefit exists for leaving the termite hole now versus in ten minutes? Psychologists, in contrast, explore the mechanistic level, typically concentrating on cognitive mechanisms involved in decision making. For instance, what information does the chimpanzee use to decide when to leave, and how does she acquire this information? Regrettably, the functional and mechanistic studies of decision making have remained largely separate endeavors, with many behavioral biologists and psychologists reluctant to cross disciplinary boundaries. Yet, the emergence of cognitive ecology and evolutionary psychology as fields demonstrates a recent push to integrate behavioral function and mechanism across species (e.g., Barkow et al. 1992; Dukas 1998; Hammerstein and Hagen 2005; Kacelnik 2006; McNamara and Houston 2009). This integration should be taken seriously when constructing models of cognitive mechanisms and evolutionary outcomes. Here, I highlight how an integration of evolutionary and psychological approaches is integral to an understanding of decision making. First, I discuss the importance of decision mechanisms and review two general approaches to studying decision making. In particular, the bounded rationality approach proposes simple mechanisms by which decisions are made. This emphasis on the decision mechanisms and the cognitive capacities required for the mechanisms may yield a more realistic understanding of how humans and other animals make decisions. Thereafter, I explore a particular class of decisions that address the future. Specifically, I focus on how individuals make decisions that yield benefits in the future and what kinds of cognitive capacities and representations of the future are needed for these decisions.

Mechanisms of Decision Making

Broadly defined, a decision is the result of an evaluation of possible options. This definition does not commit to a particular process (conscious or otherwise) and can be applied across a wide range of taxa (potentially to plants as well; Kacelnik 2003). Decisions can take a variety of forms, including both inferences and preferences. Inferences go beyond the information given to make predictions about the state of the world; for instance, knowing the color of a fruit, can a decision maker infer its ripeness and sugar content? In contrast, preferences rank the desirability of options; for instance, would a decision maker prefer to receive a small food item now or a large food item tomorrow? Though I distinguish between inferences and preferences as separate entities, they can interact such that inferences can feed into preference decisions and vice versa.

Approaches to Rationality

The nature of rational decision making has been debated for centuries. Over this time, two perspectives on decision making have emerged: unbounded rationality and bounded rationality.

Unbounded Rationality

Historically, many models of decision making have been based on the *Homo economicus* or "economic man" perspective in which decision makers can access all information relevant to a decision and arrive at optimal inferences via rules of logic and statistics (e.g., Bayes's rule, linear regression) or exhibit optimal preferences via rules of probability (e.g., expected utilities). An unboundedly rational decision maker uses all information available to arrive at the decision producing an optimal outcome. Proponents of unbounded rationality focus on the optimal outcomes and typically skirt claims about the process of decision making by stating that agents behave "as if" they are rational (Berg and Gigerenzer 2010). Nevertheless, any claims of unbounded rationality require that agents possess sophisticated mental inference or preference functions that, when supplied with all relevant information, output the optimal decision. Deviations from the norms of linear regression, Bayes's rule, or expected utility are considered normatively "irrational" behavior.

The unbounded rationality models imply an implausibly omniscient, temporally unconstrained, and computationally unlimited decision maker. There are, however, examples in which agents seem to make unboundedly rational decisions (Glimcher 2003; Glöckner 2008). Yet, typically these models are feasible only in specific, "small-world" circumstances (Savage 1954), and the generality of their application remains unclear. Moreover, even if organisms possess the ability to use higher-order cognitive skills such as optimal decision making, they do not necessarily do so when simpler solutions will suffice. For instance, cotton-top tamarins (*Saguinus oedipus*) use simpler, more approximate amount-based mechanisms when discriminating different quantities of food, even though they can use more sophisticated and precise number-based mechanisms in other situations (Stevens et al. 2007). Thus, though unboundedly rational models are mathematically tractable and elegant, they do not offer realistic accounts of decision-making mechanisms in complex environments.

Bounded Rationality

An alternative to the omniscience and unlimited computational power required of *Homo economicus* is a perspective that emphasizes a more realistic view of tools available to decision makers. The bounded rationality approach advocates a plausible notion of the capacities of and constraints on the mind, as well as the interaction of the mind and the decision-making environment (Gigerenzer and Selten 2001; Simon 1956). This bounded rationality approach implies a set of computationally simple heuristics that use only partial information to make good, robust decisions that apply to specific decision-making environments (Payne et al. 1993; Gigerenzer and Gaissmaier 2010). That is, rather than having general-purpose statistical devices that require extensive information and complicated computations, decision makers often succeed by using less information and simple heuristics specifically adapted to their environment. The simple-heuristics approach makes explicit predictions about the decision process, the outcomes, and the conditions under which heuristics will work.

An evolutionary perspective on decision making highlights the gap between unbounded and bounded rationality. Many models of decision making in animals use optimization to find the best solution to a decision problem. However, despite using unboundedly rational models, behavioral biologists do not suggest that animals use optimal decision mechanisms. Optimization models are used only because natural selection approximates an optimizing process under constraints. Instead, biologists often assume that animals use rules of thumb (heuristics) that approach optimal outcomes. Consequently, the evolutionary perspective on decision making distinguishes between optimal outcomes and feasible mechanisms that can approach those outcomes.

Animals use rules of thumb in a number of important decision-making contexts, ranging from navigation to nest construction (Marsh 2002; Hutchinson and Gigerenzer 2005; Stevens and King 2011). As an example, biologists have investigated the use of simple rules in the "patch-choice" model of foraging (Stephens and Krebs 1986; Wilke et al. 2009) described in the chimpanzee termite-fishing example. Recall that in this scenario, foragers must decide when to leave a patch and move on to another. The optimal policy recommends leaving when the intake rate at the current patch equals the average intake rate for the remaining patches under this policy. Calculating or estimating this average intake rate in the environment may be computationally difficult in complex environments. A number of researchers have proposed simple patch-leaving rules that avoid some of the complicated computations (Figure 7.1). For instance, rather than comparing the current intake rate to the average rate, animals may just leave a patch when the current intake rate drops below a critical threshold. Other even simpler rules dispense with the requirement of directly monitoring the current intake rate and instead indirectly estimate this rate. Animals using these rules may leave after consuming a certain number of prey items (fixed number rule), after a certain time period after arriving to a patch (fixed time rule), or after a certain time period of unsuccessful foraging (giving-up time rule). Empirical evidence suggests that different species use these various rules in different foraging situations (Stephens and Krebs 1986; van Alphen et al. 2003; Wajnberg et al. 2003).

The use of simple rules and heuristics by animals is not surprising. This perspective, however, has stimulated more controversy when applied to human decision making (see Todd and Gigerenzer 2000 and subsequent commentaries). Do humans use simple heuristics for important decisions? Gigerenzer and colleagues argue that in certain environments heuristics can achieve good outcomes. Given that the human brain has been built by evolution through natural selection, we might suppose that the costs of decision computations weigh heavily in the evolution of decision mechanisms, and mechanisms with simple

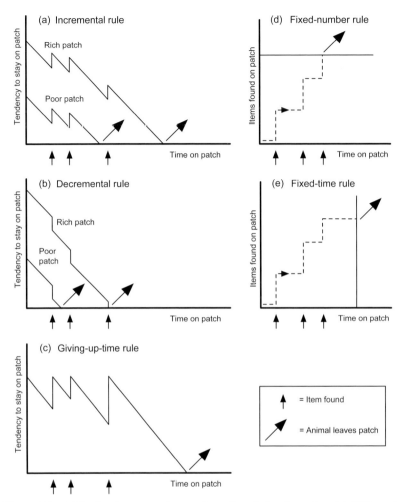

Figure 7.1   Biologists have tested a number of patch-leaving rules. (a) With an incremental rule for deciding when to leave a patch, each resource capture (indicated by small arrows) increases the probability of staying in a patch. (b) With a decremental rule, each resource capture reduces the probability of staying. (c) With a giving-up time rule, the tendency to stay in the patch declines with unsuccessful search and is reset to a maximum with each resource found. (d) With a fixed-number rule, a patch is left after a fixed number of items have been found. (e) With a fixed-time rule, the patch is left independent of the number of food items found. Reprinted with permission of the Cognitive Science Society from Wilke et al. (2009).

decision rules tend to prevail over complex computations when yielding similar outcomes.

The bounded rationality approach involves not only an exploration of heuristics and other decision mechanisms but also an investigation of the cognitive capacities that underlie these mechanisms. This is particularly useful when studying the evolution of decision making, because species differ in their underlying capacities and therefore may differ in which decision mechanisms they can implement. Consequently, carefully outlining the required capacities is critical for studying the mechanism. As an example, though tit-for-tat and similar strategies have been promoted as simple decision rules that can generate cooperation (Axelrod and Hamilton 1981; Nowak 2006), the underlying capacities needed to implement these strategies have not been well studied (Stevens and Hauser 2004). When measuring memory capacity, for instance, it seems unlikely that even humans have the memory structure and accuracy required to implement tit-for-tat (Stevens et al. 2011). Thus, consideration of the underlying cognition needed for decision rules will help constrain the possible list of feasible mechanisms.

To summarize, the unbounded rationality approach to decision making focuses on optimal outcomes, whereas the bounded rationality approach emphasizes the cognitive mechanisms of decision making. In addition to testing decision heuristics, the bounded rationality approach highlights the importance of investigating the underlying cognitive capacities needed for decision mechanisms. With this general overview of bounded rationality in hand, we can now focus on a more specific class of decisions.

Making Decisions about the Future

Most of the decisions made by animals, humans included, involve some aspects of the future. Individuals must make inferences about the future (e.g., predicting the presence of a predator at a goal destination) as well as preferences about the future (e.g., investing in social partners to achieve future rewards). Here, I focus on a subset of preferences about the future known as *intertemporal choices*; that is, choices between options with future rewards (Read 2004; Stevens 2010b).

The termite-fishing chimpanzee introduced earlier in this chapter faces an intertemporal choice. Should she continue fishing in the current termite mound to extract more food or move on to another mound? From searching for food and mates to investing in territory, offspring, and social partners, intertemporal choices are ubiquitous in animal decision making. Researchers have studied these kinds of questions under a host of different names: delayed gratification, impulsivity, patience, self-control, temporal discounting. The key feature of these decisions is that animals act now to influence their future state, sometimes at a cost to their current state. Can animals forgo immediate benefits for delayed ones?

The Psychology of Intertemporal Choice

Some of the most amazing instances of waiting for delayed rewards in animals come from species that cache food for the winter. Nutcrackers (*Nucifraga columbiana*) can bury 33,000 pine seeds each winter and wait months to re-cover them (Vander Wall and Balda 1977). Every year, these birds make thousands of intertemporal choices in which they choose between an immediate, smaller (relative) payoff versus a larger (relative) payoff in the future. How do they and the myriad other caching species make these decisions? Do they have a concept of the harsh conditions facing them in the coming months and plan accordingly? Or are there other ways to solve this problem? Animals can make intertemporal choices in a variety of ways. Indeed, many kinds of inter-temporal choices do not require a representation of the future or any kind of planning ability. Though there are likely more, below I explore four types of mechanisms that may yield intertemporal choices: simple rules, reinforcement decay, reinforcement rate, and temporal discounting.

Simple Rules

In many cases, animals may use simple rules to make intertemporal choices. These rules do not require a representation of the future, and they may not even need any estimates of time. This is likely the case in many instances of caching. Rather than anticipate the future dearth of food, caching species implement simple strategies that respond to salient environmental variables. For caching, this probably entails a propensity to cache modulated by hormonal variations that result from changes in day length. Indeed, in the laboratory, experimenters elicit caching behavior in seasonal caching species by reducing the daily light:dark ratio (e.g., Pravosudov et al. 2010). This is not to say that caching is not flexible. On the contrary, much of the evidence of caching in corvids suggests remarkable flexibility in their caching decisions, depending on social context and the caching environment (Clayton et al. 2005; Emery and Clayton 2001).

As another example, parasitoid wasps (*Leptopilina heterotoma*) lay more eggs in lower-quality hosts when an impending storm is coming (Roitberg et al. 1992). Rather than assessing the future uncertainty of the storm and dump-ing eggs in anticipation of possibly losing the opportunity to lay, the wasps respond directly to manipulations of barometric pressure. Thus, various spe-cies use rather simple rules to convert environmental input into intertemporal choices. In these situations, the animals do not represent the future or any ele-ments of time or reward magnitude. Instead, they respond rather directly to environmental cues.

Reinforcement Decay

In their natural habitats, animals continually face intertemporal choices. Yet, most of the work on intertemporal choice in animals occurs in the laboratory under operant conditions (e.g., Green and Myerson 2004). These studies often present two stimuli to signal the options. For instance, choosing a blue circle results in a smaller food amount available sooner, and choosing a yellow square yields a larger food amount available later. Laboratory studies offer the advantages of tight control over the reward magnitudes and delays, allowing precise manipulation of relevant factors for intertemporal choices. The artificial nature of the task, however, allows alternative accounts of the phenomenon of interest. Rather than choosing between future rewards, the animals may simply be choosing between two reinforcement decay rates; that is, the strength of the association between the stimuli and the reward decays with the time since last reinforcement. Therefore, choices may be based on the past reinforcement history (decaying stimulus strength) instead of the future payoffs. Using operant paradigms does not necessitate the decay explanation, but it does offer an alternative that does not consider future states.

One solution is to replace the arbitrary stimuli with the actual rewards, so that subjects choose between the rewards rather than stimuli (Stevens et al. 2005c; Rosati et al. 2007). An additional solution is to switch from a purely temporal task to a spatial task. In these tasks, animals choose between smaller, closer rewards and larger, more distant ones (Stevens et al. 2005c; Mühloff et al. 2011). Therefore, the animals can see both the rewards and the cost required to obtain the rewards (the spatial distance). These kinds of spatial tasks mimic natural foraging problems (Janson 2007; Noser and Byrne 2007) and can mitigate reinforcement decay explanations of intertemporal choice.

Reinforcement Rate

As an alternative to the reinforcement decay explanation, animals may be attending to reinforcement rate or intake rate; that is, the number of rewards per unit time. To use these rates, individuals must have some estimate of the reward magnitudes and time delays. Research in numerical competence and timing suggests that animals can estimate both quantity and time (Brannon 2006; Gibbon 1977; Haun et al. 2010). Moreover, combining quantity and time into a rate is a core principle of behavioral ecological studies of foraging (Stephens and Krebs 1986) and psychological accounts of learning (Skinner 1938; Gallistel 1990).

Animals can use at least two types of reinforcement rates. Short-term rates focus only on the delay from choice to reward acquisition, whereas long-term rates include the time it takes to consume rewards as well as the time between trials. Intertemporal choice studies using blue jays (*Cyanocitta cristata*) and cotton-top tamarins (*S. oedipus*) are consistent with using short-term rates (Stephens and Anderson 2001; Stevens et al. 2005b), whereas choices of bonobos (*Pan paniscus*) may be consistent with long-term rates (Rosati et al. 2007).

After the rates are estimated, two different decision rules can be employed to make a choice: maximizing and matching. Maximizing predicts that individuals will compare the rates of available options and exclusively choose the option with the higher rate. Matching, in contrast, predicts the distribution of choices in proportion to the relative rates across the options. If, for example, one option offered a reinforcement rate that is twice as high as that from another option, the higher rate option would be chosen in approximately 67% of the choices (Herrnstein 1961). An extended debate on the importance of matching versus maximizing remains unresolved (Commons et al. 1982; Logue et al. 1990) and has not been properly separated from the short- versus long-term rate issue.

Temporal Discounting

Probably the most commonly studied explanation of intertemporal choice is temporal discounting (Frederick et al. 2002). The discounting approach suggests that the present value of a future reward decreases with the delay to receiving that reward. The discounted value function requires estimates of both reward magnitude and future delay, so this mechanism requires an understanding of the future. In fact, some argue that temporal discounting and future planning or prospective memory are intertwined (Critchfield and Madden 2007).

Much of the work on animal intertemporal choice attributes the choice to discounting without testing whether a discounting mechanism is at work (Green and Myerson 2004). Indeed, the work on human intertemporal choice also relies on the discounting explanation. When making a choice between, say, $100 today and $105 in 3 weeks, economists suggest that people discount the value of the future reward. The discounting approach assesses how the present value of the delayed reward decreases with the time to receiving the reward. In both humans and other animals, this value appears to decrease with time delay in a hyperbolic way; that is, the rate of discounting decreases as the delay increases (Figure 7.2).

This hyperbolic pattern of choices, though consistent with a discounting explanation, is not unique to discounting. In fact, the reinforcement rate approach also produces behavior consistent with a hyperbolic decrease in value (Figure 7.2). In addition, a simple rule can account for this pattern, a rule that humans could be using. Rubinstein (2003) and Leland (2002) suggest that rather than making intertemporal choices based on discounting, humans may compare the two reward amounts or the two time delays and assess their similarity. If one attribute (amount or delay) is similar but the other not, then the decision maker would ignore the similar attribute and just focus on the other one. In the monetary example, for instance, one might consider $100 and $105 similar, thereby using the delays to decide and choosing the sooner option. When this rule can be used, it can outperform the discounting models in some situations (Stevens 2009), suggesting that simple rules may account for some instances of discounting-like behavior.

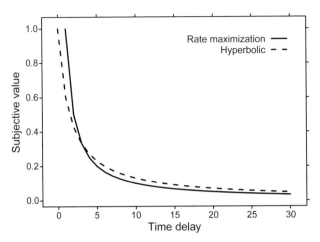

Figure 7.2   Temporal discounting explanations assume that individuals devalue future rewards. Though the hyperbolic discounting model fits animal data quite well, other mechanisms of intertemporal choice, such as rate maximization, also show a hyperbolic pattern.

Intertemporal Choice Mechanisms

Numerous mechanisms exist that allow organisms to make intertemporal choices, and I have provided by no means an exhaustive list. The critical point is that considering the mechanism has important implications for how we study intertemporal choice. First, it influences what kinds of models are relevant. The bulk of work on intertemporal choice uses temporal discounting models to investigate this behavior, both for humans and other animals. In the experimental paradigms of intertemporal choice, however, alternative nondiscounting mechanisims may account for these choices. When given binary forced choices between two options, humans may use similarity rather than discounting. Similarly, animals may use reinforcement rate or decay to make their choices in operant experiments. Again, though most studies of intertemporal choice assume temporal discounting, few spell out and test a clear discounting mechanism.

A mechanistic approach also highlights the underlying cognitive capacities needed to implement the mechanisms. Simple rules used by the parasitoid wasp require only a barometer. The similarity rule proposed for human intertemporal choices needs the ability to categorize amounts and times as similar or different. Temporal discounting involves an understanding of the future, but the type of understanding is not well studied. How do individuals assess the future? How is the future incorporated into the decision-making mechanism? Which types of future cognition are required and which types are optional? For instance, though mental time travel might be a useful capacity to have when implementing temporal discounting decisions, it may not be necessary for them to be made. However, other theories of intertemporal choice frame the choices as a problem of "multiple selves" in which one must mentally travel in time to determine which future self would be best (Frederick et al. 2002). Clearly, these models require a different set of cognitive abilities.

Though formulating different decision mechanisms is useful, empirically testing between these mechanisms may be difficult. In many cases, they make similar predictions at the behavioral level. Thus, purely behavioral outcome measures may not suffice to discriminate among them. Instead, measures of process are needed to test between mechanisms (Schulte-Mecklenbeck et al. 2010). These measures may include reaction times, eye tracking, active information search, and physiological and neurological measures. Shapiro, Siller, and Kacelnik (2008), for instance, propose a model of intertemporal choice that successfully uses process data to predict choices in starlings (*Sturnus vulgaris*). Their sequential choice model takes reaction times (response latencies) to a single option in the absence of choice to predict choices when multiple options are presented simultaneously. At the moment, few intertemporal choice models are well specified enough at the mechanistic level to provide appropriate process predictions. The sequential choice model provides a nice example of the importance of incorporating decision mechanisms into models of intertemporal choice.

Summary

A truly integrative study of decision making must synthesize evolutionary and psychological approaches. Though the emerging fields of cognitive ecology and evolutionary psychology have begun this integration, much work remains. The bounded rationality approach offers a promising perspective that highlights the importance of studying simple mechanisms of decision making. In contrast to unbounded rationality's assumptions of omniscient agents with limitless time and computational ability, bounded rationality begins with reasonable approximations of how the mind works. Boundedly rational agents often use rather simple heuristics when they perform well. Moreover, this approach emphasizes the cognitive capacities that must be in place to implement various decision mechanisms.

The bounded rationality approach can assist us in understanding decisions about the future. In particular, intertemporal choices involve future benefits, and a number of explanations have been proposed to account for these decisions. Yet, these explanations have not been fully worked out at the mechanistic level, and each mechanism requires different cognitive capacities and representations of the future. Temporal discounting seems to require some kind of understanding of the future, but other explanations can account for many instances of intertemporal choices without the need for a representation of the future. More specific mechanistic models are needed to better understand how organisms make decisions about the future.

Acknowledgment

Parts of this chapter are based on work from an earlier Ernst Strüngmann Forum (Stevens 2008).

8

Status of Nonhuman Memory Monitoring and Possible Roles in Planning and Decision Making

Robert R. Hampton

Abstract

In this chapter, the concept of monitored and unmonitored memory and cognition is introduced, and behavioral as well as neurobiological findings are used to link the application of these concepts in humans and other animals. Techniques are described that assess cognitive monitoring in nonverbal species, which indicate some of the putative differences in function associated with monitored and unmonitored cognition. Difficulties in characterizing the mechanisms which support the monitoring of cognition are highlighted, and thoughts on how this work might best proceed are provided.

Introduction

Monitoring of cognitive processes may improve decision making by conditionalizing behavioral choices on the availability of needed knowledge. The dichotomy between memory that is accessible to monitoring (explicit) and that which is not (implicit) is at the theoretical core of human cognitive neuroscience. The explicit-implicit distinction has not, however, been systematically applied in nonhumans, creating a significant gap in our understanding of the relations between human and nonhuman cognition, and cognitive evolution in general. The failure to apply these concepts in nonhumans likely results from the fact that humans usually demonstrate access to cognitive processes by providing verbal commentaries on their experience of cognition that are not available from nonverbal animals. In the absence of parallel data from nonverbal animals, some have concluded that nonhuman species do not possess accessible memory (e.g., Tulving and Markowitsch 1994), or that it is impossible to determine whether or not they do (Shettleworth 2010b). However, new techniques using memory monitoring paradigms (Washburn et al. 2006; Hampton 2001; Smith et al. 2003; Hampton et al. 2004b; Kornell et al. 2007; Inman and Shettleworth 1999) may permit us to apply the explicit-implicit distinction in nonhuman species. Accessible explicit memory and cognition may be used more flexibly in decision making than inaccessible knowledge and may be especially critical for planning. While some forms of metacognition depend on accessible explicit representations, many others do not, so all metacognition should not be equated with access to explicit cognition or memory. The connection between metacognition or memory monitoring and consciousness remains unclear and is probably beyond the scope of studies using nonhuman subjects. In future work, we should endeavor to move beyond functional demonstrations of metacognition and aim to identify the diversity of stimuli, cognitive processes, and neural substrates that explain it. This shift in focus will help develop an understanding of cognitive monitoring in both nonhumans and humans that is mechanistic and avoids invoking nonexplanatory homunculi.

Monitored and Unmonitored Memory and Cognition

Vertebrate brains are widely recognized to contain multiple individual memory systems, each specialized for different cognitive demands (Sherry and Schacter 1987; Cohen and Eichenbaum 1994). In popular taxonomies of human memory systems, a major distinction is made between memory systems that are consciously accessible to monitoring (explicit or declarative) and those that are unconscious (Cohen and Eichenbaum 1994). Human memory monitoring is associated with consciousness and is most often identified on the basis of verbal reports of private experience (e.g., "I knew" versus "I guessed"). Because nonhuman species cannot verbally report their experience of memory as do humans, it has been difficult to establish behavioral criteria that unambiguously capture the phenomenon of accessibility in nonhumans. Discriminating between accessible and inaccessible memory in nonhumans is further complicated by the fact that much learning and cognition in humans occurs without conscious awareness (e.g., some forms of classical conditioning, skill learning, and priming). It is not obvious a priori which kinds of learning and memory might require, or be associated with, cognitive access. Understanding this dimension of nonhuman memory, and the evolution of memory generally, therefore requires disciplined interpretation of studies designed to discriminate between accessible and inaccessible memory and cognition.

Extensive progress has been made in identifying the functional properties and the neural substrates of nonhuman memory, and this progress has been made without techniques for characterizing findings with respect to the accessibility of memories. Most of this work has been done under the (probably correct) assumption that phenomenal consciousness is not a helpful construct in studies of nonhumans because it is not clear what evidence would indicate the presence of such consciousness in nonhumans. Even as they focus on functional and mechanistic properties of memory, investigators often claim, directly or indirectly, that distinctions among memory systems establish parallels with conscious and unconscious memory in humans. For example, conscious memory is often identified with cognitive flexibility of the type that supports rapid adaptation to changing conditions, whereas unconscious memory may serve precisely honed but relatively inflexible behavior. When we focus on the most obviously functional traits of nonhuman memory, progress may appear to be rapid; however, our capacity to test for parallels between human and nonhuman memory would be greatly improved if behavioral criteria were established to capture the more subtle phenomena of accessibility. Determining which, if any, nonhuman memories are accessible to monitoring will allow us to sharpen distinctions between nonhuman memory systems and permit a better comparison of memory systems across species.

An objective study of cognitive processes must involve functional and mechanistic, rather than phenomenological, characterizations of the processes under study (Hampton 2001, 2005; Hampton et al. 2004b; Shettleworth 2010b). A functional approach might begin by posing the question (e.g., Shea and Heyes 2010): What can an organism with memory awareness do that one without it cannot do? In answering this question we can arrive at operational definitions of memory access that capture important functional capacities while avoiding the pitfalls associated with attempts to study phenomenology in nonverbal species. Such an approach is also directly relevant to the functional features upon which evolution can act in selecting for specific characteristics of memory systems. For memory monitoring to have evolved by natural selection, it must have had behavioral benefits that improved the ability to survive and reproduce. Memory monitoring allows humans to discriminate between knowing and not knowing. For example, when making a phone call, humans are able to determine whether or not they know the number before dialing and adapt their course of action: call when the number is known versus select a different course of action (e.g., look up the number, delay the call, send email) when it is unknown.

In traditional tests of memory in nonhuman animals, subjects are given "forced-choice" tests which require them to do their best based on the available information. In such tests there are no behavioral options analogous to a human looking up a phone number when uncertain. However, paradigms do exist that allow animals alternatives, thus more precisely paralleling situations in which humans make adaptive choices based on memory monitoring. A subset of these paradigms arguably allows us to discriminate between explicit and implicit memory in nonverbal species. In some of these experiments, rhesus monkeys are given a choice between taking a memory test and declining the test, which is analogous to a human saying "I remember" or "I forgot," respectively. Monkeys demonstrate that they can accurately monitor memory in these paradigms by either selectively declining tests or by gathering more information, when their memory is poor during the test. (Kornell et al. 2007; Hampton 2001; Hampton et al. 2004b; Smith et al. 2003; Smith et al. 2006). One example of this type of test is shown in Figure 8.1. Currently, this ability to monitor memory and cognition has only been reliably demonstrated in monkeys. Pigeons have repeatedly failed tests of memory monitoring (Inman and Shettleworth 1999; Sutton and Shettleworth 2008; Roberts et al. 2009),

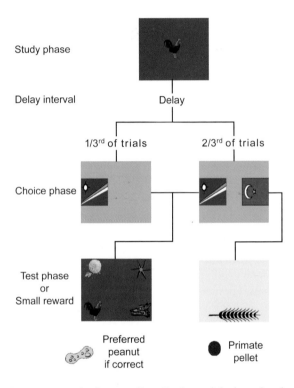

Figure 8.1   A memory monitoring paradigm. Each panel depicts what the subject sees on a touch-sensitive computer monitor at different stages in a trial. *Study phase*: At the start of each trial the animal studies an image. During the *delay interval* the subject will often forget the image. *Choice phase*: On 67% of trials, the subject then chooses between taking a memory test (right panel, left-most stimulus) and declining the test (right panel, right-most stimulus). For the remaining 33% of trials, the subject is required to take the memory test; only the option leading to the test is offered (far left panel). *Test phase*: Subjects receive a preferred reward after correct responses or a less-preferred reward after declining tests. No reward follows incorrect choices. To maximize reward, therefore, subjects should take the test when they remember and decline when they have forgotten. Better average performance on freely chosen tests compared to forced tests indicates memory monitoring. The animal knows when it remembers and declines to take tests when it does not. Importantly, the choice to decline the memory test is offered *before* the monkey sees the memory test. Thus, the decision to decline tests is based on memory, rather than on a reaction to the test display.

and the status of rats is still ambiguous (Foote and Crystal 2007; Jozefowiez et al. 2009).

Interaction among Memory Systems

Understanding how different memory systems act together or independently to control decision making and behavior poses a major challenge in the study of the brain's multiple memory systems (Packard and McGaugh 1996; McDonald and White 1993). Multiple memory systems participate in even "simple" behavioral experiments. In a particularly clear example, rats were trained in a plus-shaped maze to start from the same location in each trial and travel to a consistently baited arm of the maze (Packard and McGaugh 1996). Because the same start and goal arms were used across training trials, rats could solve the maze by learning either to navigate to a particular place in the room (as defined by landmarks; that is, a place strategy), or by learning to turn in a particular direction (e.g., turn right; that is, a response strategy). On probe trials the rats started from the arm directly opposite the start location used on training trials. These probe trials tested whether the rats were using the place or response strategy because the two strategies resulted in entry into opposite arms of the maze. Early in training, rats used a place strategy, but after extensive training they followed the response rule. Furthermore, by inactivating the dorsal striatum or hippocampus on probe trials it was found that the place strategy required the hippocampus whereas the response strategy required the dorsal striatum. Most interesting was the finding that inactivation of the striatum after extensive training resulted in the clear expression of the place strategy again, demonstrating that both the place and response strategies were available but that under normal conditions, the response strategy controls behavior late in training. This pattern of the development of automaticity parallels in some ways the development of human expertise and may underlie the difficulty experts can encounter when trying to describe the basis of their performance to a novice. Experts may often lack easy introspective access to the cognitive basis of their performance. Other animal work strongly suggests that multiple simultaneously active memory systems are the rule rather than the exception. If this is indeed the case, then understanding most forms of decision making will require identification of the specific memory systems involved and understanding of the interactions among them. Essentially no work has addressed the extent to which interacting memory systems are differentially accessible to monitoring in nonhumans species. Determining the extent to which cognitive monitoring plays a role in controlling the expression of memory systems in nonhumans will likely inform our understanding of decision making.

The Hippocampus

The hippocampus is widely recognized to play a critical role in the expression of many accessible memories in humans. The accessibility of spatial memory has not been studied in nonhumans. However, across species as diverse as fish, birds, rats, and primates, the role of the hippocampus in supporting the memories underlying spatial navigation is well established (Rodriguez et al. 2002; Hampton et al. 2004a). This extensive conservation of the spatial function of the vertebrate hippocampus begs for specification of the extent to which other functions of the hippocampus, including support of accessible memory, have also been conserved through evolution. Recent work on the role of the hippocampus in human nonspatial memory indicates that the contribution of the hippocampus may be critical but quite circumscribed (Hampton and Schwartz 2004; Vargha-Khadem et al. 2001). Hippocampal damage in humans causes robust and devastating memory deficits. However, studies of so-called developmental amnesics with extensive hippocampal damage show that they can develop normal language, IQ, and can succeed in school. Despite these competencies, developmental amnesics almost completely lack episodic memory (i.e., the ability to remember events as having occurred in one's own past). In contrast to these clear deficits in episodic memory seen in humans, some studies of nonspatial memory in monkeys with hippocampal damage find no deficits whatsoever (Murray and Mishkin 1998). This difference in the ease with which nonspatial memory impairments are detected in humans and monkeys shows that measuring some functions of the hippocampus in nonhumans, such as a possible role in episodic memory, can be challenging and may require the development of new behavioral tests. Whether or not a specific memory test measures hippocampal function may depend on subtle differences in training and testing procedures that bias monkeys toward different approaches to memory testing (Zola et al. 2000).

Our current tests for nonhumans fail to measure important components of memory. It has been proposed that the hippocampus is critical for performance in recall tests, whereas adjacent cortex supports recognition test performance based on familiarity (e.g., Eichenbaum et al. 2007; Sauvage et al. 2008; Brown and Aggleton 2001; Ranganath et al. 2004). At present, there are no widely applicable recall tests for nonhumans, though some elegant paradigms do suggest a distinction between familiarity and another memory process in nonhumans. Rats with hippocampal lesions displayed intact recognition of previously presented odors but, unlike control rats, they could not correctly identify the order in which odors were presented (Fortin et al. 2002). This dissociation suggests that nonhuman animals may have a memory system similar to that which supports recall in humans. However, further studies are needed before this issue can be resolved. Studies of memory monitoring have the potential to contribute to measurements of recall in nonhumans.

Work on memory monitoring in monkeys (Hampton 2001; Smith et al. 1998; Kornell et al. 2007) arguably demonstrates that monkeys have access to at least some types of memory and that they use this access to discriminate between knowing and not knowing. In addition, because monkeys can at least sometimes adaptively choose to take or decline a memory test even before it appears, monkeys may base their decision about whether to take a test or not on whether they can successfully recall a studied image even in the absence of the image (Hampton 2001; Figures 8.1 and 8.2). The ability to recall memories may have implications for planning and decision making, because recall performance is much less directly tied to currently experienced stimuli. Recall can take place when animals are spatially or temporally distant from a decision point, exactly when planning would be most useful.

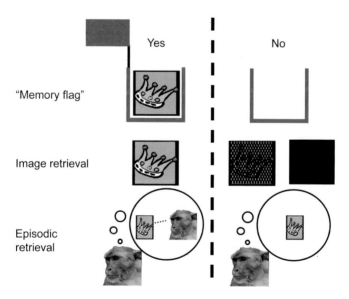

Figure 8.2   Three ways in which monkeys might generate behavior that looks like recall in memory monitoring experiments. The three rows in the figure represent three possible mechanisms underlying private memory monitoring. The two columns depict the target of monitoring when the monkeys choose to take ("yes") or avoid ("no") the test. The first row depicts the simplest mechanism for memory monitoring: a "memory flag" indicates the presence or absence of memory, but the contents of memory are inaccessible. The "image retrieval" model proposes that the monkeys attempt to "bring to mind" the sample image: if the retrieved image is clear, the monkey chooses to take the test; if it is degraded or blank, the monkey declines the test. In the "episodic retrieval" model, the monkey either recovers details of the study episode and takes the test, or fails to retrieve these details and avoids the test.

Relation to Planning

A conspicuous feature of planning is that it requires the processing of stimuli which are not currently present. Planning is thus critically dependent on memory. While imagination can construct representations of events that have not, and may never, transpire, memories provide the raw material for these constructions. Many researchers have emphasized the importance of memory, and the neural substrates for memory, in planning (e.g., Buckner 2010). Indeed, memory of the past exists to promote successful behavior in the present and future. Natural selection could not act on the ability to remember the past unless it promoted adaptive behavior, for idle reminiscence is a waste of energy from an evolutionary point of view.

While the inaccessible memories sufficient to support skills like those needed for food processing or prey capture certainly prepare animals for future behavioral needs, such memories probably cannot enter into planning as we normally think of it. Accessible memories appear to be subject to manipulation in flexible ways not evident with inaccessible memories, for example in making transitive inferences (Smith and Squire 2005). Such flexibility and manipulability would support the mental exploration of options to permit effective planning. More concretely, knowing what you know is important in situations in which specific knowledge will be required for upcoming behavior, as described by the earlier example about deciding whether to dial a number, look up the number first, or use email. Such an example seems to qualify as short-term planning, at least, and the logic would extend to longer-term planning.

Relation to Decision Making

Except in a few limited circumstances, such as deciding whether to take a test based on whether you know the answer, there are few cases where access to memory is obviously necessary for adaptive decision making. It is possible, but not demonstrated to my knowledge, that memory monitoring aids in contrasting alternative courses of action even when these alternatives do not differ in terms of required knowledge. Humans certainly ponder alternatives consciously, especially when uncertain, but the nearly automatic decision-making process of true experts may be generally more effective. It seems clear that access is often involved during the learning of new skills (e.g., driving), where initially a great deal of mental "supervision" is required. However, it is much less obvious *why* access is required initially, particularly when expert behavior is less dependent on access.

Examples that highlight the importance of memory monitoring in humans are relatively easily generated. For nonhuman animals outside of the laboratory, it is less obvious how access to knowledge contributes to adaptive behavior in ways that could not be accomplished without access. Developing an inventory of natural situations in which nonhumans would benefit from memory monitoring would be a significant contribution to this area of research. Such an inventory would begin to capture the important functional capacities provided by access and would establish a solid basis for the comparative study of memory monitoring. In developing this inventory, it is probably important to distinguish between the types of experimental situations necessary to demonstrate memory monitoring and the sorts of situations arising in nature in which memory monitoring would be of adaptive value. Ideal experimental conditions prevent subjects from solving the experimental problem by any means other than memory monitoring; thus success demonstrates memory monitoring. Such restrictive conditions would not be necessary for memory monitoring to evolve. Rather, memory monitoring need only provide a selective advantage in some problem domain, not a unique solution. For example, nest parasitic cowbird females scout for nests of other birds that contain some eggs, but not a complete clutch, in which to lay their own egg the following morning. It might be adaptive for a cowbird to stop scouting for nests and return to foraging for food, as soon as she has located and memorized the locations of one or two that are suitable. Metacognition could be useful in determining when this state of sufficient knowledge has been achieved, but other mechanisms (e.g., shifting from scouting to foraging whenever a threshold level of hunger is reached) might also provide a somewhat less fine-tuned, but effective, solution. Whether metacognition would evolve in this situation is not determined by it being the only solution to the problem, but rather by it providing an adaptive advantage over other solutions sufficient to outweigh the costs in terms of neural structure, brain metabolism, and other investments required to support it.

Relation between Memory Monitoring and Metacognition

Memory monitoring is just one type of metacognition. Often loosely defined as "thinking about thinking" (e.g., Flavell 1979), metacognition allows one to monitor and adaptively control cognitive processing (Nelson 1996). Monitoring and control of cognition could be manifest in a number of ways, including the regulation of time spent studying, reviewing, or seeking more information when forgetting has occurred, or the selective avoidance of situations where information is required but not available. In humans, metacognition is commonly associated with conscious introspection. In some contexts (e.g., in educational research), it refers, however, to the capacity to monitor or control the status of cognition by almost any means. Such a broad definition has both positive and negative consequences: It prevents "hair-splitting" arguments and allows investigators to continue their work without getting defused by arguments about the status of specific putative cases of metacognition. However, it may also conceal distinctive features of specific instances of metacognition that make them unusual and exciting.

What Does Metacognitive Behavior Tell
Us about Cognitive Systems?

Metacognition in humans is often associated with conscious awareness of one's own cognitive states (e.g., Nelson 1996; Koriat 1996) and is therefore presumed to reflect private monitoring of those states. Monitoring can be accomplished using discriminative stimuli that can be categorized into two types: *Private* monitoring depends on the privileged access of the subject to its own cognitive state. *Public* monitoring depends on discriminative stimuli, such as the perceivable difficulty of a problem or the subject's reinforcement history with particular material, to control the metacognitive response in an adaptive manner. Consider the following: (a) a colleague asks whether you remember the title of B. F. Skinner's first book; (b) a friend asks whether you can answer a question that his six year old has about psychology. In the first case, you would attempt to retrieve a memory of the book title and privately monitor the success or failure of that attempt. If you were able to bring the title to mind, it would be clear to you (though not yet to anyone else) that you were successful, and you could confidently reply, "Yes, I remember the title." Your metacognitive judgment, therefore, depends on your success or failure at privately retrieving the relevant explicit memory. The specificity and privacy of this example contrasts with the second case, in which your friend has not even asked you to retrieve a specific memory. If you are an expert in psychology, you might feel confident that you can answer the question of a six year old. Your confidence would not depend on a private evaluation of your ability to retrieve any particular memory, but rather on knowledge of your expertise, your past ability to answer such questions, and your assessment of the intellectual capacity of six year olds. Your friend's judgment about your ability to answer correctly would be about as accurate as your own. Indeed, he probably consulted you because he believes that you possess a particular level of expertise. By contrast, the introspecting individual has a distinct advantage over others in accurately evaluating the success of a completed or ongoing attempt at retrieving a specific memory because they alone know what has been privately "brought to mind." Accurate predictions of performance, even when subjects predict their own behavior, should not be equated with introspection or use of private information—such predictions result from the use of private *or* public information.

Understanding the mechanisms of metacognition in nonhumans requires more than a demonstration of accurate monitoring. Progress will depend on the development of experimental procedures that allow us to specify what information subjects use to assess their ability to remember or perform, and how they use that information. At least four possible classes of stimuli could be effective for cognitive control and will be summarized briefly here. Future work might benefit from considering this framework for contrasting the possible cognitive mechanisms that underpin metacognition. Although this review focuses on experiments that involve nonhuman subjects, it is probable that this reasoning extends to humans as well.

Environmental Cue Associations

Some stimuli are more difficult to discriminate or remember than others, as are some test conditions more challenging than others. Stimulus magnitude, image similarity, and delay interval are all types of publicly available information that indicate the difficulty of a particular test trial. Subjects performing tests with such stimuli might use the identity, magnitude, similarity, delay, or other publicly available information as a discriminative cue for declining tests or rating confidence. For example, if subjects have experienced low rates of reward with stimuli in a specific magnitude range, they could learn to avoid tests with all stimuli in that range (for the same argument, see Kornell et al. 2007; Shettleworth and Sutton 2003; cf. Smith et al. 2006). In a somewhat more subtle version of this account, extra-experimental events which might interfere with attention or performance (e.g., randomly occurring noises in the test environment, itches, or bouts of auto-grooming) can become discriminative stimuli for the metacognitive response (e.g., Hampton 2001, 2005). Generalization tests are the best way to evaluate the contribution of environmental cue associations to metacognitive performance. If performance generalizes immediately to new test conditions or new stimuli, it is safe to conclude that metacognitive responding was not controlled by stimuli that were changed for the generalization test.

Behavioral Cue Associations

This account of metacognitive behavior is similar to environmental cue associations, with the exception that the discriminative stimuli controlling the use of the metacognitive response are systematically generated by the subject in a way that correlates with accuracy in the primary task. For example, subjects may vacillate when they do not know the correct response on a given test (Tolman 1948). Vacillation might reflect the subjects' introspection that they do not know the answer, but it may just as likely be an unmediated result of not knowing how to respond. Because vacillation and response latency correlate with accuracy, subjects can use these self-generated cues as discriminative stimuli for the metacognitive response, for example, by declining tests on which they experience a relatively long response latency. In this case, the subject does not introspectively "know they do not know," but rather they "know they are slow." Response latency can be eliminated as a discriminative cue by using prospective metacognitive judgments, in which subjects choose to take or decline tests before seeing them and therefore before the latency of any response is available (see Figure 8.1).

Figure 8.3 Left: a rhesus monkey, ignorant of the food's location (unseen trial), makes the effort to bend down and collect more information by looking through the ends of the opaque tubes before making a choice. Right: an informed monkey makes a choice without making the effort of confirming the location of the food (seen trial). Such selective information seeking suggests that the monkey knows when he knows and more information is sought only as it is needed.

Response Competition

In most reports of metacognition in nonhumans, subjects are confronted with the primary discrimination problem or memory test and the secondary meta-cognitive response option simultaneously (see Figure 8.3; Smith et al. 1995; Smith et al. 1998; Shields et al. 1997; Hampton et al. 2004b; expt. 1 in Inman and Shettleworth 1999; Call and Carpenter 2001; Basile et al. 2008; Washburn et al. 2006). Because subjects can only make one response (a primary test response or a secondary decline test response), simultaneous presentation puts these two behaviors in direct competition. On trials with no prepotent primary test response, the probability that the subject will make the secondary meta-cognitive decline test response is greater, simply because no other competing response occurs immediately. On correct trials, when the inclination to make a primary test response is strong, it may dominate the tendency to decline the test. Response competition can be ruled out as an account for metacognitive responding by presenting the secondary metacognitive response option either *before* or *after* the primary test, so that the two types of response do not compete directly (Hampton 2001; Kornell et al. 2007).

Introspection

Metacognition could also be mediated by a private, introspective assessment of the subject's mental states. By the introspection account, the discriminative stimulus controlling a metacognitive response (e.g., declining to take a test) is the private experience of uncertainty (Smith et al. 2003) or the weakness of memory (Hampton 2001, 2005). Memory assessment might be accomplished through several mechanisms, which vary in sophistication from detecting whether a memory is present (while knowing nothing of the content of the memory) to attempting to retrieve the relevant memory and determining the success of that effort (Figure 8.2). The important difference between this account and the preceding three is that use of the metacognitive response is based on privileged introspective access to the subject's cognitive states, rather than on publicly available information or response competition. Introspection is probably the most interesting and most controversial mechanism for metacognitive performance because it invokes access to mental states. As such, it is potentially a tool for distinguishing between implicit and explicit mental processes in nonhumans.

Relation to Implicit and Explicit Representation

Some investigators may want to limit the use of the term metacognition to cases where conscious awareness and introspection can be inferred, and many might argue that private introspective metacognition is the most interesting case. Certainly, private introspective metacognition has the most potential to establish parallels between human explicit and implicit memory and nonhuman memory systems. Thus, paradigms that rule out adaptive control by public mechanisms are of high interest, yet it appears that only a minority of studies have done this to date.

If the study of metacognition is motivated by the possibility that it provides a means for studying something akin to introspection in animals, then we need to be thorough in our use of procedures that rule out other sources of stimulus control. Studies of meta-memory, in particular, are aimed at determining whether we can make a distinction between implicit and explicit mental representations in nonhuman species that parallel those made in humans (Hampton 2001, 2003, 2005, 2006; Hampton and Hampstead 2006; Hampton et al. 2004b). Perhaps the first studies to address explicit representation in nonhumans were the "blindsight" studies done in monkeys (Cowey and Stoerig 1995; for later studies, see Cowey 2010). These studies demonstrated that monkeys can accurately localize a stimulus even when they report that no stimulus is present in a present-absent discrimination. Similar techniques were subsequently used in experiments that assessed metacognitive abilities. These demonstrations depend on the capacity of subjects to make what Weiskrantz (2001) terms a "commentary response," which is interpreted to reflect some assessment by subjects of their subjective perceptual experience. It may still be premature to conclude that any case of observed metacognition in nonhumans depends on introspection involving explicit representations, but when sources of public stimulus control are eliminated, it is more likely that introspection underlies metacognitive performance.

9

Planning, Memory, and Decision Making

Amanda Seed, Nicola Clayton, Peter Carruthers,
Anthony Dickinson, Paul W. Glimcher,
Onur Güntürkün, Robert R. Hampton, Alex Kacelnik,
Murray Shanahan, Jeffrey R. Stevens, and Sabine Tebbich

Introduction

Animals make a variety of choices, and it is a fair start to assume that the psychological mechanisms underpinning their choices will be adaptive in the sense of maximizing their net gain of resources, reproductive opportunities, predator avoidance and ultimately their fitness.[1] Even choices that initially appear simple can be complicated because adaptive decisions often involve trade-offs along multiple dimensions. All other things being equal, we would expect an animal to delay consumption of an immediately available green apple until it is ripe but not so long that it gets moldy, but all things are rarely equal, and an ideally optimal consumer is only a theoretical abstraction. Implementing ideally optimal choices may be seen as being tuned to how the fruit matures: to current temperature and humidity, to present and future needs, to competition with other consumers, etc. These are the complex trade-offs that cognitive mechanisms implement.

In this chapter we are motivated by the following sorts of questions: What sorts of information do animals use to make decisions, and what mechanisms underpin the actions of different animal species in different contexts? Can they act now to secure an outcome with value in the future, even if it has limited value in the present? Can they integrate disparate sources of information, and recognize when they do not have enough information to make a good choice?

---

[1] It is customary to frame biological research around the notion that traits are designed to maximize fitness. This is the approach we adopt because the psychological abilities that are at the center of this contribution are of course biological traits. The many virtues and vices of this approach have been discussed extensively so we will not belabor them here.

To what extent do these decisions result from deliberation, as opposed to the sculpting effect of consequences, either over the course of evolution or the life history, and how can we tell the difference from studying animal brains and behavior?

Although answers to these questions will vary for different species in different contexts, comparative study can help us to extract common evolutionary and psychological principles. Impressive progress toward answering these questions has been made in the past decades within several disciplines, but substantial disagreements about how to interpret findings persist, and there is plenty still to learn. Our aim has been to outline the state of the art, to clarify the points of disagreement, and to suggest future directions.

Decision Making: Who Decides, How, and Why?

What Is a Decision?

Stevens (this volume) broadly defines a decision as the results of an evaluation of possible options. This definition encompasses the study of decision making from several different perspectives, with the fundamental difference between them being who (or what) decides (i.e., evaluates) the options to determine the resulting choice (e.g., natural selection, the mind, neural networks). From an evolutionary perspective, decision making or "choice" simply describes the selection of one among a set of possible targets. Similarly, in economics, the processes by which decisions are reached do not figure among the list of priorities in the study of choices and preferences: preferences and decisions are what the subject does, not what it thinks about it or how it achieves it.

The psychological approach, however, is critically concerned with the process by which options are evaluated in the minds of individuals. Determining what counts as a "decision" from a psychological perspective is slightly more controversial. One possible definition of a decision is any process (at the psychological, algorithmic or neural level) that leads to choices and preferences. An alternative definition is that only a subclass of such processes qualifies as decision making. For example, Dickinson argues that if choices result from no additional mechanisms than those generating action when an option is presented without competition, then this process implies choice without decisions. Dickinson uses the sequential choice model (SCM) as an example (Shapiro et al. 2008). In this model, when the agent encounters a source of reward, its actions toward it tend to reflect the value of this source relative to its context. The strongest and most quantifiable measure of this value is the frequency distribution of latencies to respond to the stimulus. More valuable options produce, on average, shorter latencies. The SCM postulates that when two sources of reward in the environment are met simultaneously, the same distributions are elicited as when each is met on its own, and their outcomes simply cross-sensor each other, since exerting one action removes the opportunity to use the alternative. In this case there is no special evaluation of the difference between the alternatives in the brain (or mind) of the animal. In other words, choices result from a horse race, and acting toward some option simply occludes the expression of any process addressed toward the competition. The SCM makes an important prediction: observed latencies toward any reward source in choice contexts should be shorter than those toward the same source when met alone, simply because only the left tail of each distribution is expressed and recorded by the observer. This is the opposite of what might be expected if choice involved an evaluation mechanism at the time of choice. Kacelnik and colleagues have provided empirical evidence in favor of SCM in several different paradigms in starlings, but whether this applies very generally across the animal kingdom (while interesting) is not crucial here (for data that SCM has difficulty explaining, see Mazur 2010).

The point is that, for Dickinson, if SCM were a correct description of the process underlying choice, then choice occurs without a decision, whereas for Kacelnik, SCM describes a mechanism for decision making that happens not to involve evaluation at the time of choice. This is to some extent a terminological distinction, but one that is important to keep in mind for interdisciplinary exchanges, as it exemplifies how different research programs need to toil to achieve mutual understanding.

From a neural perspective, the critical issue is how psychological choices (or decisions as broadly construed above) are physically realized. Before we explore the psychological processes that underpin decisions and actions, let us review the state of the art from this point of view for a particular taxon.

The Neural Mechanisms for Decision Making in Primates

Over the course of the last decade, significant advances have been made in our understanding of the basic architecture for decision making in humans and old world monkeys (for a review, see Glimcher 2011; Kable and Glimcher 2009). Current data strongly suggest that decision-making circuits in these animals can be described as being constructed from two sets of tightly interconnected networks. The first of these networks, located primarily in the frontal cortex and the basal ganglia, appears to be involved in learning and representing the values of the objects of choice. When, for example, a monkey repeatedly samples each of two food dispensing levers, regions in these areas of the brain come to represent the values of those two actions. While there is no doubt that many subsystems contribute to this valuation process, it is now widely accepted that the neurotransmitter dopamine participates in this process by encoding the difference between expected and obtained reward and broadcasting that signal throughout these areas. Multiple subsystems are now known to use these dopaminergic signals to compute and represent the values of action. Current evidence thus suggests the existence of interconnected sets of valuation mechanisms that interact to yield an overall value for each action, good, or option. While significant debate has taken place over the structure of the interactions between these multiple systems, current evidence leans toward the suggestion that these interactions are largely additive in nature within the timescale of a single decision, although that interaction may be significantly more complex over longer timescales.

Current evidence then suggests that these learned values are projected to a decision-making network located in the frontal and parietal cortices which effectively selects, from among the currently available options, that single option which has the highest "value" (i.e., the highest firing rates in the frontal valuation networks). These data, gathered mostly from physiological recordings in monkeys, suggest that topographically organized maps encode the values of each available action or option as a firing rate at a distinct point in the topography in these frontal and parietal networks. Algorithmically, choice is proposed to occur when change in the intrinsic excitatory and inhibitory tone of these networks forces a competition between different points in one or more of these topographic maps. The result of this winner-take-all competition is the unique identification of the most highly valued option, a burst of neural activation which then gains access to the motor control circuitry through a biophysically fixed thresholding mechanism. It should also be noted, however, that the separation of the valuation and choice circuits appears to be one of degree rather than an absolute categorical boundary. Neurons in the frontal cortex and the basal ganglia clearly encode chosen actions, and there is good reason to believe that the winner-take-all process, though synchronized across many brain areas, might well be driven from more than one point in the network under different conditions. For this reason, the clear presence of mechanisms in frontal areas and in the basal ganglia must not be taken as excluding the possibility that choice, the winner-take-all process, involves these areas as well under some conditions.

Comparing Species

Historically, there has been little integration between the different approaches to the study of decision making, but the value of cross-fertilization of ideas, paradigms, concepts, and species models between approaches is increasingly being recognized. The comparative psychological approach to decision making allows for the exploration of relevant evolutionary pressures that can shape decision mechanisms. Though decision making is investigated in a variety of species, we have only a handful of cases in which socioecological factors are considered. To show the benefit of this approach, we outline two examples.

Just as cats can be skinned in many ways, but look the same once the deed is done, actions can be generated by many different neural and/or psychological processes yet appear the same when the animal behaves. If behaviors look the same, then how can we identify the different processes underlying them? If different processes cause the same behavior, then why have divergent species evolved convergently toward these behaviors? Conversely, why do animals behave differently when faced with exactly the same choice, even if they are closely related and presumably using similar neural and cognitive processes to execute their choices? Can we use these similarities and differences among species to extract general evolutionary principles?

Different Mechanisms, Convergent Behavior

In many cases, two processes can cause the same behavior in one class of problems, but they would typically show different outcomes when circumstances are modified. If behavior is the same under all sorts of environmental transformations, then the underlying processes may still differ but not be distinguishable by behavioral experiments. In such cases, analysis at the neural level might be revealing. For instance, the same learning algorithm may account for data in mammals and insects, but surely the neural architecture underlying the process in each species would differ (albeit not necessarily at cellular level).

An interesting case is when distant species use clearly different mechanisms to generate similar behavior. In such cases one may conclude that there must be something important about the behavioral outcome that caused convergent evolution or selects for the maintenance of the trait. This may be illuminating when the behavior's function is not clear, as it may guide the functional analysis.

A concrete example, developed by Kacelnik and his colleagues, may help. These authors describe how choice can be controlled by the state-dependent value of reinforcement. For instance, if a subject learns about a food source when hungry and about another when satiated, the subject may overvalue the source found when in greater need, because the memory for the reinforcement experienced at the time of acquaintance is stronger. This may even occur if the animal possesses a veridical representation of the properties of the reward sources. For instance, in one study, starlings were trained with a blue key when hungry and with a red key when partly satiated (Pompilio and Kacelnik 2005). In one condition, pecking the blue key (in hungry sessions) resulted in food with a 15-second delay, while pecking at the red key (in partially satiated sessions) resulted in food after a 10-second delay. When the birds' preferences were tested at a later stage, they chose the blue key, even though their pecking behavior showed that they possessed accurate representations of both delays. In other words, preference was not due to the animals storing a distortedly short delay when hungry, because their pecking shows that the representation of the interval was accurate. Instead, a different valuation tag had been attached to the keys during training. Similarly, when locusts were trained with two odors signaling equally sized blades of grass when hungry or satiated, later they preferred the odor experienced in hungry sessions (Pompilio et al. 2006). In this case, however, the mechanism appears to be different at both neural and algorithmic levels. Preexisting neurobiological information suggests that the modulation due to hunger is brought about by state-dependent differences in the odor receptors. The locusts seem to smell the odor associated with greater need more intensely. In summary, two distant species overprefer alternatives that have been met in the past when hungrier, but one does so in spite of remembering their properties accurately and the other by modulating the amplitude of the sensory receptors.

This being the case, the issue is why would such different species (the phenomenon is also observed in fish) end up choosing according to state at the time of learning, if this can cause the wrong outcome (as when starlings choose the more delayed reward)? Searching for the answer may be guided by the comparative observation itself, and especially by the divergence in underlying mechanisms: if locusts, fish, and starlings show a state-dependent valuation effect but they achieve it by different means, we infer that the net selective pressure is sufficiently strong to favor these mechanisms in the majority or more significant problems, even if they may occasionally be suboptimal. In this case, the comparative approach points to the likely existence of an adaptive explanation and helps us to infer what the decision process may be like in other species.

Different Decisions, Homologous Mechanisms

The comparative approach also allows us to explore how evolutionary pressures can shape decision mechanisms by testing decision making in closely related species that differ in key aspects of their ecology. This question has been tested in the study of risky and intertemporal choice.

Risky choices involve opting for alternatives that vary in the probability of receiving rewards of different sizes. In the laboratory, this is often tested by offering individuals a choice between a smaller, certain reward and a larger, more variable reward (e.g., 4 for sure vs. a 50% chance of 1 and a 50% chance of 7). Dozens of studies across a broad range of species, including insects, birds, and mammals, suggest that many species are averse to variance in reward amounts (Kacelnik and Bateson 1996). Heilbronner and colleagues (2008) tested whether foraging ecology could shape preferences in risky choice situations in chimpanzees and bonobos. Both species consume fruit. Chimpanzees, however, engage in cooperative hunting activities in which the group hunts monkeys or other small mammals. This foraging strategy involves a variance in whether the group is successful and whether an individual will receive any meat. Bonobos, in contrast, forage on terrestrial herbaceous vegetation, an abundant food resource. If foraging ecology shapes risk preferences over evolution, chimpanzees may be willing to accept more risks than bonobos. An experimental study on risky choice in both species is consistent with this hypothesis (Heilbronner et al. 2008). When given a choice between a fixed and variable option, chimpanzees are more risk seeking than bonobos and even show a preference for the variable option.

In the related topic of intertemporal choice, individuals choose between options that vary in the timing and size of rewards, such as between smaller rewards available sooner and larger rewards available later. To test the effects of foraging ecology on intertemporal choice, Rosati et al. (2007) compared chimpanzees and bonobos in a choice task. Hunting in chimpanzees not only involves the risk of not capturing any prey but also involves a significant delay between making the decision to hunt and actually receiving the food. Bonobos face very little time delay when consuming vegetation because of its abundance in the environment. The foraging ecology hypothesis predicts, therefore, that chimpanzees will have evolved a greater willingness to wait for long delays than bonobos. Rosati et al. (2007) tested these species in an intertemporal choice task and again found results consistent with the foraging ecology hypothesis: chimpanzees waited longer than bonobos. A similar study on cotton-top tamarins and common marmosets also suggests that species differences in temporal preferences match temporal aspects of their foraging ecology (Stevens et al. 2005b). Thus, we have a number of cases in which comparisons across species can help resolve evolutionary questions about the selective pressures relevant for the evolution of decision mechanisms.

Let us now focus our attention on the different psychological mechanisms that underpin animal decision making; namely the processes by which information in the environment is translated into action.

Goal-Directed Behavior

As described above, animals can make choices based on past experience of the value of different options without knowing what they want, or how to get it; that is, behavior does not have to be goal directed in the psychological sense for animals to make good "decisions" from an evolutionary perspective. Nevertheless, it may be beneficial for animals to be able to adjust their behavior in accordance with up-to-date information about the value of different alternatives and the causal relationship between their efforts and the attainment of those goals. As Dickinson (this volume) explains, for animal behavior to be psychologically goal directed, the behavior must be shown (usually experimentally) to satisfy two criteria:

1. The goal criterion: Behavior must be immediately sensitive to changes in the value of the goal, such that changing the value of the goal in another context has immediate effects on actions that produce that goal, even when there has been no direct experience of the (updated) consequences of that action.

2. The instrumental criterion: Behavior must be sensitive to the causal relationship between an action and its consequences, such that if the

contingency between an action and its outcome is disrupted, behavior can be flexibly changed or ceased.

Taken together, the criteria were designed to bring about a 2 × 2 classification:

		Instrumental Criterion	
		Present	Absent
Goal Criterion	Present	Goal-directed behavior	Habits
	Absent	Pavlovian conditioning (some forms)	Pavlovian conditioning (other forms)

In contrast to habitual action, goal-directed behavior is rational and intelligent, as animals are shown to represent what they want and what they have to do to get it when they act. Does this framework, however, capture all cases of such behavior?

Are There Classes of Behavior that Defy This Classification?

Consider sophisticated forms of navigational behavior of the sort undertaken by honeybees, mediated by a cognitive map (see Menzel, this volume): a complex representation. A bee has become lost and wants to return to the hive, or to a particular feeder. When it locates a known landmark on its cognitive map, it calculates the direction and distance that it needs to fly to reach its goal and sets out accordingly. The resulting behavior is entirely novel and cannot be considered a conditioned response to a stimulus, nor explained in any merely associative way. Do cases in which navigation through space is mediated by a representation (e.g., cognitive map) and desire (outcome value) argue for a conferral of goal-directed status, according to a belief-desire psychology (see Dickinson, this volume)?

It seems unlikely that the bee knows that flying a particular vector will cause it to achieve its goal, for it seems unlikely that bees possess the concept of cause at all (nor indeed the action concept, flight). Rather, once the appropriate vector has been calculated, motor instructions for flight are issued, and the direction of flight is thereafter guided by matching the intended vector against current directional information calculated from the position of the sun or from polarized light. This causes the bee to fly in the correct direction. However, the bee itself does not represent its own actions as causing it to go in the right direction. It just acts, thereby, as a matter of fact, going in the right direction (given the correctness of its map-based representations and current calculations). One could thus argue that there are two distinct forms of goal-directed behavior represented in the animal kingdom: one in which the causal status of the animal's own action is represented, and one in which it is left implicit as in navigation toward a goal.

Another potentially problematic example is sophisticated tool use, as carried out by humans and perhaps other animals. Sometimes individuals use a tool without knowing how it works (e.g., a television set's remote control). When the contingency between using the remote control and changing the channel breaks down, the mechanically naive individual stops trying to use it, or could feasibly learn to point it away from the television set to make it work. By responding flexibly to changes in the instrumental contingency, the action passes the instrumental criterion. However, other forms of tool use (e.g., raking food toward you with a stick) might be mediated not only by a representation of the causal relationship (raking causes goal attainment) but also of the specific generative mechanism (by contacting the object and exerting force on it). Such beliefs may be particularly robust to changes in the instrumental contingency; for example it would be hard to learn to push the reward away from you in order to pull it in. Some studies have provided evidence that some large-brained animals (such as corvids and apes) display knowledge of properties such as connection, weight, and solidity when solving problems, but whether this knowledge is integrated into a causal framework is an open question (Seed and Call 2009).

Dickinson (this volume) suggests that with these queries in mind, passing the instrumental criterion should be downgraded from being "necessary" for the assignment of goal-directed status to being "sufficient" (along with the goal criterion, which is necessary). In cases which fail the instrumental criterion, additional evidence would then have to be invoked to show that apparently maladaptive behavior (under what is in effect an "omission" contingency) is mediated by a belief about a generative causal mechanism to retain the goal-directed status. Developing paradigms that can provide convincing evidence of this is an important goal for future work.

Behaviors that Meet the Criteria Need Psychological Accounts

How can we explain goal-directed behavior at an algorithmic level? Dickinson provides two categories of explanation: one "rational" (belief-desire psychology), the other associative (the associative-cybernetic model, which is an example of simulation theory). One might ask if both classes of explanation are right at different levels of analysis. From a folk psychological perspective, the computation can be described as behavior driven by a belief (that acting causes a specific goal) and a desire (for that goal). At the algorithmic level, this can be cashed out in associative terms (e.g., simulation theory). An immediate problem with this idea is that it assumes that the current associative models can account for the computations for which animals are capable. Some findings, as described by Dickinson (this volume), such as causal reasoning about events in rats (Blaisdell et al. 2006) and some future oriented behavior in scrub jays (Raby et al. 2007) are not amenable to associative explanations, as they are currently modeled, and therefore may demand recourse to a more sophisticated, representational architecture capable of inference and induction.

A parallel can be drawn with different approaches to planning deployed in cognitive robotics. The symbolic approach inherited from so-called classical artificial intelligence involves reasoning with sentences in a propositional language. The goal state, initial state, and effects of actions are represented in this language, and a reasoning system carries out deductive inference with these representations to find a sequence of actions that will achieve the goal. By contrast, a simulation approach uses so-called analogical representations, in which the structure of the representational medium reflects the structure of what is being represented. These spatially organized structures (such as two-dimensional arrays) are used to represent spatial structure (of an image, say), arranged over time, as in a movie. Using this approach, a simulation (based on past experience) is run forward from the initial state until a goal state is reached (Marques and Holland 2009; Shanahan 2006; Ziemke et al. 2005). One limitation of the use of a simulator for planning is that other forms of reasoning, such as explanatory reasoning, require additional mechanisms, whereas in the symbolic approach such reasoning is carried out within the same representational and inferential framework as planning (Shanahan 2006).

Further conversations between those trying to model artificial intelligence and real animal intelligence could be productive in trying to describe how rational, goal-directed action is algorithmically realized. It is fascinating to note that so far, some recourse to propositional representations is needed both to explain what animals do and to produce robots capable of doing the same.

Why Isn't All Behavior Goal Directed?

Rats and probably many other species show the capability for goal-directed behavior, in the sense defined by Dickinson (this volume). Given the additional flexibility afforded by goal-directed behavior compared to habits and conditioned responses, we might ask why, from an evolutionary perspective, it is limited to certain contexts, and why actions can become habitual (autonomous of the current value of the goal) in contexts that are extensive such as overtraining (Adams 1982).

One possible advantage of habitual behavior under stable ecological circumstances might arise from the fact that it is evidence based. Animals may simply repeat what has worked in the past because this is a safe and normally predictive cue for what will follow. This may imply that behavior is less flexible than it would be if the animal were persistently evaluating the best route to achieve a goal, but it would run less risk of getting it wrong. Furthermore, because it is computationally simpler, it might be faster.

Choice behavior in very stable environments has been well studied in non-human animals. In a typical experiment, a rat, pigeon, or monkey faces a choice between two or more actions which offer different quantities of or delays to the same resource (e.g., Herrnstein 1961; Lau and Glimcher 2005). The findings point toward conditioned rather than goal-directed behavior in such contexts, although note that in cases where the two options yield different outcomes (e.g., different types of food), behavior always appears to be goal directed. The general observation is that under certain conditions, subjects distribute their choice between the two or more actions in a way that matches the ratio of pay-offs from the actions; this is the matching law. By itself, this is surprising be-cause it implies not allocating all behavior to the action with higher payoff, and many authors differ in their view of how much the data really support matching when its outcome is clearly poorer than maximizing. Here, however, we stay out of this controversy and focus instead on how mechanisms that produce matching can be modeled. Modeling studies suggest that the subject is engaged in straightforward reinforcement learning (e.g., Corrado et al. 2005; Lau and Glimcher 2005). Interestingly, very little attention has been given to the ques-tion of how the learning rates for these behaviors are set (i.e., how quickly the distribution of choices is adjusted to the ratio of payoffs). One reason for this omission is that in the variable interval environments which have been studied most extensively, it is not possible to say what learning rate is optimal for a given set of environmental conditions.

One approach to this problem has been to study choices under condi-tions in which optimal learning rates can be defined precisely and then to ask whether different species produce behaviorally observed learning rates that are well correlated with these normative solutions. Studies of this kind now underway (Glimcher, pers. comm.), in which monkeys have to choose over water rewards, suggest that the learning rates observed in well-trained animals (animals with hundreds of thousands of trials of experience) do in fact approximate normative solutions. When environments are highly vari-able in reward magnitude or probability, then learning rates must be high to allow animals to track the rapidly changing environment. When environ-ments are stable, the reverse is true: learning rates should be low to allow maximally precise estimates of the values of competing actions. In fact, not only is this broad pattern observed, but monkey subjects yield learn-ing rates that are very close approximations of the precise optimal rates. The same cannot, however, be said of humans performing the same tasks for monetary rewards. Humans do, broadly speaking, adjust their learning rates in the same directions after thousands of trials of training, but they do so in a much less precise manner. One observes that under these conditions, recent re-wards appear to influence the behavior of the subjects more strongly than they should; in effect, the humans show learning rates that are too high (Glimcher, pers. comm.).

Why is there this species difference? It could be due to the differences in de-gree of training or in reward type, but another possibility may be considered: a second system for valuation may be operating in humans which interacts with the (in this case) more normatively valuable reinforcement learning system. To begin to test this latter possibility, one can require that human subjects, while performing tasks of this kind, also perform secondary concurrent tasks that may consume the time or resources of the hypothesized second system. To this end, DeWitt and Glimcher (pers. comm.) have human subjects perform a standard n-back number recall task while also performing the task described above. Under these conditions, it was found that the learning rates of the subjects were much closer to the normative rates observed in the monkeys. One possible conclusion that can be drawn from this observation would be that the n-back task effectively suppresses the output of a secondary system active under these conditions in the humans but not the monkeys.

In procedures employed by human cognitive psychologists (e.g., choice reaction time procedures), it is also observed that behavior appears to become automatic in the sense that responses can be performed in parallel (excluding, of course, peripheral interference) and are impervious to the imposition of a cognitive load. At present we do not know whether the behavioral autonomy (from current goal value) that characterizes habitual behavior and automaticity are the product of the same or different processes. Within the context of animal cognition, we need to develop paradigms for imposing an independent cognitive load while the animal is performing a goal-directed or habitual behavior. For example, the opportunity to perform a goal-directed or habitual (target) action could be provided during the retention interval of a delayed conditional discrimination so that the animal has to remember the identity of the stimulus while performing the target action. If the imposition of the memory task interferes with goal-directed but not habitual performance, we would demonstrate a concordance between automaticity and autonomy in the same behavior.

This line of reasoning suggests that goal-directed behavior, when held up as a contrast to automatic or autonomous behavior, is volitional and effortful. This contrast sounds remarkably like the distinction between conscious and unconscious processing made in humans. Later, in the section on consciousness, we will investigate the applicability of this contrast, which has been well studied in human psychology, to the study of animal consciousness.

Goal-directed actions are sensitive to the current value of an action's outcome. However, some animals go beyond this and take actions toward outcomes that will have value in the future, sometimes even when their current incentive value is low (food-caching birds and mammals such as squirrels can be full of acorns and nevertheless continue to forage for them to hoard the excess for the winter). This raises another controversial question: Are animals capable of imagining likely future events and needs?

Animal Future Planning

In classically associative models of valuation and choice, changes in the state of a chooser, such as changes in hunger state, can alter current valuation. In goal-directed action, as discussed above, these changes in value can feed into action so that animals act appropriately given their current needs. However, in these models, anticipated future changes in the state of a chooser which have not yet been experienced cannot affect value or choice. Here we consider whether animals other than humans are able to forecast changes in the future state of the world (e.g., the anticipated future prevalence of a reward) and use this information to influence current decision making in a manner for which traditional associative models cannot account. This could be an adaptive ability for animals that experience large fluctuations in food availability, such as food-caching animals, which hide acorns and other foods that are only available at certain times of the year, and then live on those stores of food throughout the coming months.

The question of animal planning is controversial because it has been proposed that in humans, the ability to forecast future states of the world is intrinsically linked to episodic memory and that both stem from an ability of the individual to engage in "mental time travel" (Corballis, this volume). Episodic memory—the ability to recall specific prior states of the world visited by the individual—allows individuals to return effectively to those prior world states and to reexamine values, choices, and motivations at those prior times. The central idea of the mental time travel hypothesis is that future world states can also be sampled in this way, constructively, by creating future episodes and prospectively evaluating objects like values, choices and motivations under those hypothesized future conditions. Critically, Corballis maintains that, at least in its fully fledged form, this is a uniquely human ability. Studying nonhuman planning is, of course, crucial to evaluate this claim, and Clayton, Dickinson, and their colleagues have conducted a number of experiments on food-caching by western scrub jays to evaluate this claim. The first step along that path, however, does not come directly into conflict with the mental time travel hypothesis. As Dickinson (this volume) explains, we first need to demonstrate that animals act in the present in ways that cannot be accounted for by traditional associative accounts grounded in the animals' present values and preferences. One can ask whether nonhuman animals, in their decision making, can take into account future internal and external states of the world even if they have never directly experienced the relationship between those states and the subject's actions/decision. Only if the answer to this question is positive will an inquiry into exactly how such a computation is algorithmically realized (through mental time travel or some other mechanism) become pertinent.

Dickinson (this volume) reviews a number of recent experiments in which animals have been shown to take an action in the present (cache food, or select and transport a tool) for a future need (a lack of that food, or the opportunity to access an apparatus where a tool, if brought along, could be used to get food). Some of these experiments can be explained by an associative account supplemented with a memory mechanism to bridge the temporal gap between the action and the goal (mnemonic-associative theory), although not all recent research is designed to be subjected to such an analysis. In particular, the work with primate tool retention is in its infancy, and we need to know more about the current motivational state of the animals, the incentive values of the food and tools on offer, and how value is generalized across tools that have similar perceptual or physical properties. This will allow the assumptions of the mnemonic-associative theory model to be fully tested. This is obviously an important direction for future research.

Controversies and Future Paradigms

Although the mnemonic-associative theory can account for many of the patterns of caching behavior arising from the scrub-jay experiments, the experiment conducted by Raby et al. (2007) on the ability of scrub jays to cache food for tomorrow's breakfast is a notable exception (see Dickinson, this volume). Having been trained that peanuts were available in one compartment at breakfast time, and kibbles in the other end compartment at breakfast time, the birds spontaneously cached kibbles in the compartment that served peanuts for breakfast and peanuts in the compartment that served kibbles for breakfast. In this experiment, the birds received a novel test of caching and therefore they could not have associated caching a particular food with either compartment. This experiment has been criticized (Shettleworth 2007) on the grounds that the birds may simply employ a heuristic to spread their caches of a particular food type rather than any cognitive plan of where they should cache the food tomorrow. According to this cache-spreading hypothesis, the jays will show a preference to cache peanuts away from sites previously associated with peanuts, an explanation that does not refer to the prospective aspect of mental time travel.

One way to test whether the jays can cache in the service of future needs while controlling for cache spreading is to ensure that all of the cache locations are associated with all food types, but at different times. For example, one could design a "kibble-for-breakfast, peanuts-for-tea" study in which the birds are given the opportunity to eat powdered kibbles in one compartment in the morning and then receive powdered peanuts in the same compartment in the afternoon, while also experiencing the reverse temporal pattern of feeding in the other end compartment. If the birds then at test cache with respect to the type of breakfast food available in each compartment, this preference would demonstrate that their behavior accorded with the temporal order of future needs in a way that could not be explained by cache spreading. In short, this would indeed be evidence of future planning.

A second test of such prospective cognition that transcends mnemonic-associative theory processes would be a test of novel rule integration. Consider the following two-phase experiment: Suppose that the jays are first trained that one food decays with time after caching, whereas the other food ripens—something that these jays readily learn (de Kort et al. 2005). In the second phase they are given the opportunity to cache both a nonperishable and nonripening food, such as peanuts, in two visuospatially distinct caching trays. Thus, in phase 2 they learn that they can recover the caches they have made from one tray after a short delay, and from the other tray after a long delay. At issue is whether, when given the opportunity to cache the ripening and decaying foods from phase 1 in the two caching trays used in phase 2, the jays will prefer to cache the decaying food in the tray associated with a short delay and the ripening food in that associated with the long delay.

Such behavior on the novel test would be problematic for mnemonic-associative theory because the jays have never previously had the opportunity to associate the memory of caching the perishable and ripening food items in these trays with the ripened and decayed states of the foods. It does, however, call upon prospective processes in that the jays must integrate the anticipation of the future states of the food with those of the opportunity to recover from the two trays.

At present, the priority for research in the domain of animal planning will be to gather more evidence to bolster the claim that animals plan for the future in ways that transcend associative models, perhaps through experiments like those proposed above. For the present, therefore, researchers will continue to use terms such as "episodic-like memory" which sidestep the issue of whether the animals actually mentally experience or construct personal past or future events. In the next two sections, we will assess the evidence that animals reflect on their own memories and knowledge, and the extent to which any animal thinking resembles human conscious processing.

Metacognition: What We Know and What We Know We Don't Know

As Hampton (this volume) explains, most paradigms in this research area require animals to discriminate between cases in which they know what they need to know in order to succeed at a particular test (e.g., discriminating stimuli, matching-to-sample, or locating a food reward) and when they don't. Metacognition can be broadly defined as monitoring or controlling cognition by whatever mechanism works. Several dependent measures have been used to assess this ability, including the use of a "declining test" response to avoid making mistakes and ensure a low-value reward, "betting" on performance, or searching for more information. A brief overview of the main paradigms that animals can successfully solve is given below (for more details, see Hampton 2009):

- *Perceptual metacognition*: Animals are trained on a perceptual task, such as classification of fields of dots as either sparse or dense. The difficulty of this primary task can be varied from easy to difficult. Animals are simultaneously offered a "decline test" response which allows them to avoid particular tests and progress to another. Metacognition is inferred when monkeys use the decline test response more on difficult than on easy trials. This pattern has been reported several times (for a review, see Smith 2009).

- *Retrospective betting*: Monkeys initially perform a perceptual task, much as described above. After completing tests, the monkeys are able to "give confidence ratings" by gambling either a large or small number of pellets on being correct. Metacognitive monkeys should gamble more food rewards following accurate responses and fewer on inaccurate responses. They do so, and they generalize to new tasks (for a review, see Kornell 2009).

- *Prospective memory*: Monkeys match to sample at delays long enough to produce considerable forgetting. At the end of memory delays, but before presentation of the test stimuli, monkeys choose between progressing to the memory test or declining the test. Declining is followed by a poor quality reward. Accurate matching is rewarded with a highly preferred food. Inaccurate test responses are followed by no reward. While most delay intervals end with a choice between taking the test and declining the test, sometimes only the choice to take the test is available. Monkeys demonstrate metacognition by being more accurate on trials they choose to take than on those they were forced to take.

- *Searching for information*: Subjects are presented with a set of opaque tubes in which a food reward is hidden. Subjects either witness the baiting or do not. At test, subjects can bend over and look down the length of the tubes to locate the food if they choose to, select a single tube and collect the reward, if correct. Subjects demonstrate metacognition by collecting information more often when they have not witnessed the baiting than when they have. Human children, chimpanzees, orangutans, and rhesus monkeys clearly showed this pattern of behavior, and while the case for capuchin monkeys was less clear, some capuchins made this differentiation under at least some conditions (Hampton 2009).

As Hampton (this volume) explains, metacognitive performance, as broadly defined, requires some type of discriminative stimulus that distinguishes between trials on which the animal knows the answer and trials on which it does not. Effective discriminative stimuli can take the form of either publicly available stimuli (such as the objective difficulty of the test) or private stimuli available only to the subject (e.g., a representation of one's own knowledge, the strength of a memory trace, a "feeling of uncertainty," or an emotional state such as anxiety). Carruthers (2008, 2009) has argued that there is no evidence to date that the discriminative stimulus used by subjects in the paradigms described above involves representations about one's own mental states (do I know or do I remember some specific thing), which we could refer to as metacognition in the narrow sense, or meta-representation (Box 9.1). It will be important for work in this field to move beyond demonstrations of metacognitive patterns of behavior to reductive analyses of the stimuli and processes controlling performance, in order to decide which of these two definitions is justified in a particular circumstance. For now, however, we will consider the adaptive value of metacognition, in its broadest sense, and consider hypotheses for the selective pressures that may have caused it to evolve.

Box 9.1 Defining metacognition.

Carruthers (2008, 2009) argues that most of the data alleged to support metacognition in the narrow sense admits to a common sort of anxiety-involving explanation. In each case the animal knows the structure of the experiment: it knows, for example, that it has to select the more dense of two patterns, or that it has to touch the longest of nine lines, or that it has to select the object that had previously been displayed on a screen. In cases where the patterns are hard to discriminate, the animal will experience anxiety at the thought of selecting either one of them, for it knows that the result is likely to be loss of a desired reward followed by a period of "time out." The negative valence component of anxiety motivates the animal not to press either of the primary response keys. In contrast, the "opt out" key is known to move the animal on to the next trial without delay, and hence will not be negatively valenced. As a result, that is what the animal selects.

Likewise in the retrospective betting paradigm, animals know that if they select the "high stakes" symbol, they face large gains if they have already made the correct discrimination (e.g., touching the longest line), but large losses if they have not. In psychophysically difficult cases, the chances of gaining a large reward will be appraised as low and, again, the animals will experience anxiety at the thought of pressing the "high stakes" symbol. The "opt out" key, in contrast, will be mildly positively valenced, since it issues in a guaranteed small reward.

Similarly in the prospective memory paradigm, animals know that to gain the desired reward, they have to select the item that had originally been shown on the screen. In cases where that item has been forgotten (or is only imperfectly recalled), an appraisal of low chances of success, issuing in anxiety, should be expected. This need not mean that the animal knows (i.e., meta-represents) that it has forgotten. Rather, failing to find an answer to a non-meta-representational question (e.g., what was on the screen), the animal feels anxious at the thought of accepting the test.

Some instances of motivated search behavior admit of the same pattern of explanation. Lacking information that is needed for success in some task, the animal feels anxious before making a choice, and this then cues a fairly stereotyped "bending down to look" response. (Note that search, in general, cannot require metacognition in the narrow sense, or almost all creatures will turn out to be metacognitive. Rather, failing to find a representation of food, say, on its mental map, the animal automatically initiates a search.) However, experiments in which the animals not only bend to look, but on the first trial move around to adopt the appropriate position for looking into an unfamiliar container (Krachun and Call 2009) suggest that the animals have some understanding of visual perspective, as well as of the actions that they should take to achieve a required perspective. This might show metacognition for perceptual access, if not for belief or memory.

Adaptive Value of Metacognition

To address the potential adaptive value of metacognition, we should distinguish between situations in which metacognition is empirically demonstrable and situations in which it might be of adaptive value. To demonstrate the use of metacognition in nonverbal individuals, we must create situations in which metacognition is the only solution that would work. We must, however, bear in mind that metacognition (and other forms of cognition such as future planning, theory of mind, etc.) does not require these strict situations to evolve. Metacognition can evolve whenever it gives a selective advantage; to evolve, it does not require a problem for which metacognition is the only solution.

The putative biological significance of metacognition may be seen by relating it to choice under uncertainty. In a canonical test of metacognition in nonhumans, a subject is presented with a choice between a safe payoff versus taking a test whose outcome depends on knowledge. If we label the safe payoff as F(ixed) and the alternative as R(isky), the task is characterized by the relation $R_{low} < F < R_{hi}$, where the subscripts *low* and *hi* denote the payoffs in the test option if knowledge is low or high. A further condition that is helpful to add is that

$$F > \frac{R_{low} + R_{hi}}{2}. \tag{9.1}$$

This means that if the subject has no additional information other than the structure of the problem, when it has no sensitivity to its knowledge state, the two payoffs of the risky option are equiprobable, and then a higher expected payoff would result from choosing F.

To increase the accuracy of the comparison, let us add the probability of being in a high state of knowledge, (p) to the equation. Now, to maximize payoff, the subject must consider whether

$$F > p \times R_{hi} + \left((1-p) \times R_{low} \right). \tag{9.2}$$

If p is sufficiently small, this inequality will be true and then F should be chosen. The variable p is determined by the subject's knowledge about its state of low or high potential performance in the test. Tests of metacognition assume that the problem lies in the animal being well tuned to p, so as to choose whatever maximizes the expected payoff. Note, however, that this assumes that the expected payoff, and not its variance, is the only factor considered. If the subject values payoffs nonlinearly, then even in the absence of any additional knowledge about its knowledge state, it may prefer risky or fixed. If, in fact, the subject is sensitive to variance, in the sense that its behavior is not designed so as to maximize expected (average) payoff per se, then the results may be more difficult to interpret. For instance, if there is surviving threshold T so that $F < T < R_{hi}$, then the subject should choose the test whatever its state of knowledge.

This reflection can, of course, be made more rigorous and detailed, but suffice it to say that the putative biological value of metacognition is obvious when it is considered as an equivalent of p when the latter is a property of the distribution of probabilities in the world. Metacognition is as adaptive as knowledge of the probabilities of low or high outcome caused by factors other than knowledge.

Here we suggest a number of contexts in which being tuned in to the state of one's own knowledge might lead to a maximization of pay-offs, in the hope that this exercise might stimulate ideas for future research paradigms.

Knowing When to Stop

Much of the work on metacognition has focused on paradigms that require animals to be sensitive to known unknowns (so as to opt out or search for information). Yet knowing when you know enough could be an adaptive feature in contexts such as search, sampling, exploration and practice, so as to devote no more than an optimal amount of time to these activities. Consider the case of HM, the deeply amnesic patient who had debilitating deficits in episodic memory. Although he was unable to remember any declarative information (memories and facts), he was able to remember procedural information, such as how to mirror write. Yet, although he knew how to mirror write, he did not know that he knew how to do so (Milner 1962). This distinction between procedural and declarative memory is critical and has implications for metacognition: because HM lacked any awareness of his memory, he did not know when to stop practicing.

Avian brood parasites provide a nonhuman example. These are bird species that instead of building their own nests and raising their young, they lay eggs in the nests of other species and exploit their hosts' parental care. Successful parasitism depends on laying in nests that are in the right phase; namely, where the host is still on a laying period and has not yet started to incubate. This matters because otherwise the parasite hatchling could be born later than the hosts and be outcompeted for food. To achieve this synchronicity, parasites such as the shiny cowbird in South America seem to scout for suitable nests during daytime, so as to use this knowledge on the following dawn to visit one of them and lay her own egg. Sampling here is costly and it only pays up to a point: knowledge of one suitable nest is close to enough, although knowing a few more may be a suitable insurance, should the preferred option be predated overnight. Thus, once a female cowbird has located one or a few suitable nests, she should stop searching and focus on foraging, necessary to complete the formation of the eggs that she will lay in the future. Some amount of knowledge is "enough," and the bird should act as if it knows that it already knows what it needs, and then stop searching. Here, then, is a potential benefit for a response of behavior to knowledge.

Avoiding Temptation

Most discussion thus far has focused on sensitivity to knowledge about some facet of the environment (e.g., memory of a food location). Sensitivity to one's own desires could, however, also be beneficial, if desires for short-term or immediate payoffs get in the way of larger long-term benefits. For example, an individual that is trying to give up smoking may avoid going to a bar or buying a packet of cigarettes, because she knows that these actions will increase her desire to smoke. To take an example from nonhuman animal behavior, sitting close to a receptive female may increase the desire to try to mate, but doing so may lead to retribution from the dominant male. Some evidence for animal's engaging in these kinds of behavioral strategies comes from temporal discounting studies that require an animal to inhibit taking an immediate small reward in order to receive a larger reward some time later. Some capuchin monkeys engage in self-distraction activities, such as looking away from the small food item, or in paradigms in which the smaller item must be retained and exchanged for the larger one, holding it at arm's length (Dufour, pers comm). Similarly, sensitivity to the fragility of a memory trace might increase behavioral strategies that increase one's chances of retaining information, such as marking a location or avoiding distraction. As in the previous example, behavioral steps are taken in the present to influence a future mental state. Again, these behavioral strategies need not be based on metacognitive abilities, but a putative advantage can be envisaged.

Mind Reading

The debate about animal metacognition (in the narrow sense; see Box 9.1) is linked to two competing accounts of the evolution of meta-representational capacities. In one account, first-person forms of meta-representation evolved first, for purposes of metacognitive control. In the other, third-person forms of meta-representation evolved first, for "Machiavellian intelligence" or for social cognition more generally. In the first account, mind reading grows out of metacognition. In the second, metacognition results from turning one's mind-reading abilities on oneself. From this latter perspective, we might predict that animals already capable of simple forms of mind reading should display matching forms of metacognition (in the narrow sense). Selective pressure for the evolution of this ability would therefore come from the social environment, leading to the prediction that animals living in complex societies would be more likely to show metacognitive performance.

In this context, it is important to note that developmental psychologists often distinguish between two forms of mind reading. There is a kind of goal/perception/knowledge-ignorance psychology which emerges early in development, followed somewhat later by an understanding of false belief, pretence, and misleading appearances. Likewise, Call and Tomasello (2008) have argued that apes understand goals, perception, and knowledge states, while being incapable of reasoning about false belief. Thus, even if animals cannot monitor their own beliefs and memories, they might be capable of reasoning about their own goals and their own perceptual access to objects. Examples of animals reasoning about their own goals might include the scrub jays who plan for what they will want for breakfast the next day (Raby et al. 2007), and the monkeys who use distraction from desired objects to maximize their longer-term rewards (Dufour, pers. comm.). An example of animals reasoning about their own perceptual access might be the study by Krachun and Call (2009) in which apes moved around to the appropriate place to look into an unfamiliar container.

Future Directions

The central question for future work will be to discover which discriminative cues are used by animals for metacognitive control. It will be particularly important to devise paradigms that can distinguish between different sorts of internal cues (anxiety-based or meta-representational). It might be possible to test the anxiety-involving explanations of metacognitive behavior proposed in Box 9.1 through manipulations of mood. Animals put into a good mood are likely to experience less anxiety, whereas those put into a bad one are likely to experience more. One might predict, then, that animals in the first group would use the "opt out" key less than usual, whereas animals in the second group would use it more. There is no reason why a metacognitive account (in the narrow sense) should predict such a result.

A possible advantage of meta-representation over an anxiety-based discriminative cue might be that an agent can monitor which information is missing and search for the relevant information more specifically. One could test this with a variation of the matching-to-sample memory paradigms presented by Hampton (this volume). In this task, an animal is required to match to sample after some delay. In contrast to Hampton's example, the stimulus that has to be remembered has two dimensions (e.g., a certain odor and a certain color), but, as in Hampton's tasks, the animal has two options: (a) to decline the task and receive a small fixed reward or (b) take the test, where accurate matching is rewarded with a highly preferred food and inaccurate matching with no reward. In the proposed task, normal trials are interspersed with trials in which the information about one stimulus dimension is missing. In these trials the animal has an additional choice to the two just described: to peck at a key that reveals additional information about one of the two stimulus dimensions, color or odor, which is followed by the task presentation. Under the assumption that animals can monitor which information they still need, they should only choose to decline if the key with the irrelevant information is presented and continue if the key for the relevant information is presented.

Part of what makes goal-directed behavior, future planning, and metacognitive performance fascinating is because when humans perform these tasks, they do it through conscious reflection and manipulation of representations. To study these topics in nonhuman animals we usually operationalize them in terms of measurable behavior and try to model them algorithmically in terms of inputs and representations and even neural circuitry. This has been very productive. However, when traditional models of animal learning and choice fall short, the question of whether or not the animal manipulates representations of different options to make a decision (causal beliefs, future values, or past events) becomes pertinent. Is this a tractable question for us to ask of a nonverbal creature? Next we consider how we study this question in human animals, to see if some lessons can be learned.

Animal Consciousness: Insights from Human Psychology

The scientific study of consciousness has come a long way since the conference on "Animal Mind – Human Mind" (Griffin 1982), at which time the very possibility of applying the scientific method to consciousness was viewed with widespread skepticism. The methodological progress that has been made, however, is largely confined to the human case. In this final section, we ask whether observations and theories about the difference between conscious and unconscious thought in humans can be usefully applied to animal psychology.

Experimental Study of Consciousness in Human Psychology

Numerous experiments in this area are based on the idea of contrastive analysis (Baars 1988, 1997). In a contrastive analysis paradigm, closely matching conscious and unconscious conditions are compared and contrasted. For example, in a backward visual masking experiment (Breitmeyer and Öğmen 2006), the subject is presented with a series of visual images, which includes a target image quickly followed by a second image. By manipulating the timing between the target and its successor, two conditions can be obtained. In the masked (or unconscious) condition, the subject is unable to report the target even though it can be shown to have had a priming effect on a subsequent task. In the unmasked (or conscious) condition, the subject can report the target image. Having established the requisite contrasting conditions, neural activity in the conscious and unconscious conditions can then be compared, for example, using MRI or MEG (for an overview, see Dehaene et al. 2006a).

One advantage of contrastive analysis is that it sidesteps many of the philosophical difficulties attendant on the amorphous subject of consciousness and moves directly to the study of a distinction—the distinction between conscious and unconscious conditions—that is more amenable to empirical study. The challenge in the present context is how to transfer such paradigms to the nonhuman case, where we cannot rely on verbal reports as an index of the conscious condition. Candidate methods for indexing the conscious condition in a nonhuman animal include post-decision wagering and nonverbal reports (for an overview, see Edelman and Seth 2009).

On the theoretical front, a number of overarching frameworks have been proposed. One of the most widely accepted is the global workspace theory (Baars 1988, 1997). According to global workspace theory, the conscious/unconscious distinction is realized in a brain with an architecture that comprises a large cohort of parallel processes and a global workspace. According to the theory, the parallel processes, or coalitions of these processes, compete for control of the global workspace, which is in essence a communications infrastructure capable of disseminating influence and information throughout the brain. So the winning coalition of processes can be thought of as broadcasting out to the full cohort of parallel brain processes, and the overall dynamic comprises episodes of broadcast punctuated by periods of competition (Shanahan 2010, chapter 4). Against the backdrop of a global workspace architecture, the theory hypothesizes that the unconscious condition corresponds to localized activity in the parallel processes, whereas the conscious condition results when widespread brain activity arises, mediated by the global workspace.

A further postulate of global workspace theory is that the conscious condition is cognitively efficacious in that it confers simultaneous access to numerous neural resources, including those associated with language, working memory, episodic memory, and mental time travel in general. In addition, the conscious condition permits the formation of novel coalitions of processes whose membership might be drawn from diverse areas of micro-expertise. It can thus be thought of as an integrative condition which, in the terminology of a modular theory of mind, allows the strict boundaries of specialist modules to be transcended, promoting cognitive flexibility (Shanahan and Baars 2005).

Neural Correlates in Human Brains

An obvious question for advocates of global workspace theory concerns what the neural substrate of the putative global workspace might be. According to Dehaene and colleagues, the global neuronal workspace should be sought in the cerebral white matter of the human brain (Dehaene et al. 1998; Dehaene and Naccache 2001), which carries long-range corticocortical and thalamocortical fiber tracts. Recent diffusion imaging studies of human cerebral white matter have produced connectivity matrices that can be analyzed using the mathematical theory of networks (e.g., Sporns 2010). This allows us to explore the question of whether white matter connectivity can support the neurodynamics required of a global neuronal workspace at a theoretical level. In particular, Shanahan (2010, chapter 5) has suggested that a modular small-world network with connector hubs is the right topology to support both the integrative and communicative functions attributed to a global workspace.

The question for this discussion is whether these two lines of inquiry that have proved fruitful in the study of human consciousness—namely, experiments that yield behavioral signatures of consciousness and the topological signatures that can be observed in neuroanatomy—could be usefully applied to nonhuman animals.

Topological Signatures in Animal Brains

Insofar as the tenets of global workspace theory are applicable in the context of animal cognition, it should be possible to establish a related set of results for nonhuman neuroanatomy. If the relevant white matter tractography can be conducted and the necessary connectivity matrices extracted for these species, then it would be possible to test whether the topological features, which are hypothesized by the theory to underpin the conscious condition in humans, are present in the cognitively well-endowed nonmammalian species such as corvids, parrots, and perhaps the octopus.

Another issue of importance is the relevance of midline thalamic activation to consciousness. Significant neurological evidence now suggests that activation levels in certain thalamic circuits are tightly correlated with levels of consciousness. Artificial activation of these areas can even induce apparently conscious states in persistently vegetative patients. Conversely, damage to these areas appears to reduce the level of consciousness in human patients. This suggests that the neurobiological signature of consciousness will likely include these areas.

There is already some evidence for some of these features in mammalian and avian brains. A systematic investigation would do well to include as many variables as possible to look at the covariation between the communicative and integrative features of the network and its potential to provide associating emotional experience as evidenced by the type of connectivity.

Possible Future Experiments Based on Human Psychology

Backward Masking

Animals are obviously unable to report verbally on whether or not they have seen a cue. However, experiments by Cowey and Stoerig (1995) on monkeys with blindsight (lateralized lesions of primary visual cortex) gained "reports" from the monkeys about whether or not they had seen a presented cue using two keys: one for presence and one for absence. They also trained them on a spatial discrimination. In the intact field, monkeys successfully performed both the presence/absence and the spatial discriminations (i.e., they reported both that they had seen the cue, and where it had been located). In the "blind" field they reported "no stimulus" but correctly performed the spatial discrimination. An analog of the backward masking experiments described above could use this procedure to present nonlesioned individuals with short exposures to visual cues and manipulate presentation time to see if there is a point at which, like humans, monkeys report "no stimulus" but can still locate it.

Directed Forgetting

Directed forgetting is a paradigm that has been used to test for working memory in nonhumans. The idea is that if working memory involves some active processing, rather than the passive decay of memory traces, the procedures that interrupt the active maintenance of memory will impair performance. In contrast, if memory involves only passive decay of traces resulting from study, then such interfering events should have little or no effect on performance. Several studies have addressed this using match-to-sample paradigms. In these studies animals are trained with a "remember" cue and a "forget" cue. Animals come to expect a test of memory following a remember cue and to expect no test following a forget cue. On probe trials, subjects are exposed to the forget cue but unexpectedly tested anyway. The evidence supporting active working memory is that performance is typically worse on tests that follow a forget cue.

These studies, however, have been vulnerable to a variety of criticisms that weaken the case for active memory. One problem is that tests following the forget cue are unexpected, and presenting tests when they are not anticipated may be disruptive to memory. A related concern is that in most paradigms, the forget cue signals nonreinforcement. Signaling nonreinforcement may cause animals to have negative emotional states or have other consequences that lead to behaviors incompatible with correct choice behavior on probe trials (Zentall et al. 1995). Some experiments may adequately control for these alternatives and still show directed forgetting, but they are a distinct minority (Kaiser et al. 1997). Nevertheless, improving on these paradigms might be a useful direction for future research.

Spatial Memory

Cook et al. (1985) assessed active use of working memory by testing whether rats can use working memory strategically by shifting from a retrospective to a prospective code to control working memory load. Rats working on a 12-arm radial maze were removed from the maze for 15 minutes after visiting various numbers of arms. The interpolated delay of 15 minutes impaired performance according to a U-shaped function. If the delay was interposed after a few arms had been visited, or after most arms had been visited, the impact was small and accuracy remained high. The delay had greatest effect when rats had visited about half of the arms. The interpretation is that the rats strategically regulated working memory load by initially remembering which arms it had visited (a retrospective code) but then switched to remember which arms it had yet to visit (a prospective code) when the number of visited arms exceeded the number of to-be-visited arms.

Dual Tasking

As discussed in the section on goal-directed behavior, paradigms that require an animal to perform two tasks—one of which must be solved by holding information in working memory (e.g., a delayed match to sample) and one which can be shown to require goal-directed action—could potentially present animals with problems if they are holding and manipulating multiple representations "in mind." Manipulating the amount of training on the instrumental task to shift the behavior from goal-directed action to autonomous habit would be hypothesized to improve overall performance if this is the case. Some tasks with multiple components have already been run with nonhumans, which perhaps have some of these characteristics. Chimpanzees that had previously learned to move food away from a trap using their hands over the course of over a hundred trials were better able to solve a similar task if they were able to use the same action to move the reward. Subjects with the same experience that had to use a tool on the transfer task did instead worse, but some still performed above chance levels. Subjects with no experience either of the type of discriminative task, or the tool-using action, could not find the solution at all (Seed et al. 2009).

The ability to manipulate representations consciously seems to be relevant for several of the abilities that we have discussed in the previous sections, as well as the abilities discussed in the contributions on mind reading and communication. The development of paradigms that contrast conscious and unconscious processing could allow us to make a comparative study of working memory capacity in different species. Evolutionary change in this capacity could have an important role in enabling or constraining psychological adaptations based on representations (Coolidge and Wynn 2001; Seed and Byrne 2010).

Conclusions

In this chapter we have discussed the nature and potential adaptive value of complex cognitive traits in the context of animals making choices and decisions in their physical environments. Repeatedly, we have raised the difficulty of distinguishing complex skills, such as meta-representation, future planning and conscious reflection, from simpler alternatives—skills that are thought by many to be uniquely human. Sometimes the behavioral output of humans and animals in an experimental task is the same, yet we cannot assume the underlying processes are similar. This statement seems obvious, but controversy arises because some scientists argue that when comparing humans with other apes, the most parsimonious Darwinian assumption is that the underlying processes are homologous (e.g., de Waal 2009). We argue, however, that a truly Darwinian approach dictates that the best mechanism is not necessarily the most complex (nor the simplest) but one that optimizes costs and benefits. From this perspective, mechanisms that need a lot of processing power or expensive neural substrate should only evolve if they are subject to strong selection pressure. Consequently, apes should share a costly human cognitive trait only if they receive benefits that exceed the costs.

As we have seen in this chapter, experimental methods for identifying underlying cognition can render ambiguous results. Better knowledge about neural bases could provide a solution to these methodological limitations. We have outlined several cases in which neurological research can inform our understanding of cognitive mechanisms, such as choice under uncertainty, state-dependent learning, and contrastive analysis of conscious and unconscious processing. The study of cortical substrates has also informed our understanding of goal-directed action (Balleine and Dickinson 1998).

Another essential source of information for a meaningful assessment of adaptive value is to study animals in the wild to ascertain whether a certain species is likely to encounter problems that demand such cognitive abilities (Kamil 1987). An acknowledgment of the fact that similar selective pressures could have led to human-like abilities in distantly related taxa has recently led to a valuable expansion of the research field. A truly comparative approach includes both the comparison of distantly related species that have similar ecological demands, which may have led to a convergence in their cognitive abilities, and the comparison of closely related species that differ in their ecology and may therefore differ in their cognitive abilities.

If we are to approach a deeper understanding of how thought has evolved in both human and nonhuman species, we must continue to integrate ecological, cognitive, and neurological research across carefully planned species comparisons.

Communication

10

Where Is the Information in Animal Communication?

Julia Fischer

Abstract

Communication is a central topic in animal behavior studies and yet the dispute over what constitutes communication is far from settled. Over the last few years, a number of papers have revisited the core issues in this field and have advanced divergent views regarding the explanatory power of the concept of "information." After a review of this debate, an integrative framework is proposed that conceives communication in its elementary form as an interaction between two individuals (sender and receiver) and involves the use of signals by the sender as well as the processing of and responses to those signals by the receiver. Signals are structures or behaviors that have evolved because their effects on other individuals benefit the sender on average, irrespective of whether or not the behavior of the receiver has evolved to be affected. Receivers have been selected to make inferences about the environment, including the behavior of conspecifics. Signals may in this sense be informative to the receiver, because they can be used to assess the state, identity, or subsequent behavior of others. Thus, signals contain "potential information," which turns into "perceiver information" once processed by a receiver. The value and amount of this information can only be defined from the receiver's perspective. This framework thus defends the concept of information but rejects the notion that senders have generally been selected to "provide" that information, and that information is "encoded" within a signal. The notion that animals process information also creates a bridge from studies of communication to those assessing the cognitive underpinnings of communicative behavior.

Introduction

Explaining the evolution of communication is a major challenge, and despite many years of research, a number of conceptual issues remain unresolved. This has led to both confusion and sometimes unproductive friction. Some of the disputes appear to stem from diverging initial points in the analyses: some focus on signal evolution, others on responses to signals. Apparently, these different foci have profound implications for the conceptualization of communication. While each approach has its merits as well as shortcomings, the real challenge is to incorporate insights from both to develop a full understanding of the complexity of communication.

In this chapter, I examine accounts that focus on explaining signal evolution and contrast them with accounts that have been adopted to explain the processing of signals. I review the recent critical discussion of the term "information" in animal communication and argue that this concept should be retained. I believe that the concept of information is indispensable for understanding not only the cognitive mechanisms which underpin the responses to signals, but also the selective pressures operating on receivers.

What Is Communication?

Definitions of communication commonly involve the use of signals and incorporate at least a signaler and a receiver. Notably, in one of the most influential contributions, Maynard Smith and Harper did not even bother to provide a definition of communication in "Animal Signals," but instead restricted the discussion to the evolution of signals (Maynard Smith and Harper 2003:388). Indeed, the term "communication" is not even indexed in the book. Because a number of researchers who seek to explain the evolution of communication refer to that text, they in turn put more emphasis on the sender's side than on the receiver's (Stegmann 2005; Scott-Phillips 2009). Analyses which follow Maynard Smith and Harper's emphasis on the sender have been labeled "adaptationist," because they have a strong focus on identifying the selective pressures that shape signal design and affect the costs associated with signaling.

A broad definition was put forward by Todt (1986), who characterized communication as "interactions with signals." This definition stresses the notion of communication as an integral part of social behavior. Moreover, it facilitates the application of insights from pragmatics, a field in linguistics that has to date only played a minor role in animal communication studies (see Wheeler et al., this volume). One complicating issue in any analysis of communication is that most communicative interactions do not only involve two individuals but rather several subjects, hence the concept of "communication networks" (McGregor and Peake 2000). This is particularly important when different receivers have divergent interests and exert different selective pressures on signalers (Skyrms 2010). For the sake of simplicity, however, this aspect will not be further elaborated here.

What Is a Signal?

An "adaptationist" account seeks to explain the evolution of signaling behavior and the maintenance of honest signaling. Game theoretical models which take into account the costs and benefits associated with signaling are employed to identify evolutionary stable strategies. Such models have shown that the distribution of interest is crucial for understanding the conditions under which honest signaling can arise. Specifically, when interests diverge, signaling must be costly to maintain honesty. When interests overlap, or when subjects interact repeatedly, cheap signaling may evolve (for an excellent introduction, see Searcy and Nowicki 2005).

Within this framework, there is a strong focus on distinguishing signals from other forms of behavior. Maynard Smith and Harper proposed that signals can be defined as "any act or structure which alters the behavior of other organisms, which evolved because of that effect, and which is effective because the receiver's response has also evolved" (Maynard Smith and Harper 2003:3). A similar stance was taken by Diggle and colleagues (2007) in a paper that aimed to integrate concepts from animal communication and sociobiology with the phenomenon of quorum sensing observed in bacteria. Quorum sensing is defined as the "accumulation of 'signaling' molecules [that] enables a…population as a whole [to] make a coordinated response" (Diggle et al. 2007:1245). The term "quorum sensing" has also been invoked to refer more broadly to all phenomena when the behavior of individuals of a social group depends on the number of other individuals performing that behavior (Fischer and Zinner 2011). Diggle and colleagues distinguished between signals, cues, and coercion on the basis of whether or not they had evolved "owing to the effect on the sender" and whether or not it "benefits the receiver to respond" (Diggle et al. 2007:1242)

Scott-Phillips (2008:388) provided an extension of that definition and described signals as "any act or structure that (a) affects the behavior of other organisms, (b) evolved because of those effects, and (c) which is effective because the effect (the response) has evolved to be affected by the act or structure." Within this framework, signals are distinguished from cues and coercion based on the presence or absence of specific evolution on the signaler's and receiver's side, respectively (Table 10.1).

Both accounts assume that for communication to occur, the interests of the signaler and receiver must overlap, otherwise there would be no reason to assume that the receiver's response evolved "to be affected." According to this view, the term "signal" is reserved solely for a narrow range of communicative interactions. Whenever interests diverge, these behaviors are defined

Table 10.1 Distinguishing between signals, cues, and coercion within the adaptationist approach to explain the evolution of signaling behavior. Adapted from Scott-Phillips (2008).

	Signaler's behavior evolved to affect receiver	Receiver's response evolved to be affected by signaler's behavior
Signals	+	+
Cue	−	+
Coercion	+	−

as coercion. The advantage of the distinction between signals and coercion is that it stresses the importance of considering the distribution of interests when seeking to explain the evolution of communicative "acts or structures" (Searcy and Nowicki 2005). However, overlap of interest is not a binary variable; instead, it constitutes a continuum ranging from a full overlap to total divergence. The degree of overlap of interest may vary in relation to the coefficient of relatedness, for instance, but also the cost functions associated with responding. An example is found within the realm of parent-offspring conflict, where the overlap of interest changes continuously over time. Imagine a needy youngster who expresses hunger or distress. Early on, caretakers benefit from investing in their offspring and respond immediately with nurturing behavior. However, at some point in time, it becomes more beneficial for the parent to invest in further offspring, creating a conflict (Trivers 1974). In nonhuman primates, such conflicts are often accompanied by tantrums and long bouts of screaming and wailing. Although mothers will initially give in to such attempts to reestablish contact and nurse, they will eventually behave aggressively toward the infant until the youngster gives up ("weaning conflict"). If one adopted the definition provided in Table 10.1, one would need a criterion to decide when the communicative behavior (screaming) turns from a signal to coercion. Because the structure of the behavior may even stay constant, while only the receiver's response changes, I believe that the distinction between signal and coercion is not helpful. In the following, I will therefore adopt a broader definition and use the term "signal" for all acts or structures that have evolved for the purpose of altering the receiver's behavior—irrespective of whether or not the receiver's behavior has also evolved for that purpose. Furthermore, the adaptationist approach does not do justice to the receiver's contribution to the equation. Tellingly, a wording such as "receiver's response evolved *to be affected* by signaler's behavior" [italics mine] carries the connotation that the receiver is a passive receptacle, unable to evolve its own strategies. It has long been known that this is not the case (Krebs and Dawkins 1984).

What Is Information?

A large body of research in animal communication is implicitly or explicitly based on the assumption that communication can be characterized as the transfer of information from the signaler to the receiver (reviewed in Rendall et al. 2009). The concept of information transmission was adapted from information theory. Although information theory was initially developed to study the processes of message encryption and their subsequent retrieval in technical systems (Shannon and Weaver 1949), it quickly found its way into communication studies. A number of authors have pointed out that such a concept is misleading because signalers do not benefit from "providing information," at least not when interests diverge. Instead, the argument goes that the senders benefit from influencing others to behave in a way that is in their own interest (Dawkins and Krebs 1978; Rendall et al. 2009). Moreover, it is questionable whether information can be determined independently from the receiver, calling into question not only the concept of information transmission, but also that of information content of a signal. Thus, it is argued that the concept of information is useful as a by-product, at best (Scott-Phillips 2008), or not at all (Rendall et al. 2009). Others have taken a more balanced view (Scarantino 2010) or have attempted to defend the concept of information (Seyfarth et al. 2010; Wheeler et al., this volume).

A critical view of the informational stance is not particularly novel. Dawkins and Krebs, for example, argued that "it is probably better to abandon the concept of information transfer altogether" (Dawkins and Krebs 1978:309; cf. Krebs and Dawkins 1984). However, in the subsequent edition of the same textbook, their view became more nuanced, casting the evolution of communication as an interplay between mind reading and manipulation, thus giving credit to both roles commonly invoked in communication (Krebs and Dawkins 1984).

As a number of authors have pointed out, one drawback of information theory is that it is agnostic with regard to the semantic aspects of signaling. Thus, it is not suited to capture the content of communication (Scarantino 2010). Indeed, the mathematical theory of information centers on the general statistical properties of the environment, whereas biological systems will only respond to statistical variation that has fitness consequences for them (i.e., that is related to conditions and events meaningful to the individual). This is the fundamental difference between Shannon information and biological information. One important insight from information theory, however, is that signals may undergo potential changes during transmission. This view has highlighted the selective pressure that different habitats may have on signal design; another valuable insight is the importance of noise. More importantly, the *conception* of information as a reduction of uncertainty to the receiver has proven to be useful. Thus, information theory offers some useful insights for understanding the receiver's behavior, because it connects communication to learning theory. Although it is difficult to provide exact quantifications of the information content of a given signal, Skyrms suggested that "the natural way to measure the information in a signal is to measure the extent that the use of that particular signal changes probabilities" (Skyrms 2010:8).

As Krebs and Dawkins (1984) wrote, any animal could benefit if it could behave as if predicting the future behavior of other animals in its world, or, as Humphrey put it, animals are "nature's psychologists" (cf. Krebs and Dawkins 1984:387). Thus, the question is whether animals can use signals (or cues, for that matter) to predict subsequent behaviors and upcoming events. There is ample evidence that this is the case. Learning theory offers tools to analyze and predict how animals form associations between stimuli, stimuli and responses, as well as behaviors and outcomes of these behaviors.

Consider threat signals. The evolution of threat signals (and display signals) can be explained on the grounds of an assumption that it benefits both the signaler and the receiver to avoid the costs of fighting. Both parties of an interacting dyad should attempt to resolve conflicts at the lowest possible cost; for instance, by using signals that communicate the signaler's intent or that reflect the signaler's quality. Because interests typically diverge in such situations, it pays for the receiver to distinguish between honest or reliable signals and unreliable ones.

For the present purposes, whether a given signal reliably predicts a certain action is of particular interest. If a receiver has been threatened by a higher-ranking animal, but chooses to stay anyway, and has subsequently been attacked, it will most likely learn that threat signals predict aggression. This view mirrors that put forward by Krebs and Dawkins (1984): they proposed that signalers should benefit from paying attention to other animal's intentions. Here, "intention" is used loosely without reference to the mental state of the animals, and it does not imply that the animal intends to communicate its intentions. Likewise, animals can learn that the occurrence of alarm calls predicts the appearance of a predator (this falls into the category of environmental information sensu Krebs and Dawkins 1984). Signals can be viewed as informative because they have the potential to reduce the uncertainty about what will happen next. Because animals benefit from ceasing to respond to unreliable (or uninformative) signals, one can make clear predictions under which circumstances animals learn to ignore specific signals. The same is true for indexical signals that are related to sender properties, such as size or hormonal state. It is important to stress that whether or not a signal reduces uncertainty can only be determined from the receiver's perspective and depends on the context of occurrence, previous experience, preceding signals, and so forth.

Skyrms distinguished between the informational content of a signal and the quantity of information in a signal. He suggested that "the informational content of a signal consists in how the signal affects probabilities," while the "quantity of information in a signal is measured by how far it moves probabilities" (Skyrms 2010:34).[1] Variation in structures or behaviors that allows receivers to predict upcoming events, gauge the quality of a sender, or detect changes in the environment has the potential to provide information as well. It is not trivial to distinguish between signals and other classes of behaviors. For instance, "walking" is part of locomotion. "Walking toward another animal,"

---

[1]   Skyrms (2010:34) goes on to explain this as follows: "It is easy to see the difference. Suppose, for instance, that there are two states, initially equiprobable. Suppose that signal A moves the probabilities to 9/10 for state 1 and 1/10 for state 2, and that signal B moves the probabilities in exactly the opposite way: 1/10 for state 1 and 9/10 for state 2. Even without knowing exactly how we are going to measure quantity of information, we know by considerations of symmetry that these two signals contain the same amount of information. They move the initial probabilities by the same amount. But they do not have the same information content, because they move the initial probabilities in different directions."

however, may also be a signal of dominance. Likewise, looking in a particular direction provide the animal with information about what is going on in that area. In nonhuman primates, eye gaze provides an important cue (Teufel et al. 2010); looking *at* some other animal may indicate that an approach or an attack will follow. A third example is the clearing of the throat, which may indicate a cold or signal the intent to begin a speech. Thus, some behaviors function as a signal, although the form or structure was not specifically selected for communicative purposes.

At the same time, one needs to be aware that all sorts of other variation in the environment ("data") have the potential to be informative. Therefore, signals constitute only a small subclass of the data that organisms are selected to process. For instance, it has been shown that animals respond adaptively to changes in acoustic signals that can be used to gauge signaler distance, such as effects due to reverberation. In fact, Rendall et al. (2009:237) noted that "perceivers have evolved sensory systems to detect, localize and discriminate *important features* of the environment" [italics mine]. I suggest that the "important features" might as well be termed "potential information." What is important can only be determined from the signaler's point of view; hence replacing "information" with "important features" does not provide a more accurate insight into animal communication than the application of the concept of information.

In the very strict sense, therefore, communication does not consist of information transmission, and signals do not contain information. Instead, information is generated by the receiver. Accordingly, statistical regularities in the environment are potentially informative, and signals contain *potential* information. Once this is clarified, however, I argue in favor of a mildly relaxed use of the terminology. For instance, I think it is acceptable to say in shorthand that information transmission has occurred once a signal has been intercepted by a receiver. Likewise, signals can be characterized in terms of their information content, in the sense that a researcher might be interested in studying, for instance, the association between signal variation and some physiological variable, as long as it is understood that this is only potential information.

Message and Meaning

The notion that communication entails the encoding of information on the sender's side and its decoding on the receiver's side has also been criticized because of its supposed implicit symbolic connotation (Scarantino 2010). Yet, some terminology is needed to describe the process of how, for instance, signaler features are related to signal features. Although frequently correlational, there is now ample evidence that in the acoustic domain, specific aspects of the call vary with signaler fighting ability, body size, and hormonal state (Fischer and Zinner 2011). To circumvent the connotation of symbolic communication, one might prefer to avoid the phrase that "information has been encoded." However, whenever there is variation in signal structure in relation to subsequent behavior, sender quality, or changes in the environment, one might say that this pattern constitutes "potential information." This is equivalent to the distinction between message and meaning (Seyfarth and Cheney 2003a). The message is thus the variation in signal structure (or usage) that is related to some aspect of the signaler or the context of signaling. The meaning is generated by the receiver, who processes and interprets the signal, and chooses the appropriate response in light of all the available evidence (i.e., contextual cues).

On conceptual grounds, it is important to distinguish between meaning and responses. In principle, the meaning could be defined as the information the receiver obtains from the signal, in the sense that a signal has been associated with a particular context, the emotional state of the signaler, or some change in behavior. Empirically, however, the meaning can only be inferred from the responses, and therefore, responses and meaning have often been (in my view incorrectly) conflated. Smith (1977), for instance, proposed that signals attain meaning by a combined assessment of signal features and the context in which they are given, but I suggest that it is more accurate to say that the responses are chosen on the basis of signal information as well as contextual information. In other words, the decision rule takes in the occurrence or variation in a signal, as well as variation in context. For instance, vervet monkey responses to acoustic signals have been shown to vary with call type ("alarm call") as well as sender identity (Cheney and Seyfarth 1988). That is, listeners process who is calling, and they may vary their responses in relation to signaler reliability. The amount of information extracted in terms of identifying the caller remains the same. At the same time, the same signal may elicit quite distinct responses, depending on the context in which it occurs. Although it has not been demonstrated experimentally, it is conceivable that receivers are able to classify a call as belonging to a certain category ("alarm call") while varying their response in relation to context ("no predator in sight" vs. "a lion right in front of me"). This issue warrants further investigation.

It has been argued that studies of (nonhuman primate) acoustic communication should consider the influence that specific acoustic properties have on broadly conserved sensory and affective systems in listeners (Owren and Rendall 2001; Rendall et al. 2009). It is certainly true that sharp onsets may elicit startle responses. Likewise, it seems plausible that most nonhuman primates would respond to aversive loud and noisy screams with avoidance responses. The diversity of alarm calls in different species, such as growls, barks, twitters and hoots, however, rejects a simplistic explanation. Given that nonhuman primate vocalizations are largely innate, it is not surprising that the same broad call types may be used in different contexts (Fischer et al. 2004). Therefore, multiple selective pressures, including those related to function, as well as evolutionary constraints must be taken into account when trying to link signal structure to function. Furthermore, nonhuman primates quickly learn to pay attention to the alarm calls of other species, such as the whistles and snorts of antelope, the calls of birds, or the growls of leopards. Even more strikingly, animals may respond to the absence of a signal, such as in the "watchman's song" found in meerkats, *Suricata suricatta*, where sentinels on guard regularly emit soft sounds. If they cease vocalizing, this signals danger to their conspecifics (Manser 1999). Clearly, such a behavior cannot be reduced to a simple physiological response.

Referential Signaling

Rendall and colleagues (2009:233) lamented that "animal communication studies often use analogies to human language." While this is perhaps true for the study of nonhuman primate signaling, most researchers studying olfactory communication in moths, the roaring of red deer, or electric communication in fish would probably disagree. The question really is: What do we gain and/or lose by applying linguistic concepts?

Obviously, any attempt to identify the evolutionary roots of the human language faculty (Hauser et al. 2002) will need to begin with a definition of the features that are seen as characteristic of language or speech. While largely resulting in a failure to find equivalents of the human language faculty (at least at the side of the signaler), one must concede that the linguistic approach was necessary to reach that insight. We would not know that nonhuman primate calls fail to fulfill the criteria for symbolic or iconic communication, if it were not for the adaption of a semiotic and/or linguistic stance. Given the deep human desire to make sense of the origin of language, I predict that this branch of research will expand further, and the quest is now to understand the suite of changes that occurred during evolution, which eventually allowed early humans to speak (Fischer and Hammerschmidt 2011). Such studies of nonhuman primate communication need to be complemented by other studies that are more ecologically grounded, or which look at other selective pressures that shape communication today.

One core concept in those studies that investigated which (if any) aspects of nonhuman primate signaling behavior may be linked to aspects of the human language faculty is the topic of referential signaling. The diagnostics for referential signaling are production specificity on the side of the sender and differential responses on the side of the listener (Macedonia and Evans 1993; Seyfarth and Cheney 2003b). The latter are indispensable to infer whether or not animals attribute differential "meaning" to the sounds (but see discussion above). Production specificity is frequently inferred by comparing signals that are given in different contexts; if these reveal systematic acoustic variation, it is assumed that the criterion of production specificity is met. However, production specificity can only truly be assessed if the vocalizations given in *all* contexts are sampled and compared. Obviously, production specificity tends to be overestimated when only a few selected contexts are included in an analysis. What does it tell us, however, if and when production or context specificity can be diagnosed? Initial accounts favored a view according to which the animals "denote" the predator type, for instance, or possibly the appropriate response, akin to a proposition. I would argue that we still have limited insights into the cognitive operations underlying the usage of calls in different contexts. In most of the cases where context-specific calls are found, the most parsimonious explanation is that variation in calls that allow listeners to select the appropriate response constitutes a selective advantage that leads to the evolution of increasingly different vocalizations. In other cases, variation may be related to changes in hormone levels or arousal. Whenever the variation is sufficiently systematic, listeners can make inferences about ongoing or upcoming events and adjust their behavior accordingly, despite the fact that in the strict sense, these calls do not refer to anything at all.

Another issue in this realm is that signals can be placed on a referential-to-motivational continuum. Scarantino (2010:E3) noted that "the notion of a continuum makes theoretical sense only on the condition that approaching one end entails moving away from the other." He argued that no such trade-offs exist. I do not believe, however, that this is the problem. First, Marler and colleagues (1992) conceived the referential-to-motivational continuum as variation along two different dimensions. Thus, in principle, a signal could show no variation in relation to external referents, but substantial variation in relation to motivation.

My main criticism of the "motivational-to-referential" continuum is of a different sort; namely, it sets up a false dichotomy. "Motivational" change can also be "functionally referential." Consider the case of rhesus monkey screams that vary in relation to the dominance of the aggressor (Gouzoules et al. 1984), and let us assume that this leads to different degrees of aversion, which in turn causes the animals to produce calls that vary in terms of noise. This is a clear case of a change in the signal in relation to motivation. A receiver may now be able to infer that animal X has been attacked by a high- or low-ranking individual. In this sense, the signal now functions referentially. In other words, "motivation" refers to signal production, whereas "referentiality" refers to the receiver's ability to understand the link between signal structure and occurrence, or context, or some other variable. Given that nonhuman primates and the majority of other terrestrial mammals have little volitional control over the structure of their vocalizations (reviewed in Hammerschmidt and Fischer 2008), it is safe to assume that the production of all acoustic signals is largely motivational. Todt (1986) distinguished between three components of the internal state: an affective one representing the animal's evaluation of the situation; a motivational one related to the tendency to exhibit a given behavior; and an arousal component related to the propensity to respond to incoming sensory information and the immediacy of a given response. This idea is closely related to the proposal that responses, particularly to predators, may vary in relation to predator class but also to the imminence of the danger (response urgency). At present, it is difficult to determine whether the sight of different predators, for instance, leads to changes in affect and/or motivation (probably both). In the framework of explaining acoustic variation, I suggest that the referential-to-motivational continuum be abandoned. It may be more illuminating to test whether such a three-dimensional construct as the one presented above provides a useful framework to understand variation in nonhuman primate signals. It might also provide a conceptual link to studies that seek to explain variation in the expression of emotion in the human voice.

Conclusion

In the strict sense, information can only be defined from the receivers' perspective, because statistical regularities in the environment are only turned into information by the receiver. Statistical regularities in the environment should thus be conceived as potential information, whose value and content depends on the state of the receiver. Communication consists of the use of specific structures or behaviors that have evolved because they affect the behavior of others, as well as the processing of these signals by the receiver. Communication can only be understood at the ultimate and proximate level if the interdependence between signaler and receiver is considered.

Acknowledgments

I thank Kurt Hammerschmidt for being such a wonderful friend and intellectual sparring partner, and Robert Seyfarth, Dorothy Cheney, Tabitha Price, Urs Kalbitzer, and Matthis Drolet for inspiration and discussion.

11

Communication in Social Insects

Sophisticated Problem Solving by Groups of Tiny-Brained Animals

Christoph Grüter

Abstract

Collective intelligence allows groups of individuals to solve problems which otherwise could not be solved by a single individual. Insect workers have tiny brains, but by functioning as part of a self-organized colony, they find sophisticated solutions to vital organizational problems (e.g., finding a suitable new home or exploiting the best food sources in a changing environment). In consensus decision making, unanimity among workers is crucial. In contrast, combined decision making requires that different groups of workers within the colony chose different options. Communication and learning are often fundamental in collective decision making. However, as workers gain experience, communication may lose importance as an information source for workers. How social insects collectively solve problems parallels decision making in other biological systems (e.g., neuronal networks), and investigation into social insect collective decision making has inspired new solutions to optimization problems in areas such as computer sciences and the organization of communication networks.

Introduction

Insect societies, like human societies, confront many organizational challenges. These include the collection and transport of resources (e.g., food or building material), the establishment and maintenance of transportation routes, the removal of waste materials, and the defense of colony resources. Over the last 100 years, an impressive number of communication signals have been identified that help organize these tasks in social insects. Most of these are chemical signals; however, tactile signals and, to a lesser degree, signals perceived via the other sensory modalities, can also be important. The vast majority of the studied signals regulate recruitment activities, either to food sources, new nest sites, or sites of aggressive interactions with intruders (Hölldobler and Wilson 1990, 2009; Wilson 1971). During recruitment, workers communicate with other workers. Queen signals are important in regulating the reproductive division of labor (Winston 1987), whereas brood signals modulate division of labor among workers (Pankiw et al. 1998).

Work in insect societies is not centrally organized (e.g., by a leader giving orders); instead, self-organization is the process by which activities are regulated (Camazine et al. 2001). Each worker acquires and responds to information from the immediate environment, often by adhering to simple behavioral rules that have been shaped by natural selection. Individual insect workers may not have the cognitive capabilities of some of their vertebrate counterparts, but by functioning collectively in groups, they show an astonishing ability to solve organizational problems. The ability of a group to solve a problem in a way that goes beyond the capacities of individuals is often called *collective intelligence* (also referred to as collective cognition or swarm intelligence; Couzin 2009; Krause et al. 2010).

This chapter reviews recent progress in our understanding of the remarkable collective problem-solving abilities of social insects and the role of communication in decision making. In some cases, problem solving is largely based on the emission and response to a single signal, as in the case of the waggle-dance signal during nest-site selection in honeybees or trail selection in the black garden ant (*Lasius niger*). Others (e.g., the organization of a particular task) may involve multiple signals, such as the different pheromones in ant foraging (Dussutour et al. 2009; Jackson and Ratnieks 2006). Social cues (i.e., information provided inadvertently by other individuals) deliver further social information to help organize tasks (Detrain and Deneubourg 2009; O'Donnell and Bulova 2007). In honeybee foraging, at least six signals are thought to be involved in the organization of foraging (Anderson and Ratnieks 1999; Grüter and Farina 2009; Seeley 1998). However, the meaning of a signal is often not fixed but can be context dependent, and its usefulness varies with the experience of the receiver (Hölldobler 1999).

Communication and Collective Intelligence

Honeybee Nest-Site Selection

Nest-site selection in European honeybees (*Apis mellifera*) nicely illustrates how a group solves a problem that cannot be resolved by an individual worker. When a honeybee colony swarms, about 5,000–10,000 workers and a queen leave the hive and settle nearby in a cluster (Lindauer 1955; Seeley 2010). During the following hours or days, the bees explore their surroundings and locate 10–30 potential new nest sites of varying quality (Lindauer 1955). Choosing a good nest site is important because the quality of the nest site affects the survival chances of the colony (Seeley 2010).

The swarm is able to solve this problem despite the fact that none of the few hundred scout bees involved in the decision-making process knows more than one or two of all the options (Seeley and Buhrman 1999). If a scout discovers a cavity that fulfils her innate preferences, she advertises her find through a waggle dance (Lindauer 1955). Originally studied in the context of foraging communication, the waggle dance (Figure 11.1) is a highly stereotyped dance-like behavior (von Frisch 1967). Karl von Frisch discovered that by means of dancing, foragers advertise the existence, odor, and location of a profitable food source to nest mates inside the hive (von Frisch 1967). Scouts perform waggle dances on the swarm cluster to (a) tell their nest mates the location of the nest site and (b) provide their opinion about the quality of the nest site. The better the quality, the longer a scout dances (Lindauer 1955; Seeley and Buhrman 2001; Seeley and Visscher 2008). Because scouts dance longer after finding a good nest site, they recruit additional bees, some of which will also perform waggle dances on the swarm after inspecting the cavity. As a consequence of this positive feedback, the amount of dancing for a very good cavity increases. At the same time, the number of dances for suboptimal cavities decreases (Seeley and Buhrman 1999) because individual scouts have an intrinsic tendency to cease dancing gradually (Seeley and Visscher 2008; Visscher 2007) and because the number of new recruits advertising the site is lower than the number of bees which discontinue dancing. In this way, groups of scouts advertise different locations until the number of scouts favoring one

Figure 11.1 Depiction of a honeybee performing a waggle dance and four follower bees. The dancer performs a waggle run, then turns to one side, circles back to the starting point of the waggle run, then starts another waggle run and usually turns to the other side and so on. Some bees perform more than 100 waggle runs during one single dance. Dancers produce airborne sounds, create airflows, cause vibrations in the comb, and releases chemicals into the air. Followers often touch the dancer with their antennae. Illustration by N. Stadelmann; reprinted with permission from Grüter and Farina (2009).

particular site reaches a threshold or quorum. Once scouts sense that the critical number of scouts at the nest site has been reached, they initiate the next stage of house hunting (Seeley and Visscher 2004). These scouts start producing a piping sound which stimulates other bees on the swarm to warm up their flight muscles and prepare for lift-off (Seeley and Tautz 2001). Shortly before lift-off, scouts excitedly run on top of and between other bees on the swarm to announce that lift-off is imminent (Seeley 2010).

Foraging Trail Selection in Ants

Ant foragers provide another example of how groups of insects solve complicated problems. In a complex environment, such as the forest floor, it is usually impossible to locate a straight path between the nest and the food source. An ant colony (e.g., aphid-tending species like *Formica spp.* or *Lasius spp.*) will often visit the same food location for weeks or even months (Quinet and Pasteels 1996; Rosengren and Fortelius 1986; Salo and Rosengren 2001). Hence, to save energy and reduce exposure to predators, it is important to find the shortest of a large number of possible paths (Beckers et al. 1992), a challenge similiar to a problem known in mathematics as the "traveling salesman problem." Here, a salesman has to find the shortest path to visit N cities exactly one time. So, how do ants do it?

After discovering a sugar food source, foragers of the black garden ant (*L. niger*), like many other ants, lay a pheromone trail back to the nest to guide other foragers to the food source. A recruit following a pheromone trail has a tendency to choose a stronger trail if she has to chose between two paths at a bifurcation (Aron et al. 1993; Beckers et al. 1993; Deneubourg et al. 1990; Detrain and Deneubourg 2008). This trail asymmetry, where there is a stronger and a weaker pheromone trail option at a bifurcation, develops as follows: two foragers might start on the same path but by chance use two different paths of unequal length around an obstacle to get to the food source (Beckers et al. 1992; Camazine et al. 2001) (Figure 11.2a). The ant using the shorter path will make more trips to the food source per unit time and thus more pheromone will accumulate on the shorter section of the path around the obstacle (Figure 11.2b). Recruited ants walking toward the food source are likely to choose the path with more pheromone when they reach the bifurcation caused by the obstacle. This positive feedback mechanism will amplify small initial differences between options and lead to a collective choice of the shorter branch (Beckers et al. 1992; Couzin 2009; Camazine et al. 2001). Again, the ability of the colony to select the best option does not depend on individuals knowing all the options and making direct comparisons between them. The choice in this type of experiment is never unanimous, as in nest-site selection, but it often leads to >80% of all ants converging on the best option. How ants solve the problem of finding the shortest path has inspired a new solution to the traveling salesman problem: the ant colony optimization algorithm (Dorigo and Stützle 2004).

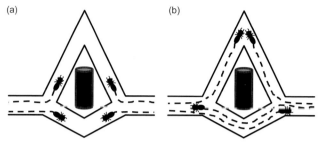

Figure 11.2   Selection of the shorter path by ants. (a) Ants laying pheromone trails to and from the food source walk on two paths of different lengths around an obstacle. (b) The shorter distance of one branch leads to a faster accumulation of pheromone on the branch. As a consequence, more ants choose the shorter branch when reaching the decision point (after Beckers et al. 1992).

Integration of Multiple Information Sources

Multiple Information Sources Used in Territorial Tournaments

Consensus decision making can involve rather complex communication processes. Perhaps the most spectacular example of how groups of insects integrate multiple information sources comes from territorial tournaments of the honey ant *Myrmecocystus mimicus*. Here, mutualistic intra-colony and manipulative inter-colony communication leads to a group decision (Hölldobler 1976b; Hölldobler and Wilson 2009).

Colonies of *M. minicus* defend their territories aggressively against conspecific intruders. If conflicts between two colonies occur, a few hundred ants are recruited by chemical signals to the tournament site where they display their fighting abilities to the opponent side through stereotyped aggressive displays (Hölldobler 1976a; Hölldobler and Wilson 2009). During the display, an ant tries to appear as big as possible to "impress" its opponent. Usually the smaller ant yields and walks away. To appear bigger, ants walk on stilted legs and raise their head and abdomen. Ants also inflate their abdomen to make it bigger. Some of the ants use an additional bluff and mount small stones to appear larger (Hölldobler and Wilson 2009). During the display, ants drum their opponent with their antennae and kick their legs against the opponent. The function of this behavior is not known. A contest lasts only a few seconds, after which the ants search for a new opponent and the procedure is repeated.

Two methods appear to be involved in reaching a group decision about which side wins: head counting and caste polling (Hölldobler and Wilson 2009). Small colonies seem to rely mostly on caste polling, in which by some unknown mechanism the ants are able to estimate the proportion of majors (large workers, sometimes called soldiers) among the ants in the tournament. The proportion of majors provides information about colony size, and combatants from smaller colonies usually retreat quickly into the nest when facing a side with a large proportion of majors (Hölldobler and Wilson 2009). If both colonies are large, head counting provides additional information. Here, a specialized group of smaller ants, the "reconnaissance ants," gathers information about the number of ants on the opposing side. They move through the tournament site and experience many short contacts with both nest mates and opponents. If necessary, these ants also recruit more combatants to the tournament site by laying pheromone trails.

The options for each side are either a collective retreat, a continuation of the tournament, or an escalated attack which can lead to the enslavement of the weaker colony. Many aspects of the group decision process are not yet understood; for example, how reconnaissance ants estimate the relative strength of both sides and how they induce a collective response. However, it seems clear that different types of information are involved in the consensus decision-making process.

Multiple Pheromones on Foraging Trail Systems

The previous examples demonstrate how consensus decision making results in a group converging on one solution. Unanimity, for example when choosing a new home, is crucial for the survival success of the group (Visscher 2007; Seeley 2010). However, there is no single optimal solution when it comes to sending foragers to different food sources because colonies need to exploit many food sources at the same time, and because the quality and location of the food source changes with time (Seeley 1995). Often, individuals must integrate more than one information source to make adaptive decisions in such a dynamic environment. In recent years, research has uncovered multiple pheromones on foraging trails. Pharaoh's ants (*Monomorium pharaonis*) use at least three different trail pheromones to organize their foraging activities (Jackson and Ratnieks 2006; Robinson et al. 2008; Robinson et al. 2005). While two attractive pheromones guide foragers along the entire trail, one repellent pheromone directs foragers away from unprofitable trails at bifurcations (Ratnieks 2008; Robinson et al. 2008; Robinson et al. 2005). Having such a "no entry" signal for unrewarding branches is likely to increase foraging efficiency (Stickland et al. 1999), but why have two different attractive pheromones? These two pheromones operate at different timescales: one is short-lived (minutes), the other lasts longer (days) (Jackson et al. 2006; Robinson et al. 2008). These different timescales provide foragers, who might otherwise not rely strongly on route memories, a kind of long- and short-term "memory" of good food sources (Dussutour et al. 2009; Ratnieks 2008). The short-lived pheromone helps colonies to respond quickly to changes, such as the sudden appearance of a food source, whereas the long-lived pheromone increases the chances of rediscovering food sources that were rewarding in the past after temporal unavailability (Dussutour et al. 2009; Ratnieks 2008).

Multicomponent Signals

The availability of multiple information sources may be separated in time and space, as in the case of trail pheromones in Pharaoh's ants, or they may be provided during the production of a single signal. Multicomponent signals simultaneously provide more than one type of information (Bradbury and Vehrencamp 1998; Partan and Marler 1999, 2005; Rowe 1999). Here, the term *multicomponent signal* refers to all communicative components of the animal's behavior that occur simultaneously (Partan and Marler 2005). The honey ant walking on stilted legs and simultaneously drumming her opponent with her antenna is a good candidate. Pheromone blends consisting of different chemical compounds, each having an effect on receiver behavior, are another example (Hölldobler 1995, 1999). Perhaps the best-known example, and one of the most complex communication behaviors in the animal world, is the honeybee waggle dance (Grüter and Farina 2009; von Frisch 1967) (Figure 11.1).

A dancing bee provides various types of information to surrounding bees. First, a dancer attracts and excites other bees and primes them to receive more information. This is probably best described as a modulatory component, increasing the motivation of surrounding bees to receive more information. Some bees will start following the movements of the dancer (Figure 11.1). A dancer also provides olfactory information: odor cues that cling to the dancer's body and are released into the air during dance maneuvers as well as odor cues present in regurgitated nectar samples, which are offered to a follower. Olfactory cues can affect the behavior of surrounding bees even if they do not physically come into contact with the dancer (Grüter and Farina 2009; Thom et al. 2007; von Frisch 1923). Food odors present on the nectar and on the forager's body indicate the type of food source the dancer has visited. Dance followers learn these odors and use this olfactory information to locate the advertised food source in the field (Farina et al. 2005; von Frisch 1967; Wenner et al. 1969). In addition, dancers also release hydrocarbons (Z-(9)-tricosene, tricosane, Z-(9)-pentacosene, and pentacosane). These chemicals seem to induce foraging behavior in bees that perceive them inside the hive (Thom et al. 2007). Two other components of the waggle-dance signal provide information about the location of the visited food source: distance and direction. Distance is encoded in the duration of the waggle phase (von Frisch 1967). The body orientation relative to gravity provides dance followers with information about the direction of the food source relative to the position of the sun (von Frisch 1967). It is still not clear which sensory modalities are involved in the decoding of the location components (Dyer 2002; Michelsen 2003). Candidates include airborne sounds, air flows produced by the wings, vibrations of the substrate, or tactile signals detected when the antennae touch the body of the dancer (for a discussion, see Dyer 2002; Michelsen 2003).

Communication and Social Learning

Learning by copying or interacting with other individuals (i.e., social learning) is common in social insects (Leadbeater and Chittka 2007, 2009). The close proximity of many workers in the nest or during the performance of collective tasks leads to many opportunities for social learning. Communication between workers, however, often does not require learning by the animals that respond to the signal. For example, there is no evidence that Pharaoh's ants learn about food locations when they follow pheromone trails (Ratnieks 2008). Similarly, the responses of insect workers to alarm pheromones of nest mates in the presence of intruders, or the response of workers to queen or brood pheromones does not seem to involve any learning.

If, however, the appropriate response to a signal is unpredictable because of environmental changes, social learning can help colonies respond adaptively to these changes. Accordingly, studies have shown that certain levels of environmental instability favor social learning versus innate responses or asocial learning (Laland et al. 1996; Rendell et al. 2010). The foraging environment of social insect colonies, for example, often changes, and social learning of currently rewarding food locations or food types is common (Leadbeater and Chittka 2007, 2009). Honeybee foragers learn about good food sources by following waggle dancers. Ants of many species follow pheromone trails while walking to a food source (Hölldobler and Wilson 1990). While pheromones guide the initial trips, ants learn about the features of the food location and the route to and from it and use these memories during later foraging trips (Collet and Collet 2002; Rosengren and Fortelius 1986; Salo and Rosengren 2001).

Another example of social learning, tandem running (Figure 11.3a), has been considered an example of teaching (Franks and Richardson 2006; cf. Leadbeater et al. 2006). During tandem running, an ant that has found a food

(a)   (b)

Figure 11.3   (a) Tandem running in the ant species *Temnothorax albipennis*. The ant with the blue paint marks, the pupil, closely follows the recruiting ant, the teacher, to a resource (photo by Tom Richardson). (b) Foragers of the ant *Lasius fuliginosus* collecting honeydew secreted by aphids. Foragers visit the same foraging locations for several months (photos by Christoph Grüter).

source guides one recruit from the nest to the food. The recruit follows by keeping antennal contact with the leader (Hölldobler and Wilson 1990). The leading ant is considered the "teacher" because she (a) modifies her behavior in the presence of the follower, (b) incurs time costs while doing so, and (c) helps the "pupil" to learn more quickly (Caro and Hauser 1992; Franks and Richardson 2006). The honeybee waggle dance is another candidate behavior which may fulfill these criteria. However, although there is clear evidence that the latter two criteria are fulfilled, the first criterion has not yet been experimentally demonstrated.

Traditions in Social Insects

Behavioral traditions are thought to be one of the foundations of culture, and it is thus understandable that research has not paid much attention to social insects when looking for examples of traditions. However, some behaviors warrant closer inspection.

Traditions can be defined as group-specific behavioral patterns that are socially transmitted from one generation to the next (Laland and Janik 2006; Leadbeater and Chittka 2007). Many social insects forage at the same food locations for weeks, months, or even years (Quinet and Pasteels 1996; Salo and Rosengren 2001) (Figure 11.3b). The ant *F. uralensis* visits very stable aphid clusters for long periods of time (Salo and Rosengren 2001). During winter, when foraging is impossible, foragers retain information about these locations, revisit them in spring, and recruit new foragers to the location. Hence, older foragers of a colony socially transmit the information about good food locations to new foragers from one year to the next (Salo and Rosengren 2001).

Another example, discussed in Leadbeater and Chittka (2007), is the social transmission of temporal foraging activities in honeybees. There is evidence that honeybee brood in cells learn about the time of peak foraging, possibly via vibrations on the comb caused by dancing, and later prefer to forage at the same time when they become foragers some 3–4 weeks later. Both examples show that one can find socially transmitted behaviors, performed beyond individual life spans, in groups of tiny-brained animals.

Communication and Memory

As workers perform a task, they often acquire information that affects the way they subsequently perform that task. Foragers, for example, can acquire route memories during foraging. On the way to the food source and back, they learn landmarks, colors and odors of food sources, how to handle them, and the timing of food abundance (von Frisch 1967). After only three visits, honeybee foragers remember the features of a food source for the rest of their life (Giurfa 2007; R. Menzel 1999). Hence, an experienced forager leaving the

nest can either use communicated information from nest mates (social information) to find a food source or rely on memory (private information) about
known food source locations. Experienced foragers frequently pay attention to
dances (Biesmeijer and Seeley 2005; Grüter et al. 2008) and may, therefore,
even encounter situations where social information and private information are
in conflict. Sometimes these dances indicate an unknown location but carry an
odor that the follower bee knows from past foraging trips to a different food
location. Here, the follower experiences a conflict between the indicated vector and the memorized route linked to this odor (Grüter et al. 2008). This can
be a common situation when a colony exploits multiple patches of the same
plant species. In this situation, honeybees seem overwhelmingly to prefer their
memory over the communicated information, if the food sources are close to
the nest and of high quality (Grüter et al. 2008; Grüter and Farina 2009).

Ant foragers face similar choices between social information, such as a
chemical trail and private information. In many ant species, the foraging trail
network of a colony has a binary tree structure (Stickland et al. 1999). Ants that
found food at the end of a branch with little or no pheromone face a conflict
between the pheromone information and their route memory at bifurcations
when the alternative branch is marked with more pheromone. As with the honeybee, memories seem to override the pheromone trail in a number of species (Grüter et al. 2011; Harrison et al. 1989; Klotz 1987; Salo and Rosengren
2001; Traniello 1989; but see Aron et al. 1993; Hölldobler 1976a). In the ant
L. niger, memory overrides social information at bifurcations after one single
foraging trip (Grüter et al. 2011). Relying on memory as an information source
during foraging makes sense if foragers learn and retrieve information depending on the quality of the food source. Indeed, there is good evidence that the
use of memory to locate food depends on the quality of the reward. In both
wasps and bees, foragers are more attached to their food source if the quality
of the experienced reward was high (Greggers and Menzel 1993; Jeanne and
Taylor 2009; Ribbands 1949). However, it is likely that other circumstances
favor the use of communicated information. If private information is outdated,
unreliable, or associated with high costs (e.g., due to the distance between the
food source and the nest), then communicated information might become more
important (Kendal et al. 2005; Laland 2004).

Similarities between Insect Colonies and Neuronal Systems

Research in recent years has uncovered similarities in consensus decision-
making processes of very different biological systems, such as insect colonies and neuronal systems (Couzin 2009; Marshall et al. 2009; Seeley 2010;
Visscher 2007). Both social insects and brains face the problem of choosing
among various options based on information that is distributed across many
subpopulations, each with only limited information. In both types of systems,

separate populations (workers in insect colonies or neurons in brains) accumulate evidence for alternative choices. In visual information processing in monkey brains, for example, different groups of neurons report information about a visual stimulus present in a small part of the visual field (Marshall et al. 2009): the stronger the stimulus, the more active the neurons. As soon as one population reaches a threshold, a decision is made for the corresponding option (e.g., moving the eye in a certain direction). In both systems, these neuron populations may be arranged in a way that leads to cross-inhibition, where the activation of one population suppresses the activity of the others (Marshall et al. 2009; Visscher 2007). In honeybee swarms, the inhibition is the removal of recruits from the recruit pool by recruitment in another group. In both honeybee swarms and neuronal systems, cross-inhibition between populations helps to sharpen the differences in signal strength between the different options (Seeley 2010; Visscher 2007).

Conclusions

By functioning in self-organized groups, insect workers are capable of solving complex problems. Communication is one of the key tools that enable colonies to solve organizational problems. In some situations, unanimity is crucial. House-hunting insects have to reach a consensus; otherwise, the colony may be unable to move to a safe home. In other situations, a colony needs to choose numerous different options simultaneously, such as the successful allocation of foragers to various food patches in foraging. This is an ongoing challenge because the foraging environment can change on a daily basis. Hence, collective decision making occurs between two extremes: consensus decision making leads to all animals of a group doing the same thing, whereas combined decision making means that each individual chooses its own option. Indeed, some decision-making processes result in a mix of consensus and combined decision making, all resulting in the creation of adaptive solutions for complex problems.

12

Language and Episodic Sharing

Michael C. Corballis

Abstract

Tulving drew a distinction between two forms of declarative memory, semantic and episodic. The notion of episodic memory as conscious, reexperienced memory for specific episodes has been extended to the notion of mental time travel, whereby we can imagine future episodes as well as past ones. The further claim that mental time travel is uniquely human has been challenged in a number of studies purporting to reveal both episodic memory and the imagining of future episodes in nonhuman species, including birds and great apes. The basic issue remains somewhat unresolved, but it is contended here that the capacity for mental time travel in humans vastly exceeds that in nonhuman animals in terms of variety, timescale, and combinatorial complexity. These properties may have built on a capacity for the generation of fantasy and the imagination of impossible events. The generativity of mental time travel is a prelude to language, whereby our mental journeys through time can be shared, and also to the generation of fictitious events, as in stories, fairy tales, and myths. The complexity and specificity of human mental time travel, and its sharing, may have been driven by the necessities of social cohesion and group planning during the Pleistocene.

Introduction

It has become commonplace in cognitive science to distinguish between declarative and nondeclarative memory (e.g., Squire 1992, 2004). Unlike nondeclarative memory, declarative memory is accessible to consciousness, and specifically to language—it is memory that can be "declared." Within this category, Tulving (1983) drew the further distinction between semantic memory and episodic memory. Episodic memory differs from semantic memory in that it refers to the reexperiencing of specific events, or episodes, in an individual's life, whereas semantic memory refers to enduring knowledge. When we call an episodic memory to mind, we think of it as *remembering* that episode, but when we bring an item of semantic memory to mind, we think of it as *knowing* that item without reexperiencing any past episode.[1] Episodic memory can

---

[1]   In some respects the term "episodic memory" is misleading, since one may know that a specific episode occurred without reexperiencing it. The distinction between *remembering* and *knowing* better captures the distinction that Tulving intended, at least in his more recent writing.

nevertheless be distinguished from autobiographical memory, which typically involves elements of both semantic and episodic memory—indeed, a meta-analysis of studies of autobiographical memory indicates different neural networks linked to the semantic and episodic components (Svoboda et al. 2006). Of special interest is Tulving's claim that episodic memory is uniquely human, whereas semantic memory is shared with other species, although we can generally suppose that the human semantic-memory store is vastly greater than that of any other species, including the great apes.

Although remembering can be distinguished from knowing, the two must nevertheless be somewhat interdependent. Tulving (2001) argues that the storage and recovery of episodic memories depends on semantic memories that are already in place, but which are then related to the self in subjectively sensed time. This allows the actual experience of the event to be processed separately from the semantic system. In this view, episodic memories could not be stored in the absence of semantic memory, which is perhaps why our childhood episodic memories do not begin until the semantic system is firmly established, at around age four or five (e.g., Levine 2004). Nevertheless there is some evidence that episodic memory can persist when semantic memory fails. People with semantic dementia, a degenerative neurological disorder that afflicts some individuals in late adulthood, show severe decline in semantic memory, but their episodic memories appear to remain remarkably and surprisingly intact (Hodges and Graham 2001). It is possible, though, that their recall of specific episodes is based on knowledge of those episodes rather than on actually remembering them (J. Perner, pers. comm.).

In most cases of amnesia, though, it is episodic memories rather than semantic memories that are lost. In one classic case, a patient with extensive damage to the frontal and temporal lobes was unable to recall any specific episode from his life, yet retained semantic knowledge (Tulving et al. 1988). Even without brain injury, people probably remember only a tiny fraction of actual past episodes (Loftus and Loftus 1980), and events are often remembered inaccurately, even to the point that people will claim with some certainty to have remembered events that did not in fact happen (Loftus and Ketcham 1994; Roediger and McDermott 1995). Of course, we also forget semantic information—who can remember everything they learned at school?—but episodic memory does seem more vulnerable and incomplete, and more open to suggestion. Tulving summarizes this as follows:

> Episodic memory is a recently evolved, late-developing, and early-deteriorating past-oriented memory system, more vulnerable than other memory systems to neuronal dysfunction, and probably unique to humans (Tulving 2002:5).

These properties suggest that episodic memory did not evolve primarily to serve as a faithful record of the past. It has been suggested, instead, that it evolved to provide for the enhancement of future planning (Suddendorf and Corballis 1997), providing a vocabulary and set of scenarios from which to construct future episodes. Of course, semantic information is also involved, as when we consult maps or travel information to plan a trip to Paris, or call upon semantic memory for our understanding of where Paris is located and what general features are to be found there. It might be helpful, though, to also remember specific details of a past visit there, to envisage the meal we had in a specific restaurant, or when we mistakenly took the metro in the wrong direction. Schacter (1996) has proposed similarly that our personal memories provide the basis for the concept of self, as well as a basis to ground future behavioral choices. The adaptive advantage of episodic memory may therefore lie in what it offers for the future, rather than in how accurately it reinstates past experience (Schacter et al. 2008b; Suddendorf and Busby 2003). By combining and recombining remembered elements from past events as well as semantic knowledge, one can imagine novel future scenarios, weigh their consequences, and act in the present to secure a future advantage. To maintain a complete record of the past, though, may be counterproductive, since this would occupy huge storage space and involve needless repetition. Forgetting itself can be adaptive, because it frees resources for future use and allows memory retrieval to continue quickly and efficiently (Anderson and Schooler 1991).

Episodic memory may thus lie on a continuum with the imagining of future episodes, creating a capacity for "mental time travel" (Suddendorf and Corballis 1997, 2007). Functional brain imaging reveals extensive overlap in the areas activated by mentally reliving past events and imagining future ones, especially in the prefrontal and parietal areas. The areas common to construction of past and future events have been termed the "core" network (Schacter et al. 2008b). The hippocampus is involved in both, with the right hippocampus engaged more than the left in the construction of imagined future events (Addis et al. 2007). Anterior and posterior regions of the hippocampus also differ functionally (Giovanello et al. 2009; Woollett and Maguire 2009) and physiologically (King et al. 2008). One current suggestion is that the posterior hippocampus is important for reinstatement of an episode in its original form, while the anterior hippocampus is involved in more flexible encoding of associative information (Jackson and Schacter 2004; Chua et al. 2007; Prince et al. 2005; Preston et al. 2004). This model suggests that increased anterior hippocampal activity for imagined future events could reflect the binding together of episodic details into novel and flexible arrangements and/or the encoding of these representations.

Is Mental Time Travel Unique to Humans?

Following Tulving's (1983, 2001, 2002) claim that episodic memory is uniquely human, Suddendorf and Corballis (1997, 2007) argued more generally that mental time travel is denied to species other than humans. The idea that even our closest nonhuman relative, the chimpanzee, has little concept of past or future was suggested by Köhler (1925) in his classic studies of chimpanzee problem solving. It has nevertheless been challenged. One difficulty is that declarative memory, including episodic memory, is generally tested verbally—indeed the very phrase "declarative memory" implies an intimate connection with language. The problem is to establish criteria for testing animal memory that might amount to a declaration and, in the case of episodic memory, to show that a particular episode was recorded and reexperienced. One suggested set of criteria has been the requirement that the animal demonstrate knowledge of *what* happened, *where* it happened, and *when* it happened; this has been dubbed "www" memory (Suddendorf and Busby 2003).

The challenge to demonstrate www memory in a nonhuman species, scrub jays, has been taken up by Clayton et al. (2003). These birds cache food in different locations and then unerringly return to the appropriate locations to recover the food. Moreover, they calibrate food recovery according to how long it has been cached. For example, if they cache worms in one location and peanuts in another, after four hours they will return to the location containing the worms, which they prefer to peanuts. However, if they have already learned that worms become inedible if left buried for too long, and if they are tested 24 hours later, they will recover the peanuts in preference to the worms. According to Clayton et al., this means that they remember *what* they have cached, *where* they have cached it, and *when* they cached it—thereby demonstrating www memory. Similar results have been reported in rats (Babb and Crystal 2005), magpies (Zinkivskay et al. 2009), and meadow voles (Ferkin et al. 2008).

There is some question as to whether the what-where-when criteria actually capture the essence of episodic memory in the "autonoetic sense" described by Tulving—or in the sense of remembering versus knowing. An animal may be considered to know where and when a particular food item was cached without appealing to the actual experience of caching it. It is possible that animals have evolved simpler mechanisms for recovering cached food, perhaps attaching some internal timing device to each location that specifies how long ago food was stored there. For instance, a distinction can also be drawn between recording *how long* an item has been cached and *when* it was cached. Roberts et al. (2008) have shown that rats, in choosing where to find food in a maze, are governed by how long ago the food was placed there rather than by when it was placed there. They take this to mean that the rats did not record the episode of actually storing the food, and therefore did not meet the www criteria. By implication, the scrub jays may also have used some measure of how long ago, perhaps through decay of a memory trace, rather than specific recording of an event located in time. Since experiments with nonverbal animals have not—and perhaps cannot—reveal the subjective aspect of episodic memory in the sense of mentally reliving past episodes, the term "episodic-like memory" is now commonly used with reference to animal studies (e.g., Babb and Crystal 2005; Clayton and Dickinson 1998; Roberts 2006).

What of mental travel into the future? Some evidence comes from scrub jays' proclivity to theft. Clayton, Bussey, and Dickinson (2003) observed that if a bird that had itself stolen food was watched while caching its own food, it later privately re-cached it, presumably to prevent the watcher from stealing it (see, however, Penn, this volume, for a critique of folk-psychology explanations of this finding). Such clandestine re-caching might suggest mental time travel into the future as well as into the past, since it might be taken to imply anticipation of a future theft. Re-caching also depended on which bird was watching and was more likely to occur if the predatory watcher was a dominant bird than if it was a subordinate bird. Thus we might add a further *w*— the birds seem to know what, where, when, and *who*. Nevertheless, even this behavior can probably be explained in terms of associative learning without supposing that the birds actually envisage a future event.

Dally, Emery, and Clayton (2006) tested more explicitly for future planning in scrub jays by allowing them, over several days, to acquire information about where food would be available the next morning. They received breakfast in different cages on alternate days. When later given the opportunity to store food in the evening, they cached more in the cage that had been the "no-breakfast" cage on that day, evidently anticipating that it would be the breakfast location the next morning. Whether this implies mental anticipation of tomorrow's breakfast is a moot point; for example, it might simply reflect a strategy to balance food sources (Suddendorf and Corballis 2008).

Although some birds seem exceptionally smart, we should probably look to our closer relatives, the primates, for closer resemblances to human memory. Schwartz and Evans (2001) have reviewed evidence that primates can remember where specific events occurred. In one example, a chimpanzee taught to use lexigrams to represent objects was able to select a lexigram for a food item and then point to a location where that item had been hidden some time beforehand (C. R. Menzel 1999). In a slightly more complicated example, Schwarz et al. (2002) report evidence that a gorilla had encoded both a food item and the person who had previously given him the food. This, however, could be a matter of simple association between the food item and the person. In none of the reviewed cases was there any evidence that the animals had coded the *time* of the past event; thus, the www criteria were not fully satisfied.

Nevertheless there has been a recent claim that orangutans and bonobos, at least, save tools not needed in the present for use up to 14 hours later, which might suggest mental time travel (Mulcahy and Call 2006), although again it is not entirely clear that the animals were not responding simply on the basis of past associations, rather than actively imagining a future one (Suddendorf 2006). The bonobo Kanzi is said to be able to lead someone to a location where he knows something to be located, but again this need not imply that he remembers the act of visiting that location previously.

Another possible example of episodic memory in orangutans is noted by Russon and Andrews (2010), although not specifically discussed in those terms. In an observational study of forest-living rehabilitant orangutans, a three-year-old orangutan was observed to be trying to extract a small stone that had pierced the sole of her foot. One of the research assistants helped extract the stone and added latex from the stem of a fig leaf to help heal the wound. Eight days later the orangutan approached the assistant, attracted her attention, and seemingly acted out the leaf treatment, and showed that the wound was now healed. The assistant interpreted this as evidence that the orangutan remembered the treatment, and even several months later the animal would display her foot whenever she saw the assistant. This was also observed by one of the authors.

These and other recent experiments have greatly extended our knowledge of the subtleties of animal behavior, but for the most part the results can be explained in terms of what the animals *know* rather than what they *remember*. This does not prove, of course, that they don't remember specific events or imagine specific future ones, and the denial of mental time travel may reflect the desire to assert human superiority so long as it is possible to do so—or, more charitably, it might be regarded as the legitimate application of Occam's razor. Conversely, though, one might argue that the mechanisms underlying animal memory and future thinking are the same as in humans, but we humans have reinterpreted them symbolically (Penn et al. 2008). A better understanding of the roles of neural mechanisms in episodic-like memory in nonhuman species, and their relation to neural mechanisms established in humans through brain imaging, might help establish whether nonhuman animals can truly remember events, as distinct from knowing about them.

A Difference of Degree?

Darwin (1896:126) famously wrote: "The difference in mind between man and the higher animals, great as it is, certainly is one of degree and not of kind." This dictum might well apply to the difference in mental time travel. There is no evidence, for example, that nonhuman species are capable of anything approaching the sheer duration of mental time travel in humans. Premack (2010) notes that the abilities of scrub jays to plan, as suggested by Raby et al. (2007), is restricted to the caching of food, and applies over fairly short intervals of time, whereas humans plan very diverse activities over very long periods. Our remembered experiences go back decades, at least if you reach my age. It might be noted that, compared to younger adults, older adults produce fewer episodic details but the same or more semantic details when reporting autobiographical memories (Levine 2004). Premack also remarks that "chimpanzees do not understand time" (2010:25), a conclusion echoed by Jane Goodall, who knows chimpanzees better than most people do. In an interview in *The Spectator* (Gray 2010), she is quoted as saying:

What's the one obvious thing we humans do that they don't do? Chimps can learn sign language, but in the wild, so far as we know, they are unable to communicate about things that aren't present. They can't teach what happened 100 years ago, except by showing fear in certain places. They certainly can't plan for five years ahead. If they could, they could communicate with each other about what compels them to indulge in their dramatic displays. To me, it is a sense of wonder and awe that we share with them. When we had those feelings, and evolved the ability to talk about them, we were able to create the early religions.

Nevertheless it is not simply the duration of mental time travel that distinguishes humans from apes. More important, perhaps, is the sheer generativity of our imaginings. Even episodic recall is an imagined construction rather than a re-living of an episode as it actually happened. Neisser (2008:88) recently wrote: "Remembering is not like playing back a tape or looking at a picture; it is more like telling a story." Remembered episodic memories are both incomplete (Loftus and Loftus 1980) and often false (Loftus and Ketcham 1994)—the induction of false memories has been incorporated into an experimental paradigm featuring in many undergraduate laboratories (Roediger and McDermott 1995). Mental time travel into the future is more obviously constructive, although built on past experience, since imagined future episodes need never happen. Rather, they serve as possibilities that can influence present behavior. For example, one might envisage the relative consequences of studying for an exam or of going to a party, and choose accordingly. Moreover, both episodic memory and the imagining of future episodes blend naturally into fantasy—the construction of stories which may even include events that are impossible, such as a cow jumping over the moon. As Boyd (2009) has suggested, stories and fantasy can be regarded as play, albeit in the mental rather than physical domain. Indeed, one might argue that fantasy preceded the incorporation of episodic memory or the imagining of future events, in evolution as in development: Children's ability to pretend emerges in the second year of life (e.g., Fein and Apfel 1979), whereas episodic memory does not emerge until about four years of age, or later (Perner et al. 2007).

How Language Evolved

A common approach to the evolution of language is that developed by Chomsky (for a recent summary, see Chomsky 2010). To Chomsky, language depends on a prior mode of thought, called internal language (I-language), which preceded the flowering of diverse forms of external languages (E-language) as actually spoken or signed. The main operation involved in I-language is what Chomsky calls "unbounded Merge," comprising the recursive merging of elements into larger elements. Since I-language is internal and presumably abstract, Chomsky argues, it cannot have evolved through natural selection and must therefore have emerged as the result of a fortuitous "rewiring," perhaps due to a mutation, in some single individual:

> Within some small group from which we are all descended, a rewiring of the brain took place in some individual, call him *Prometheus*, yielding the operation of unbounded Merge, applying to concepts with intricate (and little understood) properties (Chomsky 2010:59).

Biologically, this scenario is deeply implausible; language is complex, which makes it extremely unlikely that it evolved in a single step in a single mutation. Here, I suggest instead that it makes better sense to view the precursors of language as cognitive rather than linguistic entities, and that one such precursor is mental time travel, which seems to call for precisely the recursive, generative properties that are embedded in language itself. Moreover, these properties probably evolved gradually with the pressure for more detailed social understanding, especially over the past two million years of existence in environments requiring extensive group cohesion for survival. Nevertheless, the seed for mental time travel may well have been planted much earlier in evolution, as experiments with other species suggest.

Indeed, even honeybees may demonstrate some of the properties of mental time travel and communication about events displaced from the present. Honeybee foragers learn the type of food collected, and where and when they collected it, and their dance can convey this information to other bees (Grüter, this volume). If bees were attacked at a food source, they can emit an acoustic "stop" signal that prevents other bees from visiting that source (Nieh 2010). While this may be construed as communication about future risk, it need not imply that the bees actually envisage what would happen if they visited the dangerous source. The apparent memorial and communicative skills of the honeybee probably depend on relatively simple mechanisms dedicated to the very specific context of foraging. Human memory and communication, in contrast, is wide ranging and context free. Even so, they may be derived from the much simpler, context-bound mechanisms evident in many other species.

It is sometimes suggested that nonhuman species are capable of mental processes, such as mental time travel, but that they cannot convey them because of lack of language. This argument can be turned around: I suggest that language evolved in humans precisely because of the importance of mental time travel to a species that relied increasingly on detailed planning and social cohesion. One might even invert the concept of declarative memory to define language as "memorial declaration." Language, then, may have evolved primarily to allow us to share our mental time travels, as well as our fantasies. Humans everywhere dote on fiction, whether in the form of stories, plays, fairy tales, novels, TV soaps, operas, or simple gossip. Through shared memories, plans, and stories, we can vastly increase our knowledge of how the world works at a level of detail not possible through inherited characters or learned habits, or even through our own personal experiences. In recent history, of course, media such as moving films and television have added to the capacity to share, but for most of the history and prehistory of *Homo sapiens*, language probably played the major role, perhaps originating, as Donald (1991) suggested, in pantomime. Indeed, the study by Russon and Andrews (2010), cited earlier, suggests elements of pantomime in the gestural communications of orangutans.

Language is exquisitely designed—or adapted—to transmit information about episodes, especially those not taking place in the present. To share information about the past or future, we need solid concepts and symbols to refer to them. Most nonhuman communication does not require reference to non-present objects, but refers to events available to the senses. In human communication about non-present events, the symbols to refer to them can be abstract but need not be. Since episodes are comprised largely of combinations of known entities, such as "who did what to whom, what is true of what, where, when and why" (Pinker 2003), language has also taken on combinatorial principles, in the form of grammar. Finally, language developed markers of time to indicate whether events are located in the past, present, or future, along with various other aspects, such as whether an action was completed or ongoing, or whether it was conditional, and so on. Even fiction pays indirect homage to time in the expression "once upon a time…" In many languages, time is indicated by tense, but other indicants, such as aspectual markers or specific dates, are also used (for a more extended discussion, see Corballis 2009). Indeed, the sheer variety of languages, not only in vocabulary but also in structure, casts severe doubt on the Chomskyan notion of universal grammar, or a universal I-language, and suggests that diverse languages were invented to meet cultural imperatives (Evans and Levinson 2009; Christiansen and Chater 2008).

Language, then, enables the sharing of memories, plans, and fantasies. Personal life is thus extended to the group and helps define culture, as well as the place of individuals within social and cultural groups. Of course language is also used for other purposes, such as explaining how things work, or preaching moral or religious messages. In these respects, semantic memory is probably more critical than episodic memory, although a skilled teacher will often introduce personal recollection to help illustrate an argument. Nevertheless, my guess is that language evolved its generative character primarily in the context of experienced episodes, perhaps initially in the context of hunting and gathering. In modern-day parlance, the basic nature of language is perhaps better revealed in Twitter or Facebook than in textbooks on nuclear physics. It is perhaps an open question as to which of the two, language or episodic memory, evolved first, but the most plausible supposition may be that they coevolved, each augmenting the other.

Sharing information about events that occurred or will occur at different times and in different places requires a vast vocabulary—not only of concepts but also of words or signs to refer to them. Pinker (2007) suggests that the average literate person has some 50,000 concepts. This is based on the number of words in a college dictionary, and these concepts must also include words to refer to them. This demand for storage may well have driven the increase in the size of the human brain, which approximately tripled from around two million years ago (Wood and Collard 1999).

Conclusion

My contention in this chapter is that the capacity for mental time travel is at best only minimally present in nonhuman species. The extended understanding of time, and the ability to imagine events at different points in time, along with the implied generative capacity to combine concepts, laid the foundation for that other uniquely human capacity: language. The combinatorial capacity also gave rise to fantasy, shared in the form of stories and myths, making possible a form of mental play to supplement physical play.

This view is at odds with Chomsky's contention that language evolved through a single event, perhaps a mutation. Chomsky has argued further that this event must have occurred within the past 100,000 years, since "roughly 100,000+ years ago...there were no languages" (Chomsky 2010:58). At least some of the argument for the late emergence of language hinges on language construed as speech. For instance, P. Lieberman (2010; Lieberman et al. 1972; Lieberman 1998; Lieberman et al. 2002) has long argued, on anatomical grounds, that the capacity for articulate speech did not emerge in our species until within the past 100,000 years, and perhaps as recently as 50,000 years ago. On Lieberman's reckoning, the Neanderthals, despite their large brains, would have been denied articulate speech (see, however, Boë et al. 2002, 2007). Others have suggested that the emergence of language was responsible for the rise of modern human behavior, in the form of enhanced technology, bodily ornamentation, burial rites, cave art, and other cultural innovations over the past 90,000 years or so (e.g., Hoffecker 2005).

The alternative view is that language, along with other enhanced social capacities such as mental time travel and higher-order theory of mind, evolved its present-day characteristics over the past 2.5 million years or so, driven especially by the conditions of the Pleistocene, which forced our forebears to adapt to deforestation, climate change, and a hunter-gatherer existence (e.g., Tooby and DeVore 1987). A possibility consistent with this scenario is that language evolved from manual gestures, and that it was the conversion to speech, rather than the emergence of language itself, that underlay the rise of modernity over the past 90,000 years (Corballis 2004). The gestural theory is outlined in more detail elsewhere (Wheeler et al., this volume). This scenario suggests that, despite the extended mental and communicative capacity of humans relative to other primates, there is much greater continuity than is suggested by those who believe that language emerged as a singular event within our own species.

Acknowledgments

I am grateful to Kristin Andrews, Christoph Grüter, Randolf Menzel, Derek C. Penn, Josef Perner, and Markus Wild for their valuable suggestions, leading to considerable improvements over the initial draft of this chapter.

First column (top to bottom): Bill Searcy, Dan Margoliash, Christoph Grüter, Brandon Wheeler, Tabitha Price, Michael Owren, Markus Wild
Second column: Michael Corballis, Tabitha Price, Dan Margoliash, Markus Wild, Christoph Grüter, Julia Fischer
Third column: Brandon Wheeler, Robert Seyfarth, Morten Christiansen, Julia Fischer, Bill Searcy, Michael Corballis, Michael Owren

13

Communication

Brandon C. Wheeler, William A. Searcy,
Morten H. Christiansen, Michael C. Corballis, Julia Fischer,
Christoph Grüter, Daniel Margoliash, Michael J. Owren,
Tabitha Price, Robert Seyfarth, and Markus Wild

Abstract

This chapter reviews what has been learned about animal thinking from the study of animal communication, and considers what we might hope to learn in the future. It begins with a discussion on the importance of informational versus non-informational interpretations of animal communication and then considers what inferences can be drawn about the cognitive requirements of communication from the communicative abilities of simple organisms. Next, it discusses the importance of context to the meaning of animal signals and the possibility of asymmetries in the neural processes underlying production versus reception. Current theories on the evolution of human language are reviewed and how the study of animal communication informs these theories.

Information in Animal Communication

Accounts of animal communication have traditionally relied heavily on the concept of information. Bradbury and Vehrencamp (1998:2), for example, defined communication as the "provision of information from a sender to a receiver," and Otte (1974:385) defined communication signals as "behavioral, physiological, or morphological characteristics fashioned or maintained by natural selection because they convey information to other organisms." Running counter to these accounts of information transmission, however, has been another tradition, one that opposes interpreting animal communication in terms of information (Dawkins and Krebs 1978; Owings and Morton 1997; Owren and Rendall 2001; Rendall et al. 2009; Fischer, this volume). The anti-informational tradition has argued that, rather than informing receivers, signals should be viewed as managing (Owings and Morton 1997) or influencing (Rendall et al. 2009) receivers in the interests of the signalers. Thus receivers are viewed as responding to signals in a way that benefits the signaler rather than themselves.

Part of the criticism of the use of information transmission in interpreting animal communication has been that the term "information" has been vaguely or inadequately defined (Rendall et al. 2009). Here we use information to mean a reduction of uncertainty on the part of the receiver about the state of the environment, including the signaler as part of that environment. More formally (following Dretske 1981), information is a change in the conditional probability that the environment is in a certain state given the signal (r) and what the receiver already knows (k), relative to the probability of that environmental state given k alone. Information in our usage, then, can be considered to be "perceiver information," in the sense that it depends on how the receiver's own internal assessment of the environment changes due to reception of the signal. Once this definition is specified, it seems fair to use "information transmission" as shorthand for cases in which signals reduce receiver uncertainty regarding the state of the environment.

The anti-informational stance on animal communication begs the question of why receivers would respond in a way that benefits signalers rather than themselves. A variety of answers has been given. Perhaps the best-known hypothesis is sensory bias (Ryan et al. 1990) or sensory drive (Endler and Basolo 1998). This hypothesis proposes that the sensory and neural systems of receivers have biases that may have been favored in contexts other than signaling, such as foraging or predator detection, or which may be nonselected consequences of the ways that sensory and neural systems are put together. Signalers then evolve to exploit these receiver biases; this side of the interaction is termed "sensory exploitation." A second hypothesis is that certain signals, such as screams given by subordinate monkeys in conflict situations, have a directly aversive effect on the receiver solely because of the signals' unpleasant acoustic properties (Owren and Rendall 2001).

A concrete illustration of a non-informational interpretation of a signaling system is provided by the well-known case of the mating call of the túngara frog (*Physalaemus pustulosus*) (Ryan et al. 1990; Ryan and Rand 1993, 2003). The basic mating call of túngara frogs is a whine to which a male can add one to several chucks. Female túngara frogs prefer calls with chucks to calls lacking chucks. Ryan and colleagues proposed that this preference was due to the auditory tuning of female túngara frogs: the whine stimulates mainly the ear's amphibian papilla whereas the higher frequencies of the chucks stimulate mainly the basilar papilla, and the greater overall auditory stimulation by the whine plus chuck(s) produces the female's preference. The sensory exploitation hypothesis predicts that the female preference (for calls with chucks) should have preceded the evolution of the preferred male trait (the chucks themselves), and testing of female preferences in related species combined with phylogenetic analysis seemed to confirm that prediction (Ryan and Rand 1993). Recently, Ron (2008) measured female preferences for chucks in additional species in the túngara frog complex and, based on these data and a more extensive phylogenetic analysis, has concluded that the preference did not evolve before the chuck, thus undermining the sensory bias interpretation. A number of other cases of sensory bias have also been proposed, such as female preferences for swords in swordtail fish (Basolo 1990, 1996) and female responses to male vibratory signals in water mites (Proctor 1991, 1992).

The non-informational view of animal communication proposes that signalers manipulate receivers to behave in ways that benefit the signaler rather than the receiver. The informational view proposes that signalers evolve signals that change the behavior of receivers in ways that benefit the signalers, but adds the assumption that receiver response behavior evolves to benefit receiver fitness. Receivers will thus only respond to signals if it is, on average, advantageous to do so (see Fischer, this volume). Further, the only mechanism from which receivers can benefit by responding entails signals which vary consistently with some feature of the environment, including the sender's quality and/or subsequent behavior. In this sense, one may state that such signals provide information because they have the potential to reduce the recipient's uncertainty. The informational interpretation has been termed an "equilibrium" view of signaling (Hurd and Enquist 2005), because both signalers and receivers have evolved to a state in which their behaviors benefit them more than would any alternative, so selection does not favor any further change. Such an equilibrium is an essential feature of game theory models of animal communication, including models of mate attraction (Grafen 1990; Kokko 1997), aggressive signaling (Enquist 1985; Számadó 2008), and begging (Godfray 1991; Johnstone and Grafen 1992). A concept that only takes into account the sender's interest might represent a "non-equilibrium" view of signaling, because it is agnostic on whether receivers have evolved to a state in which their present behavior benefits them more than alternatives would. At equilibrium, signals are expected to be informative, but this is not necessarily an expectation for non-equilibrium signals (Hurd and Enquist 2005).

The distinction between informational and non-informational interpretations is relevant to the cognitive demands of communication. Cognition has been defined as "mechanisms by which animals acquire, process, store, and act on information from the environment" (Shettleworth 1998:5). Thus if communication does not involve information, it cannot depend on cognition, at least on the part of the receiver. This conclusion matches with intuition: if female túngara frogs prefer males emitting whines plus chucks over males emitting only whines, and the preference is due solely to differential stimulation of the female's peripheral auditory system, then it would seem wrong to invoke cognition to explain the female's response.

Although cases of non-informational signaling may exist, as in the instances of sensory bias discussed above, the interpretation of many animal signaling systems has been couched in terms of the concept of information. Examples include the waggle dance of the honeybee (see Grüter, this volume), alarm calls in vervet monkeys (Seyfarth et al. 1980), suricates (Manser 2001) and many other vertebrates, aggressive signaling in some songbirds (Searcy et al. 2006; Ballentine et al. 2008), and food calls in chickens and primates (Marler et al. 1986; Di Bitetti 2003). In these systems in which receivers are seen to process and act on information contained in signals, cognitive mechanisms may be involved in both producers and receivers.

If non-informational as well as informational signals exist, then definitions of communication or of signals that require signals to be informational are not sufficiently broad. One definition of signals that drops the information requirement is provided by Maynard Smith and Harper (2003:3): a signal is "any act or structure which alters the behavior of other organisms, which evolved because of that effect, and which is effective because the receiver's response has also evolved." The last criterion would seem to exclude most cases of noninformational signaling, as these systems involve signalers exploiting preexisting behavioral mechanisms of receivers that have not evolved to be affected by the signal. Therefore, we prefer a definition that omits the last criterion: signals are acts or structures that affect the behavior of other organisms and have evolved because of those effects.

A specific category of communication with possible implications for cognition is deception. In human communication, deception is said to occur when a signaler produces a signal that it knows to be false with the intention of creating a false belief in one or more receivers. Such a definition requires that the signaler be able both to form intentions and to attribute mental states to others. Biological definitions of deception, however, omit the stipulation concerning the intention to create a false belief and instead stipulate that the signaler derives some fitness benefit from conveying false information (Hauser 1996; Searcy and Nowicki 2005). Under this biological definition, we can classify as deception instances in which we are unable to determine whether signalers intend to deceive, including for example those cases in which animals give "false alarms" in contexts where they benefit from eliciting escape behavior from receivers in the absence of a predator (Wheeler 2009; Bro-Jorgensen and Pangle 2010). Moreover, we can even include cases in which all thought on the part of the signaler is precluded, as for example when orchids mimic the appearance and odor of the females of an insect species and thereby attract male insects to aid in pollination (Jersakova et al. 2006).

Communication from Single Cells to Complex Systems

As the orchid example illustrates, communication can be performed by organisms entirely lacking nervous systems, though in the orchid example it is only the signaler, and not the receiver, that fits this description. A case in which both signalers and receivers lack nervous systems is provided by quorum sensing in bacteria (Miller and Bassler 2001). Here, bacteria secrete signaling molecules termed "autoinducers," which interact with receptors in other bacterial cells to affect expression of particular genes. Bacteria are able to assess population density via the concentration of the autoinducer, so that genes for certain traits are turned on only when some threshold density is reached. The traits controlled by quorum sensing are typically ones that are effective at high population densities but ineffective at lower ones; examples include bioluminescence in *Vibro fischeri* and biofilm production in *Pseudomonas aeruginosa*. In these and other cases, autoinducers appear to have evolved to affect receiving cells, so these chemicals meet our definition of signals (Diggle et al. 2007). The fact that these signaling systems operate in organisms entirely lacking any nervous system demonstrates that simple forms of communication can be accomplished without any cognitive ability at all.

Organisms that possess nervous systems are often capable of more complex communication than seen in orchids and bacteria; nevertheless, it cannot be claimed that any tight association exists overall between the degree of development of an animal's nervous system and the complexity of its communication. To the contrary, arguably the most complex communication systems found in nonhuman animals are seen in social insects (Grüter, this volume), whose nervous systems are relatively simple compared to those of birds and mammals. Within the social insects, the waggle dance of the honeybee (von Frisch 1967; Dyer 2002) provides the most extreme known example of communication complexity.

Honeybees use the waggle dance both when deciding on a new nest site and during foraging. In the foraging context, the dance is performed by a worker that has returned from a foraging trip during which she has successfully found a food source of high quality, and the dance functions to increase and direct the foraging activity of additional workers. The dance has several communicative components (von Frisch 1967; Seeley 1997; Grüter, this volume): the angle of the dance's waggle run relative to vertical conveys the angle of the food source relative to the sun; the duration of the waggle run conveys the distance to the food; and the number of waggle runs performed per dance communicates the quality of the food source to the workers as whole. Recruits that attend to a dance often fly off in the direction and for the distance indicated (von Frisch 1967). The precision of the waggle dance is impressive; as one example, recruits following the dance are able to orient within ± 7.5° (standard deviation) of a food source sited 700 meters from the hive (Towne and Gould 1988).

Wenner and colleagues argue that the behavior of the recruits can be explained by a simpler "olfactory hypothesis," which proposes that, rather than following the dance parameters given above, recruits follow odors picked up by the dancer at the food source (Wenner and Johnson 1967; Wenner et al. 1969; Wenner 2002). The dance hypothesis, however, is firmly supported by an array of experimental results: when dancers are manipulated to dance in an incorrect direction or report an incorrect distance, recruits follow the dance to the predicted incorrect site (Gould 1975; Esch et al. 2001); and recruits displaced to a new starting point when leaving the hive fly the direction and distance indicated by the dance to a site similarly displaced from the original goal (Riley et al. 2005).

The honeybee waggle dance has the property of "functional reference." Functional reference means that a signal functions to refer to things external to the signaler (Macedonia and Evans 1993), without implying that the signal causes receivers to call up a representation of those things. The signal passes both criteria established by Macedonia and Evans (1993) for functional reference: dances exhibit production specificity, in that there is a close relationship between the signal that is produced and properties of the external object (its direction, distance, and quality), and they satisfy the perception criterion, in that the signal alone is sufficient to allow receivers to choose the appropriate response. Although referential in this sense, the waggle dance does not fulfill a number of criteria for language: it does not involve a true symbol system (with largely arbitrary relationships between signals and referents), let alone complex recursive structure (see Menzel, this volume). As functionally referential signals, the waggle dance can best be compared to vertebrate calls that also have this property, such as the alarm calls of certain mammals (Seyfarth et al. 1980; Zuberbühler et al. 1999; Manser 2001; Fischer and Hammerschmidt 2001) and birds (Gyger et al. 1987; Templeton et al. 2005). Alarm calls of some species have been shown to vary with both predator type and "response urgency." For example, suricates (*Suricata suricatta*) simultaneously vary their alarm calls based on both predator type and the proximity of the predator (Manser 2001), whereas Barbary macaque alarm calls vary with predator type and appearance of the predator (Fischer et al. 1995). Nevertheless, it is clear that for the systems of vertebrate alarm calls thus far studied, all fall short of the honeybee waggle dance in terms of communicative complexity and precision.

Honeybees have some advanced cognitive abilities. They are able, for example, to learn the concepts of sameness and difference, and to transfer the concept from one modality (e.g., olfaction) to another (e.g., vision) (Giurfa et al. 2001). Honeybees also have numerical abilities akin to counting (Dacke and Srinivasan 2008) and sophisticated spatial memory (Menzel, this volume). Their brains, though tiny in absolute terms, are large for their body size, though not necessarily large relative to other social insects (Mares et al. 2005). Although the navigational skills and learning abilities of honeybees are impressive, further claims for honeybee cognition are limited; they are not claimed, for example, to have episodic memory or theory of mind. In other words, a highly developed communicative system does not necessarily entail highly developed cognitive machinery.

Pragmatics and Contingency in Animal Communication

In human language, the interpretation of a given utterance depends not only on the linguistic knowledge of speaker and listener but also on the context in which an utterance is made. Linguistic pragmatics studies how context can influence the way in which an utterance is understood. "Context" in language can include ongoing events; memory of past events; the status, age, or sex of those involved; and the inferred intent of the signaler.

As in language, responses of recipients to animal signals can be influenced by external context or prior knowledge to varying degrees. For example, worker honeybees which have recently observed a food source in location B and then view a waggle dance that indicates a food source in location A will often not use the vector of the dance but instead fly to location B, particularly if the food source at B is of high quality. The bees' "private" information (Grüter et al. 2008) apparently overrides the more "public" information they acquire from observing the dance (see also Grüter and Farina 2009).

Territorial songbirds offer another example. Akcay et al. (2009) demonstrated that the response of male song sparrows (*Melospiza melodia*) to the songs of neighbors was contingent on the past behavior of those neighbors. The song of a neighbor was played from a loudspeaker set in the center of a subject's territory, simulating a territorial intrusion. After a lapse of 45 minutes, a second playback was staged from the subject's boundary, using either the song of the first "bad neighbor" or the song of another unoffending neighbor as a control. Subjects responded more aggressively to the song of the bad neighbor. In a subsequent experiment, Akcay et al. (2010) used song playback to simulate an intrusion by a bad neighbor, not on the subject's own territory, but on the territory of another neighbor—the "victim." In response to subsequent playback from the subject's boundary, subjects were more aggressive toward songs of bad neighbors than toward songs of victims. Response to song is thus contingent not only on an individual's own experience with the singer but on what is inferred from the experience of others.

In baboons (*Papio hamadryas ursinus*), individuals appear to use social context when inferring the intent of the signaler. In one set of experiments, Engh et al. (2006) waited until one adult female, D, had directed aggression against a lower-ranking female, E. After the two had separated, the experimenters played female D's threat-grunt to female E. On another day, the experiment was repeated after D and E had groomed. After prior aggression, E responded strongly to D's threat-grunt: she acted as if the call was directed at her. By contrast, after prior grooming E showed little response to the threat-grunt: she acted as if the call was directed at someone else. E's responses, moreover, were specific to particular individuals: prior aggression or grooming with D did not affect E's responses to the threat-grunts of other high-ranking animals. Female baboons, therefore, used their memory of prior interactions with particular individuals to infer a speaker's intent and to decide how to respond to a vocalization (for other examples, see Cheney and Seyfarth 2007).

Research on the role of contextual cues carries important implications for the study of communication and cognition in animals. Context, after all, is ubiquitous in nature. It is extremely difficult to imagine an animal signal whose meaning does not have the potential to be influenced by the context in which it is given. The pervasiveness of contextual cues suggests that natural selection has acted strongly to favor receivers who can integrate relevant signal properties with cues acquired from memory or from the circumstances in which the signal is given.

Moreover, while virtually all animals have a relatively small repertoire of signals, these limited signal types can generate an enormous variety of responses (Smith 1977). The richness of animal communication can, in many cases, be traced to the cognitive operations by which receivers integrate signal and context to create meaning. This integration of signal and context may be the step where cognitive abilities are taxed, and where the performance of higher vertebrates such as birds and primates exceeds that of honeybees and other social insects. This hypothesis deserves further testing, by additional experiments on the ability of higher vertebrates to modify response based on complex contextual variables, and especially by parallel experiments on effects of context on communication in social insects such as honeybees. Testing a broad range of species would be particularly valuable for understanding at which point (or points) such abilities evolved (see Bshary et al., this volume).

Some contextual cues play an important role in communication whereas others, apparently, do not. Signaler identity, for instance, affects communication in many species (Tibbetts and Dale 2007); by contrast, it remains unclear whether any animal species includes knowledge about the signaler's thoughts or beliefs as part of context. A baboon may attribute to others an intent to communicate *to her*, but the attribution of other mental states remains controversial (Penn, this volume).

The importance of context provides a possible tie between animal communication systems and human language.

Animal Communication and Human Language

Asymmetries in Signal Production and Perception

An important observation for animal communication is that signaling is not an inherently symmetrical process—at any level of analysis. While symmetry can and does exist in some aspects, the best starting assumption is that the development, mechanisms, adaptive function, and phylogenetic history of communication can be significantly different for signalers and perceivers. In ontogeny, for example, full-fledged signal production may emerge before, simultaneously with, or after functional responding to the very same communicative events. An illustration from nonhuman primates is that infant vervet monkeys show semantic-like, predator-specific alarm call production well before any understanding of the significance of those calls is evident on the receiver side (Seyfarth and Cheney 1986). Mechanistically, that outcome may be traceable to an asymmetry in the strength of direct cortical control of vocal production versus response that is evident in nonhuman primates, and which has implications for the evolution of human speech (Seyfarth and Cheney 2010).

The vocal pathway in terrestrial mammals (and many other taxa) involves different subsystems, contributing to different degrees in the initiation and structural properties of vocalizations. The first pathway runs from the anterior cingulate cortex via the midbrain periaqueductal gray (PAG) into the reticular formation of the brainstem, and from there to the phonatory motoneurons. The second pathway runs from the motor cortex via the reticular formation to the phonatory motoneurons. This pathway has been shown to include two feedback loops: one involving the basal ganglia and the other involving the cerebellum (Jürgens 2009). Both pathways are linked to the different motoneurons that innervate the respective muscles for vocal fold, lip, jaw, and tongue movements via the reticular formation. The comparison of vocalization pathways among terrestrial mammal species has revealed that only humans exhibit strong direct connections from the motor cortex to the motoneurons controlling the laryngeal muscles, which can be understood as a third pathway. While this appears to be a derived trait in humans, connections between the limbic cortex and the motoneurons constitute an ancestral trait found in many nonhuman species (for reviews, see Jürgens 2002, 2009; Hammerschmidt and Fischer 2008).

The degree to which these pathways exhibit ancestral or derived characteristics needs to be evaluated cautiously. Because long-distance tract tracing in postmortem human brains is challenging, the putative direct pathway is supported only by electrophysiological studies. Neuroanatomy remains poorly explored in cetaceans, the other comprehensive example of mammalian vocal learning. In birds, direct forebrain projections to syringeal and laryngeal motoneurons—an equivalent "third" pathway—is well-established in songbirds and parrots (e.g., Wild 1993; Striedter 1994) and may also be represented in other groups. There is compelling evidence and broad (but not universal) consensus of homology between avian and mammalian forebrain (Reiner et al. 2004; Wang et al. 2010), so descending pathways might also be preserved. The evidence that basic pattern-generating circuitry in the brainstem has been conserved for perhaps 450 million years since early fishes also indicate that descending forebrain vocomotor projections target ancestral networks (Bass et al. 2008).

The first pathway described above, involving the anterior cingulate cortex and the PAG, seems to be responsible for the initiation of some classes of vocalizations. The PAG apparently controls the production of involuntary sounds, such as a cry of pain given in response to a painful stimulus (Jürgens 2009). The anterior cingulate cortex controls the voluntary production of such sounds. Macaques, in which this area is intact, can learn to increase their vocalization rate for a food reward, whereas individuals with lesions in this area are unable to master this task (Sutton et al. 1974). The second pathway, running from the motor cortex through the reticular formation, is responsible for the patterning of vocalizations (Jürgens 2009). The third pathway, in which the motor cortex connects directly to phonatory motoneurons, is presumably the one that allows humans the ability to perform vocal learning (i.e., the learning of vocal production through imitation). Vocal learning is defined in distinction to auditory learning, which is the ability to learn the meaning of sounds produced by others. Vocal learning is known to be present in three groups of birds (songbirds, parrots, and hummingbirds) and in four clades of mammals (bats, cetaceans, elephants and humans) (Jarvis 2004; Jarvis et al. 2000; Poole et al. 2005). Evidence for vocal learning is scarce for other mammals and in particular for nonhuman primates (Egnor and Hauser 2004; Snowdon 2008). Auditory learning, by contrast, seems to be universal among the higher vertebrates.

Although some nonhuman primates have vocalizations that are functionally referential (Seyfarth et al. 1980; Manser 2001), the number of such vocalizations is consistently quite limited within any one species. The expansion of the repertoire of referential vocalizations necessary for the evolution of human speech presumably required the acquisition of vocal learning, and the evolution of vocal learning, in turn, presumably required the evolution of more direct cortical control of phonatory motoneurons, as seen in humans. The evolution of neural pathways allowing such cortical control of phonation can thus be considered one of the major steps in the evolution of human speech. Comparative work on the neural pathways controlling vocal production in cetaceans, bats, and elephants might aid in understanding the evolution of such pathways in the human lineage.

Syntax and Recursion

One controversial view of human language holds that the crucial cognitive ability that allows language, and which only humans possess, is the capacity for recursion (Hauser et al. 2002). To determine the importance of recursion for the evolution of language and its relation to nonhuman communication systems, it is imperative to evaluate the empirical data on recursive linguistic behavior. It is important to note that there are different kinds of recursive structures in language. Simple kinds of recursion involve left- and right-branching structure (also known as tail recursion), as for example, when using multiple adjective phrases in "the big, fat, gray cat." This kind of recursion can be accommodated within a finite-state grammar, in which only the transition from the current state to the next state is represented. More complex recursion can be found in the form of center-embedding and cross-serial dependencies; this is the kind of recursion that is typically at the center of discussions about recursion in language. In English, complex recursion is employed when phrases are embedded within phrases such as "the cat that the dog chased ran away." A further level of center-embedding would be "the cat that the dog that Alex owned chased ran away." The existence of complex recursion has been said to require sophisticated grammar machinery beyond so-called context-free grammars

(Chomsky 1957). Importantly, though, computational machinery of this sort is only needed if infinite depths of recursion have to be processed.

Gentner et al. (2006) challenged the assertion that recursion is unique to human language by testing the ability of starlings to distinguish sequences of rattles (R) and warbles (W) that either had a complex recursive structure, R_nW_n, or a tail recursive structure, $(RW)_n$. The two categories of song elements, R and W, each contained eight different exemplars, so that the actual combinations of rattles and warbles were randomly chosen. An example of a complex recursive series with three levels of recursion would be *R7R1R5R3W6W7W2W5*. The corresponding tail recursive version of this series would be *R7W6R1W7R5W2R3W5*. Strictly speaking, the complex recursive series represent counting recursion rather than center-embedding, as the latter requires that embedded elements exhibit dependencies between the two categories of elements (such as noun-verb agreement in number) that are not actually present here. After extensive training, the starlings were eventually able to discriminate both the complex and tail recursive sequences from those not obeying these conditions. Since the actual examples of rattles and warbles were varied randomly from trial to trial, the birds could not have been learning specific sequences, but must have somehow grasped something about the different underlying structures.

It has been suggested that the starlings in the Gentner et al. (2006) study could have discriminated between the test sequences they were presented with using simpler heuristics (Corballis 2007; Hilliard and White 2009; ten Cate et al. 2010; but see Gentner et al. 2010). Many of the alternative mechanisms for discrimination, such as learning that complex recursive patterns always start with two rattles and tail recursive patterns do not, are eliminated by the starlings' responses to additional agrammatical probe stimuli presented by Gentner et al. (2006). Corballis (2007) has suggested a further alternative: that the starlings might have determined, by counting or subitizing, the number of successive Rs and then the number of successive Ws, and accepted the sequence as R_nW_n if the numbers matched. Whether this alternative is more parsimonious than mastering complex recursion is arguable.

Although definitive evidence is not available that any nonhuman animal can master true center-embedded recursion, it should be realized that human performance on complex recursive constructions is in turn rather limited. For example, in corpus analyses of seven European languages, Karlsson (2007) found that doubly center-embedded sentences practically never occur. Psycholinguistic data show that people are unable to understand such sentences (Blaubergs and Braine 1974; Hakes et al. 1976; Hamilton and Deese 1971; Wang 1970) and receive little benefit from explicit training on them (Blaubergs and Braine 1974; Stolz 1967). Moreover, children appear to acquire their (limited) ability for recursive sentence processing gradually in a piecemeal fashion (Dickinson 1987)—construction by construction—indicating that recursion is not a fundamental part of the grammar that is initially limited by memory or other developmental constraints (Christiansen and MacDonald 2009). Importantly, there is also considerable variation across languages with regard to the amount of recursion used (Evans and Levinson 2009). Finally, the same type of recessive recursive construction can vary dramatically across languages in how easy it is to process (Hawkins 1994; Hoover 1992).

Further work is clearly needed on the ability of both humans and nonhumans to utilize recursion and, in particular, to understand complex forms of recursive constructions such as center-embedding. In undertaking such work, it is important to approach human abilities on recursion tasks with the same skeptical stance that has been applied to work on recursion in nonhuman animals. It is also important to keep in mind that the ability to process recursive material, like any other biological trait, almost certainly evolved gradually (Margoliash and Nusbaum 2009), so that precursors at some level are very likely to be present in nonhuman animals.

Developmental Genetics and Language Evolution

Recent progress on the genetic foundations of speech may have implications for the evolution of language. One gene that appears to be involved in vocal production is *FOXP2*, which was identified in a British family with specific language impairments (Hurst et al. 1990). Molecular analysis has revealed that there is only a single amino-acid difference in the FoxP2 protein of chimpanzees and mice, but two additional amino-acid differences between chimpanzees and humans (Enard et al. 2002). These findings suggest that the substitutions in the human lineage underwent positive selection, perhaps due to effects on some aspects of speech and language (Fisher and Scharff 2009). The amino-acid changes that created the human version of FOXP2 are likely to have taken place before about 500,000 years ago, because analysis of the Neanderthal genome indicates that they had the human version of FOXP2 (Krause et al. 2007).

Importantly, *FOXP2* is not a language gene but is rather a gene for a transcription factor that affects the function of many genes, including ones involved in the development of the lungs, heart, and other organs (Fisher and Marcus 2006). Its precise effects in the phenotype affecting language development have been a matter of some debate. Affected individuals have problems with sequential speech production that can lead to major problems with intelligibility. They also have more general difficulties with language, made evident in their written language and in language comprehension (Bishop 2009). Whereas prior human studies of *FOXP2* have involved rare mutations, Mueller et al. (in preparation) found that a common polymorphism in the promotor region of this gene is associated with variation in language ability as well as the ability to learn visually presented sequential structure.

Studies of the effects of FoxP2 protein in animal models revealed that complete absence of the protein in mice leads to premature death, while conditional knock-out in birds impairs the accuracy with which birds learn to sing (Haesler et al. 2007; Fischer and Hammerschmidt 2011). Mice carrying the "human variant" of the *Foxp2* gene show a higher density of medium spiny neurons in the striatum and slightly altered ultrasonic vocalizations (Enard et al. 2009). Intriguingly, the striatum plays a crucial role in the kind of sequential learning that Mueller et al. (in preparation) found to be associated with a common polymorphism in *FOXP2*. In sum, while there is some evidence that links *FOXP2* to vocal behavior, the precise mechanisms remain unclear. Continued research on the *FOXP2* gene will be critical to determine in what way it was involved in the emergence of human language.

Ancestral Stages in the Evolution of Human Speech

A major question in the evolution of language is the nature of the ancestral stages that preceded the evolution of spoken language. Here a natural theory is that spoken language evolved from the systems of vocal communication found in nonhuman primates (Seyfarth 1987; Cheney and Seyfarth 2005). An alternative theory holds that human language emerged initially from manual gestures, with human language only secondarily becoming spoken (Hewes 1973; Corballis 2002; Tomasello 2008; Arbib et al. 2008).

The ability to use symbols has been suggested as an important precursor to language (Christiansen and Kirby 2003; Jackendoff 1999); consequently, the extent to which other animals use vocal and gestural signals to refer to objects or events in the environment is relevant to the two theories. The vocal theory is supported by the finding that many species of primates produce "functionally referential" alarm calls, whereby the production of a specific call type is dependent on the appearance of a particular predator type, and reception of the call allows receivers to choose a response appropriate to that predator type. Functional reference in this sense has been supported for the alarms of vervet monkeys, guenons, lemurs, tamarins, and capuchin monkeys (Seyfarth et al. 1980; Zuberbühler et al. 1999; Fichtel and Kappeler 2002; Kirchhof and Hammerschmidt 2006; Wheeler 2010). Although the alarm calls of great apes have not been shown to have a similar level of functional reference, food calls of captive chimpanzees have been found to vary for different food types, and playback of the calls guided the search behavior of one test subject (Slocombe and Zuberbühler 2005). Other primate vocalizations provide listeners with detailed cues to events in their social environment. Among baboons, for example, certain calls are given only in highly predictable social circumstances: threat-grunts are solely given by higher-ranking to lower-ranking animals, and screams are given only by lower-ranking to higher-ranking animals. Playback experiments indicate that listeners monitor the vocalizations exchanged by others in their group, and in this way learn about changes in their social relationships. When listeners hear a higher-ranking animal give threat-grunts and a lower-ranking animal scream, they show little response, but when they hear a lower-ranking animal's threat-grunt followed by a higher-ranking animal's scream they respond strongly (Cheney et al. 1995). Listeners' response to an apparent rank reversal is particularly strong if the interaction suggests that the member of a lower-ranking matriline has risen in rank above the member of a higher-ranking matriline (Bergman et al. 2003). These results suggest that highly specific, functionally referential vocalizations in nonhuman primates are not limited to alarm calls but instead can be found throughout the animals' repertoire of vocal signals.

By contrast, evidence for the referential use of manual gestures by nonhuman primates is scarce (Arbib et al. 2008) and mostly limited to imperative "pointing" gestures by captive apes during interactions with humans (Leavens et al. 1966; Call and Tomasello 1994; Miles 1990). A referential gesture, "the directed scratch," has been suggested for chimpanzees in the wild; here, an exaggerated scratching movement on a part of the body is used to elicit grooming of this area (Pika and Mitani 2006). The use of iconic gestures (gestures that bear a physical resemblance to an external referent) has been reported only in one bonobo and one gorilla (Tanner and Byrne 1996); therefore, the use of iconic gestures by great apes remains controversial (Tomasello and Call 2007a). Whether pointing gestures function referentially or whether receivers respond as a result of stimulus enhancement remains unclear. Gestures, especially in the wild, are often more difficult to record, categorize, and play back than are vocalizations, so the lack of evidence for functional reference in primate gestures may be due to a lack of appropriate research. More work on the use of primate gestures in natural communication with conspecifics is needed, especially work that employs experimental methods. The majority of what is known about gestural communication comes from studies of captive apes, compared to vocal research that is more often carried out on free-ranging monkeys. Studying vocal and gestural communication simultaneously within a species would also address this imbalance in knowledge and make direct comparisons of these two signaling modalities easier.

Although nonhuman primates typically possess rather small repertoires of vocal signals, the communicative power of these restricted repertoires can be substantially augmented by the receiver's ability to integrate vocalizations with contextual cues. We have already provided one example of how context can influence one primate's response to another's vocalization: baboons' response to the threat-grunt of another individual depends upon their recent interactions with that individual (Engh et al. 2006). In much the same way, the response of Diana monkeys to playback of a Diana monkey's leopard alarm call can be influenced by contextual cues. Normally, whenever a Diana monkey hears another Diana's leopard alarm call, she gives a leopard alarm call of her own. However, if the listener has recently heard (and responded to) the growl of a leopard coming from the same area, she no longer responds to the sound of an alarm call with her own alarm, presumably because she already knows that a leopard is in the area (Zuberbühler et al. 1999).

Research in functional linguistics (e.g., Clark 1996; Levinson 2000) suggests that pragmatic context also plays a crucial role in language processing and makes it possible to interpret the linguistic signal given the context. The importance of context in both human language and primate vocal communication provides an element of evolutionary continuity between the two, continuity that is less apparent in semantics and syntax. This interpretation does not preclude, of course, that humans may have evolved more sophisticated sociopragmatic skills than nonhuman primates, but the difference and impact on communication would be a matter of degree and not of kind.

One problem already discussed for the theory of language evolution from primate vocalizations is the weakness of direct cortical control of phonatory neurons in nonhuman primates—a weakness that largely precludes vocal learning and limits the ability to control when to produce or not produce vocalizations. Gestural theory does not suffer from this problem, as neocortical control of manual movements is well developed in primates (Gentilucci and Corballis 2006). This difference in cortical control of vocalizations versus gestures may explain why attempts to teach great apes to speak have failed, whereas at least moderate success has been attained from the use of simplified forms of sign language, or keyboards containing abstract symbols (Gardner and Gardner 1969; Savage-Rumbaugh et al. 1998).

Proponents of the gestural theory emphasize flexibility in the form and use of gestures, as an important step in the evolution of symbolic communication and language (Tomasello and Call 2007b). Studies of all great ape gestural repertoires have identified idiosyncratic gestures used by single individuals (Goodall 1986; Pika et al. 2005), suggesting that some gestures are invented through ontogenetic ritualization (Tomasello and Call 2007b). However, variability alone does not increase signal meaning. For gestures to be used communicatively, their variation must relate in some consistent way either to internal states or to external objects and events. For vocal signals, acoustic analysis and playback experiments present a reliable way to assess whether structural variation is meaningful to conspecifics (e.g., see Fischer 1998). Similarly, quantitative measures of variability and experimental validation of whether signal variation affects receiver response are needed for gestural signals, before such signals are accepted as communicative.

The observation that signed languages of the deaf have essentially all of the linguistic, semantic, and pragmatic properties of spoken language has also been used as an argument for the plausibility of the gestural theory (Armstrong et al. 1995; Stokoe 2001; Armstrong and Wilcox 2007). Others would argue, however, that these properties of signed languages have been found in fully evolved humans, rather than human ancestors, and thus may be a reflection of communication abilities evolved in another context, such as the vocal one. Finally, the dominance of the left hemisphere of the brain is apparent both in right-handedness and in the control of speech, suggesting a close tie between manual and vocal activity (Corballis 1989). There is, however, ample evidence that nonhuman primates also reveal a left hemisphere dominance in the processing of vocalizations, indicating that hemispheric lateralization per se is not a good diagnostic (reviewed in Fitch 2010).

Gestural theory has recently received support from the discovery of mirror neurons in primates in areas of the cortex responsible for control of manual movements. These neurons fire both when a monkey makes intentional movements with its hands and when the monkey sees another individual making the same movements. These neurons also respond to the *sounds* of manual gestures, but they do not respond to vocalizations (Kohler et al. 2002). Mirror neurons were first discovered in monkeys in areas of the brain considered to be homologous with Broca's area. Mirror neurons are now understood to be part of a larger network, called the *mirror system*, which includes areas in addition to Broca's that are homologous to ones important to language. Altogether, the parieto-frontal mirror system in primates corresponds very closely to the language circuits in the left hemisphere of the human brain (Rizzolatti and Sinigaglia 2010). Evidence for mirror neurons in humans, however, is a subject of debate (e.g., Turella et al. 2009).

Rizzolatti and colleagues have proposed that the mirror system in monkeys is in essence a system for understanding action (Rizzolatti et al. 2001; Rizzolatti and Craighero 2004). That is, the monkey understands the actions of others in terms of how it would itself perform those actions. This is the basic idea underlying what has been called the *motor theory of speech perception*, which holds that we perceive speech, not in terms of the acoustic patterns it creates, but rather in terms of how we ourselves would articulate it (Liberman et al. 1967). The mirror system provides a natural substrate, though grounded in gesture rather than vocalization. Still, there is ample evidence that the perception of sounds in general and the acquisition of sound-referent relationships are widespread and independent of the ability to produce these sounds. An extreme example, perhaps, is, Rico: a border collie that learned the names of over two hundred toys and was able to retrieve them correctly on command (Kaminski et al. 2004). In contrast, his vocal repertoire was limited to some barks and growls, suggesting that a close perception-action link is not a prerequisite for the processing of acoustic stimuli (reviewed in Fischer 2010).

Although the discovery of mirror neurons responsive to manual movements has widely been taken to support the gestural theory of the origin of language, it should be noted that mirror neurons have recently been shown to also exist in the song system of songbirds (Prather et al. 2008). Mirror neurons may eventually prove to be widely distributed in the brains of higher vertebrates, and thus not to be strong evidence in favor of any particular theory of language origin (see also Hurford 2004 for discussion). Moreover, it is also important to remember the many continuities that exist between human and nonhuman primates in the perception of conspecific vocalizations (Gil-da-Costa et al. 2004), lateralization in the perception of such calls (Poremba et al. 2003; Poremba et al. 2004), the integration of faces and voices (Ghazanfar et al. 2005), and the recognition of individual speakers (Scott 2008). These continuities are just what we would expect to find if human language had emerged from an ancestral vocal system of communication.

The greatest problem for the primate vocal theory for the evolution of language, as stated above, is the absence of direct cortical control of vocal production in nonhuman primates and the presumed difficulty of evolving such control. The greatest problem for the gestural theory is that, even if our ancestors started with gestural language, the switch to spoken language still must have been made at some point (Burling 2007). That switch, whenever it occurred, would have required the evolution of cortical control of vocal production. A communication system dependent on manual gestures does not require cortical control of vocal production, and thus does nothing to pave the way for such an adaptation. Put another way, the vocal theory assumes the sequence primate vocal communication to human spoken language, whereas the gestural theory assumes the sequence primate gestural communication to gestural language to spoken language. Corballis (2010) has suggested that the latter transition might have occurred by face movements gradually becoming more important than hand movements in gestural communication, with the eventual addition of voicing and movements of the vocal tract to facial gestures. Nevertheless, if the intermediate step of gestural language does not simplify the second transition, then the vocal theory, with one transition, can be claimed to be more parsimonious than the gestural theory, with two.

An intermediate view might be that the vocal-facial and manual pathways coevolved. There is good evidence for a close link between specific facial expressions and specific vocalizations (Haesler et al. 2007). Further studies should examine the link between hand movements and vocalizations, including its neural basis, in more detail.

Coevolution of Language and Cognition

Corballis (this volume) argues for the importance of episodic memory and mental time travel in providing the selective impetus for the evolution of language. The ability to review past events and to plan for the future is enhanced by improvements in language skills; thus the fitness benefits of episodic memory and future planning might have provided a primary selective advantage for the evolution of language. Others have made a similar argument with respect to theory of mind. A full blown theory of mind requires language, for example, to derive explanations for the behavior of others that depend on inferences about their mental states (Malle 2002). If so, the selective benefits of having a theory of mind would also provide a selective advantage for the evolution of language.

The argument can be reversed; that is, it can be argued that cognitive skills, such as theory of mind and episodic memory, enhance language skills. Thus the ability to engage in joint attention, an aspect of theory of mind, seems to be important to word acquisition in humans (Baldwin 1993). It is also sometimes claimed that the ability to infer the intention to communicate in others, another theory of mind skill, is important to language learning (Malle 2002). According to Grice (1989), ordinary conversation is dependent on knowing what is in the minds of others, to the point of requiring a specialized theory of mind module (Sperber and Wilson 2002), although Millikan (1984) and others have criticized this idea as making conversation more complicated than it actually is. Improvements in memory certainly must have been important as human ancestors expanded their vocabulary of signals beyond those found in other primates, and episodic memory may have played a role here.

The conclusion, then, is that language enhances cognitive skills and cognitive skills enhance language. The primary benefit of both sets of skills may have been in dealing with social complexity (Cheney and Seyfarth 1990b; Dunbar 1998b; see also chapters in the section on Knowledge, this volume). Cognition and language then would have coevolved, though not in the sense that species coevolve (e.g., as in host-parasite interactions) by putting reciprocal selection pressures on each other. Rather, cognition and language would coevolve in the sense that both attributes would evolve gradually over the same time period, with each enabling improvements in the other. The degree to which such coevolution would have resulted in specific biological adaptations for language is, however, unclear given the possibility that language itself might have evolved by way of cultural evolution (e.g., Chater et al. 2009; Christiansen and Chater 2008).

Conclusions

Although the bulk of animal communication involves the integration of signal and context, and thus potentially relies on cognition, the actual cognitive demands of many signaling systems seem rather modest. This conclusion is brought home by the observation that some forms of communication are managed by organisms, such as bacteria, which lack nervous systems altogether, as well as by the fact that the most complex forms of communication known in nonhuman organisms are accomplished by social insects with relatively modest nervous systems. Nevertheless, we see a role of advanced cognitive abilities in certain aspects of animal communication, especially in the integration of signals with context. Such integration occurs more obviously at the receiver end, when the response of receivers to signals is contingent on a combination of present circumstances and memories of past circumstances. Integration can also occur at the signaler end, when senders make decisions about whether or not to signal or on the form of the signal, which is again contingent on context. Moreover, the complex context-dependence of signal production and interpretation found in particular in the communication of nonhuman primates provides an important element of continuity between animal communication and human language. Eventual understanding of the evolution of language will depend on an analysis of how the context-dependent, partially referential signaling systems of our ancestors were gradually elaborated through the co-evolution of language and the other cognitive abilities that both support and require language.

Knowledge

14

How Intelligent Is Machiavellian Behavior?

Redouan Bshary, Felice Di Lascio,
Ana Pinto, and Erica van de Waal

Abstract

The hypothesis that the complexity of social life selects for large brains is currently very prominent. Somewhat surprisingly, this functional hypothesis has been mainly tested by experiments which aim to identify the cognitive processes/mechanisms that may underlie social behavior. Such research is inherently challenging because it is extremely difficult to design experiments that conclusively allow the exclusion of simple cognitive processes as an explanation for successful behavior. Here it is argued that cognitive scientists should not focus on processes only but rather test quantitatively what animals can do with their brain: how fast, how precise, how much can they learn depending on the problem at hand. Many differences between species concerning cognitive tasks in the social domain are quantitative in nature: the number of group members and their past behavior that an individual has to recognize respectively, the number of opportunities for social learning or cooperation that arise per time unit, etc. Tests on how such quantitative differences between species translate into quantitative cognitive performances should be addressed in many species to permit a comparative approach, where predictions about relative performance can be made based on detailed knowledge of each study species' ecology. Comparative approaches are methodologically challenging but can be tackled through large-scale cooperation between scientists.

Introduction

The evolution of sociality has been a key research focus in evolutionary biology for a long time. One likely reason why so many evolutionary biologists find this question so interesting is that humans are highly social animals. In social species, an individual's main challenge for successful survival and reproduction is competition with fellow group members over access to limited resources like food and mates. At the same time, group members can be important alliance partners against predators and neighboring groups. Cooperation and conflict are thus the two opposing forces that affect virtually any decision of individuals, selecting for cognitive abilities that allow individuals to cope with the complexity of decision making in this dynamic social world. Two related hypotheses, the *Machiavellian intelligence hypothesis* and the *social brain hypothesis*, propose that the challenges linked to social life caused the evolution of increased cognitive abilities and, correspondingly, an increase in relative (allometric) brain size in social species, more precisely of particular parts of the brain (e.g., the neocortex).

The social brain hypothesis (Dunbar 1992; Barton and Dunbar 1997) stresses a link between social complexity and neocortex size evolution in mammals without specifying what aspects of social life might be particularly cognitively demanding. A basic assumption of this approach is that relative brain size is a good proxy for the developmental and running costs of a brain, while accepting that there will be unexplained variation because changes in cell density, connectivity, receptor density, and neurotransmitter concentration may provide alternative ways to increase or reduce costs. Initial analyses focused on group size as a correlate of social complexity and obtained positive correlations between group size and neocortex ratio (neocortex size regressed against the size of the rest of the brain) in primates, carnivores, and bats (Barton and Dunbar 1997). However, several other variables correlate positively with neocortex ratio and hence it remains unclear what aspects of social life may cause an enlargement of the neocortex (Healy and Rowe 2007). The Machiavellian intelligence hypothesis, in its original form (Byrne and Whiten 1988; Whiten and Byrne 1997) took a wide, permissive perspective on the variety of socio-cognitive adaptations through which an individual may exploit the potential benefits of its social world, as well as dealing with the hostile aspects of it: social knowledge, discovery techniques, social curiosity, social problem solving, innovation, flexibility, social expertise, social play, mind reading, self-awareness, imitation, and culture were all explicitly included. However, a more refined hypothesis emerged which focuses on the importance of gaining influence and power for an individual's fitness. In this view, key cognitive abilities of individuals are (a) the ability to understand and remember relationships between other group members in order to form strategic alliances and (b) skills in manipulation and deception of group members. The refined version corresponds well to several key questions that were addressed at the Forum:

- What do different kinds of animals know about the relationships between others?
- What do they know about each other's intentions and motivations?
- What do they know about each other's knowledge and beliefs?
- How does social knowledge affect communication?
- What is the difference between social and physical cognition?
- How can we relate the findings to the social brain hypothesis?

Answers to several of the questions raised above rely heavily on our ability to design conclusive experiments. Interestingly, while the social brain hypothesis and the Machiavellian intelligence hypothesis are evolutionary hypotheses that address a functional question (Under what conditions do the benefits of a more expensive brain outweigh the costs?), most attempts to answer the question focus on mechanisms; namely, on the presence/absence of "complex" cognitive processes, like perspective-taking, experience projection, planning, or imitation learning. In fact, the hypothesis that Machiavellian intelligence is linked to neocortex size (or the size of functionally homologous structures) is largely based on the assumption that social animals not only successfully solve the complexity of their social environment but that they actually evolved some understanding about why a certain behavior causes a response in a social target that leads to the acquisition of a goal (Byrne and Whiten 1988). This has spurred a major debate and much research effort into trying to find out whether large-brained social species are able, for example, to understand what other individuals want, feel, or believe; that is, whether they have a theory of mind (Premack and Woodruff 1978). We refer to this approach as qualitative because one cannot plot different cognitive processes along an axis.

Designing experiments that would allow conclusive tests for theory of mind is a particularly difficult task (Penn and Povinelli 2007b; also discussed further below). In most species, we do not really know how intelligent Machiavellian behavior is at the mechanistic level because identifying "complex" cognitive processes by ruling out simpler explanations is inherently difficult. Current studies on cognitive processes fail to explain why some species have relatively larger brains than others. This is because, based on evolutionary logic, one should define "complex" cognitive processes as processes that demand more brain power and hence are more expensive to use. It remains an open question whether the "complex" cognitive processes are complex according to our definition (though we consider it likely to be the case), and we think that too strong a focus on cognitive processes misses out on the advantages of having cognitive research firmly based on evolutionary theory. Natural selection favors any solution which makes individuals more adapted to their environment. Many adaptations concern the ability to gain, store, and update relevant information. The selection on the amount of information an individual of a given species can retain to make appropriate behavioral decisions may be highly variable between species that otherwise use the same cognitive processes to gain information and to make decisions. We refer to studies that try to evaluate the knowledge of species as quantitative because here one can plot the amount of information available for decision making along an axis.

Such a quantitative approach fits well with questions about the social intelligence of different species as many social challenges have a strong quantitative component. For example, the question for many social (vertebrate) species is not really whether individual recognition exists but how many individuals must be recognized and with what amount of additional information this recognition must be combined so that an individual can make suitable decisions (see also Shettleworth 2009). We develop this complementary approach, which focuses on the ecology of each species, as already promoted by Kamil (1998) and Shettleworth (1998), and propose four key aspects:

1. A shift from the qualitative mechanistic approach that studies underlying cognitive processes to a more quantitative functional approach that measures an animal's ability to solve social problems.
2. The use of ecological information to generate precise hypotheses about a species' performance in a specific cognitive task.
3. The need to study a great variety of species rather than a few "usual suspects" species with presumably high cognitive abilities.
4. The need to conduct field observations and field experiments.

The Quest to Demonstrate Complex Cognitive Processes

Providing convincing evidence that nonhuman animals use or do not use complex cognitive processes has turned out to be one of the main challenges in animal cognition (Heyes 1993, 1998). In some areas, a shift in experimental design has provided encouraging results. For example, there is now convincing evidence that a variety of species is able to learn through imitation of conspecifics, at least under laboratory conditions (Whiten et al. 2004). With respect to the theory of mind debate, we still await more definite results. Ever more sophisticated experimental designs have provided evidence that animals can foresee the actions of other animals, but two alternative explanations have emerged: (a) the mind-reading hypothesis postulates that animals have mental concepts that they can use to predict the behavior of others, whereas (b) the behavior-reading hypothesis says that animals base their behavioral responses solely on what is observable, without any need of mental concepts (Lurz 2009). The difficulty here is that even if animals are mind-readers (i.e., possess a theory of mind), the starting point of their decision making will be based on behaviors, cues, or information from their environment that they can "capture." Thus, both hypotheses are intrinsically linked, since both have the same causes and the same outcomes (responses) in most cases.

Consider the experimental design by Hare et al. (2000): in this paradigm a subordinate and a dominant look into a room from opposite ends. Two food items are placed at equidistance to both subjects, each close to a barrier. One barrier blocks the dominant's view on the food item while the other barrier is not functional. The subordinate is released into the room shortly before the dominant and hence has to choose which food item to approach. Typically, subordinates go to the food that is hidden from the dominant's view. This choice can be based on the subordinate's knowledge of what the dominant can or cannot see, but the dominant's orientation behind the door could also be used as a cue to choose the food that will be less likely contested (Shettleworth 2009).

Major advances have been made by researchers who tested better-defined cognitive processes that are considered to be cognitively complex. For example, the ability to take another individual's perspective (being able to predict what another individual may or may not be able to see) has been documented in several primates (Tomasello et al. 1998), other mammals (Bräuer et al. 2004; Kaminski et al. 2005), and in ravens (Bugnyar et al. 2004). In scrub jays, there is experimental evidence for so-called experience projection: young jays develop an aversion for being watched during food caching if they are given the opportunity to raid the caches of others (Emery and Clayton 2001).

Unfortunately, tests on the presumably complex cognitive processes which underlie social behavior are restricted to few study species, mainly primates and a few select other mammals and bird species, in particular corvids. Such research is most likely to determine the upper limits of nonhuman cognitive processes. However, such a focus prevents us from knowing whether nonprimate and noncorvid species would have similar cognitive processes at their disposal. Part of the problem may have to do with publication policies. Imagine you have to referee or decide to print a manuscript with a great experimental design that provides negative results for experience projection in a spider species. Such studies are necessary, because to make an assumption that spiders don't use such cognitive processes without any tests is not very scientific. In any case, we argue that cognitive research which focuses solely on the processes that underlie social behavior will fall short of providing a complete picture of the link between social complexity and brain evolution. Without trying to promote the position of Macphail (1982), who proposed that all nonhuman animals possess the same cognitive toolbox, we consider it highly unlikely that differences in relative brain size or brain-part size (always to be seen as a correlate of costs) between two species can be explained sufficiently by differences in the cognitive toolbox for social behavior. Instead, species may have the same cognitive processes in place but differ in quantitative rather than qualitative aspects. For example, species that live in large groups need to recognize more individuals and keep track of more third-party relationships than species that live in smaller groups, which may select for larger brains in the former without evoking more sophisticated processes.

A broad evolutionary approach should aim at placing any study species into the bigger picture. Suppose that eventually an experiment or a series of experiments demonstrated beyond doubt that chimpanzees know what others believe. Also suppose that fancy brain scans demonstrate that in chimpanzees certain well-developed neocortex areas are activated during tasks in which the chimpanzees attribute beliefs to others, and that these areas are much smaller for example in baboons, which turn out to fail in the task. Under such a scenario, we would have understood quite a bit about chimpanzee intelligence and the evolution of the chimpanzee brain. Maybe, we could conclude that the attribution of beliefs indeed needs a large brain and certain structures (in mammals). However, we would not have gained an understanding of the larger picture, especially as many comparative brain analyses provide strong support for the hypothesis that the social domain is the most important selective force acting on the evolution of relative brain size: Why do baboons have a larger neocortex ratio than other monkeys if all failed to evolve the (supposedly) most sophisticated social cognitive tool? Why do primates and cetaceans generally have larger neocortex ratios than other mammalian clades (Jerison 1973) if, supposedly, complex cognitive processes appear to be largely absent in primates and cetaceans? If we want to understand relative brain size evolution, the evolution of substructures in the brain, and the link between brain structures and an animal's social cognitive abilities, we need to study as many (vertebrate) species as possible. With respect to social cognition, amphibians and reptiles may turn out to be challenging as they generally show little social behavior. In contrast, fishes are very diverse in their social behaviors and have demonstrated sophisticated social learning as well as cooperation (Brown et al. 2006; Kendal et al. 2009; Raihani et al. 2010). We reemphasize that we should explore the possibility that quantitative differences rather than qualitative differences in cognitive abilities may explain differences in brains.

The Evolutionary Approach to Social Cognition

Much information can be gained by focusing on what problems animals can solve and how fast, how precise, and how much animals can learn rather than getting stuck with the underlying processes. Consider, for example, the triangulation method developed to test whether animals know what others know: animals have to respond correctly to a change in condition on the first trial so that fast conditioning can be excluded and more complex processes be accepted (Heyes 1998). While this experimental setup has not provided evidence that animals know what others know, it could be very well used to compare many different species and test how fast they learn to adapt to a new situation. On the functional level, a species that is able to learn a new situation after just one exposure can be virtually as efficient as a species that has the ability of insight and knowledge about what others know. The relative efficiency will depend on how often an animal encounters any given situation: the more often a situation occurs, the less important it becomes that conditioning takes longer to produce appropriate behavior.

In any case, appropriate behavior relies on the animal's ability to identify the relevant cues of a situation. Therefore, selection will favor individuals that are able to solve problems quickly; in particular, the most important problems an animal faces during its life. Each species or even each population will be unique with respect to its list of key problems and/or their precise ranking of importance. Therefore, different species or populations within species must be selected to solve different tasks. Detailed knowledge about a species' ecology will thus allow the formulation of very precise predictions about the kind of cognitive tasks where it will excel relative to other species with different ecologies. The predictions are (a) purely functional and not concerned about the underlying cognitive processes and (b) quantitative in nature: species X should learn a certain task linked to its ecology faster or more precisely than species Y for which the problem presented in the task is not, or less, ecologically relevant. A classic study along this line of thinking is the comparison of spatial memory abilities in three corvid species that differ with respect to their dependency on retrieving cached food to survive the winter (Balda and Kamil 1989). Spatial memory was most developed in the most dependent species. Selection apparently worked specifically on spatial memory but not on memory per se, as the three species did not differ in a memory task on colors.

Many social tasks are quantitative in nature and thus very suitable for the functional approach. For example, social vertebrates share some important cognitive abilities like individual recognition, memory of past interactions with specific individuals, and the ability to learn about third-party relationships. Regarding the latter, countless experiments on a great variety of species have tested and confirmed the *communication network theory* that predicts that individuals eavesdrop on ongoing interactions to gain information for later use (McGregor 2005). However, the degree to which animals are able to recognize individuals, to remember past interactions with them, and to know about their relationships with third parties should all be linked to a species' typical "functional" group size; that is, the number of individuals with which it has individualized relationships (Dunbar 1992). These quantitative predictions can be tested by confronting species that differ in group size with operant tasks where subjects get rewarded for learning faces, linking specific faces to rewards, or learning to respond correctly to third-party interactions. A comparison of learning curves can reveal whether more social species learn the tasks faster and whether they perform with higher precision than less social species.

Applications of the Evolutionary Approach to Machiavellian Intelligence

We think that the evolutionary approach provides interesting perspectives for at least three topics. First, it is interesting to ask under which conditions animals use their cognitive abilities and to specify the advantages of the use. Second, using quantitative field observations, we can then explore which aspects of social behavior may be correlated with the evolution of relative brain size. Answers provided through the second approach will help formulate predictions concerning the third topic; namely, the cognitive processes that underlie "intelligent" social behavior.

Testing the Use of the Cognitive Toolbox

Classic field studies on social knowledge in wild vervet monkeys and wild baboons show, for example, that vervet monkeys recognize mother-offspring pairs and baboons know the entire matrilineal hierarchy in their group (Cheney and Seyfarth 1990b; Bergman et al. 2003). In addition, evidence indicates that vervets could be more likely to help a group member in a conflict if they had a recent grooming interaction with that group member; when subjected to a loudspeaker that played back calls suggesting an agonistic encounter with the group member in question, vervets took longer to respond (for a similar study on baboons, see Cheney et al. 2010).

The next important step is to test how far animals are able to use their knowledge and the (scientifically demonstrated) predictability of group member decisions to their advantage. Can we design experiments that would allow the amount and precision of information used by different species to be quantified while addressing such questions as:

- Are individuals more likely to seek a conflict with a third party after they groomed a dominant potential alliance partner?
- Do they "know" (and hence make use of this knowledge) that dominants are more tolerant toward them after being groomed?
- Do they adjust their behavior to the presence or absence of specific individuals?
- Do they loosen the tie with individuals that often deceive?
- How easily can individuals learn to produce false alarm calls if they are given the experimental opportunity, and how quickly would group members adjust to that?

Some results on vervet monkeys (Cheney and Seyfarth 1990b) show that repeated playbacks of specific alarm calls from one individual (e.g., to a leopard) leads other group members to ignore these specific leopard alarm calls, but not other alarm calls made by the same individual. More experiments of this type are necessary.

**Back to Basic Observations to Get Ideas on What Makes
Social Interactions More Complex than Nonsocial Tasks**

The hypothesis that social complexity is more cognitively demanding than aspects of the physical environment is largely based on the perception that the former is less stable than the latter. Color or smell consistently indicates ripeness of fruit, objects consistently fall to the ground, stone is harder than wood, etc. In contrast, social behavior depends, for example, on motivational states of individuals, history of interactions, and dominance relationships. Motivation can frequently change as can rank order, group composition, and coalition partners, making individual behavior more difficult to predict than the physical environment. However, while the logic of this argument seems to be quite convincing, we are unaware of any quantitative data that explicitly evaluates the degree of social instability as a measure of social complexity. The highest levels of complexity may actually be achieved at intermediate levels of instability, whereas very high levels of instability may lead to simple decision rules.

In species with stable group composition, we think that social instability can be described with long-term field observations. Actually, we believe that many primatologists have the right data to address this issue. Data on group composition, hierarchy, conflicts, grooming, nearest neighbors, etc., belong to the standard protocols of most field studies. These data could be used to calculate indices of group composition stability, hierarchy stability, or coalition partner stability. More recently, social network analysis has been developed to describe social relationships within groups (Sih et al. 2009). The network could be analyzed on a monthly or yearly basis and an index created to assess the similarity between subsequent network structures. A large comparative data set might reveal that species differ significantly in these indices, and it could then be tested whether the differences correlate with differences in neocortex ratio or other brain indices. Such tests would certainly help to reduce the long list of candidate social cognition tasks listed in the Machiavellian intelligence hypothesis that may indeed have a major effect on the evolution of relative brain size.

Is Machiavellian Intelligence More about Cooperation or Deception?

Originally posed by Whiten and Byrne (1997), a clear answer to this question would help in making predictions of the key cognitive processes that underlie social behavior (Brosnan et al. 2010). Mutual interdependence between group members may lead to rather unconditional forms of cooperation, where the evolution of positive emotions like empathy could play a major role to ensure cooperative behavior (Jaeggi et al. 2010). In contrast, conflicts are likely to select for more strategic behavior and watchfulness regarding the behavior of other group members. Currently, it seems unclear which processes would need larger brain powers (Brosnan et al. 2010). In humans, deception and cooperation apparently invoke different brain areas (Lissek et al. 2008), suggesting that these two antagonistic forces of social behavior may affect brain evolution in different ways. Methods which allow comparison between species with respect to cooperativeness versus competitiveness would enable us to evaluate their relative importance for the evolution of relative brain size and structure.

Methodological Considerations

In this section, we propose a shift in experimental paradigms so that experiments can closely reflect problems faced by an animal under natural conditions.

In addition, we highlight the importance of conducting experiments on wild animals and discuss major concerns about the comparison between species that will invariably differ in (many) ways that could affect their performance in cognitive tasks.

Experimental Paradigms

The theory that social challenges are the key selective forces involved in the evolution of more costly (larger) brains is very popular, in particular, among primatologists. Thus it is surprising that few laboratory experiments address the cognitive processes underlying social strategies. It appears that it is quite difficult to design good social experiments in the lab. From our perspective, two key problems in experimental designs on social cognition contribute to this: experiments often involve an important technical component (like pulling a string or a lever), and typically use food as a reward. Technical components of a task may be difficult to solve in their own right and therefore distract the animals from the social component. For example, the design by Melis et al. (2006a)—where two chimpanzees had to pull simultaneously on a string to drag a platform with food toward them—may be technically challenging for many species that are not used to pull. Using food as a reward can be problematic because most animals compete over food rather than share it. Food as reward is thus ideal to test for the strategic abilities of animals in a contest situation (Hare et al. 2000), but may easily cause negative results in cooperative tasks. It is therefore very important to devise new experimental designs and alternative rewards when planning future research on the link between cognition and cooperation. Stable cooperation may readily emerge if the experimental design allows animals to avoid a negative stimulus or obtain access to a sharable resource (e.g., a sleeping spot, a shady place, water, or a mechanic grooming device).

The most important aspect for an experimental design is that the situation and the benefits need to be based on a species' ecology. Allowing animals to perform naturally occurring behavior to achieve naturally occurring benefits of cooperation or manipulation will most likely produce positive results. Furthermore, following the ecological approach, the same situation can be used on species that usually are not confronted with the situation under natural conditions to test whether selection acts specifically on the ability of exposed species to solve the problem at hand. Ideally, both information acquisition abilities and underlying processes should be studied. For example, Bond et al. (2003) compared a highly social and a more solitary jay species with respect to the use of transitive inference. Both species solved the tasks but the more social pinyon jays learned faster and more accurately (quantitative difference). The differences were at least in part due to differences in the underlying mechanisms (qualitative difference): pinyon jays seemed to learn the relations between stimuli, whereas scrub jays learned associations between stimulus pairs.

Field Experiments

An important step for future research is to conduct experiments under field conditions. While laboratory studies have revealed exciting evidence about the cognitive processes that may underlie animal behavior, there is doubt whether wild conspecifics would ever perform as well: laboratory animals are well fed, the experiments are often the most exciting aspect of their daily life, they don't have to worry about predators or all other group members, separations ensure close proximity, etc. We do not know how important these variables are for "success" that is observed in laboratory experiments, and how the lack of these conditions hinders the use of the same cognitive processes in nature.

As it stands, evidence for imitation learning is restricted to laboratory evidence (Whiten and Mesoudi 2008). More than twenty years after the first publication on Machiavellian intelligence (Byrne and Whiten 1988), evidence for tactical deception in wild primates is still largely anecdotal. With respect to the one major exception in a field study on capuchins (Wheeler 2009), we note that the underlying cognitive processes remain currently unclear. Nevertheless, some laboratory experimental designs can be transferred to the field (van de Waal et al. 2010), and new paradigms adapted to field conditions can be developed.

Methodological Considerations Concerning the Comparative Approach

It is very clear that direct comparison of information acquisition, precision of performance, and flexibility of different species in different social tasks is full of potential pitfalls, especially when different clades are being compared. Species may differ with respect to their main sensory systems (e.g., visual, acoustic, olfactory) or within their main sensory systems (e.g., presence or absence of color vision or UV vision, differences in acoustic frequency range). In addition, two species may perceive the same color stimulus in very different ways, depending on the importance of the particular color in their ecology. For example, zebrafinch males may perceive an orange stimulus as aggressive whereas a male sparrow would perceive it as neutral.

Another methodological problem with the comparative approach is that differences between species in their performance in cognitive tasks may not necessarily reflect differences in their cognitive toolbox. Species *A* may succeed, for example, in a social learning task where species *B* fails because the task requires close proximity between model and subject, and hence a level of social tolerance that is only present in species *A*. Furthermore, testing wild animals on tasks that are relevant for individuals of some species but not for others means that ontogenetic effects will be potentially important.

Because of the various potential methodological problems, there seems to be no general optimal solution for the comparative approach. Three possibilities emerge where the generality of the conclusions would differ. First, one could design an experiment such that the design is optimally adapted to the ecology of one species and try to keep the design as similar as possible for other species. This approach seems to be particularly feasible to contrast the hypothesis that selection acts on specific performances with the hypothesis that large-brained species generally perform better than species with small brains. Second, one could choose a problem and adjust the experimental design to the ecology of each study species separately, trying to optimize the results for each species. The results could then be compared for speed of learning, precision of performance, etc. Finally, one could develop optimal designs for each species and then test all study species on all the designs. If species *A* performs better than species *B* in both experiments, then it would appear to be relatively safe to conclude that species *A* is more able to solve the general problem at hand *if* the experiments were conducted in the field or on wild caught individuals. For animals born and raised in captivity, holding conditions may have important effects that are difficult to control. For example, we consider it a legitimate question to ask whether captive young chimpanzees develop the same social foraging strategies as their wild counterparts when so many potentially important variables differ (e.g., the distribution, quantity, and quality of food or interindividual distance between group members and group composition). Nevertheless, we accept that differences between wild animals may also be due to ontogenetic differences, but at least these would be linked to ecological differences.

Conclusions

Major advances in our understanding of the social cognitive abilities of nonhuman animals will rely on the following points. Most importantly, we need to make a strong link between evolutionary theory and research on animal cognition. Evolutionary theory allows us to make predictions about the cognitive problems each animal species should be able to solve with relative ease. We argue that the ease with which different species solve particular problems is related to their ability to identify important cues as well as their ability to gain, store, and use information that is relevant to solve the problem at hand. It is less obvious that evolutionary theory allows predictions about the precise underlying cognitive processes that individuals of a species use to solve a problem. The success of the evolutionary approach is strongly based on detailed knowledge about the ecology of each study species. Only such knowledge allows making precise predictions about differences between species with respect to their ability to solve a specific cognitive task, irrespective of underlying processes. Therefore we think that research on animal cognition should have a much stronger field component, ideally conducting experiments in the field or on wild caught individuals, to complement standard laboratory experiments. The overall aim should be to compare a broad range of species belonging to different (vertebrate) clades and with differing relative brain sizes and structures. This goal presents a major challenge with respect to both methodological problems and research effort. Ideally, both issues should be addressed simultaneously in large collaborations between scientists who specialize in different species, and who are therefore able to develop appropriate experimental designs for a joint cognitive question. Having a framework in place that would permit (and even reward) such collaborative efforts might be a good way to demonstrate that humans are indeed intelligent, because we are able to cooperate on large scales!

15

Simple Reactions to Nearby Neighbors and Complex Social Behavior in Primates

Charlotte K. Hemelrijk

Abstract

Simple behavioral reactions to nearby neighbors may result in a greater variety of patterns of social interactions, social relationships, and social organization than has been previously assumed. Here, such transitions of micro-rules to macro-patterns are shown for primates in computer models. They concern the emergence of patterns of aggression, including the formation of coalitions and patterns of affiliation, such as reconciliation and grooming reciprocation. It is generally believed that these behavioral patterns require high cognition. While the high cognitive capacities of primates are not denied, these simulations suggest that primates may be less calculative in their daily lives. Simple behavioral reactions and self-organization may suffice to explain their patterns of social behavior.

Introduction

Compared to many other animal taxa, the social behavior of primates is generally regarded to be more complex in its patterns and underlying cognition. This complexity has often been overestimated, because the same patterns of social behavior are found in taxa that are supposed to be cognitively less sophisticated and recently, for these patterns, cognitively simpler explanations have been given (discussed below).

In earlier empirical studies, coalitions of primates were considered more complex than those of other species, and this was taken as evidence of calculative behavior (Harcourt and de Waal 1992). In later studies, however, coalitions of hyenas proved to be similar (Smith et al. 2010), and coalitions of primates were found to be explainable by simple behavioral rules (Range and Nöe 2005). The same holds for patterns of affiliative behavior in primates. Whereas early empirical studies suggested that affiliative patterns, such as reconciliation and reciprocation, require sophisticated cognitive deliberations (de Waal 1982), they were later found in species presumed to have less sophisticated cognition, such as goats, hyenas, and dolphins (Aureli and de Waal 2000). The mechanisms thought to underlie reconciliation (a conciliatory tendency, the "deliberation" to reconcile fights with more valuable partners more often, and the ability to distinguish between relationships of different value; Aureli and de Waal 2000) were later considered too complex for these animals (Silk 2007a). Furthermore, record keeping and "moralistic feelings" in primates were initially thought to be the basis of reciprocation and exchange (de Waal 1982); later simple behavioral responses were proposed to explain the observed patterns of behavior (Hemelrijk 1996a). Thus, empirical explanations proceed from assuming complex deliberations to simpler behavioral rules.

This transition from cognitively complex causes to simple ones is also observed in studies of artificial intelligence, for example, in computer models and the building of robots (Pfeifer and Scheier 1999). It appears that the discovery of cognitively simpler explanations is furthered by the use of self-organization models (Camazine et al. 2001; Hemelrijk 2002, 2005).

In this chapter, I discuss to what extent complex patterns of social behavior can be generated without resorting to sophisticated cognition and how they may arise through self-organization from spatial interactions among individuals who follow simple behavioral rules. To avoid the confusion that often surrounds these models, I indicate from the outset what these models can and cannot achieve. The models presented in this chapter are a kind of "null model": they show that little cognition is needed for primates to generate the observed patterns of social interaction. If simple behavioral reactions can generate certain complex patterns similar to those observed in primates, then this complex behavior can no longer be seen as proof of the sophisticated higher-level cognition that has been presumed to underlie it. Thus, these models illustrate that even if primates have sophisticated cognition (such as, possibly, "knowledge" about social relationships of others), they may not use it in (most of) their daily behavior. This also holds for humans. These models cannot rule out the possibility that complex cognitive processes are used in these social interactions. They show, however, that explanations may be more parsimonious and cognitively simpler explanations should be preferred.

Social Organization, Interactions, and Relationships

Primates are supposed to use their highest cognition in their aggression, such as their coalitions, and affiliative behavior, such as in exchange and reciprocation of services and in reconciliation of fights (Byrne and Whiten 1997). The model, DominanceWorld, and its extensions, GroupWorld and GroofiWorld, show, however, that these behavioral patterns may arise from simple social habitual "responses" and the spatial structure in the group. I begin with an outline of the model and then discuss the emergence of aggression patterns in it that resemble those in real primate groups. One pattern, intersexual dominance, is used to make predictions which are subsequently confirmed with empirical data. Finally, I show the emergence of patterns of affiliation (reciprocation and reconciliation).

DominanceWorld and Its Extensions, GroupWorld and GroofiWorld

DominanceWorld (DomWorld) represents an artificial world consisting of a homogenous space inhabited by artificial individuals that group and compete, but do nothing else (Figure 15.1). In this world, encounters among individuals are not random; they are dependent on the spatial proximity of individuals. Grouping arises from rules of attraction. If individuals are sufficiently close to others (i.e., they have someone in NearView), they continue along their movement direction. Thus, unlike models of schooling (e.g., Hemelrijk and Hildenbrandt 2008), individuals do not align their heading to that of others.

If, however, another individual is too close (i.e., in the personal space of "ego," PersSpace), a competitive or dominance interaction may take place (it

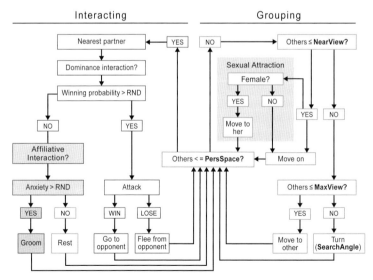

Figure 15.1 Outline of behavioral rules in DomWorld and GroofiWorld. The gray-shaded area "sexual attraction" is activated for males in certain runs only. The areas representing "affiliative interaction" were added later in GroofiWorld (gray-shaded). RND: random number drawn between 0 and 1 (see text for explanation).

is not specified what the cause of this competition is, such as food or a sexual partner). After a fight, the winner chases the opponent and the defeated individual flees. Individuals are sensitive to the risk of losing a fight: the greater its chance to be victorious, the more inclined an individual is to undertake an aggressive interaction. An individual's capacity to be victorious is represented through its dominance value. Individuals observe each other's dominance value upon meeting each other. Initially, it is the same for all individuals. Thus, during the first encounter, chance decides who wins. Subsequently, the higher-ranking individual has a greater chance to win. Changes in dominance values reflect the self-reinforcing effect of victories and defeats (Hsu et al. 2006). In the model, this is implemented by an increase of the dominance value of the victorious individual after its victory and a decrease of that of the defeated one by the same amount. Further, the impact of a conflict or the change in dominance values differs depending on the likelihood of an outcome (Hogeweg and Hesper 1985). Thus, when an individual unexpectedly defeats a higher-ranking opponent, this outcome causes a greater change in dominance values of both opponents than when, as would be expected, the same individual conquers a lower-ranking opponent. In this way, rank reversals are made possible.

Intensity of aggression (which ranges in primates from staring to biting) is represented by a fixed scaling factor, called StepDom. This factor is multiplied with the change in dominance value per fight. A high value of StepDom (of 1.0) implies that the impact of a single interaction may be high (e.g., biting); a low value (of 0.1) represents low impact (e.g., threats and staring). As reported later, this will be used to represent differences in fierceness of aggression between species as well as between the sexes.

Parameters are set so that on the computer screen the grouping of individuals resembles that of a macaque group: the number of individuals (8–12) reflects the number of adults in groups of macaques; high and low values of StepDom are set such that there is a great difference between both settings. The behavior of the modeled individuals is analyzed by means of behavioral units and statistical methods similar to those used when studying real primates. For a complete description, see Hemelrijk (1999b, 2000).

One of the shortcomings of the model has been suggested to be the lack of individual recognition among group members, which is clearly present in real animals. However, in DomWorld, individuals recognize the precise rank of others. In reality, this may come about in various ways: by recognizing others individually and remembering the outcome of previous fights with each opponent, by having observed the outcome of fights of that individual with others, or, in the absence of individual recognition, by directly perceiving the health and attitude of the other at the moment of the interaction (e.g., body posture, hair erection), or a combination thereof. In another model, we have studied which aggression patterns result when each individual, a so-called estimator, memorizes its experiences with each opponent and estimates the fighting power of the other on the basis of this memory (Hemelrijk 2000). The results appear to be similar to those of DomWorld without such memory, but they are weaker because everyone has a somewhat different experience with everyone else, and thus a different assessment about the dominance of everyone. Here, I confine myself to the model with clearer patterns in which the precise mechanism of perception of dominance is not specified.

Results of DomWorld

Spatial Structure, Dominance Style, Egalitarian and Despotic Societies

The social system, type of society, or dominance style of many species (e.g., insects, birds, and primates) has been classified as egalitarian or despotic, depending on the way in which benefits are distributed. These benefits include access to mates, food, and safe locations. When benefits are strongly biased toward higher-ranking individuals, the society is called "despotic"; when access to resources is more equally distributed, it is called "egalitarian." Egalitarian and despotic primate species, such as macaques, differ in many traits. Despotic macaques display aggression that is fiercer (biting rather than staring), less frequent, and more unidirectional. Spatial configuration of individuals in a despotic group is structured with dominants in the center (Itani 1954; Imanishi 1960; Yamada 1966). Usually these differences are explained by optimization of single traits through natural selection. However, Thierry (2004) suggests that in macaques these differences are due to covariation with only two inherited differences: degree of nepotism (i.e., cooperation among kin) and intensity of aggression.

DomWorld delivers an even simpler hypothesis; namely that a mere difference in intensity of aggression produces both types of societies. Analysis of the model specifies in detail how these societies may arise (Hemelrijk 1999b). By increasing only the value of intensity of aggression from mild to fierce, the artificial society switches from a typically egalitarian dominance style to a despotic one. For instance, compared to egalitarian artificial societies, despotic ones are more dispersed, show a lower frequency of attack, their behavior is more rank-related, aggression is more unidirectional, and spatial centrality of dominants is clearer. All of these differences between fierce and mild societies arise via a feedback between the development of the hierarchy and spatial structure that happens only when aggression is fierce (Hemelrijk 1999b, 2000). The steep hierarchy (Figure 15.2a) develops from the fierce aggression, because each outcome has a strong impact. Pronounced rank-development causes low-ranking individuals to be continuously chased away by others and thus the group spreads out (Figure 15.2b). As a result, the frequency of attack diminishes, hierarchy stabilizes, and, because low-ranking individuals flee from everyone they encounter, this automatically brings them at the periphery,

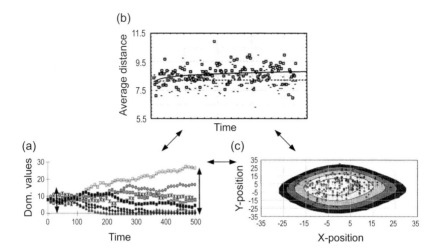

Figure 15.2 Mutual reinforcement between dominance hierarchy and spatial structure: (a) dominance values (winning tendencies) of each group member (of a single sex) over time; (b) average distance among group members for fierce aggression (open blocks) and mild aggression (short strokes) (Hemelrijk 1999b); (c) dominants are in the center. Darker shades indicate lower dominance rank of group members.

leaving dominant individuals in the center. Thus, a spatial-social structure develops (Figure 15.2c).

In short, the model shows that behavioral traits are interdependent and that a single change of the parameter representing the intensity of aggression causes a switch from a society resembling egalitarian macaques to despotic ones (Hemelrijk 1999b). In real macaques, these differences may be interconnected as they are in the model. In addition to fierce aggression, frequent aggression can cause this switch (Hemelrijk 1999a) because it also leads to a steeper hierarchy. A higher frequency of aggression may, for instance, arise from spatial confinement (e.g., in captivity). Thus, we can expect that captive groups of one and the same species are often more despotic than free-ranging groups.

Dominance style (egalitarian or despotic) is usually considered to be *species specific*, but Preuschoft et al. (1998) suggest that it may also be *sex specific*. In their study of the competitive regime of both sexes of Barbary macaques, Preuschoft et al. found that females behave more despotically than males. This was unexpected because females have a smaller body size and milder aggression. However, the despotic behavior of females should not be regarded as a separate adaptation, because it also occurs in DomWorld. In DomWorld, the sexes are distinguished only by the smaller fighting capacity of the females (i.e., a lower initial dominance and lower aggression intensity). Greater despotism among females was unexpected because of their weaker aggression intensity (Hemelrijk and Gygax 2004), but in DomWorld it is due to the lower initial dominance of females compared to males (which represents, among other things, sexual dimorphism in body size). Consequently, single events of victory and defeat have more impact on the overall power of females and cause the greater hierarchical differentiation among females than among males: the smaller the initial dominance of females (compared to males), the more despotic the dominance style of females (compared to that of males). The conclusion is that the degree of sexual dimorphism may influence the competitive regime of each sex, both in the model and in real primates.

The Socio-Ecological Theory

According to the socio-ecological theory (van Schaik 1989), dominance style is supposed to be a consequence of the degree of clumping of food sources and of different degrees of competition within and between groups. This theory suggests that despotic societies evolve when food is clumped and competition is high within groups, and egalitarian societies result when competition is high between groups, but low within groups. In line with this, when explicit foraging behavior and food distributions of different degrees of clumping are incorporated in DomWorld (Hemelrijk and Wantia 2005), high clumping of food leads to a despotic society (Hemelrijk et al. 2003). In contrast to the socio-ecological theory, in GroupWorld (an extension of DomWorld to several groups), competition between groups appears to favor despotic rather than egalitarian societies (Wantia 2007). In DomWorld as in real primates, high-ranking individuals usually participate in encounters between groups (Cooper 2004). In GroupWorld, competition between groups with different dominance styles appears to be won, under most conditions, by the group which has a more despotic style. This is due to the greater power of individuals of the highest rank as a consequence of the stronger differentiation of the hierarchy in despotic groups. The outcome of fights between groups depends on the details of the fights and the composition of the groups. When participants of intergroup conflicts fight in dyads or in coalitions of equal size, the despotic group outcompetes the egalitarian one. If, however, individuals of despotic groups fight in smaller coalitions or if their coalitions include fewer males than those of the egalitarian groups, the despotic group runs the risk of losing. Thus, the main conclusion is that group composition and details of what happens in fights between groups should be studied to increase our understanding of the formation of dominance style. This complexity confirms empirical findings on inter-group competition (e.g., see Majolo et al. 2005; Robbins and Sawyer 2007).

Model-Based Predictions Concerning the
Relative Dominance of Both Sexes

The value of a model becomes clear when the model produces predictions that are subsequently confirmed by empirical tests. DomWorld, for instance, predicts greater female dominance over males, both when the hierarchy is steeper and when the percentage of males in the group is larger. In a meta-analysis of the relative dominance of males and females in groups of 22 species throughout the primate order, both hypotheses have been confirmed (Hemelrijk et al. 2008).

Although in primate species (apart from Lemuriformes), females are smaller than males and milder in their aggression (due to their relatively smaller canines and weaker muscular structure), they still may be dominant over some males. In DomWorld (and in our accompanying empirical studies, Figures 15.3c, 15.4b, and 15.5), we measured the relative dominance position of females compared to males by the ratio of the summed number of males ranking below each female, divided by its maximum (Hemelrijk 1999a). Although females in DomWorld differ from males only in their inferior fighting capacity, the model shows that, unexpectedly, females become more dominant over males when species-specific aggression is fiercer (Hemelrijk 1999a; Hemelrijk et al. 2003). This results from the stronger hierarchical differentiation, which causes some males to rank very low and over these males females become dominant (Figure 15.3b). This prediction has been subsequently confirmed in macaques: female dominance over males is greater in despotic macaques than in egalitarian ones, even though the degree of sexual dimorphism in both types of species is the same (Hemelrijk et al. 2008) (Figure 15.3c). Earlier incidental observations of greater dominance of despotic female macaques over males, as opposed to egalitarian females over males, have been attributed to their stronger cooperation to suppress males (as a consequence of their supposedly stronger genetic relatedness) (Thierry 2004). DomWorld shows that greater female dominance may also simply arise as a side-effect of more pronounced hierarchical differentiation. In turn, their higher rank may facilitate the cooperation among females in attacks against males.

In DomWorld, frequent aggression also causes hierarchical differentiation to be pronounced and, as a result, female dominance to be greater. This may explain the difference in female dominance between pygmy chimpanzees and common chimpanzees. Despite their similar sexual dimorphism, female dominance in pygmy chimpanzees is higher than among common chimpanzees. This is usually attributed—just as for despotic macaques—to a higher frequency of the formation of coalitions among pygmy females against males (Parish 1996). However, in line with DomWorld, it may also be a side-effect of the difference in density (proximity to neighbors) and thus frequency of aggression between both species (Hemelrijk et al. 2003; Hemelrijk and Wantia 2005). Both are higher in groups of pygmy chimpanzees than in common ones (Stanford 1998). This hypothesis should be tested by comparing different groups of pygmy chimpanzees and by studying the relationship between female dominance and frequency of aggression.

Furthermore, DomWorld predicts that when species-specific aggression is fierce, female dominance is higher when there are more males in the group (Figure 15.4a) (Hemelrijk et al. 2008). This arises because a higher proportion

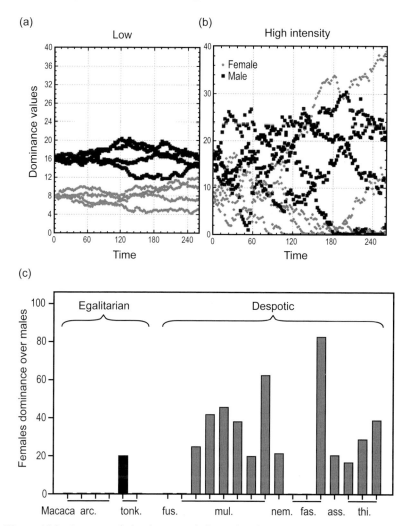

Figure 15.3 Intersexual dominance relations: female dominance in DomWorld is shown over time for (a) mild and (b) fierce aggression (Hemelrijk 1999b). (c) Empirical data of female dominance in groups of egalitarian macaques (left side) and in groups of despotic macaques (right) (Hemelrijk et al. 2008).

of males causes both sexes to interact more often with males. As a result of being the victim of attacks by males more often, some males become very low in rank and females may become dominant over these males (Figure 15.3b). This is not the case when aggression is mild, because here the hierarchy hardly develops (Figure 15.3a). This has been confirmed in real primates at several levels (Figure 15.4b and Figure 15.5b, d) for all species combined (also if we partial out effects of sexual dimorphism in body size), for several groups of a single species (rhesus macaques), and for several species of despotic macaques.

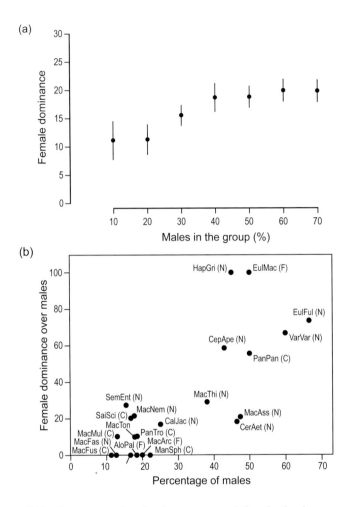

Figure 15.4 Percentage of males in a group and female dominance over males (Hemelrijk et al. 2008) in (a) model (average and SE) and (b) real data from primates. Six-letter codes indicate species. Data analysis was based on the independent contrasts method. Environmental conditions: N = natural, F = free-ranging, C = captive condition.

In egalitarian species, both in a single egalitarian species (stump-tailed macaques) and in several ones (Figure 15.5a, c), female dominance (like in the model) was independent of the percentage of males in the group.

In summary, relative dominance between the sexes is not a fixed trait that results merely from sexual dimorphism. Instead, it can be caused by the self-reinforcing effects of dominance interactions; through the frequency and strength of the self-reinforcing effects, female dominance may become dependent on group density and composition.

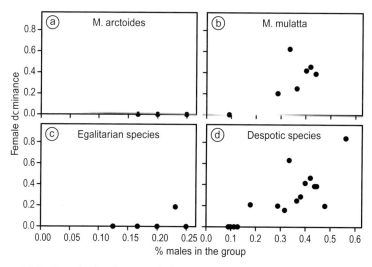

Figure 15.5   Female dominance relative to males in macaques and percentage of males in the group. (a) Groups of *Macaca arctoides* (Kendall rank correlation, $N = 4$, Tau = 0.33, not significant). (b) Groups of *M. mulatta* ($N = 7$, Tau = 0.62, $P < 0.05$ two-tailed). (c) Groups of several egalitarian species ($N = 6$, Tau = 0.36, not significant). (d) Groups of several despotic species of macaques ($N = 16$, Tau = 0.62, $P < 0.01$ two-tailed, partial for sexual dimorphism, $P < 0.001$ two-tailed).

Sexual "Exchange"

Sexual attraction in real animals is usually thought to be accompanied by strategies of exchange. For instance, chimpanzee males are described as exchanging sex for food with certain females (e.g., see Goodall 1986; Gomes and Boesch 2009). Yet, despite detailed statistical studies in which statistical dependency of recurring individuals were taken into account, no evidence has been found to support the idea that males copulate more (or have increased offspring) with precisely those females with whom food has been shared (Hemelrijk et al. 1992; Hemelrijk et al. 1999). Recently, Gomes and Boesch (2009) claim to have found such patterns, but they did not take statistical dependency into account. In general, males have been found to share food with females more often and to be more tolerant toward females during estrus despite the absence of noticeable benefits for males. Thus, another explanation is needed, and DomWorld provides it.

DomWorld represents sexual attraction of males to females by giving the males a greater inclination to approach females than males (by one step), whereas females ignore sexual identity (Figure 15.1). This sexual attraction appears to increase relative female dominance over males, due to the higher frequency of intersexual interactions. Thus, males are more tolerant of females, not as a kind of exchange, but as a kind of "timidity." Increase in female dominance occurs both when females cycle synchronously and asynchronously and

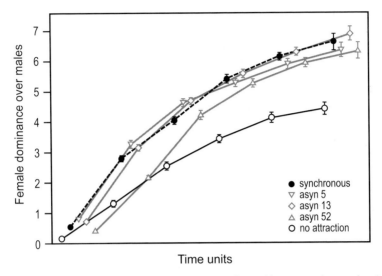

Figure 15.6 Female dominance over males over time without sexual attraction (control: no attraction) as well as when attracted to females that cycle synchronously (synchronous) and asynchronously (asyn); 5, 13, 52 are arbitrary intervals between subsequent periods of estrus (Hemelrijk et al. 2003; Hemelrijk and Wantia 2005).

for different cycle lengths (Figure 15.6) (for details of the underlying mechanisms, see Hemelrijk et al. 2003). These results are in line with the observation that female dominance in chimpanzees increases when males are sexually attracted to the females (Yerkes 1940). Studies are needed to determine whether female dominance over males increases during sexual attraction in other species as well.

Coalitions: Reciprocation of Support

Coalitions occur when a third individual aggressively intervenes in a dominance interaction between two opponents. Coalition formation is considered a sign of intelligence because it requires simultaneous negotiations with two or more individuals (Harcourt and de Waal 1992). When reciprocation of support at a group level was found in chimpanzees and macaques, this was thought to have resulted from a desire to pay back in return for services received by keeping records of acts given to and received from each group member (de Waal and Luttrell 1988). In a coalition, an intervener is not only supposed to "support" one of the opponents, she is also supposed to intentionally "oppose" the one she attacks (de Waal and Luttrell 1988). When chimpanzees (but not macaques) appeared to reciprocate "opposition," de Waal and Luttrell interpreted this as evidence for the higher intelligence of apes compared to macaques.

However, in a subsequent study of the same group of chimpanzees, reciprocation of opposition was absent not only among males, but also among females as well as all adults (Hemelrijk and Ek 1991). This difference may have resulted from two important shortcomings in the methods of analysis used by de Waal and Luttrell (1988): First, in contrast to Hemelrijk and Ek, de Waal and Luttrell included data collected ad libitum and merged data collected over five consecutive summers, although several changes in group stability had occurred, and males had switched ranks and changed coalition partners. Second, their statistical method did not take into account individual variation, whereas the Kr test used by Hemelrijk and Ek does (Hemelrijk 1990).

Furthermore, studies of DomWorld have shown that reciprocation of support in fights may also emerge in the absence of any intention to help others or to reciprocate, or to keep records of acts given and received (Hemelrijk 1996b, 1997). In DomWorld, where individuals merely group and perform self-reinforcing dominance interactions, support is recorded if, by accident, a third individual attacks one of two individuals that were opponents in a preceding activation. Reciprocation at a group level occurs in the model, just as in empirical data, when individuals appear to support more often those partners from whom they have received support more frequently (tested by means of the TauKr correlation between a matrix of support given and received) (Hemelrijk 1990). This occurs in about 50% of the runs. Reciprocation appeared to arise from a kind of social facilitation due to tit-for-tat-like interactions. There were strings of immediate reciprocation of support when two collaborators (A and B in Figure 15.7) together chased away a third individual (C): By fleeing from

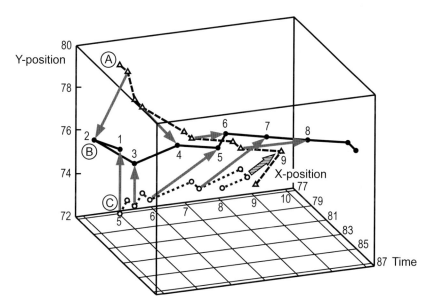

Figure 15.7   Series of events during immediate reciprocation of support. Arrows indicate acts of attack. The accompanying numbers indicate subsequent events. At the ninth time step (thick arrow) one of the supporters attacks the other (Hemelrijk 1997).

one opponent, the victim ended up in the attack range of the other. Such a series ended, for example, when C fled outside the attack range of both collaborators, or when the collaborators entered each other's attack range (and thus, attacked each other), or when uninvolved individuals happened to come too close and thus sparked an interaction with one of the three. In dense groups, uninvolved individuals are often in close proximity to others. Consequently, such series were interrupted sooner and thus, reciprocation happened less often than in sparser groups (Hemelrijk 1996b). Series of immediate reciprocation arise, therefore, from the intertwined effects of aggression and social cohesion, but without the supposed underlying cognition.

Reconciliation of Fights, Reciprocation, and the Exchange of Grooming

Grooming the fur of others has been considered an altruistic trait (i.e., one that is more beneficial to the receiver than the actor). According to the theory of reciprocal altruism, grooming should be either reciprocated or exchanged for other services. Regarding exchange, it has been suggested that individuals groom others of higher rank more often, because more effective support can be expected in return (Seyfarth 1977). Therefore, primates are expected to groom up the hierarchy, particularly in despotic societies. This pattern was not expected for egalitarian societies, because the differences in power, and thus in efficiency of support, are small (Barrett et al. 1999). In addition, individuals were supposed to keep track of the number of grooming acts given and received (de Waal and Luttrell 1988).

Primates have been observed to groom a former opponent more often immediately after a fight than at other times (Aureli and de Waal 2000)—a behavior known as "reconciliation." To reconcile, individuals are supposed to remember a former fight, be selectively attracted to the opponent, and have a conciliatory disposition. Individuals appeared to reconcile more often with those partners that were more "valuable" (i.e., with whom they groomed more often outside the context of a fight). To explain these findings, primates were supposed to cognitively evaluate and trace the value of an affiliative relationship (Aureli and de Waal 2000). Remarkably, the conciliatory tendency appeared to be higher in egalitarian than in despotic species. This was explained by arguing that in egalitarian societies more reconciliation is needed because individuals are less certain about their relationships due to the similarity of their dominance ranks (Thierry 1990).

All of these patterns (including the differences between egalitarian and despotic societies) emerge, however, in DomWorld when a single, cognitively simple, rule is added to groom others (Figure 15.1) (Puga-Gonzalez et al. 2009): when individuals encounter others in their personal space, they consider grooming only when they estimate that they will lose a fight; when they are more anxious, their inclination to groom is greater (Keverne et al. 1989; Schino and Troisi 1992). This rule is based on the well-known calming and rewarding effect of grooming (see also Shutt et al. 2007). In the model, increased stress is caused by fighting as well as by the time elapsed without grooming (Keverne et al. 1989). To determine how patterns emerge in the model, now called GroofiWorld (Puga-Gonzalez et al. 2009), experiments were conducted in which some of the assumptions, such as that grooming depends on spatial proximity, were omitted. This led to the following explanations.

Reciprocation of grooming emerges without record keeping in the model. It emerges because individuals have a greater chance to groom certain individuals than others, because they are more often closer to them than others. This spatial heterogeneity, in turn, results from aggressive interactions.

In our model, as in baboons (Barrett et al. 1999), individuals groom up the hierarchy when it is steep (thus when aggression is fierce), but not when it is weak. In contrast to what was suggested for primates (Seyfarth 1977; Barrett et al. 1999), this happens *without* the intention of individuals to obtain support in return. In the model, individuals groom others more often the higher the rank of the partners when rank differences are so great that lower-ranking individuals are inhibited to attack out of fear of being defeated. Consequently, they often groom higher-ranking ones instead.

To our astonishment, individuals in GroofiWorld also "reconcile" their fights (as measured by the PC-MC method; Veenema et al. 1994). This happens even though individuals have neither a conciliatory tendency nor insight into the value of affinitive relationships. This seemingly conciliatory behavior arises because former opponents are in closer proximity after a fight than otherwise. Close proximity after a fight may be responsible for patterns that resemble reconciliation in real primates as well: the conciliatory tendency appears to be decreased when distance between opponents after a fight is made more similar to that during the matched control (Matsumura 1996; Call 1999; Arnold and Whiten 2001). Further empirical work is clearly needed.

In both the model and in reality, "reconciliation" is more frequent in societies with mild aggression and a weak hierarchy (resembling egalitarian societies) than in those with fierce aggression. In real primates, Thierry (1990) states that this higher frequency of reconciliation in egalitarian societies is necessary because individuals are less certain about relationships, due to a weak hierarchy. In GroofiWorld, however, higher frequency of reconciliation emerges even though there is no greater uncertainty about relationships. It emerges because a lower percentage of interaction time is spent on grooming when aggression is fierce than mild. This, in turn, results from spatial centrality: dominants have more opportunities to interact with others. Since they experience fewer risks, dominants are more often aggressive and groom others less frequently than lower-ranking individuals. Therefore, grooming becomes rarer when aggression is fierce than mild. Consequently, grooming after a fight is also rarer. In data of real animals, this might well be misinterpreted as if fewer fights are "reconciled."

In the model, individuals "reconcile" fights more often with their so-called "valuable" partners, although they have neither knowledge nor understanding of their affiliative relationships. This is a side-effect of dominance: individuals groom higher-ranking ones more often and "reconcile" with them more frequently. As a result, they "reconcile" more often with individuals with whom they groom more frequently (i.e., their "more valuable partners"). (This, however, only occurs when the hierarchy is steep.)

Evaluation and Future Work

These kinds of models have been used to study social organization of moving groups of locusts (Buhl et al. 2006), fish (Couzin et al. 2002; Hemelrijk et al. 2010), birds (Hildenbrandt et al. 2010) and primates (te Boekhorst and Hemelrijk 2000). They explain the complexity of social behavior by showing that, although usually attributed to cognition or genetic architecture, complexity may be determined by spatially induced (nonrandom) reactions among individuals as well as by interactions between individuals and their environment. Consequently, these models generate innovative explanations. In the studies related to primates mentioned above, such models show that many complex patterns of social interaction may result from the spatial organization of group members, the self-reinforcing effects of victory and defeat, risk sensitivity of attack, and the tension-reducing effect of grooming.

Further empirical studies are needed to test the above-mentioned parsimonious, model-based hypotheses. In particular, the interconnections between spatial structures, dominance style, intersexual dominance, and patterns of affiliation (e.g., reconciliation, reciprocation, and exchange of grooming) should be pursued.

Acknowledgments

This chapter benefited from the discussions at the Ernst Strüngmann Forum as well as from comments on an earlier draft by Kristin Andrews, Randolf Menzel, Josef Perner, Brandon Wheeler, and an anonymous referee.

16

Cooperation in Nonhuman Primates

Function and Cognition

Dorothy L. Cheney

Abstract

It has long been hypothesized that the demands of establishing and maintaining social relationships in complex societies place strong selective pressures on cognition and intelligence. What has been less clear, until recently, is whether these relationships, and the skills they require, confer any reproductive benefits, and whether such benefits vary across individuals. During the last few years, much progress has been made in resolving some of these questions. There is now evidence from a variety of species that animals are motivated to establish close, long-term bonds with specific partners, and that these bonds enhance longevity and offspring survival. The cognitive and emotional mechanisms underlying cooperation, however, are still not understood. It remains unclear, for example, whether animals keep track of favors given and received, and whether they rely on memory of past cooperative acts when anticipating future ones. Although most investigations with captive primates have indicated that cooperation is seldom contingency-based, several experiments conducted under more natural conditions suggest that animals do take into account recent interactions when supporting others. Moreover, while interactions within dyads are often unbalanced over short periods of time, pairs with strong bonds have strongly reciprocal interactions over extended time periods. These results suggest that the apparent rarity of contingent cooperation in animals may not stem from cognitive constraints. Instead, animals may tolerate short-term inequities in favors given and received because most cooperation occurs among long-term reciprocating partners.

Introduction

It has long been hypothesized that the demands of establishing and maintaining bonds in large social groups has placed strong selective pressures on animal cognition. Research over the last thirty years has demonstrated that many animals—including, in particular, nonhuman primates—may indeed recognize other individuals' social relationships, intentions, and perhaps even knowledge states (Cheney and Seyfarth 2007; Call and Tomasello 2008). What has been less clear, until recently, is whether these relationships, and the skills they require, confer any reproductive benefits, and whether such benefits vary across individuals. Doubts even persist about whether animals have the cognitive capacity or motivation to maintain long-term relationships. It remains unclear, for example, whether animals keep track of support given and received, and whether they rely on memory of past cooperative acts when anticipating future ones. Some problems are methodological, arising from the difficulties of testing cooperation experimentally under natural conditions. Others stem from the different results obtained from observations of wild animals as opposed to those living in captivity.

Here, I first describe results which suggest that the ability to maintain long-term social relationships confers significant reproductive benefits. Thereafter I discuss some of the many outstanding questions regarding the function of cooperation in animals and the cognitive mechanisms that may underlie them. My discussion is restricted to species that exhibit relatively low reproductive skew including, in particular, Old World monkeys and apes.

Cooperation among Long-Term Partners

Function

If knowledge of other individuals' relationships and mental states is adaptive, it should be possible to identify correlations between social knowledge and reproductive success. Although these have not yet been documented, there is growing evidence that animals are motivated to form social bonds, and that there is individual variation not only in the strength and consistency of social bonds but also that this variation is correlated with reproductive success.

Several studies have demonstrated that primates balance grooming exchanges with long-term partners. Among female baboons (*Papio hamadryas* spp.), for example, grooming within dyads is often unbalanced over short periods of time. However, pairs who groom each other frequently have strongly reciprocal grooming relations over extended time periods (Silk and House 2011). A similar pattern characterizes male chimpanzees (*Pan troglodytes*) (Mitani 2009b).

The close bonds that arise through long-term grooming relationships are also correlated with reproductive success. Female chacma baboons (*P. h. ursinus*) who maintain strong bonds with other adult females experience higher offspring survival and live significantly longer than females with weaker bonds (Silk et al. 2009, 2010). These effects are independent of dominance status, suggesting that close bonds may offset any fitness loss due to low rank.

Importantly, the fact that most females' partner changes are not due to the death of the partner suggests that some females may be more skilled or more motivated than others in maintaining relationships with preferred partners over time. These findings parallel evidence from humans which shows that social integration enhances longevity and health (Holt-Lunstad et al. 2010).

There remains some uncertainty about the direction of the causal links between social bonds and fitness. One causal factor may be related to stress. For example, female mice (*Mus musculus*), who often rear pups communally, reproduce more successfully when they are allowed to choose their nestmates than when nestmates are assigned randomly (Weidt et al. 2008). Rat (*Rattus norgevicus*) sisters with well-balanced affiliative relationships exhibit lower glucocorticoid levels, fewer tumors, and higher survival rates than sisters with less well-balanced relationships (Yee et al. 2008). Similarly, female chacma baboons display marked increases in glucocorticoid levels when a preferred partner dies. In the same population, females experience lower glucocorticoid levels when their grooming interactions are focused on only a small number of partners, and females with more focused grooming patterns show less pronounced responses to various stressors, including the immigration of potentially infanticidal males (Cheney and Seyfarth 2009).

Mechanisms

The psychological mechanisms that underlie animals' social interactions and relationships are not yet understood. Because we have no evidence that animals can plan or anticipate the benefits that might derive from a long-term relationship, a number of investigators have argued that animals' cooperative interactions are motivated only by short-term rewards, such as the opportunity to handle an infant or gain access to food. According to these arguments, social interactions are not founded on long-term patterns of affiliation but are based instead on short-term by-product mutualism or biological markets motivated by the likelihood of immediate reward (Noe and Hammerstein 1994). These arguments certainly have some validity. Much cooperative behavior in primates and some other animals (e.g., spotted hyenas, *Crocuta crocuta*) occurs in the form of low cost services like alliance support against lower-ranking opponents (Smith et al. 2010). Because these alliances confer direct and immediate benefits by reinforcing the status quo, they may represent a form of mutualism. Similarly, when a female baboon grooms another, she may simply be engaging in a short-term negotiation with a trading partner who controls a desirable commodity, like an infant (Henzi and Barrett 2007).

Not all social interactions, however, are based on the value and supply of alternative trading partners; many others reflect long-term patterns of affiliation. Although female baboons, for example, form long-term bonds with only a small number of other females, these bonds can endure for years despite short-term fluctuations in interaction rates. Moreover, grooming often occurs in the absence of an immediate reward, and it is seldom evenly balanced between partners within single bouts—even among partners who have strongly reciprocal grooming interactions over extended periods of time.

Contingent Cooperation

Over the last decade, there has also been increasing skepticism about the relevance of contingent-based reciprocity in the social interactions of animals. Because most cooperative interactions like grooming occur between long-term partners (often kin) for whom any single altruistic act may be relatively insignificant, many investigators are now convinced that the sort of reciprocal altruism first proposed by Trivers (1971) may be both rare and fragile in nature (Hammerstein 2003; Clutton-Brock 2009). Although there is limited experimental and correlational evidence that animals sometimes rely on memory of recent interactions when behaving altruistically toward others, interpretation has been complicated by a paucity of convincing examples, the absence of important controls in some early tests, and a number of experimental studies seeming to indicate that animals lack the cognitive or empathetic ability to sustain contingent cooperative exchanges.

Reciprocal altruism (Trivers 1971; see also Schino and Aureli 2009) occurs when the donor of an altruistic act incurs an immediate cost but receives delayed benefits when the recipient reciprocates the altruistic act at some future time. For reciprocal altruism to evolve, individuals must have a high probability of meeting again, and they must be able to detect or avoid cheaters. Reciprocal altruism can be distinguished from mutualism, in which both participants receive immediate benefits that outweigh any associated costs, and from kin selection, in which the donor gains inclusive fitness benefits despite incurring costs. Because the costs and benefits of many altruistic acts are difficult to quantify, I will here use the term *contingent cooperation* rather than *reciprocal altruism* to describe altruistic behavior whose occurrence is contingent upon a specific previous supportive act. This definition is agnostic with respect to the precise costs and benefits of the altruistic behavior; it posits only that A's support of B is causally dependent upon a previous supportive act by B toward A.

Cognitive Constraints

Doubts persist about whether animals possess the cognitive abilities to sustain contingent cooperation. These include the ability to remember specific interactions, to delay reward, to track favors given and returned, to plan and anticipate future outcomes, and to distinguish between cooperators and defectors (Stevens et al. 2005a; Henzi and Barrett 2007; Melis and Semmann 2010). Some of these objections may be unjustified. Playback experiments on baboons have demonstrated, for example, that females' behavior is strongly influenced by the memory of single interactions with specific individuals (Cheney and Seyfarth 2007). If a baboon hears another female's "reconciliatory" grunt shortly after being threatened by her, she behaves as if the grunt is causally related to the recent fight and directed specifically to her as a signal of benign intent. As a result, she is more likely to approach her former opponent and to tolerate her opponent's approaches than if she has heard the grunt of another female unrelated to her opponent. By contrast, if she hears the same female's threat-grunts shortly after grooming with that female, she acts as if she assumes that the calls are being directed at another female, because females seldom threaten a recent grooming partner. In both cases, females' responses appear to be guided by memory of the quality of a specific recent interaction. The extent to which this memory is explicit is as yet unknown.

Other purported cognitive limitations can also be questioned. There is now a large literature on animals' numerical discrimination abilities suggesting that quantity assessments are widespread across many taxa (Shettleworth 2010b). Similarly, although many tests with primates have suggested a general failure to delay rewards beyond short time periods, there appears to be considerable interindividual variation in self-imposed delayed gratification. Moreover, the ability of primates and other animals to delay gratification in contexts that do not involve food rewards remains largely untested. Thus, contingent cooperation in animals is not necessarily constrained by the inability to delay reward or to quantify past cooperative acts.

It has also been assumed that animals are not capable of contingent cooperation because it demands the anticipation of future interactions. Leaving aside for the moment the question of whether mental projections of future outcomes are necessary to sustain contingent cooperation, the assumption that animals are unable to anticipate future events may not be valid. There is a long history in experimental psychology of tests demonstrating that many animals accurately and predictably anticipate future rewards and outcomes (Shettleworth 2010b). Furthermore, a growing number of experiments suggest that primates make prospective decisions based on certainty judgments about their past behavior (Hampton, this volume).

It is also doubtful whether nonhuman primates are unable to distinguish cooperators from noncooperators. In tests conducted in captivity that require two individuals to work together to obtain a food reward, both capuchin monkeys and chimpanzees are more likely to cooperate with partners with whom rewards are shared more equitably (de Waal and Davis 2003; Melis et al. 2006b, 2009; Silk and House 2011). Chimpanzees also recognize which partners are most effective (Melis et al. 2006a) and show a limited ability to increase their rate of cooperation with partners who have cooperated with them in the past (Melis et al. 2008). They may also be able to resolve conflicts of interests when working together to achieve a common goal (Melis et al. 2009).

Emotional Constraints

In humans, inequity aversion, tolerance, and the motivation to engage in joint activities are important catalysts for cooperative behavior. Whether primates are motivated by these emotions, however, remains unclear. Some experiments have suggested that primates reject food offered by humans if a rival is receiving a better reward (e.g., Brosnan and de Waal 2003). Other studies have failed to replicate these findings and suggest that the food rejections are due not to perceived inequality but rather to frustration at seeing, but not obtaining, a preferred food item (e.g., Bräuer et al. 2006; Dubreuil et al. 2006). In captivity, chimpanzees seem generally indifferent to inequitable returns to themselves and others. In experiments in which chimpanzees have the opportunity to deliver food to a partner at no cost to themselves, for example, subjects show no sensitivity to the consequences for their partner (Silk et al. 2005; Jensen et al. 2006). They do not behave spitefully or withhold food from their partner; they simply ignore their partner's returns. In other experimental paradigms, however, chimpanzees have been observed to assist one another in collaborative tasks involving food rewards (Greenberg et al. 2010), suggesting that chimpanzee helping behavior may involve some consideration of partners' outcomes.

It has also been argued that a lack of social tolerance may contribute to the low levels of cooperation displayed by chimpanzees in many experiments. Bonobos (*Pan paniscus*) achieve higher levels of success in some cooperative tasks than do chimpanzees, seemingly because their willingness to share rewards with their partners prompts continued cooperation (Hare et al. 2007). It remains unclear, however, whether bonobos also show higher degrees of cooperation and tolerance under natural conditions, where the structure and rewards of the task are not determined by humans. It is not known, for example, whether bonobos show higher levels of cooperation than chimpanzees when hunting, or whether they share their kills more equitably. Similarly, it is not apparent whether bonobos ever engage in any behavior that is as cooperative and potentially costly as chimpanzees' patrolling behavior (Mitani et al. 2010), or if they do, whether they are more likely than chimpanzees to share risks equitably.

Taken together, results suggest that cooperation in animals may be sustained by qualitatively different mechanisms than it is in humans. Indeed, experiments explicitly designed to compare the behavior of children and chimpanzees indicate that humans may be uniquely motivated to engage others' attention, share their intentions, emotions, and knowledge, and impose sanctions on noncooperators (Tomasello et al. 2005; Warneken and Tomasello 2009; Melis and Semmann 2010). It is also possible, however, that inequity aversion may be less universal in humans than is often supposed. Surveys of people living in societies that lack large-scale religions and economic markets tend to reveal a general indifference to unfair outcomes (Henrich et al. 2010), suggesting that what is often regarded as a species-specific prosociality in humans is not entirely the result of innate psychological mechanisms.

Measuring Contingent Cooperation

For several reasons, it has proved difficult to investigate contingent cooperation under natural conditions. First, in the absence of experiments, it is almost impossible to determine whether a given altruistic act is causally dependent upon a specific prior interaction. Second, many altruistic acts occur in different currencies (e.g., grooming and alliance support) whose relative values are difficult to calibrate. Moreover, even altruistic acts that occur in the same currency may not carry equal value for each participant. In species which form dominance hierarchies, a low-ranking individual may value alliance support from a more dominant partner more highly than vice versa. As a result, the individual may provide substantially more support to the dominant partner than is received in return yet still regard the relationship as reciprocal. Given these tautological assumptions, almost any relationship can be termed reciprocal. Finally, the degree to which interactions are regarded as reciprocal may be a function of the timescale under consideration. As already mentioned, grooming exchanges within single bouts are often unbalanced and asymmetrical. Nonetheless, over longer time periods, partners with close social bonds exhibit a high degree of reciprocity in their grooming interactions.

Observational Evidence

Correlations between grooming and alliance support have been documented in a variety of primates (Silk 2007c). In a meta-analysis involving 14 primate species, Schino et al. (2007) found a weak but highly significant correlation between grooming and alliances among long-term partners over extended periods, but little evidence that alliance support is motivated by a specific recent grooming bout. Indeed, in one study of captive Japanese macaques, kin were never observed to support each other in the half hour after grooming, even when they had the opportunity to do so (Schino et al. 2007). Similarly, although female spotted hyenas form the majority of their alliances with close kin, there is no evidence that this support is reciprocal or based on the memory of a specific recent interaction (Smith et al. 2010).

Among male chimpanzees, individuals who groom most often are also those who form alliances and share meat at the highest rates. Cooperation thus involves the exchange of services in different currencies, with males reciprocating grooming for support, support for meat, and so on. Although exchanges are often asymmetrical within dyads over short time periods, they become more evenly balanced over longer periods of time and are not simply a by-product of association frequency or genetic relatedness (Mitani 2006; Boesch 2011).

The most costly cooperative behavior shown by male chimpanzees occurs during boundary patrols, when the males from one community make incursions into the territories of their neighbors (Mitani et al. 2010; Boesch 2011). These incursions are risky and sometimes fatal, because a small party or lone individual is vulnerable to attack if they encounter a larger party; incursions, therefore, cannot be undertaken alone. Although it remains unclear whether patrols are planned, they appear to involve some degree of shared intentionality and a high degree of mutual support. Little is known about the mechanisms that motivate chimpanzees to initiate and participate in these highly cooperative and potentially costly activities. It is not known, for example, whether chimpanzees take into consideration memory of another individual's behavior during previous patrols when deciding whether or not to join him in a patrol. Whether cooperation in this context is more, or less, contingent upon memory of previous events, remains unclear.

In sum, most observational studies suggest that cooperation under natural conditions is not contingent upon specific recent events. Instead, reciprocal exchanges tend to emerge gradually among regular partners over repeated interactions, despite not being balanced over short time periods.

Experimental Evidence

Although chimpanzees' interactions with preferred partners become reciprocal over extended periods of time, tests on captive subjects suggest that reciprocity is not contingency-based. For example, in one experiment with captive chimpanzees, subjects were given a choice of cooperating with either an individual who had previously helped them or one who had not (Melis et al. 2008). Although there was some evidence that subjects increased their cooperation with the more helpful partner, this effect was relatively weak, and subjects did not consistently avoid noncooperators. In another experiment deliberately designed to test whether cooperation was contingency-based, Brosnan et al. (2009) found no evidence that chimpanzees were more likely to provide food to a partner if that partner had previously provided food to them. Melis et al. (2006b) suggest that chimpanzees may be capable of contingent reciprocity, but that long-term partner preferences which develop over repeated interactions may override the decisions that chimpanzees make on the basis of immediate exchanges and rewards.

The lack of evidence for contingent cooperation in tests with captive animals may also result from the stringent standards set by these experiments, which have typically required proof of equal back-and-forth exchanges in a single currency—food—whose amounts and timing are determined by humans. These requirements may have set the bar unrealistically high, leading investigators to underestimate the extent to which a recent cooperative interaction may motivate animals to cooperate again.

Several investigations conducted under more natural conditions have provided more positive indications of contingent cooperation. Unfortunately, however, interpretation has been complicated by the lack of follow-up experiments to correct for potential confounds. For example, in the well-known study of vampire bats (*Desmodus rotundus*) most reciprocal exchanges of blood occurred among close kin (Wilkinson 1984). Although some individuals regularly exchanged blood with unrelated partners, it was not clear whether any specific act of regurgitation was contingent upon a specific recent donation.

An investigation of mobbing behavior in pied flycatchers (*Ficedula hypoleuca*) provides more convincing evidence for contingent cooperation (Krams et al. 2008). In this experiment, subjects had the opportunity to help one of two neighbors mob an owl. One of these neighbors had recently helped the subjects to mob an owl at their own nest box, while the other had been prevented from doing so by the experimenters. Subjects were significantly more likely to help previous supporters than apparent defectors, suggesting that cooperative behavior was contingent upon memory of the neighbors' behavior. However, the possibility that the birds' behavior might have been influenced by *any* recent interaction with their neighbors—not just a supportive one—was not addressed.

This confound was also present in Seyfarth and Cheney's (1984) playback experiment on wild vervet monkeys. Although subjects were more attentive to the recruitment call of an unrelated female after grooming with her than after no interaction, it remained unclear whether subjects might have been equally responsive after *any* interaction with her, including even aggression. Subsequently, Hemelrijk (1994) demonstrated that grooming increased the probability of actual alliance support in an experiment with captive long-tailed macaques.

Recently, we conducted a playback experiment with wild baboons that attempted to control for some of these confounds (Cheney et al. 2010). In the test condition, a subject was played the recruitment call of another female at least 10 minutes after she had groomed with that female and then separated without any further interactions. This playback was designed to mimic a context in which the former grooming partner was threatening another individual and soliciting aid. Each subject's responses were compared to her responses in two control conditions. The first control was also conducted after the subject and the same female had groomed and then separated for at least 10 minutes. In this case, however, no playback was conducted. This control was designed to test whether a recent friendly interaction might simply motivate the subject to approach her partner again, even in the absence of any solicitation for support. In the second control, the same female's threat-grunts were played to the same subject at least 10 minutes after the subject had threatened that female. This control was designed to test whether subjects' responses to a recruitment call were primed by any prior interaction, not just a friendly one.

Results provided some support for delayed contingent cooperation among unrelated individuals. Hearing the recruitment call of a recent grooming partner caused subjects to move in the direction of the loudspeaker and approach their former partner. When the subject and her partner were close kin, no such effect was observed. Importantly, subjects' responses were not influenced by *any* type of recent interaction, because subjects only responded to their former partner's recruitment call after grooming, and not after aggression. Similarly, their responses were not prompted only by the motivation to resume a friendly interaction, because prior grooming alone did not elicit approach. Instead, subjects were most likely to approach their grooming partner when they had also heard her recruitment call. Thus, females' willingness to attend to the recruitment calls of other individuals appeared to be prompted at least in part by memory of a specific friendly interaction.

In sum, several factors may interact to motivate contingent cooperation in animals under natural conditions: the strength of the partners' social relationship, the nature of their recent interactions, and the opportunity to reengage in some form of cooperative behavior. Animals appear to possess many of the cognitive abilities thought to be essential for the emergence of contingent cooperation, if only in rudimentary form. Nonetheless, such cooperation appears to be less common than the noncontingent cooperation that develops among kin and long-term partners.

Detection of Noncooperators

If cooperation depends in part on the memory of previous behavior, why do animals seldom avoid or punish cheaters and free-loaders? In captivity, chimpanzees continue to work with noncooperators despite receiving inequitable returns (Melis et al. 2006b, 2009). While they retaliate against an individual who steals food from them, they do not attempt to punish those who obtain disproportionate rewards, and they are not spiteful (Jensen et al. 2007b; Melis et al. 2009; Silk and House 2011).

Under natural conditions, free-loaders also appear to be tolerated. To provide two examples, individual lionesses (*Panthera leo*) vary predictably in their participation in territorial conflicts. In playback experiments that simulated the approach of an aggressive intruder, some females consistently advanced toward the source of the calls, whereas others consistently lagged behind, avoiding the potential cost of a conflict (Heinsohn and Packer 1995). Advancers appeared to be aware of the laggards' behavior, because they often looked back at them; nonetheless, they did not subsequently avoid or punish them. It is possible that advancers tolerate laggards because they derive inclusive fitness benefits through the laggards' survival and reproduction. Laggards may also cooperate in other currencies, such as hunting. It is also possible, however, that lions do not have the cognitive ability to recognize laggards as free-loaders, with the result that laggards are able to exploit advancers.

Similarly, male chimpanzees do not participate equally in boundary patrols. Some individuals are allowed to reap the benefits of territorial integrity without incurring any costs. Mitani (2006, 2009a) offers several possible explanations for chimpanzees' tolerance of free-loaders. First, the benefits of patrolling may be greater for some individuals than others. Perhaps patrolling is a costly signal that enhances an individual's dominance or access to females. Second, patrolling may yield indirect fitness benefits in the form of enhanced survival and reproduction of close kin. Thus, males with more kin in the community may engage in higher rates of patrolling. Finally, chimpanzees may lack the cognitive capacity to foster or infer deceptive intent. If true, animals may well not be capable of achieving the sort of contingent cooperation manifested by humans, which is sustained in part by inequity aversion and sensitivity to envy, spite, and deception (Jensen et al. 2007b; Melis and Semmann 2010).

This last objection, however, only denies the possibility for human-like contingent cooperation in animals; it does not rule it out entirely. The detection of cheaters does not, in principle, require the ability to impute complex mental states like deception to others. It could arise through relatively simple associative processes, by which animals learn to avoid individuals whose presence is associated with a negative experience.

Indeed, mental state attribution may be irrelevant to contingent cooperation in animals. Schino and Aureli (2009) have argued that the focus on cognitive constraints in discussions of contingent cooperation is misguided and confuses proximate and ultimate explanations for behavior. Altruistic behaviors may be favored by natural selection because of the subsequent benefits they confer, but what motivates animals to behave altruistically are the previous benefits they have received. In this view, the accumulation of multiple, cooperative exchanges over time causes animals to form partner-specific emotional bonds that prompt future altruistic behavior. Thus, reciprocity may be maintained by a kind of partner-specific "emotional book-keeping" (Schino and Aureli 2009) that permits long-term tracking of multiple partners and facilitates cooperation in different behavioral currencies. The resulting bonds that develop between preferred partners may motivate future positive interactions without the need for explicit tabulation of favors given and returned, or calculations of anticipated benefits (Aureli and Schaffner 2002). For unrelated females who interact at low rates, a single grooming bout may temporarily elevate a female's positive emotions toward her partner sufficiently above baseline to influence her immediate interactions with her. In contrast, grooming and support among females with close bonds (who are also usually kin) should be less subject to immediate contingencies and less influenced by single interactions. Many of these proximate mechanisms may also motivate social interactions in humans. It seems unlikely that the formation of close bonds among humans is driven by expectations that such bonds will enhance health and longevity.

Finally, it is important to emphasize that while the absence of punishment in animals may derive partly from cognitive constraints, a strict accounting of services given and received is likely maladaptive in stable societies where individuals establish close bonds and interact regularly in a variety of contexts. In fact, although the cognitive constraints that supposedly limit contingent cooperation in animals is often contrasted with humans' sensitivity to inequitable exchanges, human friendships are rarely contingency-based. Numerous studies have shown that people seldom keep tabs of costs and benefits in interactions with regular partners (Silk 2003a). Although people become resentful and dissatisfied when exchanges within a friendship are consistently unbalanced, tallying of favors given and received is typically reserved for infrequent associates.

These observations emphasize, again, the importance of separating proximate and ultimate explanations when considering cooperation in animals. Whether animals have the cognitive capacity to engage in contingent cooperation is one issue; whether it is adaptive for them to do is another. It may well be that the relative rarity of contingent cooperation in animals stems less from the inability to keep track of recent interactions (and even, perhaps, to anticipate future ones) than from the willingness to tolerate short-term inequities with long-term partners.

Future Directions

We are only beginning to understand the many functions of cooperative behavior in animals and the cognitive and emotional mechanisms which underlie them. There have been only a handful of direct experimental tests of contingent cooperation under natural conditions, and we do not yet understand how supportive, reciprocal relationships emerge from single interactions that are often asymmetrical. Similarly, as yet there have been few attempts to document the reproductive benefits of cooperation and strong social bonds. Here, I highlight three of many possible foci for future research.

Cognition

I have argued that contingent cooperation may not require complex cognition, such as the ability to detect cheaters or to plan future cooperative acts based on memory of previous ones. Nonetheless, some animals may engage in such mental activities. There is growing evidence that many animals have some access to their knowledge states (Smith et al. 2010). Such metacognition may permit animals to weigh alternative strategies in novel contexts; it may also serve as a precursor to reading others' minds. Playback experiments indicate that baboons remember the nature of specific interactions with specific individuals, although the extent to which this memory is explicit remains to be determined. Similarly, some forms of cooperative behavior in animals (in particular, the boundary patrols of chimpanzees) strongly suggest shared intentionality, planning, and episodic memory. To date, however, these cognitive abilities have been examined only under captive conditions, in tests whose rules and constraints are determined by humans. A challenge for future research will be to devise the experimental means to examine mental state attribution and meta-cognition under more natural conditions, in contexts where these abilities may be of survival value.

Personality

Recent evidence from baboons indicates that females vary in the strength and stability of their social relationships, and that this variation contributes significantly to individual variation in reproductive success. The fact that some females fail to maintain the same partners over time also suggests that some individuals may be less skilled or motivated than others at maintaining bonds. Although the proximate mechanisms underlying these individual differences are not yet understood, they may well be related to personality traits associated with attributes like anxiety and confidence. In female primates there tends to be no correlation between stress and dominance rank or number of kin. Instead, glucocorticoid levels are more strongly influenced by the size and stability of a female's social network (Cheney and Seyfarth 2009). These observations suggest that some individuals may be more adept than others at recruiting allies, reconciling with others, or assessing the strength and stability of others' relationships. Whatever the cause, results point to the need for a stronger focus on the relation between behavior and personality.

Personality traits are influenced not only by genetic factors but also by environmental factors that affect gene expression. In both humans and rhesus macaques (*Macaca mulatta*), for example, a specific polymorphism in the serotonin transporter gene is associated with deficits in neurobiological functioning and poor control of aggression (Suomi 2007). Mothers carrying a certain version of the allele are more likely to be abusive, and both they and their infants exhibit higher cortisol levels. Indeed, maternal effects have been shown to have a profound impact on offspring dominance, hypothalamic-pituitary-adrenal axis, and personality in a variety of species (Jablonka and Raz 2009). These effects may persist across generations. Thus, genetic variation affecting factors such as serotonin and oxytocin reactivity, anxiety, and social reward may influence the strength and stability of an individual's social bonds, which in turn exert epigenetic effects in offspring. Differences in personality traits may well explain some of the individual variation in cooperative behavior.

Integration of Field and Laboratory Studies

There is currently some disconnect between results obtained in experiments with captive animals and observations derived from field observations. For example, chimpanzees in captivity seem relatively indifferent to inequitable outcomes to others and themselves and fail to reciprocate favors in back-and-forth exchanges. In the wild, however, chimpanzees often exchange grooming, alliances, and meat with specific long-term partners. In captivity, tasks which require cooperation are easily disrupted by disparities in the participants' dominance ranks, the size of the rewards, and the degree to which rewards can be monopolized. Under natural conditions, however, chimpanzees not only share meat (if inequitably) but also regularly participate in risky boundary patrols that are obligately cooperative. These discrepancies point to the need both for more detailed investigations of cooperation in the wild and, in captivity, for experiments that carry greater external validity and relevance for the participants.

17

How Folk Psychology Ruined Comparative Psychology

And How Scrub Jays Can Save It

Derek C. Penn

Abstract

The cognitive revolution in psychology was founded on the premise that all cognitive processes result from rule-governed operations and that cognizers do not need to understand these rules to act "rationally" or "intelligently." Despite its intent to replace romantic folk psychological intuitions about how the mind works, anthropomorphism is prevalent throughout much of comparative psychology: claims that animals perform "human-like" feats find broad acceptance in the media and permeate the academic debate, while less anthropomorphic explanations are largely dismissed. To construct a viable scientific theory of nonhuman minds, comparative psychology must aim for a computationally explicit account of cognition—not just folk psychological descriptions. Given the impressive body of data that has been collected on the social cognitive abilities of scrub jays, compiling a functional specification of corvid social cognition would be a great place to start.

Introduction

Recently, a pair of papers appeared in *Current Biology* claiming that chimpanzees may have a human-like understanding of death (Anderson et al. 2010; Biro et al. 2010). In the first paper, boldly entitled, "Pan Thanatology," Anderson et al. (2010) describe how a group of chimpanzees living in a Scottish safari park "grieved" over the death of an elderly female chimp named Pansy. The researchers claim that a chimp named Chippie "appeared to test for signs of life by closely inspecting [Pansy's] mouth and manipulating her limbs" (Anderson et al. 2010:R350). They admit that Chippie also attacked the corpse three times, jumping and pounding on the body. However, the researchers suggest these acts were an expression of "denial," "frustration," and "anger toward the deceased" or perhaps an attempt at "resuscitation" (Anderson et al. 2010:R350).

The authors provide no evidence for these colorful suggestions other than the fact that the animal's behavior was, as they put it, "strikingly reminiscent of human responses to peaceful death" (Anderson et al. 2010:R350).

In an accompanying paper in the same issue of *Current Biology*, Biro et al. (2010) describe how two mothers, whose infants had died of a respiratory epidemic, carried the bodies of their dead children around for days, even after the infants' bodies had undergone complete mummification. The "fascinating" question, the authors write, is the extent to which the chimp mothers "understood" that their offspring were dead (scare quotes taken from the original). The authors do not claim, however, that the mothers "understood" that their offspring were dead and, indeed, do not believe that the evidence warrants such an interpretation. "In many ways," Biro et al. (2010:R352) point out, "[the two mothers] treated the corpses as live infants, particularly in the initial phase following death." Indeed, in all of her discussions with the media, Biro explains, "[I] made it very clear that we had no idea whether the carrying of the corpses in any way reflected an understanding of death...or whether any of the responses the mothers and other individuals in the group showed toward the dead infants had any parallels with human responses to death" (Biro, personal email Nov. 9, 2010).[1]

These two papers were cited by hundreds of mainstream media outlets as if they both supported the same anthropomorphic conclusion. *AP Press* carried the story under the headline, "Chimps deal with death like humans." *NPR* entitled their story, "Chimps May Mourn Lost Ones, Study Suggests." Like Anderson et al. (2010), the mainstream media expressed few doubts that chimps understand death in a human-like way. Indeed, *Discovery News* opined that this finding was not even particularly surprising and then published a video clip of a squirrel attempting to "resuscitate" a dead comrade (Viegas 2010). Biro et al.'s more careful assessment of the evidence was hardly mentioned.

It would be nice if one could blame this case on the hyperbole of commercial media outlets or the radical views of a fringe movement in comparative psychology. However, stories such as these are ubiquitous. Hardly an issue of *Current Biology* or *Animal Cognition* goes by without some new effigy of human cognitive uniqueness being torn down and dragged through the mud. The authors of these claims rarely bother to elucidate alternative interpretations that don't convey an anthropomorphic story line (Shettleworth 2010b). Far from being a fringe movement, Anderson et al. (2010) represent the reigning consensus among comparative psychologists when they argue that "the differences between humans and our great ape relatives aren't as marked as most people think."

---

[1] In fact, Biro says she favors the hypothesis that the chimps' behavior was a by-product of the strong mother-infant bond in chimpanzees and acknowledges that the choice of the word, "understand," was "unfortunate." It is "too bad," she writes, "that the article didn't mention the by-product explanation more explicitly—we hint at it, but having it spelt out clearly would have been the right thing to do" (Biro personal email, Nov. 18, 2010).

From tool use to metacognition, from deception to death, much of comparative psychology over the last 35 years has been driven by the single-minded goal of demonstrating that nonhuman animals are capable of "human-like" cognition. This "anthropocentric approach" to comparative psychology, as Shettleworth (2010a) calls it, has tended to emphasize the mental continuity between humans and other animals and to treat nonhuman animals as "little furry or feathered people." Vast numbers of comparative psychologists, of course, quietly continue to pursue more careful, ecologically grounded research projects (for a review, see Shettleworth 2010a). Those claiming that animals are capable of "human-like" feats have dominated the general media, commercial bookshelves, and much of the academic debate as well. Those favoring less anthropomorphic explanations have been shunned and/or ignored. The problem has been particularly egregious among researchers studying "Theory of Mind" (ToM), and it has only gotten worse over the last decade.

For the first twenty years after Premack and Woodruff's (1978) seminal claim, research on the ToM abilities of nonhuman animals was fraught with controversy (Heyes 1998). Over the last ten years, the consensus in support of attributing at least some aspects of a ToM to nonhuman animals has grown ever more widespread and confident (Suddendorf and Whiten 2001; Tomasello et al. 2003a; Hare and Tomasello 2005; Santos et al. 2006; Tomasello and Call 2006; Wood et al. 2007; Emery and Clayton 2009; Byrne and Bates 2010; de Waal and Ferrari 2010). Indeed, in some researchers' minds, the debate is all but over. In a recent review of the last thirty years of research on the ToM debate, Call and Tomasello (2008:189), for example, conclude: "We believe that there is only one reasonable conclusion to be drawn from the totality of the studies reviewed here: chimpanzees, like humans, understand the actions of others not just in terms of surface behaviors but also in terms of the underlying goals, and possibly intentions, involved." "In a broad construal of the phrase 'theory of mind,'" they go on to write, "the answer to Premack and Woodruff's pregnant question of 30 years ago is a definite yes, chimpanzees do have a theory of mind"(Call and Tomasello 2008:191).

Povinelli and colleagues have long argued that there is no evidence that nonhuman animals possess anything even remotely resembling a "theory" about the causal role mental states play in modulating others' behavior (Povinelli et al. 2000; Povinelli and Vonk 2003, 2004; Povinelli 2004; Penn and Povinelli 2007b; Penn et al. 2008; Penn and Povinelli 2011). Nevertheless, we have been spectacularly unsuccessful at changing the tide of anthropomorphism that has swept through comparative psychology, and it would serve little purpose to reiterate our arguments here.

What went wrong? How is it that so many eminent comparative psychologists are convinced that there are good scientific reasons for attributing some form of a ToM to nonhuman animals? Why is it that all the evidence and arguments against this position have been so unconvincing and unpopular?

The Revolution that Comparative Psychology Abandoned

Here is my hypothesis: One of the principal factors explaining the prevailing consensus about animals' ToM abilities is that the comparative psychologists who defend these claims have largely abandoned the fundamental tenets of the cognitive revolution.

Let us all remember that the goal of the cognitive revolution in psychology, some forty-odd years old now, was not solely to leave behind the limitations of a behavioristic approach to cognition. It was also to replace romantic folk intuitions about how minds work with a materialist psychology of mental states grounded on a computational theory of cognition (Von Eckardt 1993). Our commonsense intuitions—our "folk psychology" (Bermudez 2003; Churchland and Churchland 1996; Stich and Ravenscroft 1994)—often posit an immaterial homunculus inside our heads named, "I," who does our thinking for us, in sudden flashes of "insight" (Dennett 1991). At the heart of the cognitive revolution was the provocative claim that all mental processes (e.g., even the ineffable experience of human self-consciousness) are entirely material processes and thus ultimately explicable in terms of the mechanical, algorithmic (i.e., rule-governed) operation of a biological device. This does not mean, of course, that human or nonhuman minds bear any similarity to a digital computer or a propositional "language of thought" (see Penn et al. 2008). The cognitive revolution was supposed to refashion our folk psychological intuitions into a viable scientific theory based on a computational account of the mind.[2]

Instead, comparative psychologists regularly claim that animals have an "understanding of" or "insight into" some folk psychological concept in order to falsify claims that the animal's cognitive processes are rule-governed and unconscious. The very term, "cognitive," is now typically used as a synonym for "mentalistic," "conscious," and "insightful"—as if "cognitive" were the opposite of "mechanical," "unconscious," and "rule-governed." Nearly all the most prominent claims in support of attributing a ToM to nonhuman animals are framed using folk psychological idioms (e.g., "chimpanzees know what their groupmates do and do not know," "chimpanzees can distinguish between an experimenter that is unwilling or unable to give them food," "scrub jays can project their own experience of being a thief onto the observing bird") without any attempt to cash out these claims at a computational, algorithmic, or neural level of explanation (Marr 1982).

To be sure, the cognitive revolution is alive and well in the work of comparative researchers as disparate as Gallistel (2002), Menzel and Giurfa (2006), Kacelnik (2006), Clayton et al. (2001), and Seyfarth and Cheney (2003c), to name only a few notable examples. Even many contemporary associationists

---

[2] Whether such a scientific theory is a "representational" account or not is, of course, a matter of enormous debate. In this chapter, I take the necessity and utility of a representational account of cognition for granted. My critique of folk psychological excesses in comparative psychology should not be taken as a critique of the use of intentional predicates in general.

have embraced a more computational, information-processing orientation to learning phenomena such as cue competition effects (e.g., Stout and Miller 2007) and causal prediction (e.g., Blaisdell et al. 2006). Folk psychology has plagued every domain of comparative psychology (Penn and Povinelli 2007a; Penn et al. 2008). Research on animals' ToM abilities has, however, been held hostage by folk psychology to a degree far beyond any other domain. Effectively, most comparative researchers in this domain are not practicing comparative cognitive psychology but rather "comparative folk psychology"; that is, the study of nonhuman minds from a folk psychological perspective.

The Principles of "Comparative Folk Psychology"

Darwin probably deserves to be credited as the founding father of comparative folk psychology (Penn et al. 2008). He was certainly not the first to interpret animals in an anthropomorphic fashion. Our entire species has an inveterate predilection to interpret the world in anthropomorphic terms (for details, see Dennett 1987). Nor was Darwin the first to emphasize the continuity between human and nonhuman minds (Richards 1987). Darwin gave comparative psychology its modern, scientific justification. According to Darwin, the principles of natural selection necessarily entail that the differences between human and nonhuman minds must be "one of degree and not of kind" (Darwin 1871), and it is this Darwinian formulation that is repeatedly cited by contemporary comparative psychologists to justify describing nonhuman minds by analogy to human ones. Frans de Waal, for example, calls this the principle of "evolutionary parsimony"; that is, if two closely related species act the same, the underlying mental processes are probably the same as well (de Waal 2006).

The methodological principles of comparative folk psychology that have grown out of Darwin's mistake are simple, well established, and widely practiced:

1. Observe animals in the wild behaving in a clever way or create an experiment that causes animals to behave in a way that appears clever to human observers.
2. Rule out random guessing, innate instinct, and stimulus-bound associative learning as possible explanations for the subjects' behavior.
3. Point out what humans would be thinking if they were behaving like the subjects in that context.
4. Claim that the subjects are thinking what humans would be thinking or are thinking functionally equivalent thoughts or, at least, possess the "precursors" to those human-like thoughts.
5. Criticize any cognitive explanation of the animal's behavior that is not consistent with folk psychological intuitions as an example of "behaviorism" or as "unparsimonious," "rule-bound," or "unfalsifiable."

Do Chimps Know What Others Do and Do Not Know?

If there is one recent paper that best exemplifies the principles of comparative folk psychology, it is Hare et al.'s (2001), "Do chimpanzees know what conspecifics know?" Hare et al. (2001) placed two chimpanzees—one subordinate to the other—in separate chambers on either side of a large empty room. On each trial, the subordinate chimpanzee's door was partially raised while the food was being hidden in one of two cloth bags in the middle chamber. On some trials the dominant chimpanzee's door was also raised so that he could see where the food was hidden. In other trials, the dominant's door was kept down and the dominant could not see where the food was placed.

Hare et al. (2001) reported a number of experimental conditions based on this protocol. In only one of these experiments, however, was the critical metric statistically significant (for details, see Penn and Povinelli 2007b, note 3). In the *uninformed* condition of Experiment 1, the dominant's door was kept closed while the food was hidden and the subordinate could see that the dominant's door was closed; in the control condition, the dominant could see where the reward was hidden and the subordinate could see that the dominant was watching. The subordinate "approached" the hidden food more often in the *uninformed* condition than in the control condition.

Based on this result, Hare et al. (2001:148) concluded that "chimpanzees know what individual groupmates do and do not know; that is, what individual groupmates have and have not seen in the immediate past." Tomasello, Call, and Hare (2003a) went on to cite this experiment as "breakthrough" (p. 154) evidence that chimpanzees "understand some psychological states in others" (p. 156). Hare et al.'s (2001) protocol launched an entire generation of experiments that claim to show that nonhuman animals understand everything from what others do and do not "hear" to whether others are "willing" or "unable" to perform some act (for reviews, see Call and Tomasello 2008; Hauser and Wood 2009).

Hare et al.'s experiment and ensuing claims are a paradigmatic case of comparative folk psychology in action. First, the authors devise a situation in which chimpanzees appear to act in a clever fashion (i.e., they didn't approach food when a competitor "knew" that it was there). Second, the authors rule out a stimulus-bound associative explanation (i.e., the subordinate could not see the dominant at the time she made her choice; thus the subordinates' behavior could not simply result from learning to avoid food in the presence of a competitor). Third, the authors note that a human put in an analogous position would decide whether to approach the food based on what the competitor does and does not "know." Fourth, the authors make the same mentalistic claims on behalf of chimps.

As Povinelli and Vonk (2003, 2004) pointed out, it is hardly necessary for chimps to reason about the beliefs of their competitors in order to pass this experiment. It suffices for the chimps to reason in terms of the dominants' overt behavior in light of the way that other competitors have acted in similar situations in the past: *don't go after food if a dominant competitor has recently oriented toward food in that location.* Although Povinelli and Vonk's alternative account requires chimps to reason about abstract relationships with respect to the present and past behavior of their conspecifics—and thus is a fully cognitive and inferential account—it does not require the chimps to represent their competitors' beliefs or goals qua epistemic, representational states.

Nevertheless, in keeping with the fifth principle of comparative folk psychology's methodology, Tomasello et al. (2003b) disparaged Povinelli and Vonk's explanation as an example of "derived behaviorism," claiming that Povinelli and Vonk's "behavioral abstraction" hypothesis is "unparsimonious" because it would require animals to learn a large number of "rules." Those who favor a more human-like interpretation of the chimps' behavior "clearly have parsimony on their side," Tomasello and Call (2006) argue. "The number of different explanations required to explain the evidence is sensibly smaller" (see also Call and Tomasello 2008 for a similar critique).

In a chapter aptly titled, "Who Took the Cog out of Cognitive Science," Perner (2010) points out that Tomasello and Call's line of argument is an excellent example of the prevailing "anti-cognitivism" in comparative psychology. There is no doubt, of course, that folk psychological explanations are "simpler for us" to understand (Heyes 1998). However, comparing the simplicity of a folk psychological explanation (e.g., "chimpanzees know what others do and do not know") to the complexity of an algorithmic explanation is like comparing a marketing description of Microsoft Word (e.g., "prints, saves, and edits complex documents") to a detailed functional specification of the application's underlying code. The fact that the detailed functional specification runs to thousands of pages and the marketing pitch takes one sentence is not a reasonable metric for comparing the merits of the two descriptions (Penn and Povinelli 2007b). The problem is not that the folk psychological explanation violates Morgan's infamous canon, but rather the job of comparative *cognitive* psychology was supposed to be to open up the black box of animal minds to functional and algorithmic specification—not simply reiterate the kinds of explanations the "folk" use.

Notably, Tomasello and Call do not bother to provide their own mechanistic account of the chimpanzees' behavior. Instead, they eschew *any* rule-governed explanation of chimpanzee social cognition as being "just a theoretical possibility" for which there is little "concrete evidence." "It is more plausible," Tomasello and Call (2006:371) argue, "to hypothesize that apes *really do know* [emphasis added] what others do and do not see."

The phrase, "really do know," is telling. From a comparative folk psychologist's point of view, rule-governed explanations of any kind feel artificial and reductionist. Here is the crux of the problem: Comparative folk psychologists don't like the consequences of the cognitive revolution. Any explanation of an animal's behavior in terms of mechanistic, rule-governed operations seems to reduce an animal's thought processes to something less than true "insight." Animals "really do know" what they are thinking, comparative folk psychologists keep insisting: *They have homunculi just like we do.*

Do Scrub Jays Have Homunculi as Well?

If comparative folk psychology was only practiced by primatologists studying great apes, there would be less cause for concern. But dozens, if not hundreds, of similar claims have been published over the last decade by prominent comparative psychologists for a wide variety of species, from dogs to scrub jays (Brosnan and de Waal 2003; Call et al. 2003; Flombaum and Santos 2005; Santos et al. 2006; Clayton et al. 2007; Wood et al. 2007; Santos et al. 2007; Emery and Clayton 2008; Hauser and Wood 2009). Folk psychological intuitions have also plagued even the most astute researchers' hypotheses.

Emery and Clayton, for example, have been responsible for some of the most well-crafted and important work in comparative cognitive psychology over the last decade (for a review, see Emery and Clayton 2009). Yet even they have succumbed at times to their folk psychological intuitions. For example, Emery and Clayton (2001) famously found that young scrub jays only re-cache their food if they have previously pilfered others' food. Following step #2 of the principles of comparative folk psychology, Emery and Clayton argue that the birds' behavior cannot be "innate" because "otherwise all scrub jays should re-cache" and they rule out a "simple conditioning explanation" because "the birds never received any positive reinforcement or any punishment for re-caching" (Clayton et al. 2007:519). They cite Humphrey's (1978) and Gallup's (1982) work on self-awareness and "experience projection" as examples of how humans might reason in such a situation and suggest that scrub jays might be capable of "experience projection" as well; perhaps scrub jays use their own experiences as a thief to predict how a potential pilferer might think or behave (Clayton et al. 2007:519).

This indeed is an "exciting possibility" (Emery 2004:21), but it is certainly not the only or even the most compelling explanation. For example, all of the birds involved in this experiment had previous experience being pilfered (see discussion in Emery and Clayton 2008). However, Emery and Clayton do not explain why scrub jays have the cognitive prowess necessary to reason by analogy to their own experience as pilferers but do not have the cognitive wherewithal to realize that they should start caching once they have been victims of pilferage themselves. Nor do Emery and Clayton show why "experience projection" is computationally necessary or even, more modestly, why it is the best explanation for the birds' behavior. Perhaps the experience of pilfering triggers a developmental change in their *motivation* to re-cache rather than a change in their understanding of why re-caching is strategically advantageous

(Penn and Povinelli 2007b). There are many other cognitive—but non-folk psychological—explanations that merit consideration.

Povinelli's Challenge

Povinelli and colleagues have challenged comparative researchers to show why representations about unobservable mental states are computationally necessary to account for the social cognitive abilities of nonhuman animals (Povinelli and Vonk 2003, 2004; Penn and Povinelli 2007b, 2011). Perner (2010) has termed this "Povinelli's challenge." In a chapter entitled, "How To Build a Scrub Jay That Reads Minds," Emery and Clayton (2008) provide the most extensive critique to date of Povinelli's challenge, thus providing an excellent opportunity to understand why Povinelli's challenge has been so unpopular and unconvincing.

For example, Emery and Clayton (2008:89) claim that Povinelli's hypothesis is incapable of generalizing to novel behaviors or individuals:

> [Behavior reading] does not allow one to accurately predict the future behavior of an unknown conspecific, as behavior reading is based on computing statistical regularities over the course of a relationship between two individuals.

Although an explanation based on associative learning might be limited to associations between specific individuals, this is certainly not a limitation of all accounts of behavior reading and is clearly not a limitation of Povinelli's account in particular. Povinelli and colleagues have repeatedly emphasized that animals form "behavioral abstractions" about classes of behaviors and animals and generalize these abstractions to novel situations in an inferentially coherent fashion (Povinelli et al. 2000; Povinelli and Vonk 2004; Penn and Povinelli 2007b). Povinelli's account seems unconvincing because Emery and Clayton have underestimated its inferential flexibility.

Emery and Clayton acknowledge that Povinelli's "behavior-reading" hypothesis can account for the results of Hare et al.'s (2000; 2001) experiments and even for certain experiments conducted with scrub jays (e.g., Dally et al. 2005). They argue, however, that other cases are not so easily handled by a "Povinellian [sic]" explanation. For example, Dally et al. (2004) showed that scrub jays prefer to cache food in darker locations rather than lighter locations when being observed by potential pilferers. Emery and Clayton (2008) propose the following "mentalistic" sketch of the scrub jays' behavior:

1. The storer is in the presence of an observer with two caching trays; one in bright light, one in the dark.
2. The tray in the light is easier to <see> than the tray in the dark, and thus easier to pilfer from.
3. The storer caches in the dark tray (because the observer cannot <see> the caches as clearly as those made in the bright tray).

According to Emery and Clayton, a Povinellian explanation would look like this:

1. The storer is in the presence of an observer with two caching trays; one in bright light, one in the dark.
2. The tray in the light is more visible.
3. The storer caches in the dark tray (because observers do not pilfer as successfully from dark trays).

Emery and Clayton (2008:89) argue that the Povinellian-style explanation is less plausible because without the mentalistic clause that light trays are easier to <see> the storer would have no reason to infer that it should store food in the dark tray, and the storer's behavior would have to result from a "series of very flexible conditional rules."

Here Povinelli's account seems unconvincing because folk psychological explanations seem so much more "intuitive" and "parsimonious" than rule-governed accounts. But the cognitive revolution in psychology was founded on the premise that *all* cognitive processes result from rule-governed operations and that cognizers don't need to understand anything about why these rules work in order to be "rational" or "intelligent" (Kacelnik 2006). As Dennett quipped in reviewing Alan Turing's contribution to the cognitive revolution: Turing demonstrated that "to be a perfect and beautiful computing machine, it is not requisite to know what arithmetic is" (Dennett 2009:10,061). In other words, Turing showed that computers don't need homunculi, so neither do brains.

And neither do scrub jays. There is no reason that evolution could not have designed scrub jays to cache food in darker areas (and behind barriers and as far away as possible from thieving conspecifics) when being observed by potential pilferers without thereby endowing scrub jays with any understanding of *why* these devious acts are effective. The parenthetical "because" clauses in Emery and Clayton's sketch are unnecessary. Scrub jays don't need homunculi any more than we do.[3]

How to Build a Scrub Jay That Thinks Like a Scrub Jay

So let us imagine a rosier future in which comparative psychologists decide to abandon folk psychological explanations and study nonhuman social cognition from a *cognitive* perspective. How might a comparative cognitive psychology of nonhuman social cognition proceed?

The place to start, I think, is with corvids. Thanks in large part to the work of Clayton, Emery and their colleagues, we have a richer and more robust body of data about the social cognitive abilities of scrub jays than we do for just about any other nonhuman species (for reviews, see Clayton et al. 2007;

---

[3] To be fair, all our talk about our homunculi (e.g., "free will," "mens rea") undoubtedly plays a significant role in human cognition and human affairs.

Emery and Clayton 2009). Scrub jays have turned out to be mavens of social interactions within the context of food caching. They also have the inimitable advantage of not looking anything like cute human children. Thus, there is every reason to hope that the study of corvid social cognition might lead the rest of comparative psychology out of its folk psychological quagmire and into a more cognitively grounded future.

The first and most important step would be to define the functional specifications that any plausible model of corvid social cognition must fulfill. For example, we know that scrub jays not only remember the "what," "where," and "when" information associated with a very large number of discrete caching events in the past, they also remember "who" was present during each caching event. We know that scrub jays select which food to re-cache based on who is present and whether a competitor who is currently present was also present during particular caching events in the past. In addition, we know that, when given a choice, experienced scrub jays prefer to cache food farther rather than nearer to potential pilferers, in darker rather than lighter areas, and behind barriers rather than out in the open.

Now this short list of scrub jay cognitive features barely scrapes the surface of the scrub jay cognitive feature set. Yet already it is obvious that scrub jays require a quite remarkable cognitive architecture. Clearly the scrub jay is not only capable of representing and keeping track of the particular features of particular objects (e.g., the spatiotemporal and physical attributes associated with each cache), but also of encoding the relation between particular constituents (e.g., "who" was present for "what" caching event) such that common inferences can be made across similar relations that have novel constituents (e.g., *for any S and C, <if S was present when C was cached, re-cache C when S is absent>*). To put this in Emery and Clayton's (2008:89) terms, scrub jays do indeed possess "a series of very flexible conditional rules which can be applied to different individuals across a variety of different but particular contexts."

Some basic principles of learning together with species-typical behavior and situation-specific predispositions clearly play an important role in explaining how these rules are acquired, and Shettleworth (2010a) is right to castigate comparative psychologists for glossing over these general learning mechanisms too quickly. But associations alone won't suffice to explain how the birds encode, update, and use the relevant information. For example, not only are scrub jays updating their representations of *who* was present for *what* caching event on a one-shot basis without any immediate reinforcement from the environment, they are keeping track of the relation between numerous cache sites and various potential pilferers in a compositional fashion. In other words, given $Obs(S,C)$—the "observing" relation between subject S and cache site C—scrub jays are somehow capable of encoding and using $Obs(S_1, C_1)$ without confounding this representation with other similar but distinct relations such as $Obs(S_1, C_2)$, $Obs(S_2, C_1)$, and $Obs(S_2, C_2)$. This may seem like a trivial cognitive feat from a folk psychological perspective, but as connectionists have repeatedly discovered over the last quarter-century, associatively structured representations have dramatic computational limitations, not the least of which being their susceptibility to "catastrophic interference" when updating similar but distinct representations such as these (for a review of the challenges faced by connectionist models of learning, see Shanks 2005).

Moreover, the ability to act on the compositional relation between numerous cache sites and competitors in an adaptive fashion would be literally unthinkable (i.e., computationally infeasible) without some mechanism for encoding the relation between particular constituents of a representation such that when overlapping constituents have different relationships to each other, the fact that these are different *relations* is somehow manifest in the structural differences between the representations. That is, the relation $Obs(S,C)$ must be distinct from the relation $Cached(S,C)$ such that scrub jays don't confound the fact that S_1 observed food being cached in C_1 with the fact that S_1 subsequently cached food in C_2 or that S_2 had previously observed food being cached in C_1. Scrub jays are able to form syntactically structured representations about the "what," "when," "where," and "who" properties associated with concrete caching events in the past as well as about the abstract statistical regularities that hold across similar relations with different constituents. Horgan and Tienson (1996) argue that this is all it should take in order for a representational system to qualify as "syntactically structured," and I agree.

Scrub jays are hardly the only relationally intelligent creature on the planet. There are baboons as well, who, as Bergman et al. (2003) have shown, are perfectly capable of keeping track of various *kinds* of relations between their conspecifics such that rank reversals between family members do not elicit the same response as rank reversals between matrilines (see also Silk 1999, 2003b). There are domestic dogs who can keep track of the relation between a "pointing" gesture and a distal object regardless of the featural properties of the particular object being pointed at (Soproni et al. 2002). There are, undoubtedly, thousands of other less well-studied species who deserve mention as well. Thus, as I have argued in the past (Penn et al. 2008; Penn and Povinelli 2009, 2011), nonhuman animals are clearly capable of encoding, updating, and using abstract relational representations in a flexible and adaptive fashion.

Picking out the causally relevant relations amidst all the salient but spurious correlations in the world requires cognitive mechanisms substantially more sophisticated than those postulated by associative models of learning (Penn and Povinelli 2011). As Clark and Thornton (1997) put it, relations are "representation hungry" and biological cognizers require an entire panoply of top-down heuristics, tricks, and ploys to circumvent the limitations of uninformed statistical learning. There are still innumerable unanswered questions about the heuristics scrub jays employ to recognize and encode the relations that matter to them and about how learning modulates the birds' relational abilities. I suspect that if Clayton and Emery sat down and compiled a comprehensive specification of what we currently know about corvid social cognition, the resulting document would set off a nuclear explosion in cognitive science by ruling out almost all existing connectionist and associative architectures as plausible models of animal cognition. Only those cognitive architectures capable of approximating the first-order relational features of a physical symbol system will be left as plausible representational-level models of the mind (Penn et al. 2008). Even the best of these (e.g., Hummel and Holyoak 2003, 2005) would have great difficulty, I suspect, in replicating the intelligence of a scrub jay or a baboon.

At the same time, the exercise of compiling a functional specification of corvid social cognition could also expose the speciousness of comparative folk psychology's principle claims. Once one has defined the extensive vocabulary of first-order relational representations managed by the corvid mind, there will be nothing left for representations about mental states to do. And there will no longer be any need to claim that scrub jays "really know" what they are doing.

First column (top to bottom): Joan Silk, Christoph Teufel, Keith Jensen, Redouan Bshary, Joan Silk

Second column (top to bottom): Keith Jensen, Nathan Emery, Charlotte Hemelrijk, Josef Perner

Third column: Kristin Andrews, Kay Holekamp, Dorothy Cheney, Derek Penn, Kristin Andrews

18

Social Knowledge

Keith Jensen, Joan B. Silk, Kristin Andrews, Redouan Bshary,
Dorothy L. Cheney, Nathan Emery, Charlotte K. Hemelrijk,
Kay Holekamp, Derek C. Penn, Josef Perner, and
Christoph Teufel

Abstract

The social milieus of animals can be complex, ranging from almost completely asocial to monogamous pairs (no mean feat) to entire societies. To adapt to a constantly shifting environment of individuals striving toward their own goals, animals appear to have evolved specialized cognitive abilities. As appealing and intuitive as the idea of social cognition is, just defining it is difficult. We attempted to delineate social cognition, speculate on its adaptive value, and come to an understanding of what we mean when we talk about complexity. Transitive inference was often brought up as an example of a cognitive ability that is important for social animals, though the focus of much of the discussion was on theory of mind. For some, theory of mind is something of a Holy Grail, whereas for others, it is more of a McGuffin. There are a number of challenges and debates in trying to determine what cognitive abilities different animals use to solve their social problems. This chapter discusses methodological approaches and issues that are needed to propel the future of research into social knowledge.

Social Cognition: What Is It, and What Is It Good For?

What Is Social Cognition?

Simply put, social cognition comprises cognitive processes that are applied to social behavior. That may sound trivially obvious; however, there are some tricky waters to be navigated in this thimble-sized definition.

What is social and what is cognition? One important issue concerns the question of whether social cognition is, indeed, special and distinct from, say, physical cognition. Examples of behaviors and capacities that are examined under the rubric of social cognition include individual recognition, social partner preferences, development and maintenance of relationships (e.g., reconciliation and alliances), triadic relationships (including transitive inference), morality, social preferences, theory of mind, contingent social coordination, collaboration, cooperation, social executive function, synchrony in time and space, social learning (e.g., imitation), gaze following, social manipulation, deception, predicting behavior, teaching, imitation, and punishment. The challenge is to determine which cognitive processes underlie these different behaviors, as well as to analyze how different species might use different processes to achieve the same outcomes.

Behaviors are observable phenomena. We can infer from these phenomena their function, namely their adaptive value, and their underlying structure, specifically their mental processes (cognitions) and the mechanisms which underlie these (such as neurological structures and hormones, as well as associative learning mechanisms). While behavioral ecologists tend to be interested in the functions of behaviors, comparative psychologists focus more on the processes. These divergent interests are both highly informative in explaining why an animal does what it does, though disagreements do arise, in part, because specialists in these fields often talk solely about the function or the process without agreeing that they might be talking about the same phenomena. Using the same terms for these different levels of explanation (ultimate and proximate, respectively) does little to reduce the confusion, a point emphasized in our discussion of folk psychology. For cognition researchers, the functional approach to understanding behavior is very important since cognitive processes should, or at least can, be tailored to specific adaptive problems.

Social Cognition as Distinct from Physical Cognition

In theory, at least, social cognition is different from physical cognition because it addresses problems linked to interactions with other agents, whereas physical cognition deals with problems linked to a relatively passive environment. Typically, the physical environment does not change rapidly, from moment to moment, as the social environment can, and thus it is more predictable: a solution which works today will likely work as well tomorrow. For example, the physics of tool use are constant, and landmarks used for orientation typically persist over long time periods. In a social environment, however, individuals pursue their own goals, and things such as rank orders and quality of relationships are subject to change. This often leads to the situation where the optimal behavior of an individual depends on how its partner(s) behaves. A partner's behavior may be variable because many behaviors are condition dependent (e.g., hungry animals behave differently from satiated ones, reproductively active animals differently from non-reproducing ones).

In terms of sociality, game theory provides a partial answer to why social cognition might be different from physical cognition. Game theory is a formal system in both behavior ecology and economics concerned with interactions between individuals and their choices. Optimality (or choice) theory provides another modeling approach. The key difference between the two, as used in behavioral ecology (Krebs and Davies 1993), is that the optimality approach assumes that the environment is passive. Under this assumption, one best solution emerges and all animals should behave in the same way. For example, animals should only eat high quality food and ignore food of lower quality as long as the density of high quality food is above a threshold. Below that threshold, animals should eat anything they find. In the game theoretical approach, the environment is not passive but consists of other agents with their own goals. Therefore, the best behavioral strategy to adopt during an interaction often depends on what others are doing. Whether animals treat game theoretical and optimality problems differently is an open question.

Adaptive Value of Social Cognition

A behavior that is specialized in one domain may be used in another domain, making it difficult to determine whether a given ability involves physical or social cognition (or some of both). Memory, for instance, is domain general, but memory for faces may build on this due to selection pressures for a specialized trait. Adaptive social behavior would come about from selective pressures in the social domain, distinct from generalized cognitive abilities or those adapted to nonsocial problems, such as foraging. (Whether predator-prey interactions count as "social" is something that is rarely considered; the emphasis is usually on conspecifics, though this need not be the case, as in, e.g., interspecific mutualisms.) Social problems include predicting the behaviors of others (animate beings), possibly manipulating them or coordinating with them, or recognizing relationships among individuals. To determine whether a given trait is specialized for the social domain, and hence is underpinned by specialized cognitive abilities, it helps to consider the trait's adaptive function. For behaviors such as navigation, it is clear that the cognitive processes which lead to the animal getting home, for instance, are adaptive. Researchers can then manipulate components of that process and measure whether the animal achieves its goal, or not, and how it does so.

For social behavior, this can be more difficult. Consider transitive inference, inferring relationships among items. The ability to infer from one's belief that "4 is greater than 2" and "2 is greater than 1" to the belief that "4 is greater than 1" is an ability that cuts across domains, but it might be selected for in the social realm. An animal that lives in a social group may not only have some knowledge of its own relationship to other individuals in the group, say whether it is dominant to D and E and subordinate to A and B, but it may also recognize the relationships among others in the group (e.g., that B is also subordinate to A and dominant to D). Although the adaptive value of a particular cognitive ability often seems to be intuitively obvious, this is usually very difficult to demonstrate empirically. We can hypothesize, for example, that transitive inference allows animals to recognize other individuals' dominance ranks, recruit alliance partners, and assess potential rivals' fighting abilities, but it is almost impossible to assign a fitness value to these behaviors or to demonstrate any individual variation in this ability that might be related to reproductive success.

A related problem arises when we attempt to identify the mechanisms underlying a particular cognitive ability. Again, consider transitive inference. There are several ways by which an animal could infer that $B > D$ in a sequence in which $A > B > C > D > E$, etc. One way is through associative strength; that is, B is valued higher than C because of its association with A, and C is valued higher than D because of its association with B. This indirect acquisition of associative strength, or "value transfer" (von Fersen et al. 1991; Shettleworth 2010b), predicts that error rates will be higher at the end of a sequence than at the beginning, such that the discriminations B/C or B/D will be more accurate than C/D or C/E. Error rates will also increase significantly if a new item appears in the sequence. By contrast, an animal that has a linear representation of the entire sequence recognizes an item's ordinal position in the list. Transitive inference through list representation is thought to be more cognitively complex than inference through associative strength. It should be equally accurate at the end of a list as at the beginning, and it should be relatively insensitive to omissions and substitutions (Bond et al. 2003; Shettleworth 2010b). A number of tests conducted on captive animals have suggested that pigeons (*Columba livia*) make transitive inferences based on associative strength, whereas monkeys represent ordinal sequences (reviewed by Shettleworth 2010b).

An example of the difficulty involved in determining the cognitive mechanisms subsuming transitive inference comes from a comparative study of western scrub jays (*Aphelocoma californica*) and pinyon jays (*Gymnorhinus cyanocephalus*). Western scrub jays are semi-territorial corvids, living in small family groups in some areas and conditions and territorial pairs in others. By contrast, closely related pinyon jays live in large, highly structured social groups with many individual members. Bond et al. (2003) compared transitive inference in these two bird species and hypothesized that, as a result of selection pressure favoring the ability to recognize other group members' relative dominance ranks, pinyon jays would be more accurate than scrub jays. Furthermore, pinyon jays would represent the sequence as an ordinal list, whereas scrub jays would rely on associative strength. Results provided mixed support for these predictions. Pinyon jays learned the sequences more rapidly and more accurately than scrub jays, and they showed no early-order effects. However, scrub jays also learned to rank items in the sequence, though more slowly and less accurately than pinyon jays. Results such as these highlight both the value of comparative studies and their limitations. If two species can achieve almost similar results through different means, of what benefit is it to adopt the apparently more difficult method?

Is Social Cognition Complex?

Presumably, the more complex the problem to be solved, the more sophisticated the cognitive mechanism needed, although even this intuitive claim cannot be taken for granted since simple mechanisms can sometimes do the trick (Shettleworth 2010a). As a result, again presumably, a relatively larger and more energetically expensive brain is needed to solve more complex problems. Complexity is a scale of variability in the environment, and at least three dimensions of complexity are relevant to this issue. One aspect of complexity is the possible number of variations in the environment or states of the world. If the only possible states of the world are night and day, little variation exists, and the world is not very complex. However, increasing the number of possible states of the world increases the complexity of the environment. Possible states of the world give a maximum amount of variation in the environment. Patterns in these states may, however, exist and the predictability of the patterns may reduce complexity in the environment. For example, if an individual always attacks after giving a particular threat signal, the predictability of the situation reduces its complexity. If, however, following a threat, an animal sometimes attacks and sometimes bluffs, the situation becomes more complex. Finally, strategic elements of the environment influence its complexity. If aspects of the environment depend on an individual's behavior, this increases complexity because the states of the world are not fixed but respond to an individual's behavior. This dependency is captured by the notion of a strategic game in game theory (von Neumann and Morgenstern 1947; Maynard Smith 1982). Thus, when dependency exists, the world is a moving target depending on one's own behavior, thereby increasing the complexity of the environment.

Complexity is not just an objective, external aspect of the environment. In this sense, it can be quantified by an outside observer. Animals, however, do not necessarily have to track or respond to all of this environmental complexity. We may think of more subjective approaches to measure the complexity of the environment. Wildebeest (*Connochaetes* sp.) herds can number into the tens of thousands, but no individual uses social information on all other individuals in the group. Though the complexity exists objectively in the environment, it is not effectively relevant to the organism. Thus, it is important to make conceptual distinctions between objective and subjective aspects of complexity in the environment. For instance, the fact that a pair-bond in birds only involves two parties (when they are not "eavesdropping" on other pairs) does not necessarily mean that the complexity of the relationship is reduced compared to relationships among multiple parties in a larger social group. Indeed, there is good reason to think that individuals who form strong bonds process social information in a very complex manner, particularly when reasoning about others' mental states. By contrast, individuals in larger groups which do not form strong bonds process social information at a low level of complexity because they do not know or need to know as much information about other parties where relationships are not as "valuable" (van Schaik and Aureli 2000). As yet, we do not have very good measures or tests for social complexity which do not rely on assumptions about the underlying cognitive abilities required when living in a pair versus a larger group. The measures or tests will need to accommodate many different forms of sociality (social system, mating system) if they are going to prove useful tools for comparative analyses.

Complexity and the Brain

If more complex environments require more complex cognitive abilities, one would expect the brain to reflect this increase in complexity. This has been called the *social intelligence hypothesis* (Dunbar 1992, 1998a).[1] The suggestion is that processing nonsocial information, such as the location, state and type of food, does not depend on the same structure (or complexity) of cognitive abilities as social information does (though see the technical intelligence hypothesis; Byrne and Whiten 1997). A number of analyses found that there was a strong relationship between the relative size of the neocortex and mean group size, but not with other ecological variables, such as home range size or the amount of fruit in the diet (Dunbar 1992). In primates and carnivores, the relationship is not wholly uncontroversial, as no data were presented on the relatively solitary orangutans in the original analysis, and primates living in the largest social groups, such as baboons (*Papio* sp.) and macaques (*Macaca* sp.), do not necessarily have the largest neocortices. The relationship between social complexity and brain size varies among the extant families of mammals, with some families failing altogether to conform to predictions of the social brain hypothesis, but others conforming very well (Finarelli and Flynn 2009). Recent analyses have further confused the issue because pair-bonding also correlates with brain size in many mammals (ungulates, bats, and primates; Dunbar and Shultz 2007). Many bird species display very complex forms of social behavior, but would be predicted to demonstrate poor correlations between brain size and flock size using similar analyses performed with primates (Emery 2006). In birds, there is a strong relationship between the size of the forebrain (the best neuroanatomical data available from one source) and pair-bonding (Emery et al. 2007; Shultz and Dunbar 2010).

The main problem with the social brain hypothesis is what the two variables in the analysis actually represent. Mean group size was originally chosen as a proxy measure of social complexity or level of social information processing. For example, a species that lives in a pair ($n = 2$) is more limited by the number of potential relationships ($n = 1$) than is a species that lives in a larger social group (say, 5 individuals) because the number of potential relationships

---

[1]   Emery and colleagues propose to apply the social brain hypothesis to prosocial behavior and the Machiavellian intelligence hypothesis to the more strategic (i.e., deceptive) aspects of social behavior.

in the larger group ($n = 10$) is greater than in the dyad. The natural assumption is that the greater the amount of information that can be processed in a larger group (e.g., tracking of previous relationships, dominance hierarchies, reciprocity), the larger the processor that is required, as reflected by a larger brain (or neocortex).

There is evidence that this relationship between brain size and social group size does not hold. Analysis of the vocal recognition of chacma baboons (*Papio ursinus*) and closely related geladas (*Theropithecus gelada*) found that the geladas, which live in larger social groups, did not recognize all the individuals they encounter based on their vocalizations, whereas the baboons did (Bergman 2010). This suggests that there is "missing social knowledge" in geladas, such that not all potential relationships between group members are treated equally. Thus, using mean group size as a proxy for social complexity may not be appropriate for all species. There are also intriguing data from social insects which show that, even with their very small brains (and total lack of neocortex), they can remember specific individuals and the context in which they were remembered (i.e., tracking relationships) for very long periods (Sheehan and Tibbetts 2008).

In addition, it is assumed that the brain area chosen as a variable is important to social information processing. Usually, large areas of the brain (either the forebrain or neocortex) process much more than simply social information. The neural circuitry of social behavior is being investigated in various species, including primates, to a fine level of detail, but the comparative neuroanatomical data sets have yet to catch up with current knowledge, so the same old data sets are still being used (e.g., Stephan et al. 1981). As such, there are significant issues about the quality of the neural material being used in such analyses, especially if pooled across different data sets that used different methods to prepare the material and so may not present a true representation of the actual size of the brain region under study (discussed in Healy and Rowe 2007).

Why Is Theory of Mind So Sexy (and Has It Screwed up Comparative Psychology)?

Transitive inference has been discussed in the context of social complexity, with the assumption that more complex social environments will demand more complex abilities at tracking social relationships. Complex cognitive abilities do not only mean being able to track larger numbers of individuals and their relationships; knowledge of what just one other individual knows, desires, and believes is considered to be cognitively advanced, and possibly even unique to humans. The topic of "mind reading" has captivated comparative psychologists who have attempted to find this ability in other animals, but it may be that this pursuit of a cognitive "Holy Grail" may be counterproductive. Ironically, perhaps, this topic generated more discussion than any other. Below we consider the question of why theory of mind is such a provocative research issue, the evidence for and against it, and what can be done about it. We also consider whether animals can recognize something of the emotions of others. First, however, a foray into folk psychology is needed to set the stage (for more on this topic, see Penn, this volume).

Folk Psychology

Folk psychology is most generally defined as "our commonsense conception of psychological phenomena" (Churchland 1981:67). Minimally, folk psychology consists of "a set of attributive, explanatory, and predictive practices, and a set of notions or concepts used in these practices" (Von Eckardt 1994:300). The practices of folk psychology would include things such as predicting, explaining, justifying, evaluating, and coordinating behavior. Concepts of folk psychology include theoretical mental entities such as beliefs, desires, intentions, emotions, sensations, goals, and personality traits. These causal roles and patterns of behavior are agnostic on the question of mechanism, though it is generally assumed that the same kinds of behaviors can be implemented in very different ways, both at an algorithmic and physical level (Bickle 2008).

The use of folk psychology in animal cognition research is undeniable, but concerns arise when folk psychological terms are used that have greater connotations or causal implications than appropriate. For example, when the term "punishment" is used to describe an act of antagonism toward a rule-breaker, it may be an overattribution if this connotes a particular attitude toward the transgressor (such as a desire for rehabilitating the transgressor) rather than just retribution. Just as there are folk psychologies for humans across cultures (see Lillard 1998), there may be folk psychologies across species, and to do comparative psychology, it could be productive to look at both differences and similarities across species at the folk psychological level.

However, folk psychology can, and often is, taken as an end point, rather than a starting point. For instance, when saying that a baboon is reconciling with another baboon, can we state that "she is reestablishing cordial relationships"? Flowers will deceive insects, but not in the same sense in which people will deceive each other. Is it possible to avoid the cognitive and normative baggage attached to these words? The problem of shared vocabulary continues to vex evolutionary biologists, psychologists, and economists who use the same lay terms, such as altruism, but in subtly different ways. A philosopher would argue that the baboon example is a misuse of the term "reconcile" and that despite this, according to the folk psychological view, the term should still be used by comparative psychologists, though carefully. Folk psychology is the linguistic equivalent of giving guns to children and telling them to play carefully: misuse is inevitable. This is especially true for words in the lay vocabulary that have a rich connotation. For example, the use of the term "rape" by behavioral ecologists has been lambasted. Is "friendship" better? What about "love"? New words can be invented for the sake of precision, just as "moron" was a term invented in 1910 to refer to people assessed with an IQ of 51–70. Once the word escaped into the open, however, it took on unintended connotations. Thus, even words invented specifically to avoid the pitfalls of folk psychology can be misused. Overfamiliarity with terms can lead to inappropriate inferential leaps, and this is as true for human psychology as comparative psychology. Although it may be useful to start with folk psychological intuitions in understanding behavior, we need to determine whether these terms are warranted in each case. As stated earlier, those intuitions must be merely starting points and open to revision during scientific investigation.

A solution to the "other minds" problem, discussed next, is not to eliminate folk psychology altogether. A possible way forward is to decide how and when the vocabulary and intuitions of commonsense psychology should be best used. For example, the use of intentional predicates (e.g., attributing mental states and representations to nonhuman animals) might be useful to comparative cognitive science. Whether any particular term (e.g., "rape," "friendship," "reconciliation," "belief," "intention") can be appropriately applied to animals, however, is an empirical matter that must be decided on a case-by-case basis (e.g., see Silk 2002).

Theory of Mind Defined, Narrowly and Broadly

Folk psychology is hardly the only cause of confusion and misunderstanding in comparative social cognition. Research on nonhuman social cognition has been plagued by multiple and inconsistent definitions of the term *theory of mind*. Penn (this volume) suggests that theory of mind research has been particularly susceptible to the limits of folk psychology. Psychologists have long known that commonsense views are not particularly trustworthy when it comes to our own species' cognition; they are even less so, Penn argues, when it comes to the minds of other species. Premack and Woodruff (1978) originally coined the term "theory of mind" to refer to a human's ability to impute mental states (e.g., goals, intentions, beliefs, and doubts) to others and to use these unobservable entities to predict and explain their own and others' behavior. According to Premack and Woodruff, this cognitive system properly counts as a "theory" in humans because "such [mental] states are not directly observable, and the system can be used to make predictions about the behavior of others" (Premack and Woodruff 1978:515). To illustrate their point, Premack and Woodruff cited the use of propositional descriptions of the form, "Paul knows that I don't like roses."

In the narrow sense, theory of mind is the attribution of propositional attitudes to predict and explain behavior. A propositional attitude is an attribution of an intentional state (e.g., belief, desire, hope, want, fear) that takes a proposition as its content (e.g., "that snow is white" or "that there is ripe fruit in the tree"). An example of a propositional attitude, then, would be: "Gojelek hopes that there is ripe fruit in the tree." Understood narrowly in this way, theory of mind has been of primary interest in the developmental literature, where the focus has been on discovering when children are first able to attribute false belief. The motivation behind the move to understand theory of mind (narrowly defined) as the ability to attribute false belief stemmed from the idea that to determine whether an animal knows that others have beliefs, experimenters could present it with a problem where it would have to alter its own behavior in expectation of another's behavior (Bennett 1978; Dennett 1978; Harman 1978). Predicting that another will act the same way you do is relatively simple, but making predictions of her behavior when she would act differently from you is more of a challenge, because it requires that you infer the existence of someone else's beliefs, something that cannot be directly observed. However, this may not always be the case. A scholar in his office would have no difficulty understanding and predicting that a baker will get up at 3 o'clock in the morning to prepare the dough, though he would have a harder time explaining why the baker appears at work at 9 a.m. like the professor. Similarly, a young chimpanzee (*Pan troglodytes*) would have little difficulty understanding why a dominant will chase away a subordinate approaching his food source and not run away, like the young chimp would, when the subordinate approaches. Generally, though, different behavior in the same environment cannot be predicted via behavioral rules, because there would be no difference in the observable stimulus. The difference in the two cases must be conceptual, rather than environmental.

Theory of mind can also be broadly construed to refer to the ability to attribute mental states more generally to engage in social behaviors, like predicting and explaining, and indeed, Premack claims that this is what he and Woodruff originally meant when they introduced the term (Premack and Premack 2003). In this sense, a theory of mind involves the attribution of a mental state—an unobservable theoretical entity that is posited by a folk psychological theory. Examples of theoretical entities are beliefs and desires, but also include emotions, perceptions, sensations, sentiments, etc. Recent research has focused on this more general question about whether conceptual (i.e., nonobservable or theoretical) mediation occurs in social cognition. Comparative cognition research into mental state understanding centers primarily around theory of mind understood broadly, including the attribution of knowledge states, goals, intentions, perceptual states, and false belief. Although some claim that there is evidence of other animals' (or, at least, chimpanzees') ability to attribute knowledge, goals, intentions, and perceptual states, there is no experimental evidence to suggest that chimpanzees (or any other animal, for that matter) understand false belief (Call and Tomasello 2008). However, a broad use of the term sheds little light on the important social-cognitive differences between species and obfuscates the very reason why theory of mind was initially such an interesting and distinctive research domain: Do nonhuman animals, in fact, appreciate that others have unobservable mental states that modulate their behavior? Or are we the only species which understands that others have minds of their own?

Theory of Mind in Animals: Putting It into Perspective

Why is this splitting of hairs important and how can we move forward? It might seem anthropocentric to deny mental state attribution or theory of mind (in the narrow sense) to animals other than humans. However, there are a number of reasons for continuing to challenge the evidence used in favor of theory of mind. First, it is often wondered what, if anything, mental state attributions would allow a social animal to do that other processes cannot do. To be fair, when asking the question of how theory of mind evolved in humans, it does seem reasonable to look for homologs in other species. Different answers to this question suggest various potential avenues for future research. For example, the social intelligence hypothesis, especially in its Machiavellian guises (Humphrey 1978; Byrne and Whiten 1991), suggested that the attribution of belief evolved in humans to make better predictions of behavior as well as to deceive competitors more effectively, and inspired research into theory of mind (particularly false belief attribution).

Today, almost all comparative psychologists agree that social vertebrates are quite adept at predicting the observable *behavior* of other animals, including how conspecifics are likely to behave given those specific individuals' past behavior as well as the behavior of other conspecifics under similar circumstances. For humans, predictions of behavior can be made using a number of different mechanisms. One can use behavioral rules (Povinelli and Vonk 2004; Penn and Povinelli 2007b; Perner and Roessler 2010; Andrews 2005) that generalize over the target individual's past behavior, or the past behavior of other individuals. One can use group norms (Maibom 2007; Andrews 2009; Perner and Roessler 2010) to predict that others will do what they should do. One can also appeal to unobservables such as personality traits, emotions, and sensations as well as propositional attitudes such as beliefs and desires (Andrews 2011). (Note that associative learning could play some role in any of these ways of predicting behavior.) Attempts to determine how animals predict behavior has tended to pit behavioral rules (learning) against mental state understanding (propositional attitudes). This is a false dichotomy, and pluralism suggests that additional hypotheses should be considered.

It seems clear that nonhuman animals form concrete representations of the behavior of particular conspecifics as well as abstract representations of the statistical regularities in general classes of behaviors. It also seems clear that the sophistication and flexibility of nonhuman social cognition goes far beyond the limits of purely associative learning and employs what might be properly called "inferential" mechanisms and relational representations (Penn et al. 2008). One well-documented example of such inferential reasoning is the ability to make inductive generalizations on the basis of the social relation between conspecifics (see, e.g., Bergman et al. 2003; Seyfarth and Cheney 2003c). Indeed, the ability to reason about transitive social relationships appears to be fairly widespread in the animal kingdom (Otter et al. 1999; Grosenick and Clement 2007). Thus, the important question for future research in the "theory of mind" domain is not whether animals are capable of reasoning about others' social relationships and behavior (they are) but whether, in addition, animals are capable of reasoning about others' unobservable mental states and, if so, what kind, when, how, and why.

Over ten years ago, Heyes (1998) complained that comparative psychology had made little progress in answering this question, and it is far from clear whether much progress has been made since then (Penn and Povinelli 2007b). One source of difficulty today is that it is rarely clear what researchers are actually claiming when they employ folk psychological terms: "chimpanzees know what others do and do not know." For example, does claiming that one animal "knows" what another animal "knows" mean that the subject represents and reasons about how the other agent is likely to act given the other agent's past behavior and the state of the world? Or does it mean that the subject represents the other agent's representation of a particular state of the world? How exactly would one tease apart this difference empirically?

The same confusion plagues terms like "intentions," "perceptions," and even "perspective-taking." For some psychologists, evidence that animals reason about how others typically act toward objects or what others see is taken as evidence that they understand others' "intentions" and "perceptions" as psychological states (Tomasello et al. 2003a, b). For other researchers, this is only evidence that those animals can reason about others' behavioral dispositions (Povinelli and Vonk 2003). The problem with "visual perspective-taking" is twofold: one needs to distinguish between Level 1 (being able to look at some object or scene or not being able to do so) and Level 2 (seeing different things when looking at the same thing or scene; Masangkay et al. 1974), and have the ability to switch between perspectives and understand that there are two perspectives involved (Perner et al. 2002). We do think that "perspective," when properly defined, captures the central aspect of "meta-representation" which, in our view, is required for understanding false beliefs. However, another source of difficulty in studying theory of mind may be due to false presuppositions about its adaptive value and ubiquity in human social interactions. Addressing these concerns may lead to more productive future research.

Looking Ahead

In contrast to the claim that the adaptive value of theory of mind is to increase the ability to predict behavior, some might speculate that adaptive value and propositional attitude attributions are to promote social cohesion by allowing individuals to explain, justify, and evaluate abnormal or unexpected behavior (Andrews 2009; Perner 2011). For instance, when an individual witnesses something unusual, say crippling polio in chimpanzees or lack of cooperation, does it seek more information to determine the underlying social causes for atypical behaviors? Further experiments along this line will be interesting, because theory of mind could allow individuals to more subtly infer failures on the parts of their partners, to recognize innovations such as new tools, and to intentionally teach others.

In this context, we discussed an experimental paradigm that involved training a dominant and subordinate chimpanzee to work together according to a certain rule in order to acquire a preferred food. The rule was then changed, but only the dominant was informed of the change. Further, the dominant was given the opportunity to learn that the subordinate was working with a different rule. The prediction is that if the dominant understood that the subordinates' incorrect behavior was due to a different informational state, the dominant should not behave antagonistically toward the subordinate who would not engage in the behavior necessary for gaining food. However, if the dominant did not understand why the subordinate violated the rule, then, since the violation results in the dominant not gaining food, we would expect the dominant to behave antagonistically toward the subordinate. Experiments such as this are based on the view that attributions of beliefs have been adaptive for the development of social norms.

In this discussion of the mechanisms that may underlie the ability to predict and explain another's behavior in terms of mental states (i.e., theory of mind), we did not discuss a related mechanism based on introspection. Humphrey was one of the first to suggest that "mind reading" has to be based on the ability to model another's inner states (thoughts and feelings) based on one's own inner states *in the same context* (Humphrey 1980). This last point is perhaps the most important as it forms the basis for "putting yourself in another's shoes." Whether or not this method of predicting behavior involves some form of introspection (Gordon 1995, e.g., argues that it does not), it can only be adaptive if it is based on using, remembering, or "generating" (imaginative identification) previous experiences in the same or similar situation to the agent whose mental states you are modeling. There seems to be great potential for using this model to test whether nonhuman animals are reliant on reading external behavioral cues to understand anything about another's mental states. Determining what additional causal work reading minds adds over reading behavior alone is one of the most contentious issues in comparative cognition (Penn and Povinelli 2007b; Penn, this volume; Perner 2011). Hence, focusing on simulation tests may be an empirical means for getting past the behavior-reading–mind-reading trap (see also Lurz 2010).

In her criticism of theory of mind research in animals, Heyes suggested that a task based on introspection could provide clear evidence for mind reading (Heyes 1998; Penn and Povinelli 2007b). The idea is to provide an animal (e.g., a chimpanzee) with a novel first-person experience; namely goggles, one of which is translucent, allowing the wearer to see, and the other which is opaque. The only way to tell the goggles apart is by an arbitrary feature, such as the color of the frames. Without any behavioral cues from the wearers, but from his own experience, the animal should be able to predict that another individual wearing the opaque goggles (say, red frames) will not be able to see, whereas the one wearing the translucent goggles (yellow frames) will. In the case of chimpanzees, individuals should beg from experimenters wearing goggles with yellow frames and not from those with red-framed goggles. This task was proposed in response to a study in which chimpanzees had to beg from an experimenter who had a bucket on her shoulders versus one who covered her head with a bucket (Povinelli and Eddy 1996). Chimpanzees in this study failed, but Heyes' (1998) concern was that even if they had passed, this may have been due to prior experience in begging from people with visible eyes. The goggles task proposed by Heyes (1998) has yet to be performed in animals but has recently been tested in young children (Teufel et al. 2011; Senju et al. 2011). The only empirical evidence (we are aware of) related to this issue is that of *experience projection* in scrub jays. These food-caching corvids cache food for later consumption and protect their caches from thieving conspecifics by hiding them in places they cannot see or moving them to new places once a potential thief has left the vicinity (Clayton et al. 2007). What is of interest to the current discussion is the fact that only jays with the *specific* experience of stealing another's caches utilize the cache protection strategy of moving caches (re-caching) to a new location in private (i.e., unknown to the previously observing jay). This re-caching behavior is not seen in jays of the same age that were not given this thieving experience, even though they had experienced their own caches being stolen. Emery and Clayton suggest that the cachers "reflected" on their previous experience of being a thief and used this experience to model a potential thief's future intention to steal and, as such, move caches to a new location to protect them (Emery and Clayton 2001). Although a reasonable assumption, especially when taken together with the other cache protection strategies demonstrated by these birds, the issue of what psychological mechanisms may underlie this behavior continues to be the subject of much debate (Penn, this volume; Shettleworth 2010b).

An example of how we might demonstrate visual perspective-taking would be to use a naturally occurring behavior, such as food-caching in scrub jays. The experimental design follows the suggestion of Heyes (1998) described above: scrub jays can be given experience with two peepholes that allows them to see into an adjacent cage. They would also have experience that one peephole allows the competitor to see while the other does not, and have a blind they can draw to block the peephole. When caching, the bird should draw the blind down only if there is a competitor in the cage with the seeing peephole, blocking his visual access. If this happens in the absence of any behavioral cues or past experience, then it is plausible that there is a perceptual state attribution, though it would not offer evidence of a belief state attribution. However, one always needs first-person experience to find out what something is, whether it is yellow, green, hard, or soft. The same holds for transparent versus opaque. Once it has been established that one peephole is transparent and the other opaque, then one need not ascribe a mental state of "seeing" to the other individual. All that is needed is an understanding that the transparent hole needs to be blocked to prevent the other from intervening. In short, even with a clever paradigm such as this, it is hard to know what can be learned about perceptual state attribution.

One might ask whether it is possible to make any progress on the theory of mind question. Many comparative researchers bemoan the attention that theory of mind has already attracted and argue that further investment would be ill-spent. It may be more productive to focus on understanding the particular mechanisms employed by particular species in their species-typical forms of social interaction rather than in making a list of nonhuman animals' inadequacies relative to a human benchmark. A final concern is that it might not ever be possible to demonstrate this in nonlinguistic species, and that research efforts would better be directed toward more ecologically grounded pursuits.

On a positive note, the point was raised that the theory of mind approach is, in fact, a productive research paradigm that has led to the discovery of many new phenomena, whereas a "behavior rule" approach just produces post-hoc explanations of these phenomena. The question of whether nonhuman animals have human-like mentalizing abilities or tendencies makes researchers look at and try to tease out aspects of animal behavior they would not otherwise detect. However, it is a legitimate post-hoc question to ask to what degree these newly discovered aspects are the product of a theory of mind or the product of picking up mind-relevant behaviors in conjunction with behavior rules. For instance, a high sensitivity to behavior in relation to locations of desirable objects attests to the fact that animals understand *something* about the mind, even though they may not have theory of mind in the narrow sense (Perner 2010). However, being a driving force in discovering new phenomena is one thing; overinterpreting these discoveries is another.

Feeling into Others: Social Concerns

Like theory of mind, emotions are difficult to define without appealing to folk psychological terms. The issue here is not how we can assess the emotional experience of animals, but whether animals are able to do this with each other. Of particular interest to social knowledge are social concerns (also called fortunes-of-others emotions; Ortony et al. 1988).

Social concerns can either be aligned with the emotions and welfare of others, or misaligned. When aligned, the emotions of the subject match those of another individual, so that if the other individual is happy (or in happy circumstances), the subject is happy (symhedonia); if the other individual is sad (or in unfortunate circumstances), the subject is sad (empathy). Aligned emotions are positive social concerns, and it is easy to see how they can be important sources of social knowledge (for reviews, see Silk 2007b, 2009; Jensen 2011). Empathy and symhedonia should motivate prosocial behavior such as comforting, sharing, and helping. It should be noted that empathy is more than just emotional contagion, which is the automatic "catching" of emotions from another individual's expressions (Hatfield et al. 1994). Empathy requires affective perspective-taking, resulting in having emotions appropriate to the circumstances of another individual (e.g., Hoffman 1982). This is similar to the earlier argument for theory of mind in that affective perspective-taking, such as empathy, requires imputing the unobservable, not simply mirroring a behavior. Some researchers (de Waal and van Roosmalen 1979; Preston and de Waal 2002) defend the notion of empathy in animals, particularly chimpanzees. Their evidence comes largely from anecdotes, but also from observations of consolation and experiments in food provisioning. Anecdotal observations are notoriously difficult to interpret. As for consolation (i.e., providing comfort to another individual, such as after a conflict with a third party), this has been taken as being motivated by empathy. However, "consolation" may be directed at reducing the consoler's stress, rather than the target's, and it may serve the functional benefit of reducing the likelihood of redirected aggression (Koski and Sterck 2007, 2009). Consolation, then, may be motivated out of self-comfort (or self-protection), rather than out of a concern for the well-being of the recipient. Emotional contagion would produce this effect because seeing the distress of another individual would cause distress in the observers, and prompt them to seek comfort for themselves.

Affective perspective-taking, like simulation discussed earlier, involves inferences about the emotional state of others, and it can do so in the absence of emotional cues (Eisenberg et al. 1991; Hoffman 1984). This has been demonstrated in children by presenting a distressing scenario without any signs of distress in the target (Vaish et al. 2009). However, as yet, there is no evidence that, in the absence of emotional signals (but in the presence of an emotional event), animals show affective perspective-taking. This issue warrants future investigation. As for the motivations behind prosocial acts, it is difficult to determine whether empathy is the driving force, as has been suggested by de Waal et al. (2008), or whether something like empathy beyond emotional contagion is at work (Koski and Sterck 2010). The evidence for prosocial acts, in the absence of requests or distress signals, is rather uncommon in primates, the most extensively studied species so far. Chimpanzees, for instance, seem indifferent to outcomes affecting others, failing to give them food even at no real personal cost (Silk et al. 2005; Jensen et al. 2006; Vonk et al. 2008), yet they will help them achieve goals when the signal is clear (Warneken and Tomasello 2006; Yamamoto et al. 2009; Melis et al. 2010). Socially tolerant cooperative breeders, such as common marmosets have been suggested as being more inclined to provide food for conspecifics in the absence of signaling (Burkart et al. 2007), but here, too, results are mixed (Cronin et al. 2010, 2009; Stevens 2010a).

Misaligned emotions occur when the emotional state of the subject is inconsistent with the target's welfare and emotions. Envy (unhappiness at the good fortunes of others) and schadenfreude (pleasure in the misfortunes of others) are examples of negative social concerns. While not likely to lead to prosocial acts, they are valuable sources of social knowledge, allowing individuals to gauge their outcomes relative to others and to be more motivated to compete with rivals, and to do so in a more sophisticated manner. For instance, they may motivate punishment and or spiteful behaviors, the former of which are adaptive by deterring uncooperative behavior, for instance (Clutton-Brock and Parker 1995). Spitefulness is less intuitively adaptive, but may benefit the actor indirectly by preventing others from being better off (Jensen 2010). What needs to be determined is whether animals are motivated by their own immediate (or possibly) delayed outcomes, or whether they also have the suffering of others as goals. One area where negative social concerns have been suggested to manifest themselves is in disadvantageous inequity aversion. Sensitivity to fairness—being upset at having less than others is the minimal case—has been suggested as an essential component to uniquely human cooperation (Fehr and Fischbacher 2003), hence the interest in this topic. The typical approach to studying disadvantageous inequity aversion, as pioneered by Brosnan and de Waal (2003), involves one animal handing an object it just received back to the experimenter in exchange for a piece of food. The general idea—sometimes replicated, sometimes not—is that the subject is less likely to engage in the game if the partner receives a better quality piece of food, particularly if the partner does no work (i.e., exchange an object). If animals are averse to disadvantageous inequity, one would expect them to behave spitefully, to respond to the unfair outcome, and to any unfair intention, by causing their better-off rival to experience a loss. The ultimatum game is a widely used tool used by economists to probe fairness preferences (Güth et al. 1982). One person (proposer) is given an endowment (money) which he can then share with another person. The second person (responder) can refuse the offer of the proposer, causing both individuals to gain nothing; acceptance results in both getting the proposed division. Contrary to economic predictions based on rational decision making, responders reject offers perceived as unfair and, as a result, proposers tend to make fair divisions. Emotions appear to play a result in the decision to reject unfair offers, even at a cost; unfair offers are met with anger (Knoch et al. 2006; Pillutla and Murnighan 1996). On the other hand, chimpanzees, the only animal tested thus far, do not reject unfair offers in a mini-ultimatum game (Jensen et al. 2007a), despite being angry in another paradigm in which their food is taken away by a conspecific (Jensen et al. 2007b). At present, it is difficult to say whether animals have negative social concerns, taking the suffering of others into account.

Although motivational states are known to affect social decision making in animals ranging from honey bees to humans, the role of emotion in social cognition remains a rich area for future exploration. Another promising area for future work at the interface between social decision making and brain function will address questions regarding how social information is transduced into cellular and molecular change in the brain, and which genes are involved in the mediation of social behavior. At present, research linking genes, brain, and social behavior is at its early stages (Fischer and Hammerschmidt 2011).

How Do We Study Social Cognition?

A point that becomes clear from the preceding discussion is that there is no easy way to get into the heads of other animals. Trying to understand what animals do and do not know about their social worlds, and the specific processes they use to solve their adaptive challenges, is a great challenge. In our discussions, we considered three broad paths that researchers can take: computational models, observational studies, and experiments.

Computational Models

Computational modeling allows us to control variables selectively and observe their effects, and illustrates how relatively simple processes can produce complex outcomes. Agent-based models are particularly attractive for behavioral research.

One example of an agent-based model is GroofiWorld, which is based on the social behavior of primates (Hemelrijk, this volume). In GroofiWorld, when agents "meet," they may "attack" the other, "groom" it, or do nothing. The model appears to reproduce many of the grooming patterns of real primates without assuming the cognitive processes usually assumed. For example, in the model the agents reciprocated grooming and reconciled fights, especially with valued partners as well as in egalitarian rather than despotic societies. Reciprocation in the model emerges because individuals have more opportunities to groom some than others. Reconciliation is statistically found in the model because former opponents are, on average, closer together after a fight than they are otherwise. Thus they have more opportunities to groom a former opponent (called reconciliation) immediately after a fight, than at other times. Thus, "reconciliation" may be in the eye of the beholder: what we observe to be "reconciliation" need not involve an underlying "conciliatory tendency." In a similar way, "preferred reconciliation" with "valuable partners" emerges in the model without an understanding of social relationships; it emerges as a side effect of rank, because individuals in the model groom and reconcile more often with partners that are higher in rank. The model also produces a higher conciliatory tendency in egalitarian societies, because subordinates initiate interactions more often than they do in a despotic society and subordinates (compared to dominants) groom others more often. Consequently, the percentage of time spent grooming as well as the frequency of grooming immediately after a fight (i.e., the conciliatory tendency) is higher in egalitarian than in despotic societies.

One insight is that simple behavioral rules can produce behaviors that appear complex to outside observers. Reconciliatory behavior may not require an understanding of social relationships, prosocial motivations, or anything of the sort. All that may be required is risk-sensitive aggression, grooming that reduces tension, a tendency to groom if defeat is expected, and the spatial positions of individuals.

Computational models generate an abundance of hypotheses for future investigations. The GroofiWorld model points to the importance of studying the spatial positioning of individuals in a group and their relation to dominance and grooming behavior. For example, there is less reconciliation in despotic species, such as Rheusus macaques (*Macaca mulatta*), than in more egalitarian species such as Tonkean macaques (*M. tonkeana*). This difference can be fully explained by a different spatial structure in both species.

Care is advised in how strongly one interprets findings from models like these. Just because a simple rule can explain the behavior of agents in a model does not mean that only simple rules actually apply (simple rules may also be applied only in a certain percentage of cases), or that all animals use the same rules. Mice might solve conflicts based solely on proximity rules, whereas monkeys might use an understanding of social relationships, while humans will apply norms of social conduct. The behavioral outcome might be the same in each case, but the processes governing the behaviors may be very different.

For computational models to advance research into social cognition, they must reflect the real world. In other words, the variables in the model have to be valid. In addition, models must make predictions which can later be confirmed. The DomWorld model (predecessor to GroofiWorld) satisfied these criteria. It predicted that female dominance over males was higher when aggression was fiercer and when males constituted a higher percentage in the group. Both predictions were first derived from the model and subsequently tested and confirmed with empirical data. Perhaps more importantly, some variables must be shown to work less effectively than others. For instance, in GroofiWorld, it made no difference whether dominance interactions had self-reinforcing effects or not; resemblance to grooming patterns of primates largely vanished when agents chose interaction partners at random instead of interacting with those that they met close by (thus, when the spatial effects were excluded). It is sometimes suspected that many variables and many models will produce the same, or superficially similar, outcomes (see Hemelrijk, this volume).

Observational Studies

The best way to determine the validity of computational models is to see what animals actually *do*. Ideally, this should be done in the natural habitat using several groups of animals for as diverse a range of taxa as possible. The idea is to build up a portrait of the behavioral repertoire. Reports of behavior of animals in the wild continue to yield surprises and insights. Observational studies from the field have revealed a fascinating array of behaviors, some very complex (Cheney and Seyfarth 1990a, 2007). For instance, spotted hyenas (*Crocuta crocuta*) often recruit conspecifics from several kilometers away with loud vocalizations (Figure 18.1); once a sufficient number of group-mates has arrived, they solicit help to mob and displace lions (*Panthera leo*) from a carcass (Figure 18.2). How hyenas assess relative group size and probability of success, how they interpret and decide to respond to recruiting signals, and how they decide with whom to form mobbing coalitions are open questions. As hyena societies are structured exactly like troops of cercopithecine primates (Holekamp 2007), priority of access to food is determined by social rank once the hyenas gain possession of the carcass from lions. Therefore, division of the spoils is never equitable among the coalition partners who mobbed and displaced the lions. This raises the question of why low-ranking hyenas cooperate in dangerous mobbing of lions if their expected rewards will be small or nil. In her chapter in this volume, Cheney suggests that monkeys might make decisions regarding whether or not to help conspecifics contingent upon earlier or anticipated behavior of group-mates, perhaps mediated by some form of long-term "emotional book-keeping." Field studies are needed, however, to determine whether a mechanism like this might be operating among gregarious animals.

In another example, giant moray eels (*Gymnothorax javanicus*) and grouper fish (*Plectropomus pessuliferus*) were observed to hunt in a coordinated,

Figure 18.1   Spotted hyenas join forces to mob a lion (photo by Stephanie M. Dloniak).

cooperative fashion reminiscent of chimpanzee hunting (Bshary et al. 2006), which raises provocative questions about the cognitive abilities used by animals. The key conclusion from the grouper-moray study is that we cannot use observations to infer the cognitive processes underlying the behavior, something that field researchers are, quite understandably, inclined to do at times, particularly when working with species that more closely resemble humans. The old idea that behaviors or patterns uniquely described in primates/chimps/humans indicate complex cognitive processes has been shattered by many studies in other taxa.

Unfortunately, field observations can obfuscate research into social cognition. Although their strength lies in describing behavioral phenomena and their adaptive functions, field observations are more opaque when it comes to inferring mental states. For example, chimpanzee hunting and border patrols have been held up as examples of a fairly sophisticated cognitive process called joint intentionality (Boesch 2005). However, coordinated behavior does not require joint intentionality; individual agents pursuing their own goals simultaneously do not have to have the goals of others in mind (Tomasello et al. 2005). Distinguishing between the two processes can only be done experimentally.

When making observations, having an open mind without preconceptions is essential, but it also helps to have expectations about what is to be observed. It may be useful to ask anthropocentric questions such as: Does the chimp intentionally deceive his opponent? Does he understand that the opponent knows where the food is? This approach goes awry, however, when the human (folk psychological) interpretation of such behavior is viewed as the only obvious and viable interpretation. Initial exploratory anthropocentric expectations need to be verified through cognitive analysis (Perner 2010). Is attribution of every element in this analysis supported by the observed behavior?

Figure 18.2   Collective action by spotted hyenas allows them to maintain possession of a giraffe carcass also sought by a large subadult male lion (photo by Kay Holekamp).

Experiments

Ultimately, the best way to assess the cognitive processes of animals is to use experiments, both in the laboratory and in the field. Laboratory experiments are more prone to problems of ecological validity, whereas field experiments are more likely to suffer from problems of lack of control. A basic disconnect between the two appears to be far greater in the study of social cognition than in the study of other cognitive processes (e.g., navigation). Optimally, both approaches are needed when studying a particular species, but this is done less often than one would hope. In addition, if we want to understand the *adaptive* value of any particular aspect of social cognition, this can only be addressed in the field.

Playback experiments on free-ranging baboons have revealed that animals recognize the close associates, dominance ranks, and transient consort relationships of other individuals (reviewed by Cheney and Seyfarth 2007) and that they make use of this knowledge in their social interactions. For example, when a female baboon hears her opponent's "reconciliatory" grunt shortly after being threatened, she is more likely to approach her opponent and to tolerate her opponent's approach than after hearing no grunt or hearing the grunt of another female unrelated to her opponent (Cheney and Seyfarth 1997). In other playback experiments, Wittig et al. (2007) demonstrated that baboons also accept the grunt of a close relative of a recent opponent as a proxy for direct reconciliation with the opponent herself. After hearing the grunt of one of their opponent's close relatives, subjects were more likely to come into close proximity of their opponent. By contrast, hearing the grunt of a female from a different matriline had no effect on subjects' behavior.

These results suggest that baboons take into account a variety of information when deciding how to respond to a vocalization, including the identity of the caller, call type, the nature of recent interactions, and the relation between the caller and other recent partners or opponents. In the case of kin-mediated reconciliation, baboons seem to recognize that a grunt by the relative of an opponent serves the same function as a grunt by the opponent herself.

Ways Forward

A Question of Questions

There are a number of reasons to study the cognitive processes and the abilities of nonhuman animals. Our attempts to understand the processes used by animals to solve their everyday problems help us understand the evolution of such behaviors. When we see lions hunt and hyenas amass to usurp their kill, comparative psychologists and others cannot help but wonder what an animal is "thinking" or how it "knows" how to achieve its goals (though behavioral ecologists might remain agnostic on these topics). Folk psychology may inspire our pursuit, but we must remain guarded against unbridled anthropomorphism. At the most fundamental level, we need more field studies asking what animals "know" about their social worlds, and we need to learn much more about multiple aspects of social cognition in a broader array of species than has been studied to date. Only once we understand what animals know in nature will we be able to ask how they acquire and use this knowledge to make adaptive decisions.

We are also interested in animals for what they can tell us about how humans solve their social problems. This is the reason for the theory of mind research "industry," just as it was the basis of comparative psychology when it was called behaviorism prior to present-day neuroscience. Understanding the brains of animals helps us understand human brains; discovering the processes animals use for addressing their social problems, which have parallels with our own, can illuminate the processes we use. In addition, while this is not likely to be a popular view, seeing how difficult it is for animals to solve social problems can impress us with what might otherwise seem to be mundane cognitive feats, such as understanding that a cup at which someone is pointing contains food. On the other hand, seeing how easy it is for animals to solve other social problems may lead us to realize that humans may be using simpler cognitive mechanisms than previously assumed. Some very exciting work on animal cognition is done in parallel with developmental psychology (e.g., Krachun and Call 2009). Both young children and animals can be tested with paradigms that do not rely on language. This allows us to see behaviors that are not manifestly fully formed (and culturally biased), as they are in human adults.

The Future of Social Cognition

In an ideal world, one useful approach would be to compare multiple species using the same or similar methods used by teams of researchers. Consortium-level experiments have been very fruitfully applied by Joseph Henrich and others in comparing economic game theory in human cultures around the world. Similar approaches, informed by phylogenetic relatedness, are being used to choose the species most appropriate to test specific questions, such as temperament. In this way, rather than piecemeal collections of papers using different methods on few species of variable phylogenetic relatedness, researchers could begin to construct phylogenies of cognitive traits and relate these to ecological factors. While a monumental and challenging enterprise, it would be desirable to see work of this type.

Related to the use of phylogenetically corrected methods for interspecific comparisons of social cognition will be the use of these methods to inquire about the evolutionary history of specific cognitive abilities in animals, as well as the selection pressures that shape them. In the same way that Basolo (1990, 1996) was able to demonstrate that female preferences for long tails among swordtail fish evolved before the long tails themselves, study of a wider range of species should allow us to infer the evolutionary pathways through which specific cognitive abilities developed. To date, the majority of work on social cognition has been conducted with primates, and a number of specific abilities in the domain of social cognition were long thought to be unique to primates, including, for example, transitive inference. Recent work has, however, shown that this ability is also present in nonprimate mammals, birds, and fish (Engh et al. 2006; Grosenick and Clement 2007), suggesting either that its mediating mechanisms in the nervous system are very old or that this ability evolved convergently multiple times in response to a common suite of selection pressures.

Another approach is to integrate research methodologies. Having more information on the possible role of neurological mechanisms using noninvasive data recording and imaging techniques will allow us to infer more about the possible cognitive processes that are involved. Physiological data (e.g., heart rate and hormones) will add depth to questions such as the role of stress in grooming and reconciliation. If these can be experimentally manipulated, such as by administering oxytocin to see if it has an effect on prosocial preferences in other animals as it does in humans, then we will be able to say more about the role of emotional and executive processes, and the evolutionary implications of these.

In addition, modeling results need to be integrated as hypotheses for empirical data from free-living animals and for experimental procedures with captive ones. Models based on self-organization are particularly useful, because their results are close to natural observations (usually the same observation units and statistical methods are used in the model as in empirical studies). These models are usually based on simple behavioral rules known to exist in animals (e.g., grouping behavior, the calming effect of grooming) and thus can be used by scientists to become acquainted with the consequences of simple behavioral rules for patterns of social behavior and for types of social organization. By integrating effects of space, these models generate hypotheses which we cannot think of without these models; it appears that our mind is more prone to thinking intentionally than to integrating spatial constraints on behavioral interactions. Therefore, social-spatial structure must be investigated on a large scale in many species.

Over forty years ago, talk of animal cognition was taboo. Since then, it has been slow to gain traction as a respected research discipline (see Griffin 1984). Students of animal behavior were once taught that there was no possible way to peer inside the black box, nor was there any value in looking. This was the one—and possibly only—thing upon which ethologists, behavioral ecologists, and behaviorists could all agree.

Now, however, based on a cornucopia of impressive discoveries of the cognitive abilities of animals, new insights are available which, in turn, generates more questions and will hopefully lead to further discoveries. Although it is not possible to predict where the field will progress over the next ten years, we see great potential in future research endeavors.

Acknowledgments

We would like to thank all of the participants from the other groups for their insightful discussion, and in particular Jeff Stevens who contributed to this report.

Bibliography

Note: Numbers in square brackets denote the chapter in which an entry is cited.

Adams, C. D. 1982. Variations in the sensitivity of instrumental responding to reinforcer devaluation. *Q. J. Exp. Psychol.* **34B**:77–98. [9]

Adams, C. D., and A. Dickinson. 1981. Instrumental responding following reinforcer devaluation. *Q. J. Exp. Psychol.* **33B**:109–122. [6]

Addis, D. R., A. T. Wong, and D. L. Schacter. 2007. Remembering the past and imagining the future: Common and distinct neural substrates during event construction. *Neuropsychologia* **45**:1363–1377. [12]

Akcay, C., V. A. Reed, S. E. Campbell, C. N. Templeton, and M. D. Beecher. 2010. Indirect reciprocity: Song sparrows distrust aggressive neighbours based on eavesdropping. *Anim. Behav.* **80(6)**:1041–1047. [13]

Akcay, C., W. E. Wood, W. A. Searcy, et al. 2009. Good neighbour, bad neighbour: Song sparrows retaliate against aggressive rivals. *Anim. Behav.* **78**:97–102. [13]

Alenda, A., L. Ginzberg, E. Marozzi, R. Hayman, and K. Jeffery. 2010. Modulation of grid cell firing by changes in context. Program No. 100.3/KKK19. San Diego: Society for Neuroscience. [3]

Allen, C., and M. Bekoff. 1995. Cognitive ethology and the intentionality of animal behaviour. *Mind Lang.* **10(4)**:319–328. [6]

Anderson, C., and F. L. W. Ratnieks. 1999. Worker allocation in insect societies: Coordination of nectar foragers and nectar receivers in honey bee (*Apis mellifera*) colonies. *Behav. Ecol. Sociobiol.* **46**:73–81. [11]

Anderson, J. R., A. Gillies, and L. C. Lock. 2010. Pan thanatology. *Curr. Biol.* **20(8)**:R349–R351. [17]

Anderson, J. R., and L. J. Schooler. 1991. Reflections of the environment in memory. *Psychol. Sci.* **2**:396–408. [12]

Anderson, R. A., G. K. Essick, and R. M. Siegel. 1985. Encoding of spatial location by posterior parietal neurons. *Science* **230**:456–458. [5]

Andrews, K. 2005. Chimpanzee theory of mind: Looking in all the wrong places? *Mind Lang.* **20(5)**:521–536. [18]

———. 2009. Understanding norms without a theory of mind. *Inquiry* **52(5)**:433–448. [18]

———. 2011. Persons As We Know Them: A Pluralistic Approach to Folk Psychology. Cambridge, MA: MIT Press. [18]

Arbib, M. A., K. Liebal, and S. Pika. 2008. Primate vocalization, gesture, and the evolution of human language. *Curr. Anthro.* **49**:1053–1076. [13]

Armstrong, D. F., W. C. Stokoe, and S. E. Wilcox. 1995. Gesture and the Nature of Language. Cambridge: Cambridge Univ. Press. [13]

Armstrong, D. F., and S. E. Wilcox. 2007. The Gestural Origin of Language. New York: Oxford Univ. Press. [13]

Arnold, K., and A. Whiten. 2001. Post-conflict behaviour of wild chimpanzees (*Pan troglodytes schweinfurthii*) in the Budongo Forest, Uganda. *Behaviour* **138**:649–690. [15]

Aron, S., R. Beckers, J. L. Deneubourg, and J. M. Pasteels. 1993. Memory and chemical communication in the orientation of two mass-recruiting ant species. *Insectes Sociaux* **40**:369–380. [11]

Asratyan, E. A. 1974. Conditioned reflex theory and motivational behaviour. *Acta Neurobiol. Exp.* **43**:15–31. [6]

Aureli, F., and F. B. M. de Waal, eds. 2000. Natural Conflict Resolution. Berkeley: Univ. of California Press. [15]

Aureli, F., and C. M. Schaffner. 2002. Relationship assessment through emotional mediation. *Behaviour* **139**:393–420. [16]

Axelrod, R., and W. D. Hamilton. 1981. The evolution of cooperation. *Science* **211**:1390–1396. [7]

Baars, B. J. 1988. A Cognitive Theory of Consciousness. Cambridge: Cambridge Univ. Press. [9]

———. 1997. In the theatre of consciousness: Global workspace theory, a rigorous scientific theory of consciousness. *J. Conscious. Stud.* **4**:292–309. [9]

Babb, S. J., and J. D. Crystal. 2005. Discrimination of what, when and where: Implications for episodic-like memory in rats. *Learn. Motiv.* **36**:177–189. [12]

Balda, R. P., and A. C. Kamil. 1989. A comparative study on cache recovery by three corvid species. *Anim. Behav.* **38**:486–495. [14]

Baldwin, D. A. 1993. Early referential understanding: Infants' ability to understand referential acts for what they are. *Dev. Psychol.* **29**:832–843. [13]

Balleine, B. W., and A. Dickinson. 1998. Goal-directed instrumental action: Contingency and incentive learning and their cortical substrates. *Neuropharmacology* **37(4–5)**:407–419. [9]

Balleine, B. W., and J. P. O'Doherty. 2009. Human and rodent homologies in action control: Corticostriatal determinants of goal-directed and habitual action. *Neuropsychopharmacology* **35(1)**:48–69. [6]

Ballentine, B., W. A. Searcy, and S. Nowicki. 2008. Reliable aggressive signalling in swamp sparrows. *Anim. Behav.* **75**:693–703. [13]

Barkow, J. H., L. Cosmides, and J. Tooby. 1992. The Adapted Mind: Evolutionary Psychology and the Generation of Culture. New York: Oxford Univ. Press. [7]

Barrett, L., S. P. Henzi, T. Weingrill, J. E. Lycett, and R. A. Hill. 1999. Market forces predict grooming reciprocity in female baboons. *Proc. Roy. Soc. Lond. B* **266**:665–670. [15]

Barry, C., R. Hayman, N. Burgess, and K. J. Jeffery. 2007. Experience-dependent rescaling of entorhinal grids. *Nature Neurosci.* **10**:682–684. [3]

Barton, R. A., and R. I. M. Dunbar. 1997. Evolution of the social brain. In: Machiavellian Intelligence II, ed. A. Whiten and D. W. Barne, pp. 240–263. Cambridge: Cambridge Univ. Press. [14]

Basile, B. M., R. R. Hampton, S. Suomi, and E. A. Murray. 2008. An assessment of memory awareness in tufted capuchin monkeys (*Cebus apella*). *Anim. Cogn.* **12(1)**:169–180. [8]

Basolo, A. L. 1990. Female preference predates the evolution of the sword in swordtail fish. *Science* **250**:808–810. [13, 18]

———. 1996. The phylogenetic distribution of a female preference. *Syst. Biol.* **45**:290–307. [13, 18]

Bass, A. H., E. H. Gilland, and R. Baker. 2008. Evolutionary origins for social vocalization in a vertebrate hindbrain-spinal compartment. *Science* **321**:417–421. [13]

Beckers, R., J.-L. Deneubourg, and S. Goss. 1992. Trails and U-turns in the selection of a path by the ant *Lasius niger*. *J. Theor. Biol.* **159**:397–415. [11]

———. 1993. Modulation of trail laying in the ant *Lasius niger* (Hymenoptera: Formicidae) and its role in the collective selection of a food source. *J. Insect Behav.* **6**:751–759. [11]

Benhamou, S. 2003. Bicoordinate navigation based on non-orthogonal gradient fields. *J. Theor. Biol.* **225**:235–239. [4]

Bennett, A. T. D. 1996. Do animals have cognitive maps? *J. Exp. Biol.* **199**:219–224. [5]

Bennett, J. 1978. Some remarks about concepts. *Behav. Brain Sci.* **1**:557–560. [18]

Berg, N., and G. Gigerenzer. 2010. As-if behavioral economics: Neoclassical economics in disguise? *History Econ. Ideas* **18**:133–165. [7]

Bergman, T. J. 2010. Experimental evidence for limited vocal recognition in a wild primate: Implications for the social complexity hypothesis. *Proc. Roy. Soc. Lond. B* **277**:3045–3053. [18]

Bergman, T. J., J. C. Beehner, D. L. Cheney, and R. M. Seyfarth. 2003. Hierarchical classification by rank and kinship in baboons. *Science* **302**:1234–1236. [13, 14, 17, 18]

Bermudez, J. L. 2003. The domain of folk psychology. In: Mind and Persons, ed. A. O'Hear, pp. 25–48. Cambridge: Cambridge Univ. Press. [17]

Bickle, J. 2008. Multiple realizability in zalta. The Stanford Encyclopedia of Philosophy, ed. E. N. Zalta. http://plato.stanford.edu/entries/multiple-realizability/ (accessed 28 April 2011). [18]

Bierwisch, M. 2008. Der Tanz der Symbole: Wie die Sprache die Welt berechnet. In: Neuronen im Gespräch: Sprache und Gehirn, ed. H. Fink and R. Rosenzweig, pp. 17–45. Paderborn: Mentis. [2]

Biesmeijer, J., and T. D. Seeley. 2005. The use of waggle dance information by honey bees throughout their foraging careers. *Behav. Ecol. Sociobiol.* **59**:133–142. [11]

Bingman, V. P. 1998. Spatial representations and homing pigeon navigation. In: Spatial Representation in Animals, ed. S. D. Healy. Oxford: Oxford Univ. Press. [4]

Bingman, V. P., and K. Cheng. 2005. Mechanisms of animal global navigation: Comparative perspectives and enduring challenges. *Ethol. Ecol. Evol.* **17**:295–318. [4]

Bingman, V. P., A. Gagliardo, G. E. Hough II, et al. 2005. The avian hippocampus, homing in pigeons and the memory representation of large-scale space. *Integ. Comp. Biol.* **45**:555–564. [4]

Bird, C. D., and N. J. Emery. 2009. Insightful problem solving and creative tool modification by captive nontool-using rooks. *PNAS* **106(25)**:10,370–10,375. [6]

Biro, D., T. Humle, K. Koops, et al. 2010. Chimpanzee mothers at Bossou, Guinea carry the mummified remains of their dead infants. *Curr. Biol.* **20(8)**:R351–R352. [17]

Bishop, D. V. M. 2009. What can developmental language impairment tell us about the genetic basis of syntax? In: Biological Foundations and Origin of Syntax, ed. D. Bickerton and E. Szathmary, Strüngmann Forum Reports, J. Lupp, series ed. Cambridge, MA: MIT Press. [13]

Blair, H. T., and P. E. Sharp. 1995. Anticipatory head direction signals in anterior thalamus: Evidence for a thalamocortical circuit that integrates angular head motion to compute head direction. *J. Neurosci.* **15**:6260–6270. [3]

Blaisdell, A. P., K. Sawa, K. J. Leising, and M. R. Waldmann. 2006. Causal reasoning in rats. *Science* **311**:1020–1022. [6, 9, 17]

Blaubergs, M. S., and M. D. Braine. 1974. Short-term memory limitations on decoding self-embedded sentences. *J. Exp. Psychol.* **102**:745–748. [13]

Boë, L.-J., J.-L. Heim, K. Honda, and S. Maeda. 2002. The potential Neanderthal vowel space was as large as that of modern humans. *J. Phonet.* **30**:465–484. [12]

Boë, L.-J., J.-L. Heim, K. Honda, et al. 2007. The vocal tract of newborn humans and Neanderthals: Acoustic capabilities and consequences for the debate on the origin of language. A reply to Lieberman. *J. Phonet.* **35**:564–581. [12]

Boesch, C. 2005. Joint cooperative hunting among wild chimpanzees: Taking natural observations seriously. *Behav. Brain Sci.* **28(5)**:692–693. [18]

———. 2011. The ecology and evolution of social behavior and cognition in primates. In: The Oxford Handbook of Comparative Evolutionary Psychology, ed. J. Vonk and T. Shackelford. Oxford: Oxford Univ. Press, in press. [16]

Bond, A. B., A. C. Kamil, and R. P. Balda. 2003. Social complexity and transitive inference in corvids. *Anim. Behav.* **5**:479–487. [14, 18]

Bonnevie, T., M. Fyhn, T. Hafting, E. Moser, and M. M. B. 2006. Misalignment of entorhinal grid fields after hippocampal inactivation. Program No. 68.9. Society for Neuroscience. [3]

Boroditsky, L. 2001. Does language shape thought? English and Mandarin speakers' conceptions of time. *Cogn. Psychol.* **43(1)**:1–22. [5]

Bowerman, M. 1996. Learning how to structure space for language: A cross-linguistic perspective. In: Language and Space, ed. P. Bloom et al., pp. 385–436. Cambridge, MA: MIT Press. [5]

Boyd, B. 2009. The Origin of Stories: Evolution, Cognition, and Fiction. Cambridge, MA: Belknap Press. [12]

Bradbury, J. W., and S. L. Vehrencamp. 1998. Principles of Animal Communication. Sunderland, MA: Sinauer. [11, 13]

Brannon, E. M. 2006. The representation of numerical magnitude. *Curr. Opin. Neurobiol.* **16**:222–229. [7]

Bräuer, J., J. Call, and M. Tomasello. 2004. Visual perspective-taking in dogs (*Canis familiaris*) in the presence of barriers. *Appl. Anim. Behav.* **88**:299–317. [14]

———. 2006. Are apes really inequity averse? *Proc. Roy. Soc. Lond. B* **273**:3123–3128. [16]

Breitmeyer, B. G., and H. Öğmen. 2006 Visual Masking: Time Slices Through Conscious and Nonconscious Vision. New York: Oxford Univ. Press. [9]

Brodbeck, D. R. 1994. Memory for spatial and local cues: A comparison of a storing and a nonstoring species. *Anim. Learn. Behav.* **22**:119–133. [5]

Bro-Jorgensen, J., and W. M. Pangle. 2010. Male topi antelopes snort deceptively to retain females for mating. *Amer. Nat.* **176**:E33–E39. [13]

Brosnan, S. F., and F. B. M. de Waal. 2003. Monkeys reject unequal pay. *Nature* **425**:297–299. [16, 17, 18]

Brosnan, S. F., L. Salwiczek, and R. Bshary. 2010. The interplay of cognition and cooperation. *Philos. Trans. R. Soc. Lond. B* **365**:2699–2710. [14]

Brosnan, S. F., J. B. Silk, J. Henrich, et al. 2009. Chimpanzees *Pan troglodytes* do not develop contingent reciprocity in an experimental task. *Anim. Cogn.* **12**:587–597. [16]

Brown, C., K. N. Laland, and J. Krause, eds. 2006. Learning and Cognition in Fishes. Oxford: Blackwell. [14]

Brown, M. W., and J. P. Aggleton. 2001. Recognition memory: What are the roles of the perirhinal cortex and hippocampus? *Nature Rev. Neurosci.* **2(1)**:51–61. [8]

Brun, V. H., T. Solstad, K. Kjelstrup, et al. 2008. Progressive increase in grid scale from dorsal to ventral medial entorhinal cortex. *Hippocampus* **18**:1200–1212. [3]

Bshary, R., A. Hohner, K. Ait-el-Djoudi, and H. Fricke. 2006. Interspecific communicative and coordinated hunting between groupers and giant moray eels in the Red Sea. *PLoS Biol.* **4(12)**:e431. [18]

Buckner, R. L. 2010. The role of the hippocampus in prediction and imagination. *Ann. Rev. Psychol.* **61**:27–48. [8]

Bugnyar, T., M. Stöwe, and B. Heinrich. 2004. Ravens, *Corvus corax*, follow gaze direction of humans around obstacles. *Proc. Roy. Soc. Lond. B* **B271**:1331–1336. [14]

Buhl, J., D. J. T. Sumpter, I. D. Couzin, et al. 2006. From disorder to order in marching locusts. *Science* **312(5778)**:1402–1406. [15]

Burgess, N. 2006. Spatial memory: How egocentric and allocentric combine. *Trends Cogn. Sci.* **10**:551–557. [5]

Burkart, J. M., E. Fehr, C. Efferson, and C. P. van Schaik. 2007. Other-regarding preferences in a non-human primate: Common marmosets provision food altruistically. *PNAS* **104**:19,762–19,766. [18]

Burling, R. 2007. The Talking Ape: How Language Evolved. New York: Oxford Univ. Press. [13]

Byrne, R. W., and L. A. Bates. 2010. Primate social cognition: Uniquely primate, uniquely social, or just unique? *Neuron* **65(6)**:815–830. [17]

Byrne, R. W., and A. Whiten, eds. 1988. Machiavellian Intelligence. Oxford: Clarendon Press. [14]

———. 1991. Computation and mindreading in primate tactical deception. In: Natural Theories of Mind: Evolution, Development and Simulations of Everyday Mindreading, ed. A. Whiten. Oxford: Blackwell. [18]

———. 1997. Machiavellian intelligence. In: Machiavellian Intelligence II. Extensions and Evaluations, ed. A. Whiten and R. W. Byrne, pp. 1–23. Cambridge: Cambridge Univ. Press. [15, 18]

Call, J. 1999. The effect of inter-opponent distance on the occurrence of reconciliation in stumptail (*Macaca arctoides*) and rhesus macaques (*Macaca mulatta*). *Primates* **40(3)**:515–523. [15]

Call, J., J. Brauer, J. Kaminski, and M. Tomasello. 2003. Domestic dogs (*Canis familiaris*) are sensitive to the attentional state of humans. *J. Comp. Psychol.* **117(3)**:257–263. [17]

Call, J., and M. Carpenter. 2001. Do apes and children know what they have seen? *Anim. Cogn.* **4**:207–220. [8]

Call, J., and M. Tomasello. 1994. Production and comprehension of referential pointing by orangutans (*Pongo pygmaeus*). *J. Comp. Psychol.* **108**:307–317. [13]

———. 2008. Does the chimpanzee have a theory of mind? 30 years later. *Trends Cogn. Sci.* **12**:187–192. [9, 16, 17, 18]

Calton, J. L., and J. S. Taube. 2005. Degradation of head direction cell activity during inverted locomotion. *J. Neurosci.* **25**:2420–2428. [3]

Camazine, S., J.-L. Deneubourg, N. R. Franks, et al. 2001. Self-Organization in Biological Systems. Princeton: Princeton Univ. Press. [11, 15]

Capaldi, E. A., A. D. Smith, J. L. Osborne, et al. 2000. Ontogeny of orientation flight in the honeybee revealed by harmonic radar. *Nature* **403(6769)**:537–540. [2]

Caro, T. M., and M. D. Hauser. 1992. Is there teaching in nonhuman animals? *Q. Rev. Biol.* **67**:151–174. [11]

Carruthers, P. 2004. On being simple minded. *Amer. Philos. Q.* **41(3)**:205–220. [6]

———. 2008. Meta-cognition in animals: A skeptical look. *Mind Lang.* **23(1)**:58–89. [9]

Carruthers, P. 2009. How we know our own minds: The relationship between mindreading and metacognition. *Behav. Brain Sci.* **32(2)**:121–138. [9]

Cartwright, B. A., and T. S. Collet. 1982. How honey bees use landmarks to guide their return to a food sorce. *Nature* **295**:560–564. [5]

———. 1987. Landmark maps for honey bees. *Biol. Cybern.* **57**:85–93. [5]

Casasanto, D. 2008. Similarity and proximity: When does close in space mean close in mind? *Mem. Cogn.* **36(6)**:1047–1056. [5]

Casasola, M., J. Bhagwat, and A. S. Burke. 2009. Learning to form a spatial category of tight-fit relations: How experience with a label can give a boost. *Dev. Psychol.* **45(3)**:711–723. [5]

Casini, G., V. P. Bingman, and P. Bagnoli. 1986. Connections of the pigeon dorsomedial forebrain studied with WGA-HRP and (3H)-proline. *J. Comp. Neurol.* **245**:454–470. [4]

Chapuis, N., and C. Varlet. 1987. Short cuts by dogs in natural surroundings. *Q. J. Exp. Psychol.* **39B**:49–64. [5]

Chater, N., F. Reali, and M. H. Christiansen. 2009. Restrictions on biological adaptation in language evolution. *PNAS* **106**:1015–1020. [13]

Cheney, D. L., R. Moscovice, M. Heesen, R. Mundry, and R. M. Seyfarth. 2010. Contingent cooperation in wild female baboons. *PNAS* **107**:9562–9566. [14, 16]

Cheney, D. L., and R. M. Seyfarth. 1988. Assessment of meaning and the detection of unreliable signals by vervet monkeys. *Anim Behav* **36**:477–486. [10]

———. 1990a. Attending to behavior versus attending to knowledge: Examining monkeys' attribution of mental states. *Anim. Behav.* **40**:742–753. [18]

———. 1990b. How Monkeys See the World: Inside the Mind of Another Species. Chicago: Chicago Univ. Press. [13, 14]

———. 1997. Reconciliatory grunts by dominant female baboons influence victims' behavior. *Anim. Behav.* **54**:409–418. [18]

———. 2005. Constraints and preadaptations in the earliest stages of language evolution. *Ling. Rev.* **22**:135–159. [13]

———. 2007. Baboon Metaphysics: The Evolution of a Social Mind. Chicago: Univ. of Chicago Press. [13, 16, 18]

———. 2009. Stress and coping mechanisms in female primates. *Adv. Stud. Behav.* **39**:1–35. [16]

Cheney, D. L., R. M. Seyfarth, and J. B. Silk. 1995. The responses of female baboons (*Papio cynocephalus ursinus*) to anomalous social interactions: Evidence for causal reasoning? *J. Comp. Psychol.* **109**:134–141. [13]

Cheng, K. 1986. A purely geometric module in the rat's spatial representation. *Cognition* **23**:149–178. [5]

———. 2006. Arthropod navigation: Ants, bees, crabs, spiders finding their way. In: Comparative Cognition: Experimental Explorations of Animal Intelligence, ed. E. A. Wasserman and T. R. Zentall, pp. 189–209. Oxford: Oxford Univ. Press. [5]

Cheng, K., and N. S. Newcombe. 2005. Is there a geometric module for spatial orientation? Squaring theory and evidence. *Psychon. Bull. Rev.* **12**:1–23. [5]

Cheng, K., S. Shettleworth, J. Huttenlocher, and J. J. Rieser. 2007. Bayesian integration of spatial information. *Psychol. Bull.* **133**:625–637. [5]

Chomsky, N. 1957. Syntactic Structures. The Hague: Mouton. [13]

———. 2010. Some simple evo devo theses: How true might they be for language? In: The Evolution of Human Language, ed. R. K. Larson et al., pp. 45–62. Cambridge: Cambridge Univ. Press. [12]

Christiansen, M. H., and N. Chater. 2008. Language as shaped by the brain. *Behav. Brain Sci.* **31**:489–558. [12, 13]

Christiansen, M. H., and S. Kirby. 2003. Language evolution: Consensus and controversies. *Trends Cogn. Sci.* **7**:300–307. [13]

Christiansen, M. H., and M. C. MacDonald. 2009. A usage-based approach to recursion in sentence processing. *Lang. Learn.* **59 (1)**:126–161. [13]

Chua, E. F., D. L. Schacter, E. Rand-Giovannetti, and R. A. Sperling. 2007. Evidence for a specific role of the anterior hippocampal region in successful associative encoding. *Hippocampus* **17**:1071–1080. [12]

Churchland, P. M. 1981. Eliminative materialism and the propositional attitudes. *J. Philosophy* **78(2)**:67–90. [18]

Churchland, P. M., and P. S. Churchland. 1996. The future of psychology, folk and scientific. In: The Churchlands and Their Critics, ed. R. N. McCauley. Cambridge: Blackwell. [17]

Clark, A., and C. Thornton. 1997. Trading spaces: Computation, representation, and the limits of uninformed learning. *Behav. Brain Sci.* **20**:57–90. [17]

Clark, H. H. 1996. Using Language. Cambridge: Cambridge Univ. Press. [13]

Clayton, N. S., T. J. Bussey, and A. Dickinson. 2003. Can animals recall the past and plan for the future? *Nature Rev.* **4**:685–691. [12]

Clayton, N. S., J. Dally, J. Gilbert, and A. Dickinson. 2005. Food caching by western scrub-jays (*Aphelocoma californica*) is sensitive to the conditions at recovery. *J. Exp. Psychol. Anim. Behav. Proc.* **31**:115–124. [7]

Clayton, N. S., J. M. Dally, and N. J. Emery. 2007. Social cognition by food-caching corvids: The western scrub-jay as a natural psychologist. *Philos. Trans. R. Soc. Lond. B* **362(1480)**:507–522. [17, 18]

Clayton, N. S., and A. Dickinson. 1998. Episodic-like memory during cache recovery by scrub jays. *Nature* **395**:272–274. [12]

Clayton, N. S., D. P. Griffiths, N. J. Emery, and A. Dickinson. 2001. Elements of episodic-like memory in animals. *Roy. Soc.* **356**:1483–1491. [17]

Clutton-Brock, T. H. 2009. Cooperation between non-kin in animal societies. *Nature* **462**:51–57. [16]

Clutton-Brock, T. H., and G. A. Parker. 1995. Punishment in animal societies. *Nature* **272**:209–216. [18]

Cohen, N. J., and H. Eichenbaum. 1994. Memory, Amnesia, and the Hippocampal System. Cambridge, MA: MIT Press. [8]

Collet, M., T. S. Collet, S. Bisch, and R. Wehner. 1998. Local and global vectors in desert ant navigation. *Nature* **394**:269–272. [5]

Collet, T. S., and M. Collet. 2002. Memory use in insect visual navigation. *Nature Rev. Neurosci.* **3**:542–552. [5, 11]

Collett, T. S., and P. Graham. 2004. Animal navigation: Path integration, visual landmarks and cognitive maps. *Curr. Biol.* **14(12)**:R475–R477. [2]

Commons, M. L., R. J. Herrnstein, and H. Rachlin. 1982. Quantitative Analyses of Behavior: Matching and Maximizing Accounts. Cambridge, MA: Erlbaum. [7]

Cook, R. G., M. F. Brown, and D. A. Riley. 1985. Flexible memory processing by rats: Use of prospective and retrospective information in the radial maze. *J. Exp. Psychol. Anim. Behav. Proc.* **11(3)**:453–469. [9]

Coolidge, F. L., and T. Wynn. 2001. Executive functions of the frontal lobes and the evolutionary ascendancy of *homo sapiens*. *Cambridge Archaeol. J.* **11(2)**:255–260. [9]

Cooper, M. A. 2004. Inter-group relationships. In: Macaque Societies: A Model for the Study of Social Organization, ed. B. Thierry et al. Cambridge: Cambridge Univ. Press. [15]

Corballis, M. C. 1989. Laterality and human evolution. *Psychol. Rev.* **96**:492–505. [13]

———. 2002. From Hand to Mouth: The Origins of Language. Princeton: Princeton Univ. Press. [13]

———. 2004. The origins of modernity: Was autonomous speech the critical factor? *Psychol. Rev.* **111**:543–552. [12]

———. 2007. Recursion, language, and starlings. *Cogn. Sci.* **31**:697–704. [13]

———. 2009. The evolution of language. *Ann. NY Acad. Sci.* **1156**:19–43. [12]

———. 2010. Mirror neurons and the evolution of language. *Brain Lang.* **112**:25–35. [13]

Corrado, G. S., L. P. Sugrue, H. Sebastian Seung, and W. T. Newsome. 2005. Linear-nonlinear-poisson models of primate choice dynamics. *J. Exp. Anal. Behav.* **84(3)**:581–617. [9]

Correia, S. P., A. Dickinson, and N. S. Clayton. 2007. Western scrub-jays (*Aphelcma california*) anticipate future needs independently of their current motivational state. *Curr. Biol.* **17**:856–861. [6]

Couzin, I. D. 2009. Collective cognition in animal groups. *Trends Cogn. Sci.* **13**:36–43. [11]

Couzin, I. D., J. Krause, R. James, G. D. Ruxton, and N. R. Franks. 2002. Collective memory and spatial sorting in animal groups. *J. Theor. Biol.* **218(1)**:1–11. [15]

Cowey, A. 2010. The blindsight saga. *Exp. Brain Res.* **200(1)**:3–24. [8]

Cowey, A., and P. Stoerig. 1995. Blindsight in monkeys. *Nature* **373(6511)**:247–249. [8, 9]

Cressant, A., R. U. Muller, and B. Poucet. 1997. Failure of centrally placed objects to control the firing fields of hippocampal place cells. *J. Neurosci.* **17**:2531–2542. [3]

Cristol, D. A., E. B. Reynolds, J. E. Leclerc, et al. 2003. Migratory dark-eyed juncos (*Junco hyemalis*) have better spatial memory and denser hippocampal neurons than nonmigratory conspecifics. *Anim. Behav.* **66**:317–328. [4]

Critchfield, T. S., and G. J. Madden. 2007. At the crossroads of time and action: A temporal discounting primer for prospective memory researchers. In: Timing the Future: The Case for Time-Based Prospective Memory, ed. J. Glicksohn and M. Myslobodsky, pp. 117–142. Hackensack, NJ: World Scientific Publishing. [7]

Cronin, K. A., K. K. E. Schroeder, E. S. Rothwell, J. B. Silk, and C. T. Snowdon. 2009. Cooperatively breeding cottontop tamarins (*Saguinus oedipus*) do not donate rewards to their long-term mates. *J. Comp. Psychol.* **123**:231–241. [18]

Cronin, K. A., K. K. E. Schroeder, and C. T. Snowdon. 2010. Prosocial behavior emerges independent of reciprocity in cottontop tamarins. *Proc. Roy. Soc. Lond. B* **277**:3845–3851. [18]

Dacke, M., and M. V. Srinivasan. 2008. Evidence for counting in insects. *Anim. Cogn.* **11**:683–689. [13]

Dally, J. M., N. J. Emery, and N. S. Clayton. 2004. Cache protection strategies by western scrub-jays (*Aphelocoma californica*): Hiding food in the shade. *Proc. Biol. Sci.* **271(6)**:S387–90. [17]

———. 2005. Cache protection strategies by western scrub-jays (*Aphelocoma californica*): Implications for social cognition. *Anim. Behav.* **70**:1251–1263. [17]

———. 2006. Food-caching western scrub-jays keep track of who was watching when. *Science* **312**:1662–1666. [4, 12]

Damasio, A. R. 1996. The somatic marker hypothesis and the possble functions of the prefrontal cortex. *Philos. Trans. R. Soc. Lond. B* **351**:1413–1420. [6]

Darwin, C. 1871. The Descent of Man, and Selection in Relation to Sex. London: John Murray. [17]

———. 1896. The Descent of Man, and Selection in Relation to Sex, 2nd ed. New York: Appleton. [12]

Daw, N. D., Y. Niv, and P. Dayan. 2005. Uncertainty-based competition between prefrontal and dorsolateral striatal systems for behavioral control. *Nature Neurosci.* **8**:1704–1711. [6]

Dawkins, R., and J. R. Krebs. 1978. Animal signals: Information or manipulation? In: Behavioural Ecology: An Evolutionary Approach, ed. J. R. Krebs and J. R. Davies, pp. 282–309. Oxford: Blackwell Scientific Publications. [10, 13]

de Kort, S. R., S. P. C. Correia, D. M. Alexis, A. Dickinson, and N. S. Clayton. 2007. The control of food-caching behavior by Western scrub-jays (*Aphelocoma californica*). *J. Exp. Psychol. Anim. Behav. Proc.* **33**:361–370. [6]

de Kort, S. R., A. Dickinson, and N. S. Clayton. 2005. Retrospective cognition by food-caching western scrub-jays. *Learn. Motiv.* **36**:159–176. [6, 9]

de Waal, F. B. M. 1982. Chimpanzee Politics: Sex and Power among Apes. New York: Harper and Row. [15]

———. 2006. Primates and Philosophers: How Morality Evolved. Princeton: Princeton Univ. Press. [17]

———. 2009. Darwin's last laugh. *Nature* **460(7252)**:175. [9]

de Waal, F. B. M., and J. M. Davis. 2003. Capuchin cognitive ecology: Cooperation based on projected returns. *Neuropsychologia* **41**:221–228. [16]

de Waal, F. B. M., and P. F. Ferrari. 2010. Towards a bottom-up perspective on animal and human cognition. *Trends Cogn. Sci.* **14(5)**:201–207. [17]

de Waal, F. B. M., K. Leimgruber, and A. R. Greenberg. 2008. Giving is self-rewarding for monkeys. *PNAS* **105**:13,685–13,689. [18]

de Waal, F. B. M., and L. M. Luttrell. 1988. Mechanisms of social reciprocity in three primate species: Symmetrical relationship characteristics or cognition? *Ethol. Sociobiol.* **9**:101–118. [15]

de Waal, F. B. M., and A. van Roosmalen. 1979. Reconciliation and consolation among chimpanzees. *Behav. Ecol. Sociobiol.* **5**:55–66. [18]

de Wit, S., and A. Dickinson. 2009. Associative theories of goal-directed behaviour: A case for animal-human translational models. *Psychol. Res.* **73(4)**:463–476. [6]

Dehaene, S., J. Changeux, L. Naccache, J. Sackur, and C. Sergent. 2006a. Conscious, preconscious, and subliminal processing: A testable taxonomy. *Trends Cogn. Sci.* **10(5)**:204–211. [9]

Dehaene, S., V. Izard, P. Pica, and E. S. Spelke. 2006b. Core knowledge of geometry in an Amazonian indigene group. *Science* **311**:381–384. [5]

Dehaene, S., M. Kerszberg, and J. Changeux. 1998. A neuronal model of a global workspace in effortful cognitive tasks. *PNAS* **95(24)**:14,529–14,534. [9]

Dehaene, S., and L. Naccache. 2001. Towards a cognitive neuroscience of consciousness: Basic evidence and a workspace framework. *Cognition* **79**:1–37. [9]

Deneubourg, J. L., S. Aron, S. Goss, and J. M. Pasteels. 1990. The self-organizing exploratory pattern of the argentine ant. *J. Insect Behav.* **3**:159–168. [11]

Dennett, D. C. 1978. Beliefs about beliefs. *Behav. Brain Sci.* **4**:568–570. [18]

———. 1987. The Intentional Stance. Cambridge, MA: MIT Press. [17]

———. 1991. Consciousness Explained, 1st ed. Boston: Little Brown and Co. [17]

Dennett, D. C. 2009. Darwin's strange inversion of reasoning. *PNAS* **106(1)**:10,061–10,065. [17]

Derdikman, D., and E. I. Moser. 2010. A manifold of spatial maps in the brain. *Trends Cogn. Sci.* **14**:561–569. [5]

Detrain, C., and J.-L. Deneubourg. 2008. Collective decision-making and foraging patterns in ants and honeybees. *Adv. Insect Physiol.* **35**:123–173. [11]

————. 2009. Social cues and adaptive foraging strategies in ants. In: Food Exploitation by Social Insects: Ecological, Behavioral, and Theoretical Approaches, ed. S. Jarau and M. Hrncir, pp. 29–51. Boca Raton: CRC Press. [11]

Di Bitetti, M. S. 2003. Food-associated calls of tufted capuchin monkeys (*Cebus apella nigritus*) are functionally referential signals. *Behaviour* **140**:565–592. [13]

Dickinson, A. 1985. Actions and habits: The development of behavioural autonomy. *Philos. Trans. R. Soc. Lond. B* **308**:67–78. [6]

————. 1994. Instrumental conditioning. In: Animal Learning and Cognition, ed. N. J. Mackintosh, pp. 45–79. San Diego: Academic Press. [6]

Dickinson, A., B. Balleine, A. Watt, F. Gonzalez, and R. A. Boakes. 1995. Motivational control after extended instrumental training. *Anim. Learn. Behav.* **23**:197–206. [6]

Dickinson, A., J. Campos, Z. L. Varga, and B. W. Balleine. 1996. Bidirectional instrumental conditioning. *Q. J. Exp. Psychol.* **49B**:289–306. [6]

Dickinson, A., A. Watt, and W. J. H. Griffiths. 1992. Free-operant acquisition with delayed reinforcement. *Q. J. Exp. Psychol.* **45B(3)**:241–258. [6]

Dickinson, S. 1987. Recursion in development: Support for a biological model of language. *Lang. Speech* **30**:239–249. [13]

Diggle, S. P., A. Gardner, S. A. West, and A. S. Griffin. 2007. Evolutionary theory of bacterial quorum sensing: When is a signal not a signal? *Philos. Trans. R. Soc. Lond. B* **362(1483)**:1241–1249. [10, 13]

Doeller, C. F., C. Barry, and N. Burgess. 2010. Evidence for grid cells in a human memory network. *Nature* **463**:657–661. [3]

Donald, M. 1991. Origins of the Modern Mind. Cambridge, MA: Harvard Univ. Press. [12]

Dorigo, M., and T. Stützle. 2004. Ant Colony Optimization. Cambridge, MA: MIT Press. [11]

Dretske, F. I. 1981. Knowledge and the Flow of Information. Cambridge, MA: MIT Press. [13]

Dubreuil, D., M. S. Gentile, and E. Visalberghi. 2006. Are capuchin monkeys (*Cebus apella*) inequity averse? *Proc. Roy. Soc. Lond. B* **273**:1223–1228. [16]

Dudchenko, P. A., and L. E. Zinyuk. 2005. The formation of cognitive maps of adjacent environments: Evidence from the head direction cell system. *Behav. Neurosci.* **119**:1511–1523. [3]

Dukas, R. 1998. Cognitive Ecology: The Evolutionary Ecology of Information Processing and Decision Making. Chicago: Univ. of Chicago Press. [7]

Dunbar, R. I. M. 1992. Neocortex size as a constraint on group size in primates. *J. Hum. Evol.* **20**:287–296. [14, 18]

————. 1998a. The social brain hypothesis. *Evol. Anthropol.* **6**:178–190. [18]

————. 1998b. Theory of mind and the evolution of language. In: Approaches to the Evolution of Language, ed. J. R. Hurford et al., pp. 92–110. Cambridge: Cambridge Univ. Press. [13]

Dunbar, R. I. M., and S. Shultz. 2007. Evolution in the social brain. *Science* **317**:1344–1347. [18]

Dussutour, A., S. C. Nicolis, G. Shephard, M. Beekman, and D. J. T. Sumpter. 2009. The role of multiple pheromones in food recruitment by ants. *J. Exp. Biol.* **212**:2337–2348. [11]

Dwyer, D. M., J. Starns, and R. C. Honey. 2009. "Causal reasoning" in rats: A reappraisal. *J. Exp. Psychol. Anim. Behav. Proc.* **35(4)**:578–586. [6]

Dyer, F. C. 2002. The biology of the dance language. *Ann. Rev. Entomol.* **47**:917–949. [11, 13]

Edelman, D. B., and A. K. Seth. 2009. Animal consciousness: A synthetic approach. *Trends Neurosci.* **32(9)**:476–484. [9]

Egnor, S. E. R., and M. D. Hauser. 2004. A paradox in the evolution of primate vocal learning. *Trends Neurosci.* **27**:649–654. [13]

Eichenbaum, H., A. P. Yonelinas, and C. Ranganath. 2007. The medial temporal lobe and recognition memory. *Ann. Rev. Neurosci.* **30**:123–152. [8]

Eisenberg, N., C. L. Shea, G. Carlo, and G. P. Knight. 1991. Empathy related responding and cognition: A "chicken and the egg" dilemma. In: Handbook of Moral Behavior and Development, ed. W. M. Kurtines and J. L. Gewirtz, pp. 63–88. Hillsdale, NJ: Lawrence Erlbaum. [18]

Emery, N. J. 2004. Are corvids "feathered apes"? Cognitive evolution in crows, jays, rooks and jackdaws. In: Comparative Analysis of Minds, ed. S. Watanabe. Tokyo: Keio Univ. Press. [17]

———. 2006. Cognitive ornithology: The evolution of avian intelligence. *Philos. Trans. R. Soc. Lond. B* **361**:23–43. [18]

Emery, N. J., and N. S. Clayton. 2001. Effects of experience and social context on prospective caching strategies by scrub jays. *Nature* **414**:443–446. [7, 14, 17, 18]

———. 2008. How to build a scrub-jay that reads minds. In: Origins of the Social Mind: Evolutionary and Developmental Views, ed. S. Itakura and K. Fujita, pp. 65–97. Tokyo: Springer Verlag. [17]

———. 2009. Comparative social cognition. *Ann. Rev. Psychol.* **60(1)**:87–113. [17]

Emery, N. J., A. M. Seed, A. M. P. von Bayern, and N. S. Clayton. 2007. Cognitive adaptations of social bonding in birds. *Philos. Trans. R. Soc. Lond. B* **362**:489–505. [18]

Enard, W., S. Gehre, K. Hammerschmidt, et al. 2009. A humanized version of FOXp2 affects cortico-basal ganglia circuits in mice. *Cell* **237**:961–971. [13]

Enard, W., M. Prezworski, S. E. Fisher, et al. 2002. Molecular evolution of FOXP2, a gene involved in speech and language. *Nature* **418**:869–872. [13]

Endler, J. A., and A. L. Basolo. 1998. Sensory ecology, receiver biases and sexual selection. *Trends Ecol. Evol.* **13**:415–420. [13]

Engh, A. L., R. R. Hoffmeier, D. L. Cheney, and R. M. Seyfarth. 2006. Who me? Can baboons infer the target of vocalizations? *Anim. Behav.* **71**:381–387. [13, 18]

Enquist, M. 1985. Communication during aggressive interactions with particular reference to variation in choice of behaviour. *Anim. Behav.* **33**:1152–1161. [13]

Esch, H. E., S. Zhang, M. V. Srinivasan, and J. Tautz. 2001. Honeybee dances communicate distances measured by optic flow. *Nature* **411**:581–583. [13]

Evans, N., and S. C. Levinson. 2009. The myth of language universals: Language diversity and its importance for cognitive science. *Behav. Brain Sci.* **32**:429–492. [12, 13]

Farina, W. M., C. Grüter, and P. C. Diaz. 2005. Social learning of floral odours within the honeybee hive. *Proc. Roy. Soc. Lond. B* **272**:1923–1928. [11]

Fehr, E., and U. Fischbacher. 2003. The nature of human altruism. *Nature* **425**:785–791. [18]

Fein, G. G., and N. Apfel. 1979. The development of play, style, structure, and situation. *Genet. Psychol. Monogr.* **99**:231–250. [12]

Ferkin, M. H., A. Combs, J. DelBarco-Trillo, A. A. Pierce, and S. Franklin. 2008. Meadow voles, *Microtus pennsylvanicus*, have the capacity to recall the "what," "where," and "when" of a single past event. *Anim. Cogn.* **11**:147–159. [12]

Fichtel, C., and P. M. Kappeler. 2002. Anti-predator behavior of group-living Malagasy primates: Mixed evidence for a referential alarm call system. *Behav. Ecol. Sociobiol.* **51**:262–275. [13]

Finarelli, J. A., and J. J. Flynn. 2009. Brain-size evolution and sociality in carnivora. *PNAS* **106**:9345–9349. [18]

Fischer, J. 1998. Barbary macaques categorize shrill barks into two call types. *Anim. Behav.* **55**:799–807. [13]

———. 2010. Nothing to talk about? On the linguistic abilities of nonhuman primates (and some other animal species). In: Homo Novus–A Human Without Illusions, ed. U. Frey et al. New York: Springer Verlag. [13]

Fischer, J., and K. Hammerschmidt. 2001. Functional referents and acoustic similarity revisited: The case of Barbary macaque alarm calls. *Anim. Cogn.* **4**:29–35. [10, 13]

———. 2011. Ultrasonic vocalizations in mouse models for speech and socio-cognitive disorders: Insights into the evolution of vocal communication. *Genes Brain Behav.* **10(1)**:17–27. [10, 13, 18]

Fischer, J., K. Hammerschmidt, and D. Todt. 1995. Factors affecting acoustic variation in barbary macaque (*Macaca sylvanus*) disturbance calls. *Ethology* **101**:51–66. [13]

Fischer, J., D. M. Kitchen, R. M. Seyfarth, and D. L. Cheney. 2004. Baboon loud calls advertise male quality: Acoustic features and their relation to rank, age, and exhaustion. *Behav. Ecol. Sociobiol.* **56(2)**:140–148. [10]

Fischer, J., and D. Zinner. 2011. Communicative and cognitive underpinnings of group movement in nonhuman primates. In: Coordination in Human and Non-human Primate Groups, ed. M. Boos et al., pp. 229–244. Heidelberg: Springer Verlag. [10]

Fisher, S. E., and G. F. Marcus. 2006. The eloquent ape: Genes, brains and the evolution of language. *Nat. Rev. Gen.* **7**:9–20. [13]

Fisher, S. E., and C. Scharff. 2009. FOXP2 as a molecular window into speech and language. *Trends Gen.* **25**:166–177. [13]

Fitch, W. T. 2010. The Evolution of Language. Cambridge: Cambrdige Univ. Press. [13]

Flavell, J. H. 1979. Metacognition and cognitive monitoring: A new area of cognitive-developmental inquiry. *Amer. Psychol.* **34**:906–911. [8]

Flombaum, J. I., and L. R. Santos. 2005. Rhesus monkeys attribute perceptions to others. *Curr. Biol.* **15(5)**:447–52. [17]

Foo, P., W. H. Warren, A. Duchon, and M. J. Tarr. 2005. Do humans integrate routes into a cognitive map? *J. Exp. Psychol.* **31**:195–215. [5]

Foote, A. L., and J. D. Crystal. 2007. Metacognition in the rat. *Curr. Biol.* **17(6)**:551–555. [8]

Fortin, N. J., K. L. Agster, and H. B. Eichenbaum. 2002. Critical role of the hippocampus in memory for sequences of events. *Nature Neurosci.* **5(5)**:458–462. [8]

Franks, N. R., and T. Richardson. 2006. Teaching in tandem-running ants. *Nature* **439**:153. [11]

Frederick, S., G. Loewenstein, and T. O'Donoghue. 2002. Time discounting and time preference: A critical review. *J. Econ. Lit.* **40**:351–401. [7]

Fuchs, R., H. Winkler, J. Ross, V. P. Bingman, and G. Bernroider. 2010. Differential effects of the migratory status on forebrain regionalization in songbirds. 6th European Conf. Comparative Neurobiology, Valencia Universidad de València. [4]

Fyhn, M., T. Hafting, A. Treves, M. B. Moser, and E. I. Moser. 2007. Hippocampal remapping and grid realignment in entorhinal cortex. *Nature* **446**:190–194. [3]

Fyhn, M., S. Molden, M. P. Witter, E. I. Moser, and M. B. Moser. 2004. Spatial representation in the entorhinal cortex. *Science* **305(5688)**:1258–1264. [5]

Gagliardo, A., P. Ioalè, M. Savini, G. Dell'Omo, and V. P. Bingman. 2009. Hippocampal-dependent familiar area map supports corrective re-orientation following navigational error during pigeon homing: A GPS-tracking study. *Eur. J. Neurosci.* **29**:2389–2400. [4]

Gagliardo, A., P. Ioalè, M. Savini, and J. M. Wild. 2006. Having the nerve to home: Trigeminal magnetoreceptor versus olfactory mediation of homing in pigeons. *J. Exp. Biol.* **209**:2888–2892. [4]

Gallistel, C. R. 1990. The Organization of Learning. Cambridge, MA: MIT Press. [3, 7]

———. 2002. Language and spatial frames of reference in mind and brain. *Trends Cogn. Sci.* **6**:321–322. [5, 17]

Gallistel, C. R., and A. Cramer. 1996. Computations on metric maps in mammals: Getting oriented and choosing a multi-destination. *J. Exp. Biol.* **199(1)**:211–217. [5]

Gallup, G. G. J. 1982. Self-awareness and the emergence of mind in primates. *Amer. J. Primatol.* **2**:237–248. [17]

Gardner, R. A., and B. T. Gardner. 1969. Teaching sign language to a chimpanzee. *Science* **165**:664–672. [13]

Gentilucci, M., and M. C. Corballis. 2006. From manual gesture to speech: A gradual transition. *Neurosci. Biobehav. Rev.* **30**:949–960. [13]

Gentner, T. Q., K. M. Fenn, D. Margoliash, and H. C. Nusbaum. 2006. Recursive syntactic pattern learning by songbirds. *Nature* **440**:1204–1207. [13]

———. 2010. Simple stimuli, simple strategies. *PNAS* **107**:E65. [13]

Ghazanfar, A. A., J. X. Maier, K. L. Hoffman, and N. Logothetis. 2005. Multisensory integration of dynamic faces and voices in rhesus monkey auditory cortex. *J. Neurosci.* **25**:5004–5012. [13]

Gibbon, J. 1977. Scalar expectancy theory and Weber's law in animal timing. *Psychol. Rev.* **84**:279–325. [7]

Gibbs, S. E. B., S. E. A. Lea, and L. F. Jacobs. 2007. Flexible use of spatial cues in the southern flying squirrel (*Glaucomys volans*). *Anim. Cogn.* **10**:203–209. [5]

Gigerenzer, G., and W. Gaissmaier. 2010. Heuristic decision making. *Ann. Rev. Psychol.* **62**:451–482. [7]

Gigerenzer, G., and R. Selten. 2001. Rethinking rationality. In: Bounded Rationality: The Adaptive Toolbox, ed. G. Gigerenzer and R. Selten, pp. 1–12. Dahlem Workshop Report, J. Lupp, series ed. Cambridge, MA: MIT Press. [7]

Gil-da-Costa, R., A. Braun, M. Lopes, et al. 2004. Toward an evolutionary perspective on conceptual representations: Species-specific calls activate visual and affective processing systems in the macaque. *PNAS* **101**:17,516–17,521. [13]

Gillner, S., and H. A. Mallot. 1998. Navigation and acquisition of spatial knowledge in a virtual maze. *J. Cogn. Neurosci.* **10**:445–463. [5]

Giovanello, K. S., D. Schnyer, and M. Verfaiellie. 2009. Distinct hippocampal regions make unique contributions to relational memory. *Hippocampus* **19**:111–117. [12]

Giurfa, M. 2007. Behavioral and neural analysis of associative learning in the honeybee: A taste from the magic well. *J. Comp. Physiol. A* **193**:801–824. [11]

Giurfa, M., B. Eichmann, R. Menzel, and Srinivasan. 2001. The concepts of "sameness" and "difference" in an insect. *Nature* **410**:930–933. [13]

Glimcher, P. W. 2003. Decisions, Uncertainty, and the Brain. Cambridge, MA: MIT Press. [7]

———. 2011. Foundations of Neuroeconomic Analysis. New York: Oxford Univ. Press. [9]

Glöckner, A. 2008. How evolution outwits bounded rationality: The efficient interaction of automatic and deliberate processes in decision making and implications for institutions? In: Better Than Conscious? Implications for Performance and Institutional Analysis, ed. C. Engel and W. Singer, pp. 259–284. Strüngmann Forum Reports, J. Lupp, series ed. Cambridge, MA: MIT Press. [7]

Godfray, H. C. J. 1991. Signalling of need by offspring to their parents. *Nature* **352**:328–330. [13]

Göksun, T., K. Hirsh-Pasek, and R. M. Golinkoff. 2010. Trading spaces: Carving up events for learning language. *Perspect. Psychol. Sci.* **5(1)**:33–42. [5]

Gomes, C. M., and C. Boesch. 2009. Wild chimpanzees exchange meat for sex on a long-term basis. *PLoS One* **4(4)**:e5116. [15]

Goodall, J. 1986. The Chimpanzees of Gombe: Patterns of Behaviour. Cambridge, MA: Belknap Press. [13, 15]

Gordon, R. 1995. Simulation without introspection or inference from me to you. In: Mental Simulation, ed. M. Davies and T. Stone, pp. 53–67. Oxford: Blackwell. [18]

Gothard, K. M., W. E. Skaggs, and B. L. McNaughton. 1996. Dynamics of mismatch correction in the hippocampal ensemble code for space: Interaction between path integration and environmental cues. *J. Neurosci.* **16**:8027–8040. [3]

Gould, J. L. 1975. Honey bee recruitment: The dance-language controversy. *Science* **189**:685–693. [13]

Gould, J. L., and C. G. Gould. 1982. The insect mind: Physics or metaphysics? In: Animal Mind–Human Mind, ed. D. R. Griffin, pp. 269–298. New York: Springer Verlag. [2]

Gouzoules, H., S. Gouzoules, and P. Marler. 1984. Rhesus monkey (*Macaca mulatta*) screams: Representational signalling in the recruitment of agonistic aid. *Anim. Behav.* **32**:182–193. [10]

Grafen, A. 1990. Biological signals as handicaps. *J. Theor. Biol.* **144**:517–546. [13]

Gray, F. 2010. If we have souls, then so do chimps. *The Spectator*, 10 April 2010. [12]

Green, L., and J. Myerson. 2004. A discounting framework for choice with delayed and probabilistic rewards. *Psychol. Bull.* **13**:769–792. [7]

Greenberg, J., K. Hamann, F. Warneken, and M. Tomasello. 2010. Chimpanzee helping in collaborative and nocollaborative contexts. *Anim. Behav.* **80**:873–880. [16]

Greggers, U., and R. Menzel. 1993. Memory dynamics and foraging strategies of honeybees. *Behav. Ecol. Sociobiol.* **32**:17–29. [11]

Grice, H. P. 1989. Studies in the Way of Words. Cambridge, MA: Harvard Univ. Press. [13]

Griffin, D. R. 1981. The Question of Animal Awareness, 2nd ed. New York: Rockefeller Univ. Press. [4]

———, ed. 1982. Animal Mind – Human Mind. Berlin: Springer Verlag. [1, 9]

———, ed. 1984. Animal Thinking. Cambridge, MA: Harvard Univ. Press. [4, 18]

Grobéty, M.-C., and F. Schenk. 1992. Spatial learning in a three-dimensional maze. *Anim. Behav.* **43**:1011–1020. [3]

Grosenick, L., and T. S. Clement. 2007. Fish can infer social rank by observation alone. *Nature* **445(7126)**:429–432. [18]

Grüter, C., M. S. Balbuena, and W. M. Farina. 2008. Informational conflicts created by the waggle dance. *Proc. Roy. Soc. Lond. B* **275**:1321–1327. [11, 13]

Grüter, C., T. J. Czaczkes, and F. L. W. Ratnieks. 2011. Decision-making in ant foragers (*Lasius niger*) facing conflicting private and social information. *Behav. Ecol. Sociobiol.* **65**:141–148. [11]

Grüter, C., and W. M. Farina. 2009. The honeybee waggle dance: Can we follow the steps? *Trends Ecol. Evol.* **24**:242–247. [2, 11, 13]

Güntürkün, O. 2005. The avian "prefrontal cortex" and cognition. *Curr. Opin. Neurobiol.* **15**:686–693. [4]

Güth, W., R. Schmittberger, and B. chwarze. 1982. An experimental analysis of ultimatum bargaining. *J. Econ. Behav. Org.* **3**:367–388. [18]

Gyger, M., P. Marler, and R. Pickert. 1987. Semantics of an avian alarm call system: The male domestic fowl, *Gallus domesticus. Behaviour* **102**:15–40. [13]

Haesler, S., C. Rochefort, B. Georgi, et al. 2007. Incomplete and inaccurate vocal imitation after knockdown of *FoxP2* in songbird basal ganglia nucleus area X. *PLoS Biol.* **5**:2885–2897. [13]

Hafting, T., M. Fyhn, S. Molden, M. B. Moser, and E. I. Moser. 2005. Microstructure of a spatial map in the entorhinal cortex. *Nature* **436**:801–806. [3, 5]

Hakes, D. T., J. S. Evans, and L. L. Brannon. 1976. Understanding sentences with relative clauses. *Mem. Cogn.* **4**:283–290. [13]

Hamilton, H. W., and J. Deese. 1971. Comprehensibility and subject-verb relations in complex sentences. *J. Verbal Learn. Verbal Behav.* **10**:163–170. [13]

Hammerschmidt, K., and J. Fischer. 2008. Constraints in primate vocal production. In: Evolution of Communication Creativity: Complexity, Creativity, and Adaptability in Human and Animal Communication., ed. D. K. Oller and U. Griebel, pp. 93–119. Cambridge, MA: MIT Press. [10, 13]

Hammerstein, P. 2003. Why is reciprocity so rare in social animals? A Protestant appeal. In: Genetic and Cultural Evolution of Cooperation, ed. P. Hammerstein, pp. 83–94. Dahlem Workshop Report, J. Lupp, series ed. Cambridge, MA: MIT Press. [16]

Hammerstein, P., and E. H. Hagen. 2005. The second wave of evolutionary economics in biology. *Trends Ecol. Evol.* **20**:604–609. [7]

Hampton, R. R. 2001. Rhesus monkeys know when they remember. *PNAS* **98**:5359–5362. [8]

———. 2003. Metacognition as evidence for explicit representation in nonhumans. *Behav. Brain Sci.* **26**:346–347. [8]

———. 2005. Can rhesus monkeys discriminate between remembering and forgetting? In: The Missing Link in Cognition: Origins of Self-reflective Consciousness, ed. H. S. Terrace and J. Metcalfe, pp. 272–295. New York: Oxford Univ. Press. [8]

———. 2006. Memory awareness in rhesus monkeys. In: Diversity of Cognition, ed. K. Fujita and I. Shoji, pp. 282–299. Kyoto: Kyoto Univ. Press. [8]

———. 2009. Multiple demonstrations of metacognition in nonhumans: Converging evidence or multiple mechanisms. *Comp. Cogn. Behav. Rev.* **4**:17–28. [9]

Hampton, R. R., and B. M. Hampstead. 2006. Spontaneous behavior of a rhesus monkey (*Macaca mulatta*) during memory tests suggests memory awareness. *Behav. Proc.* **72**:184–189. [8]

Hampton, R. R., B. M. Hampstead, and E. A. Murray. 2004a. Selective hippocampal damage in rhesus monkeys impairs spatial memory in an open-field test. *Hippocampus* **14**:808–818. [8]

Hampton, R. R., and B. L. Schwartz. 2004. Episodic memory in nonhumans: What, and where, is when? *Curr. Opin. Neurobiol.* **14**:192–197. [8]

Hampton, R. R., A. Zivin, and E. A. Murray. 2004b. Rhesus monkeys (*Macaca mulatta*) discriminate between knowing and not knowing and collect information as needed before acting. *Anim. Cogn.* **7**:239–254. [8]

Harcourt, A. H., and F. B. M. de Waal, eds. 1992. Coalitions and Alliances in Humans and Other Animals. New York: Oxford Univ. Press. [15]

Hare, B., J. Call, B. Agnetta, and M. Tomasello. 2000. Chimpanzees know what conspecifics do and do not see. *Anim. Behav.* **59(4)**:771–785. [14, 17]

Hare, B., J. Call, and M. Tomasello. 2001. Do chimpanzees know what conspecifics know? *Anim. Behav.* **61(1)**:771–785. [17]

Hare, B., A. P. Melis, V. Woods, S. Hastings, and R. W. Wrangham. 2007. Tolerance allows bonobos to outperform chimpanzees on a cooperative task. *Curr. Biol.* **17**:619–623. [16]

Hare, B., and M. Tomasello. 2005. Human-like social skills in dogs? *Trends Cogn. Sci.* **9(9)**:439–444. [17]

Harman, G. 1978. Studying the chimpanzees' theory of mind. *Behav. Brain Sci.* **1**:576–577. [18]

Harrison, J. F., J. H. Fewell, T. M. Stiller, and M. D. Breed. 1989. Effects of experience on use of orientation cues in the giant tropical ant. *Anim. Behav.* **37**:869–871. [11]

Hartley, T., E. A. Maguire, H. J. Spiers, and N. Burgess. 2003. The well-worn route and the path less traveled: Distinct neural bases of route following and wayfinding in humans. *Neuron* **37**:877–888. [5]

Hatfield, E., J. T. Cacioppo, and R. L. Rapson. 1994. Emotional contagion. Cambridge: Cambridge Univ. Press. [18]

Haun, D. B., F. M. Jordan, G. Vallortigara, and N. S. Clayton. 2010. Origins of spatial, temporal and numerical cognition: Insights from comparative psychology. *Trends Cogn. Sci.* **14**:552–560. [7]

Hauser, M., and J. Wood. 2009. Evolving the capacity to understand actions, intentions, and goals. *Ann. Rev. Psychol.* **61(1)**:303–324. [17]

Hauser, M. D. 1996. The Evolution of Communication. Cambridge, MA: MIT Press. [13]

Hauser, M. D., N. Chomsky, and W. T. Fitch. 2002. The faculty of language: What is it, who has it, and how did it evolve? *Science* **298(5598)**:1569–1579. [10, 13]

Hawkins, J. A. 1994. A Performance Theory of Order and Constituency. Cambridge: Cambridge Univ. Press. [13]

Hayman, R., M. Verriotis, A. Jovalekic, A. A. Fenton, and K. J. Jeffery. 2011. Anisotropic encoding of three-dimensional space by place cells and grid cells. *Nat. Neurosci.*, in press. [3]

Healy, S. D., E. Gwinner, and J. R. Krebs. 1996. Hippocampal volume in migratory and non-migratory warblers: Effect of age and experience. *Behav. Brain Res.* **81**:61–68. [4]

Healy, S. D., and T. A. Hurly. 1998. Rufous hummingbirds' (*Selasphorus rufus*) memory for flowers: Patterns or actual spatial locations? *J. Exp. Psychol. Anim. Behav. Proc.* **24**:396–404. [5]

Healy, S. D., and J. R. Krebs. 1991. Hippocampal volume and migration in birds. *Naturwiss.* **78**:424–426. [4]

Healy, S. D., and C. Rowe. 2007. A critique of comparative studies of brain size. *Proc. Roy. Soc. Lond. B* **274**:453–464. [14, 18]

Heilbronner, S. R., A. G. Rosati, J. R. Stevens, B. Hare, and M. D. Hauser. 2008. A fruit in the hand or two in the bush? Divergent risk preferences in chimpanzees and bonobos. *Biol. Lett.* **4(3)**:246–249. [9]

Heinsohn, R., and C. Packer. 1995. Complex cooperative strategies in group-territorial African lions. *Science* **269**:1260–1262. [16]

Hemelrijk, C. K. 1990. Models of, and tests for, reciprocity, unidirectional and other social interaction patterns at a group level. *Anim. Behav.* **39**:1013–1029. [15]

———. 1994. Support for being groomed in long-tailed macaques, *Macaca fascicularis. Anim. Behav.* **48**:479–481. [16]

———. 1996a. Dominance interactions, spatial dynamics and emergent reciprocity in a virtual world. In: From Animals to Animats, ed. P. Maes et al., pp. 545–552. Cambridge, MA: MIT Press. [15]

. 1996b. Reciprocation in apes: From complex cognition to self-structuring. In: Great Ape Societies, ed. W. C. McGrew et al., pp. 185–195. Cambridge: Cambridge Univ. Press. [15]

———. 1997. Cooperation without genes, games or cognition. In: 4th European Conf. on Artificial Life, ed. P. Husbands and I. Harvey, pp. 511–520. Cambridge, MA: MIT Press. [15]

———. 1999a. Effects of cohesiveness on intersexual dominance relationships and spatial structure among group-living virtual entities. In: Advances in Artificial Life, ed. D. Floreano et al., pp. 524–534. Lecture Notes in Artificial Intelligence, J. G. Carbonell and J. Siekmann, series ed. Berlin: Springer Verlag. [15]

———. 1999b. An individual-oriented model on the emergence of despotic and egalitarian societies. *Proc. Roy. Soc. Lond. B* **266**:361–369. [15]

———. 2000. Towards the integration of social dominance and spatial structure. *Anim. Behav.* **59**:1035–1048. [15]

———. 2002. Understanding social behaviour with the help of complexity science. *Ethology* **108**:655–671. [15]

———, ed. 2005. Self-organisation and Evolution of Social Systems. Cambridge: Cambridge Univ. Press. [15]

Hemelrijk, C. K., and A. Ek. 1991. Reciprocity and interchange of grooming and "support" in captive chimpanzees. *Anim. Behav.* **41**:923–935. [15]

Hemelrijk, C. K., and L. Gygax. 2004. Dominance style, differences between the sexes and individuals: An agent-based model. *Interact. Stud.* **5(1)**:131–146. [15]

Hemelrijk, C. K., and H. Hildenbrandt. 2008. Self-organized shape and frontal density of fish schools. *Ethology* **114**:245–254. [15]

Hemelrijk, C. K., H. Hildenbrandt, J. Reinders, and E. J. Stamhuis. 2010. Emergence of oblong school shape: Models and empirical data of fish. *Ethology* **116**:1099–1112. [15]

Hemelrijk, C. K., C. M. Meier, and R. D. Martin. 1999. "Friendship" for fitness in chimpanzees? *Anim. Behav.* **58**:1223–1229. [15]

Hemelrijk, C. K., G. J. van Laere, and J. A. R. A. M. van Hooff. 1992. Sexual exchange relationships in captive chimpanzees? *Behav. Ecol. Sociobiol.* **30**:269–275. [15]

Hemelrijk, C. K., and J. Wantia. 2005. Individual variation by self-organisation: A model. *Neurosci. Biobehav. Rev.* **29**:125–136. [15]

Hemelrijk, C. K., J. Wantia, and M. Daetwyler. 2003. Female co-dominance in a virtual world: Ecological, cognitive, social and sexual causes. *Behaviour* **140**:1247–1273. [15]

Hemelrijk, C. K., J. Wantia, and K. Isler. 2008. Female dominance over males in primates: Self-organisation and sexual dimorphism. *PLoS One* **3(7)**:e2678. [15]

Henrich, J., J. Ensminger, R. McElreath, et al. 2010. Markets, religion, community size, and the evolution of fairness and punishment. *Science* **327**:1480–1484. [16]

Henzi, S. P., and L. Barrett. 2007. Coexistence in female-bonded primate groups. *Adv. Stud. Behav.* **37**:107–132. [16]

Hermer, L., and E. S. Spelke. 1996. Modularity and development: The case of spatial reorientation. *Cognition* **61**:195–232. [5]

Herrnstein, R. J. 1961. Relative and absolute strength of response as a function of frequency of reinforcement. *J. Exp. Anal. Behav.* **4**:267–272. [7, 9]

Hershberger, W. A. 1986. An approach through the looking glass. *Anim. Learn. Behav.* **14**:443–451. [6]

Hesslow, G. 2002. Conscious thought as simulation of behaviour and perception. *Trends Cogn. Sci.* **6(6)**:242–247. [6]

Hewes, G. W. 1973. Primate communication and the gestural origin of language. *Curr. Anthro.* **14**:5–24. [13]

Heyes, C. M. 1993. Imitation, culture and tradition. *Anim. Behav.* **46**:999–1010. [14]

———. 1998. Theory of mind in nonhuman primates. *Behav. Brain Sci.* **21(1)**:101–14; discussion 115–48. [14, 17, 18]

Heyes, C. M., and A. Dickinson. 1990. The intentionality of animal action. *Mind Lang.* **5**:87–104. [6]

———. 1995. Folk psychology won't go away: Response to Allen and Bekoff. *Mind Lang.* **10(4)**:329–332. [6]

Hildenbrandt, H., C. Carere, and C. K. Hemelrijk. 2010. Self-organized aerial displays of thousands of starlings: A model. *Behav. Evol.* **21(6)**:1349–1359. [15]

Hilliard, A. T., and S. A. White. 2009. Possible precursors of syntactic components in other species. In: Biological Foundations and Origin of Syntax., ed. D. Bickerton and E. Szathmary, pp. 161–184. Strüngmann Forum Reports, J. Lupp, series ed. Cambridge, MA: MIT Press. [13]

Hillier, B., and J. Hanson. 1984. The Social Logic of Space. Cambridge: Cambridge Univ. Press. [5]

Hodges, J. R., and K. S. Graham. 2001. Episodic memory: Insights from semantic dementia. *Philos. Trans. R. Soc. Lond. B* **356**:1423–1434. [12]

Hoffecker, J. F. 2005. Innovation and technological knowledge in the Upper Paleolithic of Northern Eurasia. *Evol. Anthropol.* **14**:186–198. [12]

Hoffman, M. L. 1982. Development of prosocial motivation: Empathy and guilt. In: The Development of Prosocial Behavior, ed. N. Eisenberg, pp. 281–338. New York: Academic Press. [18]

———. 1984. Interaction of affect and cognition in empathy. In: Emotion, Cognition, and Behavior, ed. C. E. Izard et al., pp. 103–131. Cambridge: Cambridge Univ. Press. [18]

Hogeweg, P., and B. Hesper. 1985. Socioinformatic processes: MIRROR Modelling methodology. *J. Theor. Biol.* **113**:311–330. [15]

Holbrook, R. I., and T. Burt de Perera. 2009. Separate encoding of vertical and horizontal components of space during orientation in fish. *Anim. Behav.* **78**:241–245. [3]

Holekamp, K. E. 2007. Questioning the social intelligence hypothesis. *TICS* **11**:65–69. [18]

Hölldobler, B. 1976a. Recruitment behavior, home range orientation and territoriality in harvester ants, *Pogonomyrmex. Behav. Ecol. Sociobiol.* **1**:3–44. [11]

———. 1976b. Tournaments and slavery in a desert ant. *Science* **192**:912–914. [11]

———. 1995. The chemistry of social regulation: Multicomponent signals in ant societies. *PNAS* **92**:19–22. [11]

———. 1999. Multimodal signals in ant communication. *J. Comp. Physiol. A* **184**:129–141. [11]

Hölldobler, B., and E. O. Wilson. 1990. The Ants. Cambridge, MA: Belknap Press. [11]

————. 2009. The Superorganism: The Beauty, Elegance, and Strangeness of Insect Societies. New York: W. W. Norton. [11]

Hölscher, C., T. Meilinger, G. Vrachliotis, M. Brösamle, and M. Knauff. 2006. Up the down staircase: Wayfinding strategies and multi-level buildings. *J. Environ. Psychol.* **26**:284–299. [3]

Holt-Lunstad, J., T. B. Smith, and J. B. Layton. 2010. Social relationships and mortality risk: A meta-analytic review. *PLoS Med.* **77**:e1000316. [16]

Hoover, M. L. 1992. Sentence processing strategies in Spanish and English. *J. Psycholing. Res.* **21**:275–299. [13]

Horgan, T., and J. Tienson. 1996. Connectionism and the Philosophy of Psychology. Cambridge, MA: MIT Press. [17]

Hough, G. E., II, and V. P. Bingman. 2004. Spatial response properties of homing pigeon hippocampal neurons: Correlations with goal locations, movement between goals, and environmental context in a radial-arm arena. *J. Comp. Physiol. A* **190**:1047–1062. [4]

Hsu, Y., R. L. Earley, and L. L. Wolf. 2006. Modulation of aggressive behaviour by fighting experience: Mechanisms and contest outcomes. *Biol. Rev.* **81**:33–74. [15]

Hummel, J. E., and K. J. Holyoak. 2003. A symbolic-connectionist theory of relational inference and generalization. *Psychol. Rev.* **110**:220–264. [17]

————. 2005. Relational reasoning in a neurally plausible cognitive architecture. *Curr. Dir. Psychol. Sci.* **14(3)**:153–157. [17]

Humphrey , N. 1978. Nature's psychologist. *New Scientist* **29**:900–904. [17, 18]

————. 1980. Nature's psychologists. In: Consciousness and the Physical World, ed. B. Josephson and V. Ramachandran, pp. 57–75. Oxford: Plenum Press. [18]

Hurd, P. L., and M. Enquist. 2005. A strategic taxonomy of biological communication. *Anim. Behav.* **70**:1155–1170. [13]

Hurford, J. R. 2004. Language beyond our grasp: What mirror neurons can, and cannot, do for language evolution. In: Evolution of Communication Systems: A Comparative Approach., ed. D. K. Oller and U. Griebel, pp. 297–313. Cambridge, MA: MIT Press. [13]

Hurly, T. A., and S. D. Healy. 2002. Cue learning by rufous hummingbirds *Selasphorus rufus*. *J. Exp. Psychol. Anim. Behav. Proc.* **28**:209–223. [5]

Hurst, J. A., M. Baraitser, E. Auger, F. Graham, and S. Norell. 1990. An extended family with a dominantly inherited speech disorder. *Dev. Med. Child Neurol.* **32**:352–355. [13]

Hutchinson, J. M. C., and G. Gigerenzer. 2005. Simple heuristics and rules of thumb: Where psychologists and behavioural biologists might meet. *Behav. Proc.* **69**:97–124. [7]

Imanishi, K. 1960. Social organization of subhuman primates in their natural habitat. *Curr. Anthro.* **1**:393–402. [15]

Inman, A., and S. J. Shettleworth. 1999. Detecting metamemory in nonverbal subjects: A test with pigeons. *J. Exp. Psychol. Anim. Behav. Proc.* **25(3)**:389–395. [8]

Itani, J. 1954. The Monkeys of Mt. Takasaki. Tokyo: Kobunsha. [15]

Jablonka, E., and G. Raz. 2009. Trangenerational epigenetic inheritance: Prevalence, mechanisms, and implications for the study of heredity and evolution. *Q. Rev. Biol.* **84**:131–176. [16]

Jackendoff, R. 1999. Possible stages in the evolution of the language capacity. *Trends Cogn. Sci.* **3**:272–279. [13]

Jackson, D. E., S. J. Martin, M. Holcombe, and F. L. W. Ratnieks. 2006. Longevity and detection of persistent foraging trails in Pharaoh's ants, *Monomorium pharaonis* (L.). *Anim. Behav.* **71**:351–359. [11]

Jackson, D. E., and F. L. W. Ratnieks. 2006. Communication in ants. *Curr. Biol.* **16**:R570–R574. [11]

Jackson, O., III, and D. L. Schacter. 2004. Encoding activity in anterior medial temporal lobe supports subsequent associative recognition. *NeuroImage* **21**:456–462. [12]

Jacobs, L. F., and F. Schenk. 2003. Unpacking the cognitive map: The parallel map theory of hippocampal function. *Psychol. Rev.* **110(2)**:285–315. [2, 5]

Jaeggi, A. V., J. M. Burkart, and C. P. van Schaik. 2010. On the psychology of cooperation in humans and other primates: Combining the natural history and experimental evidence of prosociality. *Philos. Trans. R. Soc. Lond. B* **365**:2723–2735. [14]

James, W. 1890. The Principles of Psychology. New York: Holt. [6]

Janson, C. 2007. Experimental evidence for route integration and strategic planning in wild capuchin monkeys. *Anim. Cogn.* **10**:341–356. [7]

Janson, C. H., and R. Byrne. 2007. What wild primates know about resources: Opening up the black box. *Anim. Cogn.* **10(3)**:357–367. [5]

Jarvis, E. D. 2004. Learned birdsong and the neurobiology of human language. *Ann. NY Acad. Sci.* **1016**:749–777. [13]

Jarvis, E. D., S. Ribeiro, M. L. da Silva, et al. 2000. Behaviourally driven gene expression reveals song nuclei in hummingbird brain. *Nature* **406**:628–632. [13]

Jeanne, R. L., and B. J. Taylor. 2009. Individual and social foraging in social wasps. In: Food Exploitation by Social Insects: Ecological, Behavioral, and Theoretical Approaches ed. S. Jarau and M. Hrncir, pp. 45–71. Boca Raton: CRC Press. [11]

Jeffery, K. J. 2007. Integration of the sensory inputs to place cells: What, where, why, and how? *Hippocampus* **17**:775–785. [3]

Jeffery, K. J., R. L. Anand, and M. I. Anderson. 2006. A role for terrain slope in orienting hippocampal place fields. *Exp. Brain Res.* **169**:218–225. [3]

Jeffery, K. J., and J. O'Keefe. 1999. Learned interaction of visual and idiothetic cues in the control of place field orientation. *Exp. Brain Res.* **127**:151–161. [5]

Jensen, K. 2010. Punishment and spite, the dark side of cooperation. *Philos. Trans. R. Soc. Lond. B* **365**:2635–2650. [18]

———. 2011. Social regard: Evolving a psychology of cooperation. In: The Evolution of Primate Societies, ed. J. Mitani et al. Chicago: Chicago Univ. Press. [18]

Jensen, K., J. Call, and M. Tomasello. 2007a. Chimpanzees are rational maximizers in an ultimatum game. *Science* **318**:107–109. [18]

———. 2007b. Chimpanzees are vengeful but not spiteful. *PNAS* **104**:13,046–13,050. [16, 18]

Jensen, K., B. A. Hare, J. Call, and M. Tomasello. 2006. What's in it for me? Self-regard precludes altruism and spite in chimpanzees. *Proc. Roy. Soc. Lond. B* **273**:1013–1021. [16, 18]

Jerison, H. J. 1973. Evolution of the Brain and Intelligence. New York: Academic Press. [14]

Jersakova, J., S. D. Johnson, and P. Kindlmann. 2006. Mechanisms and evolution of deceptive pollination in orchids. *Biol. Rev.* **81**:219–235. [13]

Johnson, A., and A. D. Redish. 2007. Neural ensembles in CA3 transiently encode paths forward of the animal at a decision point. *J. Neurosci.* **27**:12,176–12,189. [5]

Johnstone, R. A., and A. Grafen. 1992. The continuous Sir Philip Sidney Game: A simple model of biological signalling. *J. Theor. Biol.* **156**:215–234. [13]

Jones, M. A., and V. P. Bingman. 1996. A neural network analysis of navigational learning in homing pigeons. *Forma* **11**:103–114. [4]

Jones, M. A., and B. Love. 2011. Bayesian fundamentalism or enlightenment? On the explanatory status and theoretical contributions of bayesian models of cognition. *Behav. Brain Sci.*, in press. [5]

Jovalekic, A., R. Hayman, N. Becares, et al. 2011. Horizontal biases in rats' use of three-dimensional space. *Behav. Brain Res.* **222**:279–288. [3]

Jozefowicz, J., J. E. R. Staddon, and D. T. Cerutti. 2009. Metacognition in animals: How do we know that they know? *Comp. Cogn. Behav. Rev.* **4**:29–39. [8]

Jürgens, U. 2002. Neural pathways underlying vocal control. *Neurosci. Biobehav. Rev.* **26**:235–258. [13]

———. 2009. The neural control of vocalization in mammals. *J. Voice* **23**:1–10. [13]

Kable, J. W., and P. W. Glimcher. 2009. The neurobiology of decision: Consensus and controversy. *Neuron* **63(6)**:733–745. [9]

Kacelnik, A. 2003. The evolution of patience. In: Time and Decision: Economic and Psychological Perspectives on Intertemporal Choice, ed. G. Loewenstein et al., pp. 115–138. New York: Russell Sage Foundation. [7]

———. 2006. Meanings of rationality. In: Rational Animals? ed. S. Hurley and M. Nudds. Oxford: Oxford Univ. Press. [7, 17]

Kacelnik, A., and M. Bateson. 1996. Risky theories: The effects of variance on foraging decisions. *Amer. Zool.* **36(4)**:402–434. [9]

Kaiser, D. H., L. M. Sherburne, and T. R. Zentall. 1997. Directed forgetting in pigeons resulting from the reallocation of memory-maintaining processes on forget-cue trials. *Psychon. Bull. Rev.* **4(4)**:559–565. [9]

Kamil, A. C. 1987. A synthetic approach to the study of animal intelligence. In: Comparative Perspectives in Modern Psychology, ed. D. W. Leger, pp. 258–308. Nebraska Symposium on Motivation. Lincoln: Univ. of Nebraska Press. [9]

———. 1998. On the proper definition of cognitive ethology. In: Animal Cognition in Nature, ed. R. P. Balda et al., pp. 1–28. New York: Academic Press. [14]

Kamil, A. C., R. P. Balda, and D. J. Olson. 1994. Performance of four seed-caching corvid species in the radial-arm maze analog. *J. Comp. Psychol.* **108**:385–393. [4]

Kaminski, J., J. Call, and J. Fischer. 2004. Word learning in a domestic dog: Evidence for fast mapping. *Science* **304**:1682–1683. [13]

Kaminski, J., J. Riedel, J. Call, and M. Tomasello. 2005. Domestic goats (*Capra hircus*) follow gaze direction and use social cues in an object choice task. *Anim. Behav.* **69**:11–18. [14]

Karlsson, F. 2007. Constaints on multiple center-embedding of clauses. *J. Ling.* **43**:365–392. [13]

Kearns, M., W. Warren, A. Duchon, and M. Tarr. 2002. Path integration from optic flow and body senses in a homing task. *Perception* **31**:349–374. [5]

Kendal, J. R., L. Rendell, T. W. Pike, and K. N. Laland. 2009. Nine-spined sticklebacks deploy a hill-climbing social learning strategy. *Behav. Ecol.* **20**:238–244. [14]

Kendal, R. L., I. Coolen, Y. van Bergen, and K. N. Laland. 2005. Trade-offs in the adaptive use of social and asocial learning. *Adv. Study Behav.* **35**:333–379. [11]

Keverne, E. B., N. D. Martensz, and B. Tuite. 1989. Beta-endorphin concentrations in cerebrospinal-fluid of monkeys are influenced by grooming relationships. *Psychoneuroendocrinology* **14(1–2)**:155–161. [15]

King, K. G., L. Glodzik, S. Liu, et al. 2008. Anteroposterior hippocampal metabolic heterogeneity: Three-dimensional multivoxel proton 1H MR spectroscopic imaging: Initial findings. *Radiology* **249(1)**:242–250. [12]

Kirchhof, J., and K. Hammerschmidt. 2006. Functionally referential alarm calls in tamarins (*Sanguinus fuscicollis* and *Sanguinus mystax*): Evidence from playback experiments. *Ethology* **112**:346–354. [13]

Kjelstrup, K. B., T. Solstad, V. H. Brun, et al. 2008. Finite scale of spatial representation in the hippocampus. *Science* **321**:140–143. [3]

Klossek, U. M. H., J. Russell, and A. Dickinson. 2008. The control of instrumental action following outcome devaluation in young children aged between 1 and 4 years. *J. Exp. Psychol.* **137**:39–51. [6]

Klotz, J. H. 1987. Topographic orientation in two species of ants (Hymenoptera: Formicidae). *Insectes Sociaux* **34**:236–251. [11]

Knierim, J. J., and B. L. McNaughton. 2001. Hippocampal place-cell firing during movement in three-dimensional space. *J. Neurophysiol.* **85**:105–116. [3]

Knoch, D., A. Pascual-Leone, K. Meyer, V. Treyer, and E. Fehr. 2006. Diminishing reciprocal fairness by disrupting the right prefrontal cortex. *Science* **314**:829–832. [18]

Kohler, E., C. Keysers, M. A. Umilta, et al. 2002. Hearing sounds, understanding actions: Action representation in mirror neurons. *Science* **297**:846–848. [13]

Köhler, W. 1925. The Mentality of Apes (originally published in German in 1917). New York: Routledge & Kegan Paul. [4, 12]

Kokko, H. 1997. Evolutionarily stable strategies of age-dependent sexual advertisement. *Behav. Ecol. Sociobiol.* **41**:99–107. [13]

Körding, K. P. 2007. Decision theory: What "should" the nervous system do? *Science* **318**:606–610. [5]

Koriat, A. 1996. Memory's knowledge of its own knowledge: The accessibility account of the feeling of knowing. In: Metacognition, ed. J. Metcalfe and A. P. Shimamura, pp. 1–25. Cambridge, MA: The MIT Press. [8]

Kornell, N. 2009. Metacognition in humans and animals. *Curr. Dir. Psychol. Sci.* **18(1)**:11–15. [9]

Kornell, N., L. K. Son, and H. S. Terrace. 2007. Transfer of metacognitive skills and hint seeking in monkeys. *Psychol. Sci.* **18(1)**:64–71. [8]

Koski, S. E., and E. H. M. Sterck. 2007. Triadic postconflict affiliation in captive chimpanzees: Does consolation console? *Anim. Behav.* **73**:133–142. [18]

———. 2009. Post-conflict third-party affiliation in chimpanzees: What's in it for the third party? *Amer. J. Primat.* **71**:409–418. [18]

———. 2010. Empathic chimpanzees: A proposal of the levels of emotional and cognitive processing in chimpanzee empathy. *Europ. J. Dev. Psychol.* **7**:38–66. [18]

Krachun, C., and J. Call. 2009. Chimpanzees (*Pan troglodytes*) know what can be seen from where. *Anim. Cogn.* **12(2)**:317–331. [9, 18]

Krams, I., T. Krama, K. Igaune, and R. Mand. 2008. Experimental evidence of reciprocal altruism in the pied flycatcher. *Behav. Ecol. Sociobiol.* **62**:599–605. [16]

Krause, J., C. Lalueza-Fox, L. Orlando, et al. 2007. The derived *FOXP2* variant of modern humans was shared with Neandertals. *Curr. Biol.* **17**:1–5. [13]

Krause, J., G. D. Ruxton, and S. Krause. 2010. Swarm intelligence in animals and humans. *Trends Ecol. Evol.* **25**:28–34. [11]

Krebs, J. R., and N. B. Davies. 1993. An Introduction to Behavioral Ecology, 3rd edition. Oxford: Blackwell. [18]

Krebs, J. R., and R. Dawkins. 1984. Animal signals: Mind reading and manipulation. In: Behavioural Ecology, ed. J. R. Krebs and N. B. Davies, pp. 380–402. London: Blackwell. [10]

Krebs, J. R., D. F. Sherry, D. Healy, V. H. Perry, and A. L. Vaccarino. 1989. Hippocampal specialization of food-storing birds. *PNAS* **86**:1388–1392. [4]

Kuipers, B. 1978. Modeling spatial knowledge. *Cogn. Sci.* **2**:129–153. [5]

———. 2000. The spatial semantic hierarchy. *Art. Intell.* **19**:191–233. [5]

Laland, K. N. 2004. Social learning strategies. *Learn. Behav.* **32**:4–14. [11]

Laland, K. N., and V. M. Janik. 2006. The animal cultures debate. *Trends Ecol. Evol.* **21**:542–547. [11]

Laland, K. N,, P. J. Richerson, and R. Boyd. 1996. Developing a theory of animal social learning. In: Social Learning in Animals: The Roots of Culture, ed. C. M. Heyes and B. G. Galef, pp. 129–154. San Diego: Academic Press. [11]

Lau, B., and P. W. Glimcher. 2005. Dynamic response-by-response models of matching behavior in rhesus monkeys. *J. Exp. Anal. Behav.* **84(3)**:555–579. [9]

Leadbeater, E., and L. Chittka. 2007. Social learning in insects: From miniature brains to consensus building. *Curr. Biol.* **17**:R703–R713. [11]

———. 2009. Social information use in foraging insects. In: Food Exploitation by Social Insects: Ecological, Behavioral, and Theoretical Approaches ed. S. Jarau and M. Hrncir, pp. 125–136. Boca Raton: CRC Press. [11]

Leadbeater, E., N. E. Raine, and L. Chittka. 2006. Social learning: Ants and the meaning of teaching. *Curr. Biol.* **16**:R323–R325. [11]

Learmonth, A. E., L. Nadel, and N. S. Newcombe. 2002. Children's use of lansmarks: Implications for modularity theory. *Psychol. Sci.* **13**:337–341. [5]

Leavens, D. A., W. D. Hopkins, and K. A. Bard. 1966. Indexical and referential pointing in chimpanzees (*Pan troglodytes*). *J. Comp. Psychol.* **110**:346–353. [13]

Legge, E. L. G., M. L. Spetch, and K. Cheng. 2010. Not using the obvious: Desert ants, *Melophorus bagoti*, learn local vectors but not beacons in an arena. *Anim. Cogn.* **13**:849–860. [5]

Leising, K. J., J. Wong, M. R. Waldmann, and A. P. Blaisdell. 2008. The special status of actions in causal reasoning in rats. *J. Exp. Psychol.* **137(3)**:514–527. [6]

Leland, J. W. 2002. Similarity judgments and anomalies in intertemporal choice. *Econ. Inquiry* **40**:574–581. [7]

Lett, B. T. 1975. Long delay learning in the T-maze. *Learn. Motiv.* **6**:80–90. [6]

Leutgeb, S., S. Hudson, L. V. Riters, T. Shimizu, and V. P. Bingman. 1996. Telencephalic afferents to the caudolateral neostriatum of the pigeon. *Brain Res.* **730**:173–181. [4]

Lever, C., S. Burton, A. Jeewajee, J. O'Keefe, and N. Burgess. 2009. Boundary vector cells in the subiculum of the hippocampal formation. *J. Neurosci.* **29**:9771–9777. [3]

Levine, B. 2004. Autobiographical memory and the self in time: Brain lesion effects, functional neuroanatomy, and lifespan development. *Brain Cogn.* **55**:54–68. [12]

Levinson, S. C. 2000. Presumptive Meanings: The Theory of Generalized Conversational Implicature. Cambridge, MA: MIT Press. [13]

———. 2003. Space in Language and Cognition: Explorations in Cognitive Diversity. West Nyack, NY: Cambridge Univ. Press. [5]

Li, P., and P. Gleitman. 2002. Turning the tables: Language and spatial reasoning. *Cognition* **83**:265–294. [5]

Liberman, A. M., F. S. Cooper, D. P. Shankweiler, and M. Studdert-Kennedy. 1967. Perception of the speech code. *Psychol. Rev.* **74**:431–461. [13]

Lieberman, D. E. 1998. Sphenoid shortening and the evolution of modern cranial shape. *Nature* **393**:158–162. [12]

Lieberman, D. E., B. M. McBratney, and G. Krovitz. 2002. The evolution and development of cranial form in *Homo sapiens*. *PNAS* **99**:1134–1139. [12]

Lieberman, P. 2010. The creative capacity of language, in what manner is it unique, and who had it? In: The Evolution of Human Language, ed. R. K. Larson et al., pp. 163–175. Cambridge: Cambridge Univ. Press. [12]

Lieberman, P., E. S. Crelin, and D. H. Klatt. 1972. Phonetic ability and related anatomy of the newborn, adult human, Neanderthal man, and the chimpanzee. *Amer. Anthropol.* **74**:287–307. [12]

Lillard, A. S. 1998. Ethnopsychologies: Cultural variations in theories of mind. *Psychol. Bull.* **123(1)**:3–32. [18]

Lindauer, M. 1955. Schwarmbienen auf wohnungssuche. *Zt. Vgl. Physiol.* **37**:263–324. [2, 11]

Lissek, S., S. Peters, N. Fuchs, et al. 2008. Cooperation and deception recruit different subsets of the theory-of-mind network. *PLoS One* **3**:e2023. [14]

Loftus, E., and K. Ketcham. 1994. The Myth of Repressed Memory. New York: St. Martin's Press. [12]

Loftus, E., and G. R. Loftus. 1980. On the permanence of stored information in the human brain. *Amer. Psychol.* **35**:409–420. [12]

Logue, A. W., G. R. King, A. Chavarro, and J. S. Volpe. 1990. Matching and maximizing in a self-control paradigm using human subjects. *Learn. Motiv.* **21**:340–368. [7]

Lohmann, K. J. 2007. Magnetic maps in animals: Nature's GPS. *J. Exp. Biol.* **210**:3697–3705. [4]

Lohmann, K. J., C. M. F. Lohmann, L. M. Ehrhar, D. A. Bagley, and T. Swing. 2004. Geomagnetic map used in sea-turtle navigation. *Nature* **428**:909–910. [4]

Lohmann, K. J., C. M. F. Lohmann, and C. S. Endres. 2008. The sensory ecology of ocean navigation. *J. Exp. Biol.* **211(11)**:1719–1728. [5]

Lurz, R. 2009. If chimpanzees are mindreaders, could behavioral science tell? Toward a solution of the logical problem. *Phil. Psych.* **22**:305–328. [14]

———. 2010. Belief attribution in animals: On how to move forward conceptually and empirically. *Rev. Phil. Psychol.* **2(1)**:19–59. [18]

Macedonia, J. M., and C. S. Evans. 1993. Variation among mammalian alarm call systems and the problem of meaning in animal signals. *Ethology* **93**:177–197. [10, 13]

Macphail, E. M. 1982. Brain and Intelligence in Vertebrates. Oxford: Clarendon Press. [14]

Maibom, H. L. 2007. Social systems. *Phil. Psych.* **20(5)**:557. [18]

Majolo, B., R. Ventura, and N. F. Koyama. 2005. Sex, rank and age differences in the Japanese macaque (*Macaca fuscata yakui*) participation in inter-group encounters. *Ethology* **111(5)**:455–468. [15]

Malle, B. F. 2002. The relation between language and theory of mind in development and evolution. In: The Evolution of Language out of Pre-Language, ed. T. Givón and B. F. Malle, pp. 265–284. Amsterdam: Benjamins. [13]

Mandler, J. M. 1996. Preverbal representation and language. In: Language and Space, ed. P. Bloom et al., pp. 365–384. Cambridge, MA: MIT Press. [5]

Manrique, H. M., A. N.-M. Gross, and J. Call. 2010. Great apes select tools based on their rigidity. *J. Exp. Psychol. Anim. Behav. Proc.* **36(4)**:409–422. [6]

Manser, M. B. 1999. Response of foragting group members to sentinel calls in suricates, *Suricata suricatta. Proc. Roy. Soc. Lond. B* **266**:1013–1019. [10]

———. 2001. The acoustic structure of suricates' alarm calls varies with predator type and the level of response urgency. *Proc. Roy. Soc. Lond. B* **268**:2315–2324. [13]

Mares, S., L. Ash, and W. Gronenberg. 2005. Brain allometry in bumblebee and honey bee workers. *Brain Behav. Evol.* **66**:50–61. [13]

Margoliash, D., and H. C. Nusbaum. 2009. Language: The perspective from organismal biology. *Trends Cogn. Sci.* **13**:505–510. [13]

Marler, P., A. Dufty, and R. Pickert. 1986. Vocal communication in the domestic chicken: I. Does a sender communicate information about the quality of a food referent to a receiver? *Anim. Behav.* **34**:188–193. [13]

Marler, P., C. S. Evans, M. D. Hauser, et al. 1992. Animal signals: Motivational, referential, or both? In: Nonverbal Vocal Communication, pp. 66–86. Cambridge: Cambridge Univ. Press. [10]

Marques, H. G., and O. Holland. 2009. Architectures for functional imagination. *Neurocomputing* **72(4–6)**:743–759. [9]

Marr, D. 1982. Vision: A Computational Investigation into the Human Representation and Processing of Visual Information. San Francisco: W. H. Freeman. [17]

Marsh, B. 2002. Do animals use heuristics? *J. Bioeconomics* **4**:49–56. [7]

Marshall, J. A. R., R. Bogacz, A. Dornhaus, et al. 2009. On optimal decision-making in brains and social insect colonies. *J. Roy. Soc. Interface* **6**:1065–1074. [11]

Masangkay, Z. S., K. A. McCluskey, C. W. McIntyre, et al. 1974. The early development of inferences about the visual percepts of others. *Child Develop.* **45**:357–366. [18]

Matsumura, S. 1996. Postconflict affiliative contacts between former opponents among wild moor macaques (*Macaca maurus*). *Amer. J. Primatol.* **38(211–219)** [15]

Maynard Smith, J. 1982. Evolution and the Theory of Games. Cambridge: Cambridge Univ. Press. [18]

Maynard Smith, J., and D. Harper. 2003. Animal Signals. Oxford: Oxford Univ. Press. [10, 13]

Mazur, J. E. 2010. Distributed versus exclusive preference in discrete-trial choice. *J. Exp. Psychol. Anim. Behav. Proc.* **36(3)**:321–333. [9]

McDonald, R. J., and N. M. White. 1993. A triple dissociation of memory systems: Hippocampus, amygdala, and dorsal striatum. *Behav. Neurosci.* **107(1)**:3–22. [8]

McGregor, P. K., ed. 2005. Animal Communication Networks. Cambridge: Cambridge Univ. Press. [14]

McGregor, P. K., and T. M. Peake. 2000. Communication networks: Social environments for receiving and signalling behaviour. *Acta Ethol.* **2**:71–81. [10]

McNamara, J. M., and A. I. Houston. 2009. Integrating function and mechanism. *Trends Ecol. Evol.* **24**:670–675. [7]

Melis, A. P., B. Hare, and M. Tomasello. 2006a. Chimpanzees recruit the best collaborators. *Science* **311**:1297–1300. [14, 16]

———. 2006b. Engineering cooperation in chimpanzees: Tolerance constraints on cooperation. *Anim. Behav.* **72**:275286. [16]

———. 2008. Do chimpanzees reciprocate favours? *Anim. Behav.* **76**:951–962. [16]

———. 2009. Chimpanzees coordinate in a negotiation game. *Evol. Hum. Behav.* **30**:381–392. [16]

Melis, A. P., and D. Semmann. 2010. How is human cooperation different? *Philos. Trans. R. Soc. Lond. B* **365**:2663–2674. [16]

Melis, A. P., F. Warneken, A.-C. Schneider, J. Call, and M. Tomasello. 2010. Chimpanzees help conspecifics obtain food and non-food items. *Proc. Roy. Soc. Lond. B* **278(1710)**:1405–1413. [18]

Menzel, C. R. 1999. Unprompted recall and reporting of hidden objects by a chimpanzee (*Pan troglodytes*) after extended delays. *J. Comp. Psychol.* **113**:1–9. [12]

Menzel, R. 1999. Memory dynamics in the honeybee. *J. Comp. Physiol. A* **185**:323–340. [11]

Menzel, R., J. Fuchs, L. Nadler, et al. 2010. Dominance of the odometer over serial landmark learning in honeybee navigation. *Naturwiss.* **97(8)**:763–767. [2]

Menzel, R., K. Geiger, L. Chittka, et al. 1996. The knowledge base of bee navigation. *J. Exp. Biol.* **199**:141–146. [2]

Menzel, R., and M. Giurfa. 2006. Dimensions of cognition in an insect, the honeybee. *Behav. Cogn. Neurosci. Rev.* **5(1)**:24–40. [17]

Menzel, R., U. Greggers, A. Smith, et al. 2005. Honey bees navigate according to a map-like spatial memory. *PNAS* **102**:3040–3045. [2, 4]

Menzel, R., A. Kirbach, W.-D. Haass, et al. 2011. A common frame of reference for learned and communicated vectors in honeybee navigation. *Curr. Biol.* **21(8)**:645–650. [2]

Michelsen, A. 2003. Signals and flexiblity in the dance communication of honeybees. *J. Comp. Physiol. A* **189**:165–174. [11]

Miles, H. L. 1990. The cognitive foundations for reference in a signing orangutan. In: "Language" and Intelligence in Monkeys and Apes: Comparative Developmental Perspectives, ed. S. T. Parker and K. R. Gibson, pp. 511–539. Cambridge: Cambridge Univ. Press. [13]

Miller, M. B., and B. L. Bassler. 2001. Quorum sensing in bacteria. *Ann. Rev. Microbiol.* **55**:165–199. [13]

Millikan, R. G. 1984. Language, Thought, and Other Biological Categories. Cambridge, MA: MIT Press. [13]

Milner, B. 1962. Les troubles de la memoire accompagnant des lesions hippocampiques bilaterales. In: Psychologie de I'hippocampe. Paris: Centre National de la Recherche Scientifique. [9]

Mitani, J. C. 2006. Reciprocal exchange in chimpanzees and other primates. In: Cooperation in Primates and Humans: Mechanisms and Evolution, ed. P. M. Kappeler and C. P. van Schaik, pp. 107–119. Berlin: Springer Verlag. [16]

———. 2009a. Cooperation and competition in chimpanzees: Current understanding and future challenges. *Evol. Anthropol.* **18**:215–227. [16]

———. 2009b. Male chimpanzees form enduring and equitable social bonds. *Anim. Behav.* **77**:633–640. [16]

Mitani, J. C., D. P. Watts, and S. J. Amsler. 2010. Lethal intergroup aggression leads to territorial expansion in wild chimpanzees. *Curr. Biol.* **20**:R507–R508. [16]

Moser, E. I., E. Kropff, and M. B. Moser. 2008. Place cells, grid cells, and the brain's spatial representation system. *Ann. Rev. Neurosci.* **31**:69–89. [3]

Mühlhoff, N., J. R. Stevens, and S. M. Reader. 2011. Spatial discounting of food and social rewards in guppies (*Poecilia reticulata*). *Front. Psychol.* **2**:68. [7]

Mulcahy, N. J., and J. Call. 2006. Apes save tools for future use. *Science* **312**:1038–1040. [6, 12]

Muller, R. U., and J. L. Kubie. 1987. The effects of changes in the environment on the spatial firing of hippocampal complex-spike cells. *J. Neurosci.* **7**:1951–1968. [3]

Murray, E. A., and M. Mishkin. 1998. Object recognition and location memory in monkeys with excitotoxic lesions of the amygdala and hippocampus. *J. Neurosci.* **18(16)**:6568–6582. [8]

Naqshbandi, M., and W. A. Roberts. 2006. Anticipation of future events in squirrel monkeys (*Saimiri sciureus*) and rats (*Rattus norvegicus*): Tests of the Bischof-Köhler hypothesis. *J. Comp. Psychol.* **120**:345–357. [6]

Neisser, U. 2008. Memory with a grain of salt. In: Memory: An Anthology, ed. H. H. Wood and A. S. Byatt, pp. 80–88. London: Chatto and Windus. [12]

Nelson, T. O. 1996. Consciousness and metacognition. *Amer. Psychol.* **51(2)**:102–116. [8]

Newcombe, N. S. 2005. Language as destiny? Or not. (Essay review of S. C. Levinson, Space in language and cognition: Explorations in cognitive diversity). *Hum. Dev.* **48**:309–314. [5]

Newcombe, N. S., and D. H. Uttal. 2006. Whorf versus Socrates, round 10. *Trends Cogn. Sci.* **10**:394–396. [5]

Nico, D., I. Israël, and A. Berthoz. 2002. Interaction of visual and idiothetic information in a path completion task. *Exp. Brain Res.* **146**:379–382. [5]

Nieh, J. C. 2010. A negative feedback signal that is triggered by peril curbs honey bee recruitment. *Curr. Biol.* **20**:310–315. [12]

Nitz, D. 2009. Parietal cortex, navigation, and the construction of arbitrary reference frames for spatial information. *Neurobiol. Learn. Mem.* **91(2)**:179–185. [5]

Noe, R., and P. Hammerstein. 1994. Biological markets: Supply and demand determine the effect of partner choice in cooperation, mutualism, and mating. *Behav. Ecol. Sociobiol.* **35**:1–11. [16]

Noser, R., and R. W. Byrne. 2007. Travel routes and planning of visits to out-of-sight resources in wild chacma baboons (*Papio ursinus*). *Anim. Behav.* **73(2)**:257–266. [6, 7]

Nowak, M. A. 2006. Five rules for the evolution of cooperation. *Science* **314**:1560–1563. [7]

O'Donnell, S., and S. J. Bulova. 2007. Worker connectivity: A review of the design of worker communication systems and their effects on task performance in insect societies. *Insectes Sociaux* **54**:203–210. [11]

O'Keefe, J., and N. Burgess. 1996. Geometric determinants of the place fields of hippocampal neurons. *Nature* **381**:425–428. [3]

———. 2005. Dual phase and rate coding in hippocampal place cells: Theoretical significance and relationship to entorhinal grid cells. *Hippocampus* **15**:853–866. [3]

O'Keefe, J., and J. Dostrovsky. 1971. The hippocampus as a spatial map: Preliminary evidence from unit activity in the freely-moving rat. *Brain Res.* **34**:171–175. [3]

O'Keefe, J., and L. Nadel. 1978. The Hippocampus As a Cognitive Map. New York: Oxford Univ. Press. [4, 5]

Ortony, A., G. L. Clore, and A. Collins. 1988. The Cognitive Structure of Emotions. Cambridge: Cambridge Univ. Press. [18]

Osvath, M., and H. Osvath. 2008. Chimpanzee (*Pan troglodytes*) and orangutan (*Pongo abelii*) forethought: Self-control and pre-experience in the face of future tool use. *Anim. Cogn.* **11(4)**:661–674. [6]

Otte, D. 1974. Effects and functions in the evolution of signaling systems. *Ann. Rev. Ecol. Syst.* **5**:385–417. [13]

Otter, K., P. K. McGregor, A. M. R. Terry, et al. 1999. Do female great tits (*Parus major*) assess males by eavesdropping? A field study using interactive song playback. *Proc. Roy. Soc. Lond. B* **266(1426)**:1305. [18]

Owings, D. H., and E. S. Morton. 1997. The role of information in communication: An assessment/management approach. In: Perspectives in Ethology, ed. D. H. Owings et al., pp. 359–390. New York: Plenum. [13]

Owren, M. J., and D. Rendall. 2001. Sound on the rebound: Bringing form and function back to the forefront in understanding nonhuman primate vocal signaling. *Evol. Anthropol.* **10**:58–71. [10, 13]

Packard, M. G., and J. L. McGaugh. 1996. Inactivation of hippocampus or caudate nucleus with lidocaine differentially affects expression of place and response learning. *Neurobiol. Learn. Mem.* **65**:65–72. [8]

Pankiw, T., R. E. Page, and M. K. Fondrk. 1998. Brood pheromone stimulates pollen foraging in honey bees (*Apis mellifera*). *Behav. Ecol. Sociobiol.* **44**:193–198. [11]

Parish, A. R. 1996. Female relationships in bonobos (*Pan paiscus*). *Hum. Nature* **7(1)**:61–96. [15]

Partan, S. R., and P. Marler. 1999. Communication goes multimodal. *Science* **283**:1272–1273. [11]

———. 2005. Issues in the classification of multisensory communication signals. *Amer. Nat.* **166**:231–245. [11]

Payne, J. W., J. R. Bettman, and E. J. Johnson. 1993. The Adaptive Decision Maker. Cambridge: Cambridge Univ. Press. [7]

Pecker, J.-C. 2004. The provocative razor of William of Occam. *Eur. Rev.* **12(2)**:185–190. [1]

Peirce, C. S. 1931. Collected Papers. Cambridge, MA: Harvard Univ. Press. [2]

Penn, D. C., K. J. Holyoak, and D. J. Povinelli. 2008. Darwin's mistake: Explaining the discontinuity between human and nonhuman minds. *Behav. Brain Sci.* **31**:108–178. [12, 17, 18]

Penn, D. C., and D. J. Povinelli. 2007a. Causal cognition in human and nonhuman animals: A comparative, critical Review. *Ann. Rev. Psychol.* **58**:97–118. [17]

———. 2007b. On the lack of evidence that non-human animals possess anything remotely resembling a theory of mind. *Philos. Trans. R. Soc. Lond.* B **362**:731–744. [14, 17, 18]

———. 2009. On becoming approximately rational: The relational reinterpretation hypothesis. In: Rational Animals, Irrational Humans, ed. S. Watanabe et al. Tokyo: Keio Univ. Press. [17]

———. 2011. The comparative delusion: The "behavioristic"/"mentalistic" dichotomy in comparative theory of mind research. In: Agency and Joint Attention, ed. H. A. Terrace and J. Metcalfe. Oxford: Oxford Univ. Press. [17]

Perdeck, A. C. 1958. Two types of orientation in migrating starlings, *Sturnus vulgaris* L., as revealed by displacement experiments. *Ardea* **46**:1–37. [4]

Perner, J. 2010. Who took the cog out of cognitive science? Mentalism in an era of anti-cognitivism. In: Cognition and Neuropsychology: International Perspectives on Psychology Science, vol. 1, ed. P. A. Frensch and R. Schwarzer, pp. 241–261. Hove, East Sussex: Psychology Press. [17, 18]

———. 2011. Theory of mind—An unintelligent design: From behavior to teleology and perspective. In: The Handbook of Theory of Mind, ed. A. M. Leslie and T. C. German. Piscataway, NJ: Lawrence Erlbaum. [18]

Perner, J., D. Kloo, and E. Gornik. 2007. Episodic memory development: Theory of mind is part of re-experiencing experienced events. *Inf. Child Dev.* **16**:471–490. [12]

Perner, J., and J. Roessler. 2010. Teleology and causal reasoning in children's theory of mind. In: Causing Human Action: New Perspectives on the Causal Theory of Action ed. J. Aguilar and A. A. Buckareff, pp. 199–228. Cambridge, MA: MIT Press. [18]

Perner, J., S. Stummer, M. Sprung, and M. J. Doherty. 2002. Theory of mind finds its Piagetian perspective: Why alternative naming comes with understanding belief. *Cogn. Devel.* **17**:1451–1472. [18]

Pfeifer, R., and C. Scheier. 1999. Understanding Intelligence. Cambridge, MA: MIT Press. [15]

Pika, S., K. Liebal, J. Call, and M. Tomasello. 2005. The gestural communication of apes. *Gesture* **5**:41–56. [13]

Pika, S., and J. Mitani. 2006. Referential gestural communication in wild chimpanzees (*Pan troglodytes*). *Curr. Biol.* **16**:R191–R192. [13]

Pillutla, M. M., and J. K. Murnighan. 1996. Unfairness, anger, and spite: Emotional rejections of ultimatum offers. *Org. Behav. Human Dec. Proc.* **68**:208–224. [18]

Pinker, S. 2003. Language as an adaptation to the cognitive niche. In: Language Evolution, ed. M. H. Christiansen and S. Kirby, pp. 16–37. Oxford: Oxford Univ. Press. [12]

————. 2007. The Stuff of Thought. London: Penguin Books. [12]

Pompilio, L., and A. Kacelnik. 2005. State-dependent learning and suboptimal choice: When starlings prefer long over short delays to food. *Anim. Behav.* **70(3)**:571–578. [9]

Pompilio, L., A. Kacelnik, and S. T. Behmer. 2006. State-dependent learned valuation drives choice in an invertebrate. *Science* **311(5767)**:1613–1615. [9]

Poole, J. H., P. L. Tyack, A. S. Stoeger-Horwath, and S. Watwood. 2005. Animal Behaviour: Elephants are capable of vocal learning. *Nature* **434**:455–456. [13]

Poremba, A., M. Malloy, R. C. Saunders, et al. 2004. Species-specific calls evoke asymmetric activity in the monkey's temporal poles. *Nature* **427**:448–451. [13]

Poremba, A., R. C. Saunders, A. M. Crane, et al. 2003. Functional mapping of the primate auditory system. *Science* **299**:568–572. [13]

Povinelli, D. J. 2004. Behind the apes' appearance: Escaping anthropomorphism in the study of other minds. *Daedalus* **Winter**:29–41. [17]

Povinelli, D. J., J. M. Bering, and S. Giambrone. 2000. Toward a science of other minds: Escaping the argument by analogy. *Cogn. Sci.* **24(3)**:509–541. [17]

Povinelli, D. J., and T. J. Eddy. 1996. Factors influencing young chimpanzees recognition of attention. *J. Comp. Psychol.* **110**:336–345. [18]

Povinelli, D. J., and J. Vonk. 2003. Chimpanzee minds: Suspiciously human? *Trends Cogn. Sci.* **7(4)**:157–160. [17, 18]

————. 2004 We don't need a microscope to explore the chimpanzee's mind. *Mind Lang.* **19(1)**:1–28. [17, 18]

Prather, J. F., S. Peters, S. Nowicki, and R. Mooney. 2008. Precise auditory-vocal mirroring in neurons for learned vocal communication. *Nature* **451**:305–310. [13]

Pravosudov, V. V., A. S. Kitaysky, and A. Omanska. 2006. The relationship between migratory behaviour, memory and the hippocampus: An intraspecific comparison. *Proc. Roy. Soc. Lond. B* **273**:2641–2649. [4]

Pravosudov, V. V., T. C. Roth, and L. D. LaDage. 2010. Chickadees are selfish group members when it comes to food caching. *Anim. Behav.* **80**:175–180. [7]

Premack, D. 2010. Why humans are unique: Three theories. *Perspect. Psychol. Sci.* **5**:22–32. [12]

Premack, D., and A. J. Premack. 1983. The Mind of the Ape. New York: Norton. [2]

————. 2003. Original Intelligence: Unlocking the Mystery of Who We Are. New York: McGraw-Hill. [18]

Premack, D., and G. Woodruff. 1978. Does the chimpanzee have a theory of mind? *Behav. Brain Sci.* **4**:515–526. [14, 17, 18]

Preston, A. R., Y. Shrager, N. M. Dudukovic, and J. D. E. Gabrieli. 2004. Hippocampal contribution to the novel use of relational information in declarative memory. *Hippocampus* **14**:148–152. [12]

Preston, S. D., and F. B. M. de Waal. 2002. Empathy: Its ultimate and proximate bases. *Behav. Brain Sci.* **25**:1–20. [18]

Preuschoft, S., A. Paul, and J. Kuester. 1998. Dominance styles of female and male Barbary maceques (*Macaca sylvanus*). *Behaviour* **135**:731–755. [15]

Prince, S. E., S. M. Daselaar, and R. Cabeza. 2005. Neural correlates of relational memory: Successful encoding and retrieval of semantic and perceptual associations. *J. Neurosci.* **25(5)**:1203–1210. [12]

Proctor, H. C. 1991. Courtship in the water mite *Neumania papillator*: Males capitalize on female adaptations for predation. *Anim. Behav.* **42**:589–598. [13]

————. 1992. Sensory exploitation and the evolution of male mating behaviour: A cladistic test using water mites (Acari: Parasitengona). *Anim. Behav.* **44**:745–752. [13]

Pruden, S. M., S. C. Levine, and J. Huttenlocher. 2010. Individual differences in children's spatial language use predicts later spatial cognition. Paper presented at Intl. Soc. on Infant Studies: When representational systems collide: Aligning space and language, chaired by S. Roseberry and T. Goksün. Baltimore, MD. [5]

Puga-Gonzalez, I., H. Hildenbrandt, and C. K. Hemelrijk. 2009. Emergent patterns of social affiliation in primates: A model. *PLoS Comp. Biol.* **5(12)**:e1000630. [15]

Quinet, Y., and J. M. Pasteels. 1996. Spatial specialization of the foragers and foraging strategy in *Lasius fuliginosus* (Latreille) (Hymenoptera, Formicidae). *Insectes Sociaux* **43**:333–346. [11]

Raby, C. R., D. M. Alexis, A. Dickinson, and N. S. Clayton. 2007. Planning for the future by western scrub jays. *Nature* **445**:919–921. [6, 9, 12]

Raihani, N. J., A. S. Grutter, and R. Bshary. 2010. Punishers benefit from third-party punishment in fish. *Science* **327**:171. [14]

Ranganath, C., A. P. Yonelinas, M. X. Cohen, et al. 2004. Dissociable correlates of recollection and familiarity within the medial temporal lobes. *Neuropsychologia* **42(1)**:2–13. [8]

Range, F., and R. Nöe. 2005. Can simple rules account for the pattern of triadic interactions in juvenile and adult sooty mangabeys? *Anim. Behav.* **69**:445–452. [15]

Ratliff, K. R., and N. S. Newcombe. 2008. Reorienting when cues conflict: Evidence for an adaptive combination view. *Psychol. Sci.* **19(12)**:1301–1307. [5]

Ratnieks, F. L. W. 2008. Biomimicry: Further insights from ant colonies? In: BIOWIRE, ed. P. Liò, pp. 50–58. Heidelberg: Springer Verlag. [11]

Read, D. 2004. Intertemporal choice. In: Blackwell Handbook of Judgment and Decision Making, ed. D. Koehler and N. Harvey, pp. 424–443. Oxford: Blackwell. [7]

Reiner, A., D. J. Perkel, L. L. Bruce, et al. 2004. Revised nomenclature for avian telencephalon and some related brainstem nuclei. *J. Comp. Neurol.* **473**:377–414. [13]

Rendall, D., M. J. Owren, and M. J. Ryan. 2009. What do animal signals mean? *Anim. Behav.* **78(2)**:233–240. [10, 13]

Rendell, L., R. Boyd, D. Cownden, et al. 2010. Why copy others? Insights from the social learning strategies tournament. *Science* **328**:208–213. [11]

Rescorla, R. A. 1994. Transfer of instrumental control mediated by a devalued outcome. *Anim. Learn. Behav.* **22**:27–33. [6]

Ribbands, C. R. 1949. The foraging method of individual honey-bees. *J. Anim. Ecol.* **18**:47–66. [11]

Richards, R. J. 1987. Darwin and the Emergence of Evolutionary Theories of Mind and Behavior. Chicago: Univ. of Chicago Press. [17]

Riley, J. R., U. Greggers, A. D. Smith, D. R. Reynolds, and R. Menzel. 2005. The flight paths of honeybees recruited by the waggle dance. *Nature* **435**:205–207. [2, 13]

Rizzolatti, G., and L. Craighero. 2004. The mirror-neuron system. *Ann. Rev. Neurosci.* **27**:169–192. [13]

Rizzolatti, G., L. Fogassi, and V. Gallese. 2001. Neurophysiological mechanisms underlying the understanding and imitation of action. *Nature Rev. Neurosci.* **2**:661–670. [13]

Rizzolatti, G., and C. Sinigaglia. 2010. The functional role of the parieto-frontal mirror circuit: Interpretations and misinterpretations. *Nature Rev. Neurosci.* **11**:264–274. [13]

Robbins, M. M., and S. C. Sawyer. 2007. Intergroup encounters in mountain gorillas of Bwindi Impenetrable National Park, Uganda. *Behaviour* **144**:1497–1519 [15]

Roberts, W. A. 2006. Animal memory: Episodic-like memory in the rat. *Curr. Biol.* **16**:1317–1321. [12]

Roberts, W. A., C. Cruz, and J. Tremblay. 2007. Rats take correct novel routes and shortcuts in an enclosed maze. *J. Exp. Psychol. Anim. Behav. Proc.* **33**:79–91. [5]

Roberts, W. A., M. C. Feeney, K. MacPherson, et al. 2008. Episodic-like memory in rats: Is it based on when or how long ago? *Science* **320**:113–115. [12]

Roberts, W. A., M. C. Feeney, N. McMillan, et al. 2009. Do pigeons (*Columba livia*) study for a test? *J. Exp. Psychol. Anim. Behav. Proc.* **35(2)**:129–142. [8]

Robinson, E. J. H., K. E. Green, E. A. Jenner, M. Holcombe, and F. L. W. Ratnieks. 2008. Decay rates of attractive and repellent pheromones in an ant foraging trail network. *Insectes Sociaux* **55**:246–251. [11]

Robinson, E. J. H., D. E. Jackson, M. Holcombe, and F. L. W. Ratnieks. 2005. "No entry" signal in ant foraging. *Nature* **438**:442. [11]

Rodriguez, F., J. C. Lopez, J. P. Vargas, et al. 2002. Spatial memory and hippocampal pallium through vertebrate evolution: Insights from reptiles and teleost fish. *Brain Res. Bull.* **57(3–4)**:499–503. [8]

Roediger, H. L., and K. B. McDermott. 1995. Creating false memories: Remembering words not presented in lists. *J. Exp. Psychol. Learn. Mem. Cogn.* **21**:803–814. [12]

Roitberg, B. D., M. Mangel, R. G. Lalonde, et al. 1992. Seasonal dynamic shifts in patch exploitation by parasitic wasps. *Behav. Evol.* **3**:156–165. [7]

Ron, S. R. 2008. The evolution of female mate choice for complex calls in tungara frogs. *Anim. Behav.* **76**:1783–1794. [13]

Rosati, A. G., J. R. Stevens, B. Hare, and M. D. Hauser. 2007. The evolutionary origins of human patience: Temporal preferences in chimpanzees, bonobos, and adult humans. *Curr. Biol.* **17**:1663–1668. [7, 9]

Rose, J., and M. Colombo. 2005. Neural correlates of executive control in the avian brain. *PLoS Biol.* **13**:190. [4]

Rosengren, R., and W. Fortelius. 1986. Ortstreue in foraging ants of the *Formica rufa* group: Hierarchy of orienting cues and long-term memory. *Insectes Sociaux* **33**:306–337. [11]

Rotenberg, A., and R. U. Muller. 1997. Variable place-cell coupling to a continuously viewed stimulus: Evidence that the hippocampus acts as a perceptual system. *Philos. Trans. R. Soc. Lond. B* **352(1360)**:1505–1513. [5]

Rowe, C. 1999. Receiver psychology and the evolution of multicomponent signals. *Anim. Behav.* **58**:921–931. [11]

Rubinstein, A. 2003. Economics and psychology? The case of hyperbolic discounting. *Intl. Econ. Rev.* **44**:1207–1216. [7]

Russon, A., and K. Andrews. 2010. Orangutan pantomime: Elaborating the message. *Biol. Lett.* [12]

Ryan, M. J., J. H. Fox, W. Wilczynski, and A. S. Rand. 1990. Sexual selection for sensory exploitation in the frog *Physalaemus pustulosus*. *Nature* **343**:66–67. [13]

Ryan, M. J., and A. S. Rand. 1993. Sexual selection and signal evolution: The ghost of biases past. *Philos. Trans. R. Soc. Lond. B* **340**:187–195. [13]

———. 2003. Mate recognition in tungara frogs: A review of some studies of brain, behavior, and evolution. *Acta Zool. Sinica* **49**:713–726. [13]

Salo, O., and R. Rosengren. 2001. Memory of location and site recognition in the ant *Formica uralensis* (Hymenoptera: Formicidae). *Ethology* **107**:737–752. [11]

Santos, L. R., J. I. Flombaum, and W. Phillips. 2007. The evolution of human mind-reading: How non-human primates can inform social cognitive neuroscience. In: Evolutionary Cognitive Neuroscience, ed. S. Platek, pp. 433–456. Cambridge, MA: MIT Press. [17]

Santos, L. R., A. G. Nissen, and J. A. Ferrugia. 2006. Rhesus monkeys, *Macaca mulatta*, know what others can and cannot hear. *Anim. Behav.* **71(5)**:1175–1181. [17]

Sargolini, F., M. Fyhn, T. Hafting, et al. 2006. Conjunctive representation of position, direction and velocity in entorhinal cortex. *Science* **312**:754–758. [5]

Sauvage, M. M., N. J. Fortin, A. P. Owens, A. P. Yonelinas, and H. Eichenbaum. 2008. Recognition memory: Opposite effects of hippocampal damage on recollection and familiarity. *Nature Neurosci.* **11(1)**:16–18. [8]

Savage, L. J. 1954. The Foundations of Statistics. New York: Wiley. [7]

Savage-Rumbaugh, S., S. G. Shanker, and T. J. Taylor. 1998. Apes, Language, and the Human Mind. New York: Oxford Univ. Press. [13]

Scarantino, A. 2010. Animal communication between information and influence. *Anim. Behav.* **79(6)**:E1–E5. [10]

Schacter, D. L. 1996. Searching for Memory: The Brain, the Mind, and the Past. New York: Basic Books. [12]

Schacter, D. L., D. R. Addis, and R. L. Buckner. 2008a. Episodic simulation of future events: Concepts, data, and applications. *Ann. NY Acad. Sci.* **1124**:39–60. [6]

———. 2008b. Remembering the past to imagine the future: The prospective brain. *Nature Rev. Neurosci.* **8**:657–661. [12]

Schinazi, V. R., R. A. Epstein, D. Nardi, N. S. Newcombe, and T. F. Shipley. 2009. The acquisition of spatial knowledge in an unfamiliar campus environment. In: Proc. of 50th Annual Meeting of the Psychonomics Society, Nov. 19–22, 2009. Boston, MA. [5]

Schino, G., and F. Aureli. 2009. Reciprocal altruism in primates: Partner choice, cognition, and emotions. *Adv. Stud. Behav.* **39**:45–69. [16]

Schino, G., E. Polizzi di Sorrentino, and B. Tiddi. 2007. Grooming and coalitions in Japanese macaques (*Macaca fuscata*): Partner choice and the time frame of reciprocation. *J. Comp. Psychol.* **121**:181–188. [16]

Schino, G., and A. Troisi. 1992. Opiate receptor blockade in juvenile macaques: Effect on affiliative interactions with their mothers and group companions. *Brain Res.* **576(1)**:125–130. [15]

Schulte-Mecklenbeck, M., A. Kühlberger, and R. Ranyard. 2010. A Handbook of Process Tracing Methods for Decision Research. London: Psychology Press. [7]

Schwabe, L., and O. T. Wolf. 2009. Stress prompts habit behavior in humans. *J. Neurosci.* **29(22)**:7191–7198. [6]

Schwarz, B. L., M. R. Colon, I. C. Sanchez, I. A. Rodriguez, and S. Evans. 2002. Single-trial learning of "what" and "who" information in a gorilla (*Gorilla gorilla gorilla*): Implications for episodic memory. *Anim. Cogn.* **5**:85–90. [12]

Schwarz, B. L., and S. Evans. 2001. Episodic memory in primates. *Amer. J. Primatol.* **55**:71–85. [12]

Scott, S. K. 2008. Voice processing in monkey and human brains. *Trends Cogn. Sci.* **12**:323–325. [13]

Scott-Phillips, T. C. 2008. Defining biological communication. *J. Evol. Biol.* **21(2)**:387–395. [10]

———. 2009. Animal communication: Insights from linguistic pragmatics. *Anim. Behav.* **79(1)**:E1–E4. [10]

Searcy, W. A., R. C. Anderson, and S. Nowicki. 2006. Bird song as a signal of aggressive intent. *Behav. Ecol. Sociobiol.* **60**:234–241. [13]

Searcy, W. A., and S. Nowicki. 2005. The Evolution of Animal Communication: Reliability and Deception in Signaling Systems. Princeton: Princeton Univ. Press. [10, 13]

Seed, A. M., and R. W. Byrne. 2010. Animal tool-use. *Curr. Biol.* **20(23)**:R1032–R1039. [9]

Seed, A. M., and J. Call. 2009. Causal knowledge for events and objects in animals. In: Rational Animals, Irrational Humans, ed. S. Watanabe et al., pp. 173–187. Tokyo: Keio Univ. Press. [9]

Seed, A. M., J. Call, N. J. Emery, and N. S. Clayton. 2009. Chimpanzees solve the trap problem when the confound of tool use is removed. *J. Exp. Psychol. Anim. Behav. Proc.* **35(1)**:23–34. [9]

Seeley, T. D. 1995. The Wisdom of the Hive: The Social Physiology of Honey Bee Colonies. London: Harvard Univ. Press. [2, 11]

———. 1997. Honey bee colonies are group-level adaptive units. *Amer. Nat.* **150**:S22–S41. [13]

———. 1998. Thoughts on information and integration in honey bee colonies. *Apidologie* **29**:67–80. [11]

———. 2010. Honeybee Democracy. Princeton: Princeton Univ. Press. [11]

Seeley, T. D., and S. C. Buhrman. 1999. Group decision making in swarms of honey bees. *Behav. Ecol. Sociobiol.* **45**:1931. [11]

———. 2001. Nest-site selection in honey bees: How well do swarms implement the "best-of-N" decision rule? *Behav. Ecol. Sociobiol.* **49**:416–427. [11]

Seeley, T. D., and J. Tautz. 2001. Worker piping in honey bee swarms and its role in preparing for liftoff. *J. Comp. Physiol. A* **187**:667–676. [11]

Seeley, T. D., and P. K. Visscher. 2004. Quorum sensing during nest-site selection by honeybee swarms. *Behav. Ecol. Sociobiol.* **56**:594–601. [2, 11]

———. 2008. Sensory coding of nest-site value in honeybee swarms. *J. Exp. Biol.* **211**:3691–3697. [11]

Senju, A., V. Southgate, C. Snape, M. Leonard, and G. Csibra. 2011. Do 18-months-olds really attribute mental states to others? A critical test. *Psychol. Sci.*, in press. [18]

Seyfarth, R. M. 1977. A model of social grooming among adult female monkeys. *J. Theor. Biol.* **65**:671–698. [15]

———. 1987. Vocal communication and its relation to language. In: Primate Societies, ed. B. Smuts et al., pp. 440–451. Chicago: Univ. of Chicago Press. [13]

Seyfarth, R. M., and D. L. Cheney. 1984. Grooming, alliances, and reciprocal altruism in vervet monkeys. *Nature* **308**:541–543. [16]

———. 1986. Vocal development in vervet monkeys. *Anim. Behav.* **34**:1640–1658. [13]

Seyfarth, R. M., and D. L. Cheney. 2003a. Meaning and emotion in animal vocalizations. *Ann. NY Acad. Sci.* **1000**:32–55. [10]

————. 2003b. Signalers and receivers in animal communication. *Ann. Rev. Psychol.* **54**:145–173. [10]

————. 2003c. The structure of social knowledge in monkeys. In: Animal Social Complexity: Intelligence, Culture and Individualized Societies, ed. F. B. M. de Waal and P. L. Tyack, pp. 230–248. Cambridge, MA: Harvard Univ. Press. [17, 18]

————. 2010. Production, usage and comprehension in animal vocalizations. *Brain Lang.* **115**:92–100. [13]

Seyfarth, R. M., D. L. Cheney, T. J. Bergman, et al. 2010. The central importance of information in studies of animal communication. *Anim. Behav.* **80**:3–8. [10]

Seyfarth, R. M., D. L. Cheney, and P. Marler. 1980. Vervet monkey alarm calls: Semantic communication in a free-ranging primate. *Anim. Behav.* **28**:1070–1094. [13]

Shanahan, M. 2006. A cognitive architecture that combines internal simulation with a global workspace. *Conscious. Cogn.* **15(2)**:433–449. [9]

————. 2010. Embodiment and the Inner Life: Cognition and Consciousness in the Space of Possible Minds. New York: Oxford Univ. Press. [9]

Shanahan, M., and B. J. Baars. 2005. Applying global workspace theory to the frame problem. *Cognition* **98(2)**:157–176. [9]

Shanks, D. R. 2005. Connectionist models of basic human learning processes. In: Connectionist Models in Cognitive Psychology, ed. G. Houghton, pp. 45–82. Hove, East Sussex: Psychology Press. [17]

Shannon, C. E., and W. Weaver. 1949. The Mathematical Theory of Communication. Urbana, Illinois. [10]

Shapiro, M. S., S. Siller, and A. Kacelnik. 2008. Simultaneous and sequential choice as a function of reward delay and magnitude: Normative, descriptive and process-based models tested in the European starling (*Sturnus vulgaris*). *J. Exp. Psychol. Anim. Behav. Proc.* **34**:75–93. [7, 9]

Shea, N., and C. Heyes. 2010. Metamemory as evidence of animal consciousness: The type that does the trick. *Biol. Philos.* **25**:95–110. [8]

Sheehan, M. J., and E. A. Tibbetts. 2008. Robust long-term social memories in a paper wasp. *Curr. Biol.* **18**:R851–R852. [18]

Sherry, D. F., and D. L. Schacter. 1987. The evolution of multiple memory systems. *Psychol. Rev.* **94**:439–454. [4, 8]

Sherry, D. F., A. L. Vaccarino, K. Buckenham, and R. S. Hertz. 1989. The hippocampal complex of food-storing birds. *Brain Behav. Evol.* **34**:308–317. [4]

Shettleworth, S. J. 1998. Cognition, Evolution, and Behavior. Oxford: Oxford Univ. Press. [13, 14]

————. 2007. Planning for breakfast. *Nature* **445(7130)**:825–826. [9]

————. 2009. The evolution of comparative cognition: Is the snark still a boojum? *Behav. Proc.* **80**:210–217. [14]

————. 2010a. Clever animals and killjoy explanations in comparative psychology. *Trends Cogn. Sci.* **14(11)**:477–481. [17, 18]

————. 2010b. Cognition, Evolution, and Behavior, 2nd ed. New York: Oxford Univ. Press. [5, 8, 16, 17, 18]

Shettleworth, S. J., and J. E. Sutton. 2003. Animal metacognition? It's all in the methods. *Behav. Brain Sci.* **26(3)**:353–354. [8]

Shields, W. E., J. D. Smith, and D. A. Washburn. 1997. Uncertain responses by humans and rhesus monkeys (*Macaca mulatta*) in a psychophysical same-different task. *J. Exp. Psychol.* **126(2)**:147–164. [8]

Shultz, S., and R. I. M. Dunbar. 2010. Social bonds in birds are associated with brain size and contingent on the correlated evolution of life-history and increased parental investment. *Biol. J. Linnean Soc.* **100**:111–123. [18]

Shutt, K., A. MacLarnon, M. Heistermann, and S. Semple. 2007. Grooming in Barbary macaques: Better to give than to receive? *Biol. Lett.* **3**:213–233. [15]

Siegel, J. J., D. Nitz, and V. P. Bingman. 2006. Lateralized functional components of spatial cognition in the avian hippocampal formation: Evidence from single-unit recordings in freely moving homing pigeons. *Hippocampus* **16**:125–140. [4]

Sih, A., S. F. Hanser, and K. A. McHugh. 2009. Social network theory: New insights and issues for behavioural ecologists. *Behav. Ecol. Sociobiol.* **63**:975–988. [14]

Silk, J. B. 1999. Male bonnet macaques use information about third-party rank relationships to recruit allies. *Anim. Behav.* **58**:45–51. [17]

———. 2002. Using the F-word in primatology. *Behaviour* **139**:442–446. [18]

———. 2003a. Cooperation without counting: The puzzle of friendship. In: Genetic and Cultural Evolution of Cooperation, ed. P. Hammerstein, pp. 37–54. Dahlem Workshop Reports, J. Lupp, series ed. Cambridge, MA: MIT Press. [16]

———. 2003b. The evolution of cooperation in primate groups. In: Moral Sentiments and Material Interests: On the Foundations of Cooperation in Economic Life, ed. H. Gintis et al. Cambridge, MA: MIT Press. [17]

———. 2007a. Animal behavior: Conflict management is for the birds. *Curr. Biol.* **17(2)**:R50–R51. [15]

———. 2007b. Empathy, sympathy, and prosocial preferences in primates. In: The Oxford Handbook of Evolutionary Psychology, ed. R. I. M. Dunbar and L. Barrett, pp. 115–126. Oxford: Oxford Univ. Press. [18]

———. 2007c. The strategic dynamics of cooperation in primate groups. *Adv. Stud. Behav.* **37**:1–41. [16]

———. 2009. Social preferences in primates. In: Neuroeconomics: Decision Making and the Brain, ed. P. W. Glimcher et al., pp. 269–284. London: Academic Press. [18]

Silk, J. B., J. C. Beehner, T. J. J. Bergman, et al. 2009. The benefits of social capital: Close social bonds among female baboons enhance offspring survival. *Proc. Roy. Soc. Lond. B* **276**:3099–3104. [16]

———. 2010. Strong and consistent social bonds enhance the longevity of female baboons. *Curr. Biol.* **20** [16]

Silk, J. B., S. F. Brosnan, J. Vonk, et al. 2005. Chimpanzees are indifferent to the welfare of unrelated group members. *Nature* **437**:1357–1359. [16, 18]

Silk, J. B., and B. R. House. 2011. The phylogeny and ontogeny of prosocial behavior. In: The Oxford Handbook of Comparative Evolutionary Psychology, ed. J. Vonk and T. Shackelford. Oxford: Oxford Univ. Press, in press. [16]

Simms, N., and D. Gentner. 2007. Finding the middle ground: Does language help children reason about spatial relations? Poster presented at the 5th Biennial Meeting of the Cognitive Development Society, Santa Fe, NM. [5]

Simon, H. A. 1956. Rational choice and the structure of the environment. *Psychol. Rev.* **63**:129–138. [7]

Skinner, B. F. 1938. The Behavior of Organisms: An Experimental Analysis. Englewood Cliffs, NJ: Prentice Hall. [7]

Skyrms, B. 2010. Signals: Evolution, Learning and Information. Oxford: Oxford Univ. Press. [10]

Slocombe, K. E., and K. Zuberbühler. 2005. Functionally referential communication in a chimpanzee. *Curr. Biol.* **15**:1779–1784. [13]

Smith, C., and L. R. Squire. 2005. Declarative memory, awareness, and transitive inference. *J. Neurosci.* **25(44)**:10,138–10,146. [8]

Smith, J. D. 2009. The study of animal metacognition. *Trends Cogn. Sci.* **13(9)**:389–
396. [9]

Smith, J. D., J. S. Redford, M. J. Beran, and D. A. Washburn. 2006. Dissociating uncertainty responses and reinforcement signals in the comparative study of uncertainty
monitoring. *J. Exp. Psychol.* **135(2)**:282–297. [8]

Smith, J. D., J. Schull, J. Strote, et al. 1995. The uncertain response in the bottle-nosed
dolphin (*Tursiops truncatus*). *J. Exp. Psychol.* **124(4)**:391–408. [8]

Smith, J. D., W. E. Shields, and D. A. Washburn. 1998. Memory monitoring by animals
and humans. *J. Exp. Psychol.* **127(3)**:227–250. [8]

———. 2003. The comparative psychology of uncertainty monitoring and metacognition. *Behav. Brain Sci.* **26**:317–374. [8]

Smith, J. E., R. C. van Horn, K. S. Powning, et al. 2010. Evolutionary forces favoring intragroup coalitions among spotted hyenas and other animals. *Behav. Evol.*
21(2):284–303. [15, 16]

Smith, W. J. 1977. The Behavior of Communicating: An Ethological Approach.
Cambridge, MA: Harvard Univ. Press. [10, 13]

Snowdon, C. T. 2008. Contextually flexible communication in nonhuman primates.
In: The Evolution of Communicative Flexibility: Complexity, Creativity, and
Adaptability in Human and Animal Communication., ed. D. K. Oller and U. Griebel,
pp. 71–93. Cambridge, MA: MIT Press. [13]

Sol, D., N. Garcia, A. Iwaniuk, et al. 2010. Evolutionary divergence in brain size between migratory and resident birds. *PLoS One* **5**:9617. [4]

Sole, L. M., S. J. Shettleworth, and P. J. Bennett. 2003. Uncertainty in pigeons. *Psychon.
Bull. Rev.* **10(3)**:738–745. [8]

Solstad, T., C. N. Boccara, E. Kropff, M. B. Moser, and E. I. Moser. 2008. Representation
of geometric borders in the entorhinal cortex. *Science* **322**:1865–1868. [3]

Soproni, K., A. Miklosi, J. Topal, and V. Csanyi. 2002. Dogs' (*Canis familiaris*) responsiveness to human pointing gestures. *J. Comp. Psychol.* **116(1)**:27–34. [17]

Sperber, D., and D. Wilson. 2002. Pragmatics, modularity and mind-reading. *Mind
Lang.* **17**:3–23. [13]

Sporns, O. 2010. Networks of the Brain. Cambridge, MA: MIT Press. [9]

Squire, L. R. 1992. Declarative and nondeclarative memory: Multiple brain systems
supporting learning and memory. *J. Cogn. Neurosci.* **4**:232–243. [12]

———. 2004. Memory systems of the brain: A brief history and current perspective.
Neurobiol. Learn. Mem. **82**:171–177. [12]

Stackman, R. W., and J. S. Taube. 1997. Firing properties of head direction cells in
the rat anterior thalamic nucleus: Dependence on vestibular input. *J. Neurosci.*
17:4349–4358. [3]

———. 1998. Firing properties of rat lateral mammillary single units: Head direction,
head pitch, and angular head velocity. *J. Neurosci.* **18**:9020–9037. [3]

Stackman, R. W., M. L. Tullman, and J. S. Taube. 2000. Maintenance of rat head direction cell firing during locomotion in the vertical plane. *J. Neurophysiol.* **83**:393–405.
[3]

Stanford, C. B. 1998. The social behaviour of chimpanzees and bonobos. *Curr. Anthro.*
39(4):399–420. [15]

Stegmann, U. E. 2005. John Maynard Smith's notion of animal signals. *Biol. Philos.*
20(5):1011–1025. [10]

Stephan, H., H. Frahm, and G. Baron. 1981. New and revised data on volume of brain structures in insectivores and primates. *Folia Primatol.* **35**:1–29. [18]

Stephens, D. W., and D. Anderson. 2001. The adaptive value of preference for immediacy: When shortsighted rules have farsighted consequences. *Behav. Evol.* **12**:330–339. [7]

Stephens, D. W., and J. R. Krebs. 1986. Foraging Theory. Princeton: Princeton Univ. Press. [7]

Stevens, J. R. 2008. The evolutionary biology of decision making. In: Better than Conscious? Decision Making, the Human Mind, and Implications for Institutions, ed. C. Engel and W. Singer, pp. 285–304. Strüngmann Forum Reports, J. Lupp, series ed. Cambridge, MA: MIT Press. [7]

———. 2009. Models of similarity in intertemporal choice (Abstract). In: Proc. 31st Conf. of the Cognitive Science Society, p. 960. Amsterdam. [7]

———. 2010a. Donor payoffs and other-regarding preferences in cotton-top tamarins (*Saguinus oedipus*). *Anim. Cogn.* **13**:663–670. [18]

———. 2010b. Intertemporal choice. In: Encyclopedia of Animal Behavior, ed. M. D. Breed and J. Moore, pp. 203–208. Oxford: Academic Press. [7]

Stevens, J. R., F. A. Cushman, and M. D. Hauser. 2005a. Evolving the psychological mechanisms for cooperation. *Ann. Rev. Ecol. Evol. Syst.* **36**:499–518. [16]

Stevens, J. R., E. V. Hallinan, and M. D. Hauser. 2005b. The ecology and evolution of patience in two New World monkeys. *Biol. Lett.* **1**:223–226. [7, 9]

Stevens, J. R., and M. D. Hauser. 2004. Why be nice? Psychological constraints on the evolution of cooperation. *Trends Cogn. Sci.* **8**:60–65. [7]

Stevens, J. R., and A. J. King. 2011. The lives of others: Social rationality in animals. In: Simple Heuristics in a Social World, ed. R. Hertwig et al. Oxford: Oxford Univ. Press, in press. [7]

Stevens, J. R., A. G. Rosati, K. R. Ross, and M. D. Hauser. 2005c. Will travel for food: Spatial discounting in two New World primates. *Curr. Biol.* **15**:1855–1860. [7]

Stevens, J. R., J. Volstorf, L. J. Schooler, and J. Rieskamp. 2011. Forgetting constrains the emergence of cooperative decision strategies. *Front. Psychol.* **1**:235. [7]

Stevens, J. R., J. N. Wood, and M. D. Hauser. 2007. When quantity trumps number: Discrimination experiments in cotton-top tamarins (*Saguinus oedipus*) and common marmosets (*Callithrix jacchus*). *Anim. Cogn.* **10**:429–437. [7]

Stich, S. P., and I. Ravenscroft. 1994. What is folk psychology? *Cognition* **50**:447–468. [17]

Stickland, T. R., N. F. Britton, and N. R. Franks. 1999. Models of information flow in ant foraging: The benefits of both attractive and repulsive signals. In: Information Processing in Social Insects, ed. C. Detrain et al., pp. 83–100. Basel: Birkhäuser Verlag. [11]

Stokoe, W. C. 2001. Language in Hand: Why Sign Came before Speech. Washington, DC: Gallaudet Univ. Press. [13]

Stolz, W. S. 1967. A study of the ability to decode grammatically novel sentences. *J. Verbal Learn. Verbal Behav.* **6**:867–873. [13]

Stout, S. C., and R. R. Miller. 2007. Sometimes competing retrieval (SOCR): A formalization of the comparator hypothesis. *Psychol. Rev.* **114(3)**:759–783. [17]

Striedter, G. F. 1994. The vocal control pathways in budgerigars differ from those in songbirds. *J. Comp. Neurol.* **343**:35–56. [13]

Suddendorf, T. 2006. Foresight and evolution of the human mind. *Science* **312**:1006–1007. [12]

Suddendorf, T., and J. Busby. 2003. Mental time travel in animals? *Trends Cogn. Sci.* **7**:391–396. [12]

Suddendorf, T., and M. C. Corballis. 1997. Mental time travel and the evolution of the human mind. *Genet. Soc. Gen. Psychol. Monogr.* **123**:133–167. [6, 12]

———. 2007. The evolution of foresight: What is mental time travel, and is it unique to humans? *Behav. Brain Sci.* **30**:299–351. [12]

———. 2008. New evidence for animal foresight? *Anim. Behav.* **75**:E1–E3. [6, 12]

Suddendorf, T., and A. Whiten. 2001. Mental evolution and development: Evidence for secondary representation in children, great apes and other animals. *Psychol. Bull.* **127**:629–650. [17]

Suomi, S. J. 2007. Risk, resilience, and gene x environment interactions in rhesus monkeys. *Ann. NY Acad. Sci.* **1094**:52–62. [16]

Sutton, D., C. Larson, and R. C. Lindeman. 1974. Neocortical and limbic lesion effects on primate phonation. *Brain Res.* **71**:61–75. [13]

Sutton, J. E., and S. J. Shettleworth. 2008. Memory without awareness: Pigeons do not show metamemory in delayed matching to sample. *J. Exp. Psychol. Anim. Behav. Proc.* **34(2)**:266–282. [8]

Sutton, R. S., and A. G. Barto. 1981. An adaptive network that constructs and uses an internal model of its world. *Cogn. Brain Theory* **4**:217–246. [6]

———. 1998. Reinforcement Learning. Cambridge, MA: MIT Press. [6]

Svoboda, E., M. C. McKinnona, and B. Levine. 2006. The functional neuroanatomy of autobiographical memory: A meta-analysis. *Neuropsychologia* **44**:2189–2208. [12]

Számadó, S. 2008. How threat displays work: Species-specific fighting techniques, weaponry and proximity risk. *Anim. Behav.* **76**:1455–1463. [13]

Tafforin, C., and R. Campan. 1994. Ethological experiments on human orientation behavior within a three-dimensional space: In microgravity. *Adv. Space Res.* **14**:415–418. [3]

Tanner, J. E., and R. W. Byrne. 1996. Representation of action through iconic gesture in a captive lowland gorilla. *Curr. Anthro.* **37**:162–173. [13]

Taube, J. S. 2007. The head direction signal: Origins and sensory-motor integration. *Ann. Rev. Neurosci.* **30**:181–207. [3]

Taube, J. S., and H. L. Burton. 1995. Head direction cell activity monitored in a novel environment and during a cue conflict situation. *J. Neurophysiol.* **74**:1953–1971. [3]

Taube, J. S., R. U. Muller, and J. B. Ranck. 1990a. Head-direction cells recorded from the postsubiculum in freely moving rats. I. Description and quantitative analysis. *J. Neurosci.* **10**:420–435. [3]

———. 1990b. Head-direction cells recorded from the postsubiculum in freely moving rats. II. Effects of environmental manipulations. *J. Neurosci.* **10**:436–447. [3]

te Boekhorst, I. J. A., and C. K. Hemelrijk. 2000. Non-linear and synthetic models of primate societies. In: Dynamics of Human and Primate Societies: Agent-based Modelling for Social and Spatial Processes, ed. T. A. Kohler and G. J. Gumerman, pp. 19–44. Oxford: Oxford Univ. Press. [15]

Templeton, C. N., E. Greene, and K. Davis. 2005. Allometry of alarm calls: Black-capped chickadees encode information about predator size. *Science* **308**:1934–1937. [13]

ten Cate, C., C. van Heijningen, and C. Zuidema. 2010. Reply to Gentner et al.: As simple as possible but not simpler. *PNAS* **107**:E66–E67. [13]

Teufel, C., N. S. Clayton, and J. Russell. 2011. Two-year-old children's understanding of visual perception and knowledge formation in others. *J. Cogn. Develop.*, in press. [18]

Teufel, C., A. Gutmann, R. Pirow, and J. Fischer. 2010. Facial expressions modulate the ontogenetic trajectory of gaze-following among monkeys. *Dev. Sci.* **124**:437–445. [10]

Thierry, B. 1990. Feedback loop between kinship and dominance: The macaque model. *J. Theor. Biol.* **145**:511–521. [15]

———. 2004. Social epigenesis. In: Macaque Societies: A Model for the Study of Social Organisation, ed. B. Thierry et al., pp. 267–289. Cambridge: Cambridge Univ. Press. [15]

Thom, C., D. C. Gilley, J. Hooper, and H. E. Esch. 2007. The scent of the waggle dance. *PLoS Biol.* **5**:e228. [11]

Thorndike, E. L. 1911. Animal Intelligence: Experimental Studies. New York: Macmillan. [6]

———. 1931. Human Learning. New York: Century. [6]

Thorup, K., I. A. Bisson, M. S. Bowlin, et al. 2007. Evidence for a navigational map stretching across the continental U.S. in a migratory song bird. *PNAS* **104**:18,115–18,119. [4]

Tibbetts, E. A., and J. Dale. 2007. Individual recognition: It is good to be different. *Trends Ecol. Evol.* **22**:529–537. [13]

Tinbergen, N. 1963. On aims and methods of ethology. *Zt. Tierpsychol.* **20**:410–433. [7]

Todd, P. M., and G. Gigerenzer. 2000. Précis of simple heuristics that make us smart. *Behav. Brain Sci.* **23**:727–741. [7]

Todt, D. 1986. Hinweischarakter und Mittlerfunktion von verhalten. *Zt. Semiotik* **8**:183–232. [10]

Tolman, E. C. 1948. Cognitive maps in rats and men. *Psychol. Rev.* **55**:189–208. [3, 4, 5, 8]

Tomasello, M. 2008. Origins of Human Communication. Cambridge, MA: MIT Press. [13]

Tomasello, M., and J. Call. 2006. Do chimpanzees know what others see—or only what they are looking at? In: Rational Animals?, ed. S. Hurley and M. Nudds. Oxford: Oxford Univ. Press. [17]

———. 2007a. Ape gestures and the origin of language. In: The Gestural Communication of Apes and Monkeys, ed. J. Call and M. Tomasello, pp. 197–220. Mahwah, NJ: Lawrence Erlbaum. [13]

———. 2007b. Introduction: Intentional communication in nonhuman primates. In: The Gestural Communication of Apes and Monkeys, ed. J. Call and M. Tomasello, pp. 1–16. Mahwah, NJ: Lawrence Erlbaum. [13]

Tomasello, M., J. Call, and B. Hare. 1998. Five primate species follow the visual gaze of conspecifics. *Anim. Behav.* **55**:1063–1069. [14]

———. 2003a. Chimpanzees understand psychological states: The question is which ones and to what extent. *Trends Cogn. Sci.* **7(4)**:153–156. [17, 18]

———. 2003b. Chimpanzees versus humans: It's not that simple. *Trends Cogn. Sci.* **7(6)**:239–240. [17, 18]

Tomasello, M., M. Carpenter, J. Call, T. Behne, and H. Moll. 2005. Understanding and sharing intentions: The origins of cultural cognition. *Behav. Brain Res.* **28**:675–691. [16, 18]

Tooby, J., and I. DeVore. 1987. The reconstruction of hominid behavioral evolution through strategic modelling. In: The Evolution of Human Behavior: Primate Models, ed. W. G. Kinzey, pp. 183–237. New York: SUNY Press. [12]

Towne, W. F., and J. L. Gould. 1988. The spatial precision of the honey bees' dance communication. *J. Insect Behav.* **1**:129–155. [13]

Traniello, J. F. A. 1989. Chemical trail systems, orientation, and territorial interactions in the ant *Lasius neoniger*. *J. Insect Behav.* **2**:339–354. [11]

Trivers, R. L. 1971. The evolution of reciprocal altruism. *Q. Rev. Biol.* **46**:35–57. [16]

———. 1974. Parent-offspring conflict. *Amer. Soc. Zool.* **14(1)**:249–264. [10]

Trullier, O., S. Wiener, A. Berthoz, and J.-A. Meyer. 1997. Biologically based artificial navigation systems: Review and prospects. *Prog. Neurobiol.* **51**:483–544. [5]

Tulving, E. 1972. Episodic and semantic memory. In: Organization of Memory, ed. E. Tulving and W. Donaldson, pp. 382–403. New York: Academic Press. [6]

———. 1983. Elements of Episodic Memory. New York: Oxford Univ. Press. [12]

———. 2001. Origin of autonoesis in episodic memory. In: The Nature of Remembering: Essays in Honor of Robert G. Crowder, ed. I. H. L. Roediger et al., pp. 17–34. Washington, DC: American Psychological Association. [12]

———. 2002. Episodic memory: From mind to brain. *Ann. Rev. Psychol.* **53**:1–25. [12]

Tulving, E., and H. J. Markowitsch. 1994. What do animal models of memory model? *Behav. Brain Sci.* **17(3)**:498–499. [8]

Tulving, E., D. L. Schacter, D. R. McLachlan, and M. Moscovitch. 1988. Priming of semantic autobiographical knowledge: A case study of retrograde amnesia. *Brain Cogn.* **8**:3–20. [12]

Turella, L., A. C. Pierno, F. Tubaldi, and U. Castiello. 2009. Mirror neurons in humans: Consisting or confounding evidence? *Brain Lang.* **108**:10–21. [13]

Twyman, A. D., and N. S. Newcombe. 2010. Five reasons to doubt the existence of a geometric module. *Cogn. Sci.* **34**:1315–1356. [5]

Ulanovsky, N., and C. F. Moss. 2007. Hippocampal cellular and network activity in freely moving echolocating bats. *Nature Neurosci.* **10**:224–233. [3]

Uttal, D. H. 2000. Seeing the big picture: Map use and the development of spatial cognition. *Dev. Sci.* **3(3)**:247–286. [5]

Vaish, A., M. Carpenter, and M. Tomasello. 2009. Sympathy through affective perspective taking and its relation to prosocial behavior in toddlers. *Dev. Psychol.* **45**:534–543. [18]

Valerio, S., B. J. Clark, J. H. Chan, et al. 2010. Directional learning, but no spatial mapping by rats performing a navigational task in an inverted orientation. *Neurobiol. Learn. Mem.* **93**:495–505. [3]

van Alphen, J. J. M., C. Bernstein, and G. Driessen. 2003. Information acquisition and time allocation in insect parasitoids. *Trends Ecol. Evol.* **18**:81–87. [7]

van de Waal, E., N. Renevey, C. M. Favre, and R. Bshary. 2010. Selective attention to philopatric models causes directed social learning in wild vervet monkeys. *Proc. Roy. Soc. Lond. B* **277(1691)**:2105–2111. [14]

van der Meer, M. A., and A. D. Redish. 2009. Covert expectation-of-reward in rat ventral striatum at decision points. *Front. Integr. Neurosci.* **3(1)**:1–15. [5]

———. 2010. Expectancies in decision making, reinforcement learning, and ventral striatum. *Front. Neurosci.* doi:10.3389/neuro.01.006.2010. [5]

van der Vaart, E., R. Verbrugge, and C. K. Hemelrijk. 2011. Corvid caching: Insights from a cognitive model. *J. Exp. Psychol. Anim. Behav. Proc.* **37(3)**:330–340. [6]

Vander Wall, S. B., and R. P. Balda. 1977. Coadaptations of the Clark's Nutcracker and the pinon pine for efficient seed harvest and dispersal. *Ecol. Monogr.* **47**:89–111. [7]

van Schaik, C. P. 1989. The ecology of social relationships amongst female primates. In: Comparative Socioecology: The Behavioural Ecology of Humans and Other Mammals, ed. V. Standen and G. R. A. Foley, pp. 195–218. Oxford: Blackwell. [15]

van Schaik, C. P., and F. Aureli. 2000. The natural history of valuable relationships in primates. In: Natural Conflict Resolution, ed. F. Aureli and F. B. M. de Waal, pp. 307–333. Berkeley: Univ. of California Press. [18]

Vargha-Khadem, F., D. G. Gadian, and M. Mishkin. 2001. Dissociations in cognitive memory: The syndrome of developmental amnesia. *Philos. Trans. R. Soc. Lond. B* **356(1413)**:1435–1440. [8]

Veenema, H. C., M. Das, and F. Aureli. 1994. Methodological improvements for the study of reconciliation. *Behav. Proc.* **31**:29–38. [15]

Vidal, M., M. A. Amorim, and A. Berthoz. 2004. Navigating in a virtual three-dimensional maze: How do egocentric and allocentric reference frames interact? *Brain Res. Cogn. Brain Res.* **19**:244–258. [3]

Viegas, J. 2010. Video shows squirrel reacting to death. *Discovery News*, http://news.discovery.com/animals/video-shows-squirrel-reacting-to-death.html (accessed 11 June 2011). [17]

Visscher, P. K. 2007. Group decision making in nest-site selection among social insects. *Ann. Rev. Entomol.* **52**:255–275. [11]

Visscher, P. K., and S. Camazine. 1999. Collective decisions and cognition in bees. *Nature* **397**:400. [2]

Von Eckardt, B. 1993. What Is Cognitive Science? Cambridge, MA: MIT Press. [17]

———. 1994. Folk psychology. In: A Companion to the Philosophy of Mind, ed. S. Guttenplan, pp. 300–307. Cambridge, MA: Blackwell. [18]

von Fersen, L., C. D. L. Wynne, J. D. Delius, and J. E. R. Staddon. 1991. Transitive inference formation in pigeons. *J. Exp. Biol. Anim. Behav. Proc.* **17**:334–341. [18]

von Frisch, K. 1923. Über die "Sprache" der Bienen. *Zool. Jahrbuch* **40**:1–186. [11]

———. 1965. Tanzsprache und Orientierung der Bienen. Heidelberg: Springer Verlag. [2, 5]

———. 1967. The Dance Language and Orientation of Bees. Cambridge, MA: Harvard Univ. Press. [11, 13]

Vonk, J., S. F. Brosnan, J. B. Silk, et al. 2008. Chimpanzees do not take advantage of very low cost opportunities to deliver food to unrelated group members. *Anim. Behav.* **75**:1757–1770. [18]

von Neumann, J., and O. Morgenstern. 1947. Theory of Games and Economic Behavior. Princeton: Princeton Univ. Press. [18]

Waisman, A. S., and L. F. Jacobs. 2008. Flexibility of cue use in the fox squirrel (*Sciurus niger*). *Anim. Cogn.* **11(4)**:625–636. [5]

Wajnberg, E., P. Gonsard, E. Tabone, et al. 2003. A comparative analysis of patch-leaving decision rules in a parasitoid family. *J. Anim. Ecol.* **72**:618–626. [7]

Wallraff, H. G. 1974. Das Navigationssystem der Vögel. Munich: Oldenbourg Verlag. [4]

———. 2005. Avian Navigation: Pigeon Homing As a Paradigm. Berlin: Springer Verlag. [4, 5]

Wang, M. D. 1970. The role of synaptic complexity as a determiner of comprehensibility. *J. Verbal Learn. Verbal Behav.* **9**:398–404. [13]

Wang, Y., A. Brzozowska-Prechtl, and J. H. Karten. 2010. Laminar and columnar auditory cortex in avian brain. *PNAS* **107**:12,676–12,681. [13]

Wantia, J. 2007. Self-organised dominance relationships: A model and data of primates. PhD thesis, Wiskunde en Natuurwetenschappen, Rijksuniversiteit Groningen, Groningen, NL. [15]

Warneken, F., and M. Tomasello. 2006. Altruistic helping in human infants and young chimpanzees. *Science* **311**:1301–1303. [18]

Warneken, F., and M. Tomasello. 2009. Varieties of altruism in children and chimpanzees. *Trends Cogn. Sci.* **13**:397–402. [16]

Warren, W. H., B. A. Kay, A. P. Duchon, W. Zosh, and S. Sahuc. 2001. Optic flow is used to control human walking. *Nature Neurosci.* **4**:213–216. [5]

Washburn, D. A., J. D. Smith, and W. E. Shields. 2006. Rhesus monkeys (*Macaca mulatta*) immediately generalize the uncertain response. *J. Exp. Psychol. Anim. Behav. Proc.* **32(2)**:185–189. [8]

Wehner, R., and R. Menzel. 1990. Do insects have cognitive maps? *Ann. Rev. Neurosci.* **13**:403–414. [2]

Weidt, A., S. E. Hofmann, and B. Konig. 2008. Not only mate choice matters: Fitness consequences of social partner choice in female house mice. *Anim. Behav.* **75**:801–808. [16]

Weir, A. A. S., J. Chappell, and A. Kacelnik. 2002. Shaping of hooks in New Caledonian crows. *Science* **297**:981. [4, 6]

Weiskrantz, L. 2001. Commentary responses and conscious awareness in humans: The implications for awareness in non-human animals. *Anim. Welfare* **10**:S41–S46. [8]

Wenner, A. M. 2002. The elusive honey bee dance "language" hypothesis. *J. Insect Behav.* **15**:859–878. [13]

Wenner, A. M., and D. L. Johnson. 1967. Honey bees: Do they use the direction and distance information provided by their dancers? *Science* **158**:1076–1077. [13]

Wenner, A. M., P. H. Wells, and D. L. Johnson. 1969. Honey bee recruitment to food sources: Olfaction or language? *Science* **164**:84–86. [11, 13]

Wheeler, B. C. 2009. Monkeys crying wolf? Tufted capuchin monkeys use anti-predator calls to usurp resources from conspecifics. *Proc. Roy. Soc. Lond. B* **276**:3013–3018. [13, 14]

———. 2010. Production and perception of situationally variable alarm calls in wild tufted capuchin monkeys (*Cebus apella nigritus*). *Behav. Ecol. Sociobiol.* **64**:989–1000. [13]

Whiten, A., and R. W. Byrne, eds. 1997. Machiavellian Intelligence II: Extensions and Evaluations. Cambridge: Cambridge Univ. Press. [14]

Whiten, A., V. Horner, C. A. Litchfield, and S. Marshall-Pescini. 2004. How do apes ape? *Learn. Behav.* **32**:36–52. [14]

Whiten, A., and A. Mesoudi. 2008. Establishing an experimental science of culture: Animal social diffusion experiments. *Philos. Trans. R. Soc. Lond. B* **363**:3477–3488. [14]

Wiener, J. M., M. Lafon, and A. Berthoz. 2008. Path planning under spatial uncertainty. *Mem. Cogn.* **36(3)**:495–504. [5]

Wiener, J. M., and H. A. Mallot. 2003. "Fine-to-coarse" route planning and navigation in regionalized environments. *Spatial Cogn. Comput.* **3(4)**:331–358. [5]

Wiener, J. M., A. Schnee, and H. A. Mallot. 2004. Use and interaction of navigation strategies in regionalized environments. *J. Environ. Psychol.* **24(4)**:475–493. [5]

Wild, J. M. 1993. Descending projections of the songbird nucelus robustus archistriatalis. *J. Comp. Neurol.* **338**:225–241. [13]

Wilke, A., J. M. C. Hutchinson, P. M. Todd, and U. Czienskowski. 2009. Fishing for the right words: Decision rules for human foraging behavior in internal search tasks. *Cogn. Sci.* **33**:497–529. [7]

Wilkinson, G. 1984. Reciprocal food sharing in vampire bats. *Nature* **308**:181–184. [16]

Wilson, E. O. 1971. The Insect Societies. Cambridge, MA: Harvard Univ. Press. [11]

Wiltschko, R., and W. Wiltschko. 2003. Avian navigation: From historical to modern times. *Anim. Behav.* **65**:257–272. [4]

Winkler, H., B. Leisler, and G. Bernroider. 2004. Ecological constraints on the evolution of avian brains. *J. Ornithol.* **145**:238–244. [4]

Winston, M. L. 1987. The Biology of the Honey Bee. Cambridge, MA: Harvard Univ. Press. [11]

Wittig, R. M., C. Crockford, E. Wikberg, R. M. Seyfarth, and D. L. Cheney. 2007. Kin-mediated reconciliation substitutes for direct reconciliation in female baboons. *Proc. Roy. Soc. Lond. B* **274**:1109–1115. [18]

Wohlgemuth, S., B. Ronacher, and R. Wehner. 2001. Ant odometry in the third dimension. *Nature* **411**:795–798. [3]

Wood, B., and M. Collard. 1999. The human genus. *Science* **284**:65–71. [12]

Wood, J. N., D. D. Glynn, B. C. Phillips, and M. D. Hauser. 2007. The perception of rational, goal-directed action in nonhuman primates. *Science* **317(5843)**:1402–1405. [17]

Woollett, K., and E. A. Maguire. 2009. Navigational expertise may compromise anterograde associative memory. *Neuropsychologia* **47**:1088–1095. [12]

Wray, M. K., B. A. Klein, H. R. Mattila, and T. D. Seeley. 2008. Honeybees do not reject dances for "implausible" locations: Reconsidering the evidence for cognitive maps in insects. *Anim. Behav.* **76(2)**:261–269. [2]

Yamada, M. 1966. Five natural troops of Japanese monkeys of Shodoshima Island (I): Distribution and social organization. *Primates* **7**:315–362. [15]

Yamamoto, S., T. Humle, and M. Tanaka. 2009. Chimpanzees help each other upon request. *PLoS One* **4**:e7416. [18]

Yartsev, M., M. P. Witter, and N. Ulanovsky. 2010. Spatial maps in the medial entorhinal cortex of the Egyptian fruit bat. *FENS Forum Abstracts* **5**:087.25. [3]

Yee, J. R., B. Cavigelli, B. Delgado, and M. K. McClintock. 2008. Reciprocal affiliation among adolescent rats during a mild group stressor predicts mammary tumors and lifespan. *Psychosom. Med.* **70**:1050–1059. [16]

Yerkes, R. M. 1940. Social behavior of chimpanzees: Dominance between mates in relation to sexual status. *J. Comp. Psychol.* **30**:147–186. [15]

Zeigler, H. P., and P. Marler, eds. 2008. Neuroscience of Birdsong. New York: Cambridge Univ. Press. [4]

Zentall, T. R., K. L. Roper, and L. M. Sherburne. 1995. Most directed forgetting in pigeons can be attributed to the absence of reinforcement on forget trials during training or to other procedural artifacts. *J. Exp. Anal. Behav.* **63**:127–137. [9]

Ziemke, T., D.-A. Jirenhed, and G. Hesslow. 2005. Internal simulation of perception: A minimal neuro-robotic model. *Neurocomputing* **68**:85–104. [9]

Zinkivskay, A., F. Nazir, and T. V. Smulders. 2009. What-where-when memory in magpies (*Pica pica*). *Anim. Cogn.* **12**:119–125. [12]

Zola, S. M., L. R. Squire, E. Teng, et al. 2000. Impaired recognition memory in monkeys after damage limited to the hippocampal region. *J. Neurosci.* **20(1)**:451–463. [8]

Zuberbühler, K., D. L. Cheney, and R. M. Seyfarth. 1999. Conceptual semantics in a nonhuman primate. *J. Comp. Psychol.* **113**:33–42. [13]

Zugaro, M. B., A. Berthoz, and S. I. Wiener. 2001. Background, but not foreground, spatial cues are taken as references for head direction responses by rat anterodorsal thalamus neurons. *J. Neurosci.* **21**:RC154. [3]

Subject Index